*In The Name of*

# GOD

*the Beneficent, the
Merciful*

Soureh Mehr Publishing House

Center for literary Creations

## That Which That Orphan Saw
(The Prophet, From Birth to Mission)

By:Muhammad Reza Sarshar (Rahgozar).

Litography publication and Bookbinding:
First Edition 1392(2013)
Print on-demnd by H&S Media
ISBN: 978 _ 600 _ 175 _749 _5



**Rahgozar, Reza, 1332-**

That Which That Orphan Saw (The Prophet, From Birth to Mission). By Muhammad Reza Sarshar (Rahgozar).

Listing based on FIPA information.
Above the title: novel.
___: 334-[333] pp.
Muhammad, the Prophet of Islam, 53 years before the Hegira – 11 A.H. – story.
A. Soureh Mehr Publishing House.
B. Title.
C. Title: The Prophet from Birth to Mission.
BP24/84/R94A8          8Fa62/3
[297/933]
The National Library of Iran  M80-19651
That Which That Orphan Saw
(The Prophet, from Birth to Mission)
Muhammad Reza Sarshar (Rahgozar)
3rd Ed./1385 A.H.
100 copies/Raq'i.
Print: Soureh Mehr Publishing House.
ISBN: 978-600-175-749-5
Copyright protected.

**Soureh Mehr Publishing House**

Add: No 23, Rasht St.,Hafez Ave.,Tehran
15815-1144,Iran
www.iricap.com
Tel: +98 2161942
Fax:+98 2166469951

*That Which That Orphan Saw*

*The Prophet, from Birth to Mission*

---

*NOVEL*
**That Which That Orphan Saw**
**(The Prophet, From Birth to Mission)**

---

*By* **Muhammad Reza Sarshar**
**(Rahgozar)**
*Translated by* **James Clark**

"Excavate Zamzam."

"What is Zamzam?"

"That whose water doesn't spoil and doesn't decrease or finish. Excavate it and quench the thirst of the throng of pilgrims."

"Where is it? Where is it? Tell me where it's located!"

"It's in the sanctuary. Its place is covered with blood and dung."

"More signs of it. Give me more signs of it!"

"The place of the ant hills. There, where the black and white crow strikes the ground with his beak."

"I...."

The specter, dressed in white and wrapped in a silk-like mist, had disappeared. It left with that same lightness of a cloud, the subtlety of water, and the swiftness of the breeze with which it had come. It had stayed with that same distance and with that same indistinctness, and it had spoken with a subtlety mixed with that same dignity. Before giving him more time to question, it had vanished into that perfumed heavenly space.

It was a summer night. We were sleeping on a platform in the courtyard of the house when I was awakened by a voice. Abd al-Muttaleb whispered in his sleep. His face, which I saw in the moonlight, was bathed in sweat. Then he began to shake. I thought he had a fever and was ill. I gently roused him from sleep.

I awoke with the caresses of the kind hands of my wife, Samra. It was as if a pail of water had been poured over me from head to foot. I was soaked from the moisture of the sweat. I had the feeling of a pleasant pounding. I thanked the god of the Ka'ba that he had accepted those several days of chaos and the knot had been opened.

Yes, the secret in my head with those visions of that past three or four days had become evident. I was now confident that those visions were true and from God.

Only God knows how happy I was that He had blessed me and that he considered me worthy of that service.

Samrā looked upon me in amazement. She knew nothing of what had gone on inside me. For that reason, she had become very concerned and didn't know what she should do. With her Yemeni cloth, which emitted a pleasant scent, she wiped away the sweat from my forehead and neck. Then she quickly got out of the bed and picked up a clay goblet that was upside-down on the jar. She filled it with cool water from the jar, gave it to me, and said, "Drink until I see what else I can do for you."

I was very thirsty. I took the goblet from Samra's hand and drank several draughts of its water with delight. Then I gave the goblet back to her and said, "Don't worry. I am not ill."

Samra sat on the edge of the bed with the goblet in her hand and stared at me in amazement.

The moon was full. The moonlight reflected off of the white hair at the front of Abd al-Muttaleb's head and bestowed a divine splendor on his attractive figure. The cool north breeze that had begun to blow shortly before swerved among the thick and wavy hair of Abd al-Muttaleb and caused Samra to think of the drawing of Abraham on the wall inside the Ka'ba.

Abd al-Muttaleb, from far away, stared at the fortress of Qa'iqa'ān, whose black, smooth, and transparent surface appeared imaginary in the stunning light of the moon, and he was silent. Then, with a voice that seemed to arise from another world, he said, "This was the fourth time that I have seen it. The first time was four days ago. For half a day, I slept in the stone of Ismail when it appeared to me and said, 'Excavate the pure thing.'

"Without wanting more explanation at that moment, I asked, 'What is *the pure*?'

"It left, however, without giving me an answer.

On another day, I saw it again in a dream. With that same form and that same countenance, it said, 'Excavate the good thing.'

"I quickly asked, 'What is *the good*?'

"Again, though, before giving me an answer to my question, it vanished from sight.

"Last night, it came to me during sleep and said, 'Excavate the valuable thing.'

"I ran towards it and asked, 'What is *the valuable*?'

"But even before I could finish, like a breeze, it had fled.

"From then on, I was never a moment without the thought of that problem. What was *the pure*? What was *the good*? What was *the valuable*? Were those dreams divine and true? From whom were these orders? And for what?

"These are the same questions and preoccupations that have disrupted my eating, sleep, and comfort for the last few days."

Abd al-Muttaleb, like a person who, after bending over for a time under a heavy load, had been relieved of that load, let out a long breathe. He took his eyes off of the Qa'iqa'an fortress. He cast a loving glance at the face of his wife and added, "Tonight, the knot was unraveled. Now I will sleep comfortably. Relax, Samra! Your husband has been chosen to excavate the pure and blessed Zamzam well again. Zamzam is the precious heritage of our ancestor Ismail. Mecca has been designated to be the recipient of the kindness and attention of the God of the Ka'ba again!"

Samra, having regained her repose, rose from her place overflowing with spiritual happiness. She poured the water from the bottom of the goblet at the foot of the plane tree beside the wall. She replaced the goblet as it first was, upside-down on the urn, and went to bed. Before her, Abd al-Muttaleb stretched out on the bed, locked his hands over his forehead and stared at the naked and transparent sky of the city. Now, even though he had been relieved of the enigmatic and troubling question of the previous days, new thoughts were driving sleep from his eyes.

That night sleep didn't come to my eyes until the light of morning. Happiness, haste, and anxiety were all mixed together in my soul. I had wished that it was morning right then, and that I could head for the sanctuary and begin the work. Zamzam was a valuable and dear lost item, and thinking about finding it had occupied my mind for years. Not just me, but my father, Hāshem, and his father too, had been thinking about that for years.

From the time when my uncle, Muttaleb, died and the obligation to give water and food to the pilgrims at the Ka'ba fell upon me, people looked at me differently. And I, to the best of my abilities, labored to comfort them and the pilgrims of the Ka'ba. But giving water to the pilgrims never turned out the way I wanted it to because water was never as abundant as I wanted it to be. During the years when rain was scarce—and that lasted for three years—the scarcity increased. On the other hand, the thought that besides the wells of Zāher 'Asqalāni Ja'rāneh and some other wells around Mecca, other wells needed to be dug as well, continuously occupied my mind. Most particularly, the distance of those wells from the sanctuary, the dearth of persons, and my means for delivering water from those distances was a tremendous hardship and burden for me.

I was no more than thirteen or fourteen when father woke me up at the first of dawn. We always rose early in the morning. That day, from the beginning, it was evident that that day was different. Father intended to dig a well in the sanctuary!

Digging a well was nothing new. But what father wanted to do this time, to do this job himself, surprised me. When I asked him the reason, he took the story back almost two thousand four hundred and forty years ago, to the time of our ancestor, Ismail, praise be on him.

Father, earlier, had told me about the adventure of bringing the infant Ismail and his mother, Hājar, to Mecca. At that time, Mecca had been a dry and empty desert. Abraham, at the urging of his wife, Sarah, had brought his other wife, Hajar, and her child Ismail, from Palestine to here, and he himself had returned. There, with Ismail's severe thirst and Hajar's fatigue, a spring had sprung up from the spot where Ismail's heel had rubbed the ground. Then, gradually, the birds and animals of the desert, sensing the water of the spring, had gathered around that place. Several wandering tribes of the desert, upon seeing water, settled down here and stayed. Of those tribes, one was a people from which Ismail took a wife as an adult.

After Ismail, his son Thābet became the guardian

and servant of the Ka'ba and its pilgrims. When Thabet passed away, that task passed to individuals of the Jorham tribe generation by generation. They, however, upon becoming powerful, became oppressive and corrupt.

The protectors of the Ka'ba considered it their own, and they harassed and plundered strangers who entered the sanctuary.

This situation went on for nearly three hundred and thirty years, until, in the land of Yemen, the famous flood of Eram took place. At that time, the people of Khozā'eh wandered from that land and migrated to Mecca. A conflict arose among them, the Jorham, and other peoples. The Khoza'is obtained help from the Kanāneh tribe and raided Mecca. A war began, and in the end the Khoza'is won and stayed in Mecca.

From then on, a struggle began over the covering of the Ka'ba and the acceptance of the pilgrims to the Ka'ba. This struggle between the two tribes of the Jorham and the Khoza'is lasted for years and resulted in revenge, enmity, and another war. In the meantime, the Khoza'is, because of the increase in their number and warriors, overcame the Jorham and subsequently drove the Jorham out of Mecca in a harshness manner.

After some time had passed, the men of the Khoza'eh became arrogant and began to oppress the pilgrims to the Ka'ba.

My father said, "They, with the creation of harsh laws, forced the male pilgrims to take off their clothes upon entering the Mecca and to put on clothes they had given to them before visiting and circumambulating the Ka'ba. By their order, the women too had to circumambulate while naked.

Another contrived law of theirs was that pilgrims could only eat food that the Khoza'is had given to them.

In this way, by means of oppression, the Khoza'is grasped a large amount of wealth and became wealthier and more powerful every day.

Years elapsed in this way until our fourth ancestor, Qosā Kalāb, attacked them because of their oppression and corruption and, after defeating them, ran them out of Mecca.

My father, quoting his father, said, "When our ancestor, Qosā, wrested Mecca from the grasp of the Khoza'is, he found no sign of Zamzam. After much inquiry he learned that the Khoza'is, when they realized their defeat was imminent, threw the remaining possessions of the Ka'ba into the well, filled the well, and caused it to disappear.

The father and son were facing the sanctuary. Abd al-Muttaleb, shovel in hand, and with long strides, was in front, and Hares was two or three steps behind. Passersby who, in that early morning light, saw the great man of the Qureish like that asked themselves in wonderment, "What has happened that the head of the Qureish has taken a shovel in hand and has thrown a straw basket on the shoulder of his young son?! What has happened to their slaves that they have stooped to this lowly task?" But Abd al-Muttaleb's greatness and dignity dissuaded them from what they were asking and for which they wanted an answer.

Hares and Abd al-Muttaleb weaved through the uneven streets of Mecca and arrived at the level area of the city. The bazaar was in the direction of the Bani Hāshem gate, and there the sanctuary, the Ka'ba, high and splendid, covered in the green Yemeni velvet, rose up from the middle. Around it was open ground, spread out over a thousand meters. All around it, too, were walls with shades: the porches.

The ground of the sanctuary was covered in a gray and soft dirt mixed with red sand. Apart from the abode of Abraham and the stone of Ismail, there were idols of the various tribes and clans of the Arabs all around the sanctuary. Three hundred and sixty idols, and each idol was the intercessor for one day before the great god of the Ka'ba, Allah.

Father and son exhibited their respect to the Ka'ba from that spot.

Upon placing their feet inside the courtyard, Abd al-Muttaleb's heart began to race.

A shaking at the bottom of the heart. A rush of fear and doubt. A mixture of enthusiasm and waiting and fear.

"Its location is covered by blood and dung."

It is clear up to this point. It is only the place of sacrifice of the sanctuary that is like this. A short distance is left until the pilgrimage site of Hajar, between the two idols of Asāf and Nā'eleh.[1] But where

---

1. Ibn Ishaq (85-150 or 153 A.H.) said, "Asaf and Na'eleh were a man and woman from the Jorham tribe by the name of Asaf bin Bagha and

is the place of sacrifice? The surface covered by blood and dung is not a small area. And too, this surface can't be dug up from one end to the other!

Ah! A black and white crow! How could I have forgotten! "There where a black and white crow strikes the ground with its beak." But where is that crow? If it doesn't come…? But is it possible? Is it possible that the four-time dream be repeated and ….

"Father, a crow! It appears to be that same black and white crow that…."

Abd al-Muttaleb looked in surprise to the sky of the sanctuary where Hares pointed with his finger. A single crow had come out from the eastern side of the sanctuary toward the Ka'ba.

The father and son held their breath, and the beating of Abd al-Muttaleb's heart became painful.

The crow circled around the sanctuary and perched on the edge of one of the roofs of the porches surrounding it. It turned its head. It flew from the roof and landed on the head of an idol between the Ka'ba and the shades. Again, it turned its head about and flew again. This time a little nearer it sat on the head of Asaf, the female idol. From there it flew to the head of Na'eleh, the male idol opposite Asaf. There, after a short halt and turning its head around, it sat on the ground of the place of sacrifice. Heavy steps, like those of a pregnant woman, at every step the body twisting to the side…and it stopped. Another glance in each direction and the striking of its beak to the ground.

---

Na'eleh bin Dik, whom God transformed into two pieces of stone."

Striking and striking....

A short cry of happiness and surprise spontaneously sprang from the throat of Hares. Abd al-Muttaleb, frozen, placed his hand on his mouth and pushed him backwards a little. But that same sound pried the wary crow from it place and…the crow left. It seemed it had come for no other reason than to do that. It left. As if it hadn't been there at all. As if it hadn't come.

Abd al-Muttaleb rushed to the side of the place of sacrifice. The mark of the crow's hard, sharp beak could be seen on the entrance to the ant den.

Happiness, value, and haste. The basket came down from the shoulder of Hares. The shovel was placed in a corner. Abd al-Muttaleb took the green turban from his head. He removed the pale white thin muslin robe from his body. He opened the green silk belt around his waist. He placed all of them at the foot of the platform of the idol Asaf. He took the pickaxe from the basket. He spread his feet, and in the name of the God of the Ka'ba he requested assistance. He brought the first strike of the pickaxe down on the place of the crow's beak....

With the beginning of our work, it seemed that the senior men of the Qureish and the other people of Mecca had found a new event to talk about. Every day when we started to work, they would gather around us and say all kinds of things. One of them thought that my father was looking for treasure in the sanctuary and was trying to find it. Another expressed surprise that we had not employed our slaves for that task and that we were doing it ourselves. They sometimes also asked me of my father's intention. I, however, did not answer.

Father dug and I, with a basket made of palm leaves that I had found, would lift the dirt up. Until one day, I saw all the senior men of Qureish were coming in our direction. They were coming in a way that made me apprehensive.

They gathered in a circle around the hole that my father was digging and called out to him.


"Abd al-Muttaleb! O' Abd al-Muttaleb! Can you hear me?"

Abd al-Muttaleb was thirty meters down in the ground. He had sensed the presence of the shadows above him. Upon hearing the voice, he stopped working and raised his head. "I can hear you."

"I hope you are well, Abd al-Muttaleb! You are probably very tired. Don't you want to stop working a while and rest a bit?"

"With work that pleases a friend, its tiredness is both sweet and desirable."

"That's good. That's good. But the elders of the tribe have gathered to say a few words to you."

"They are welcome. But why with this urgency? It shouldn't be much longer until sundown. Once I have stopped working, I will be with you at whatever time you want. Heh! Hares!"

Hares opened a path among the group and came forward. When he reached the edge of the hole, he bent his head over it and said, "Yes father?!

"Since 'Amer came to bring the food and plates for lunch, tell him to spread out a larger cloth today next to the Ka'ba."

Abd al-Muttaleb, without waiting for Hares' answer, started to dig again. When they saw it was like that, they didn't dare insist any more.

When the sun reached the horizon, the elders of the Qureish clans were sitting at the edge of the courtyard of the sanctuary. Some were on the platform of the idols.

"He has been digging in the courtyard for several days now without asking our opinion! He has taken the leadership of the Qureish and protecting the Ka'ba on himself! But we have rights too in this affair."

"At sundown of the first day, I came here and told him that this work is disrespectful to our idols. He didn't answer me though."

"I told him the same thing. But he said, 'Zamzam, whether before or after Asaf and Na'eleh, was here, and no one ever considered its existence an insult to the idols.'"

"In that case, he did not have permission to do this without obtaining our satisfaction! What is the council for then?"

That day, after I had stopped working, I went to see them. All of them were sitting on the large cloth that my slave had spread out beside the wall of the Ka'ba, and they were awaiting me.

As always, words were spoken without anything being held back. The gist of their talk was that Ismail was the ancestor of all of us, and Zamzam belonged to us all too. Thus, I had to make them partners in the excavation of Zamzam.

I told them that I did not want the well and water merely for myself. But I could not let them share in it, because I alone had been ordered to carry out this task. And too, giving water to the pilgrims to the Ka'ba for generations was the inheritance of my fathers.

With that, they rose and insisted that they be allowed to participate in excavating Zamzam with me.

Upon seeing their suspiciousness and excuses, my heart was pained. Before that, I had felt many times that I was their leader, although in name only. Whenever their interests were threatened, they did not pay attention to what I said. Now that I had many sons, their behavior was certainly not that way with me now.

They were all waiting for my answer, and I said, "Doubtless, that which has ordered me to do this work also has the power to support me against you. Now, though, since I don't see another path available to me, I see no choice but to suggest mediation to cease this conflict. Select someone other than yourselves who is objective and intelligent to mediate between us."

Then, saddened, I looked away from them to see what they say.

For a while, they whispered among themselves, giving suggestions. Finally, Hashem Moghayreh, the leader of the Sahm clan, who was older than the others, presented the group's view. He suggested that Sa'd Hodaym, the Syrian rabbi, be the mediator between us on this issue. Thus, based on that, it was determined that one person would be selected from each clan of the Qureish and, with me and several persons of my family, would head for Ma'ān in Syria.

Three days later, we gathered our essentials for the road and set out for that land.

We had set out from Mecca fifteen days earlier, and now it was six days that we were traveling lost. Following a sand storm, the road had disappeared and we had become lost. The only thing that we saw was desert before us!

It was three days that, despite all of our forbearance, our water had finished. On the evening of that day, after tolerating a difficult day, we stuck a stick down the throats of two camels and drank the vomit-laden water of their stomachs. On the day after as well, we drank the water from the stomachs of two other camels. But from the fifth day we knew that there was no more water left in the stomachs of the camels.

At the beginning of the fifth day of wandering, one of the camels that was older knelt down in the middle of the road and would not rise. The other camels had become crazy from the intensity of thirst and hunger too and controlling them was difficult.

On the sixth day, we left them because we could see signs that they could not endure any more. I myself continued to limp along. After going a bit further and passing a some hills and sand dunes, we gave up and each collapsed where he was.

Some of my fellow travelers believed that we had continuously gotten father away from the road and had gone deeper into the heart of the desert. That alone increased our despair about going forward because, as you know, the road from Mecca to Syria is in the direction of the Red Sea. That road passes by Yathrib, and then, intruding from the left side of the course, there is a large, wide desert. Upon entering this desert, we didn't have much hope of either staying alive or being saved.

"Forty men! Forty of the flowers from the various clans of the Qureish tribe! What a tremendous loss! How quickly and easily we reached the end of our lives! We brought ourselves to our own place of death!

The years will come to an end in this manner, and our families and clans, even our corpses and bones, will not be found.

Ah! How painful for a person to die like this and for his body to not be safe from the animals of the desert.

"Man, don't be so agitated! And don't chastise yourself. No one could have foreseen such a situation or day. It has passed now, and the future is now out of our reach. Perhaps this was our fate that we should die like this far away from friend and home and with this harshness.

"I, like you, believe that our death here in this dry desert is inevitable. But a solution can be contemplated so that our bodies are taken safely to the grave."

"And how is that Abd al-Muttaleb?"

"It isn't that difficult. Let every person dig a grave for himself and sit in it waiting for death. That way, the person who dies sooner will be buried by those who are still alive, and only the body of the last person will remain above ground."

It was a worthy suggestion. In any case, having that intense amazement was better than continuing down the hopeless and intolerable road in that murderous and unmerciful desert heat. In any case, doing something, no matter how absurd, in that extremely difficult situation of hopelessness, breathed life into the lifeless bodies of those travelers.

Thus, there remained the digging of their own graves with their last bit of life….

Despair was such that, because of its intensity, the heart beat until it was going to stop. At that point, we, several of the leaders of the Qureish, chastised ourselves, openly and in private. I thought to myself about how we had given up the pleasant and cool shade of the city, the pleasant afternoons of the sanctuary, the cool and quenching drinks and colorful and tranquil foods, spouses, children, relatives, friends, and our interest and affairs, and with absurd insistence had engaged in such a journey full of suffering and had stepped into the valley of non-existence!

Oh! How late man comes to realize his mistake, such that even knowing it is late and does not achieve anything!

If man could only live twice…!

All were aware that I never feared death, but that death was not something that I longed for. My sadness at that moment was because I saw myself as an innocent victim of others.

Therefore, I did not know why I thought, "The substance of the insistence of that white-clad specter to excavate Zamzam…was it thinking of bestowing me with this ominous fate?!

After I had thought a great deal, and the darkness had dissipated from my mind, I said to myself, "Never! The God of the Ka'ba is greater and more knowledgeable than to do that with me listening to his command.

It was as if a voice from inside said to me, "O' Abd al-Mottaleb! So why were you heedless?! Arise! Arise!"

I sprang from my place and said to my companions, "Get up friends! Stop digging! It is unacceptable for a man to die like this. As long as breathes come, we mustn't cease struggling. Too, if death is our unavoidable fate, we mustn't give in to it like this.

"Get up so we can climb this sand hill. Dying on the road, even though it is still death, in this manner, like old women sitting in wait of death, is many times more superior."

Our weakness was so much that our brains had stopped working. At such a moment, it sufficed that someone like Abd al-Muttaleb open his mouth until others, without asking the reason, start following him.

With Abd al-Muttaleb in front and the others at a distance behind him, they began to climb the side of the hill with their incapable feet.

The feet going down into the sand up to the ankle; the repeated bending of the knees under the heavy bodies; the frequent falling to the ground; the slow circling of the vultures, greedy but patient companions, up above with short, sharp, hair-raising screams; the scorching of the body in the melting deluge of the sun; vertigo; headaches; the urge to vomit and empty the stomach and intestines and whatever else was in the belly; the dimness of the eyes; the heavy and fearful silence of death (only sounds from the bottom of the deep well of the throat and broken, short, and occasional screams of the vultures). Looong, looong moments.

Ah! Where are you Mecca, valley of ease and security? Where are you goblets of cold, wholesome water? Where are you cool and animating shade? Where are you life...?

They reached the top of the first hill.

What?! A mountain?!

The eyes had become bleary from fatigue and weakness, but not such that they couldn't see the mountain! In the distance, three mountain peaks could be seen, one behind the other. The sign of salvation from the deadly whirlpool of the desert. The glad tidings of finding the road again!

Behind the hill there was a wide plain. Familiar.

Though dry, it nevertheless had a kind and pleasant smell. The smell of life. The smell of men. Many thorn bushes.

The faint outline of the road. The varied coloring of the ground, from yellow fading into to red; to grey and black. Hope, hope, hope…! Life, life, life…! The kind soil of the friend….familiar peaks….

The end had come! Death had fled! The body had again become young and gained life without receiving an ounce of food or a drop of water.

What miracles hope brings!

Screams. Chuckling. Jumping in the air. Crazy actions. Hugging one another. Loud, childlike laughter. Weeping, weeping, weeping, out loud and reckless. A return to the pure nature of childhood. The toppling of the curtains of arrogance and egotism before the eyes. Kissing the heads and faces of the great men of the people. Being favored by the God of the Ka'ba.

"Forgive us Abd al-Muttaleb. Forgive us! What happened to us was doubtless the result of our selfish opposition to you and desire. Now, with renewed happiness and gratitude for this life, we are regaining ourselves and heading for our homes. May Zamzam be granted to you, O' son of Hashem. Hope, which is from your blessed hands and great position, has brought abundance and blessings to Mecca."

The air outside the hole, even though it did not have the irritating burning of outside, was however warm, heavy, and stifling. The lungs of Abd al-Muttaleb seemed to have relinquished their usual volume. Something seemed to be pressing in on them. The breaths did not go down with their normal capacity. They were short, small, and quick. But no matter how much the pressure on the body intensified, the lightness and joy of the soul increased. However much the suffering of the body intensified, Abd al-Muttaleb felt that it pleased the God of the Ka'ba more. That repeated and true dream, because it convinced him of the correctness of his action, was enough. That miraculous rescue from extinction in the desert of death had doubled his belief in this matter.

Although several days had passed since that long and innervating journey, the feeling of weakness had still not left my body. But, still, I felt better than many of my companions, because on the return journey several of them had become so weak and abject that they became bedridden and for days did not get up. The affairs of finding those swords and shields and golden gazelles in the well and the stopping of the excavation because of the obstruction of the people placed another burden on me, decreasing my ability and dissolving it.

Before I set out on that unwanted journey, I had dug almost thirty meters of the well. And more or less at that same time I could smell moisture, and I was certain not much was left before I reached what I was looking for. That is why I had so much enthusiasm and haste in pursuing my task and I did not agree to rest for even a day after returning after those recommendations my wife made.

Abd al-Muttaleb, tired but perseverant, was busy digging. In that situation, so as not to allow laxity to advance, he sang in a loud voice in praise of days gone by. And Hares, too, standing underneath the small straw shade beside the hole, slowly began to sing along with him.

"O' God,
I have answered the request of that person
Who ordered me,
And like a hasty man
Who is firm in his belief,
I have stepped and am working.
Now, my child too
Is helping and following me,
And is happy about this work.
And of the hardness and suffering he bears,
He is not complaining.
O' God,
Grant our wishes!
For
My arms
Do not engage

In those tasks you dislike."

His voice resembled the bubbling of a creek. From it, a spiritual intoxication rushed into the soul of Hares and made bearing the burning heat of the sun easy for him.

The day approached noon. The porches all around the sanctuary slowly emptied, and the straw shades and large cloths of the Qureish were gathered up.

I had realized a few moments ago that the ground beneath my pickaxe does not have its previous heaviness and hardness. The change in the sound of the strikes confirmed my realization.

Suddenly, I felt that I was digging in sandy soil rather than the earlier heavy and thick mud.

Before I could be sure, I knelt down and, with my hand, felt the soil. I had not been mistaken. The soil had become sandy. Thus, not much should be left!

Abd al-Muttaleb, with increasing speed, pursued his digging and made his strikes more solid. Hares, too, now, without needing to be told by his father every time, after emptying his pail of its dirt, would send it back into the hole.

Suddenly, a strike reflected. The pickaxe seemed to have struck something hard and had bounced back. Abd al-Muttaleb made the strikes shorter and lighter, and quicker.

A large stone, but narrow and soft and carved by a human hand and…vacuum…the sound of sand pouring into water. The heavenly and affable melody of water.

The end of long days of sadness and anticipation. The return of blessings to Mecca. The end of the yearly disturbance of delivering water to the pilgrims. Explaining those repeated dreams that had become true. Brightness. Life. Water…!

"God is great!"

Abd al-Muttaleb's saying of "God is great" was so loud and audible that it reached the far corners of the sanctuary. Persons who were moving stopped where they were.

In short, they dropped what they had in their hands and ran toward the place of sacrifice and Hares.

"The well of Zamzam has been found!"

"The son of Hasehm has finally excavated the Zamzam well!"

Amazed, several persons also hurried toward the bazaar and the quarters of the city to tell the people before others did about the rediscovery of the Zamzam well after four generations[1].

---

1. According to one tradition, the rediscovery of the Zamzam well occurred in the year 540 A.D.

The roots of this matter went back several decades. The first time, it was in that same place where I had begun to dig for Zamzam and the heads of nine clans of the Qureish had stood in opposition to me that had led to that deadly journey.

When we were saved from extinction in that dry desert and my companions had come to themselves like that and requested forgiveness from me, I thought that they would leave me to myself from then on so I could perform the task.

During the first days after returning to Mecca, that is how it was. Even though the remorse from the days ruined because of the people's spite stayed with me, I kept thinking that if I had numerous sons, they would never have had the audacity to confront my forthright words like that. Whatever it was, it was because they saw me without any helper or supporter.

That is how it was when the discovery of that treasure came about.

Abd al-Muttaleb, with clear signs of weakness in his body and arms, murmured the earlier melody under his breath and split the ground.

The air was warm, and his *dishdasha* was soaked with sweat. Large drops of sweat flowed down the crevices of his forehead like small springs and passed the barrier of his eyebrows and lingered there before going on to his eyes. Abd al-Mottaleb, out of necessity, once every few minutes, leaned the pickaxe against his thigh so as to wipe away the sweat from his forehead with his wrist.

"...O' God,
Realize our desires!
My arm,
For the work that...."
Clangggg...!
Abd al-Mottaleb's hands stopped moving. He had clearly seen the sparks that had come from the tip of the pickaxe hitting something metallic.

"What can it be?!"

"Hares, son, lower the basket!"

The basket came down. Abd al-Mottaleb poured the dirt into the basket and quickly sent it back up. He could now understand better what his pickaxe had hit: a small piece of black metal sticking out from under the dirt.

Abd al-Mottaleb, with gentle strikes, but faster than before, began to uncover the metal object. Now the ground allowed for easier digging than before.

An ancient iron shield, with flower-shaped nails with four leaves whose color time had slightly tarnished, was sticking out of the ground.

Mild happiness raced through Abd al-Mottaleb's heart like a gentle wave. This could be another sign that, until here, he had proceeded correctly.

Strength raced through his arms. This time, with greater joy, he yelled out, "Hares! Basket!"

Hares also, upon noticing the change in the tone of

his father's voice, felt that something was happening. With more strength and agility than before, he followed his father's command.

The coming up of the shield along with a lump of red dirt elicited a small scream from Hares' throat. That scream was not missed by the ears of the lounging men who had gathered around him since morning telling stories about the journey of Abd al-Mottaleb and the other heads of the clans of Qureish to Syria. The heads turned toward the opening of the hole all together, and upon seeing the shield, they all stood beside Hares.

"An ancient shield! It is surprising how its steel has remained in such good condition after all these years!"

"Yes! What fine materials too! It is certainly of fine steel. If not, it would have rusted and deteriorated."

"For sure, it comes from the time of the rule over Mecca. If I am not mistaken, the son of Hashem has come across a treasure!"

"Hares! Basket!"

"Okay father!"

A shield, six Arab scimitars of Syrian steel, then a golden gazelle, and, following that, another golden gazelle.

People had gathered around the hole.

The news spread through Mecca instantly and pulled the great men of the various Qureish clans and anyone who was in the city at that hour to the sanctuary and beside the hole.

Now, the situation had become such that Abd al-Mottaleb had to scream for his voice to reach Hares.

The steel swords and heavy golden gazelles quickly passed from hand to hand. Several times fights almost broke out between several persons.

Once the greedy desire from seeing the uncovered treasure had subsided a bit, a debate over it began. Most of the words were with Abd al-Mottaleb. Hence, again, he had to leave his work undone.

Hashem Moghayreh, with an excitement that he tried to conceal, said, "O' son of Hashem! Earlier we accepted that the honor of digging up Zamzam again only be yours, and we adhered to that. But the story of this treasure is something else. You must divide it among the ten clans of the Qureish!"

Abd al-Mottaleb, now standing on the mound of dirt of the hole, said, "The Zamzam well was unknown and unfound for years in this sanctuary and not one of you tried to find or dig it up again. At that time, when I resolved to do it, all of you opposed it. And now that a treasure has been found in it, you want a share of it?! How have you forgotten that the age-old Arab tradition is that whoever finds a treasure in the ground, all of it belongs to him!"

"But Zamzam belongs to all of the Qureish, and any treasure that…."

"These words mean nothing to us. We want…."

"Calm down! Calm down! I still…!"

"We are all saying the same thing!"

"Yes, this treasure must be divided."

At this time, Harb Omayyeh, a relative of Abd al-Mottaleb and a son of Abd Manaf, parted the mass of people and came forward. He stood beside Abd al-Mottaleb and, said in a loud voice, "This treasure belongs to the sons of Abd Manaf because one of them has found it. The other clans of Qureish should not covet the property that the gods have sent to us.

The assembly, however, were more surprised with these words. Abd al-Mottaleb's struggles to calm those angry people whose ears had become deaf to hearing any unacceptable word remained fruitless. It was as if only he did not have permission to speak among them.

Abd al-Mottaleb, even though he was not sad or greedy for the windfall of gold and treasure, neither did he turn away from the improper word or force. Bending the shoulder under the burden of the first improper pressure was the beginning of accepting future contempt and humiliation. And since Abd al-Mottaleb was a free man who had lived his whole life with greatness, he could not stand such humiliation.

At this time, and once again, he felt alone from the bottom of his soul. And sadness pressed on his heart heavily. The impudence of the people had no other aim other than to neither help nor support him.

This was the umpteenth time that the great men of the Qureish, no matter how much they knew that he was right, were united in making him accept their incorrect opinion. If he had had many brave sons, they certainly would not have acted like that with him. In this situation, although he was a great leader, he had no power. And so, every superior person causes the weaker one to waver until he fights him hand to hand and becomes determined to throw him to the ground.

If he only had ten sons!

Abd al-Mottaleb's silence, his gravity and dignity, slowly quieted the yells and screams. That initial calamity was turned into a rumble and then a whisper. In every respect, and no matter how helplessness, Abd al-Mottaleb was the leader of the Qureish and without his opinion no task in Mecca was possible. Thus, they had to listen to what he said and know what he thought.

"Huh. What do you say Abd al-Mottaleb?"

"Hesham, I have more or less said what I have to say. In this case, since I had another intention in finding Zamzam, I did not want any difficulty to come about in the matter. I suggest drawing lots."

"Lots?"

"Lots between what and whom?"

"Depending on right if possible. The right of the Ka'ba for this treasure, among all of us, is greater. Therefore, I suggest casting lots in the Ka'ba, you and I."

That day, we had to stop working. Dejected, father said to me, "Let me give the tools to our slave, 'Amer, to take to the house."

We washed our hands and faces and put our clothes on and with the senior men of Qureish left the Ka'ba.

The holder of the arrows of the Ka'ba came from that direction too. Father and the senior men of the Qureish went up the ladder leaning against the wall of the Ka'ba and entered it.

I stayed outside. The people stayed there too until

the results of the lots were known.

The arrow-keeper dropped the arrows, yellow, black, and white, onto the cylinder of the lots and mixed them up: yellow for the Ka'ba, black for me, and white for the other clans of the Qureish.

First, he threw for the swords and shields. The lots landed on my name. Then a casting of lots began for the golden gazelles, and the gazelles went to the Ka'ba. But I also granted the swords and shields to the Ka'ba.

At that moment I told the people, "In the Ka'ba, they are not proper for its god. It is better that the shields be sold and, with the money from them and the gold of the two gazelles, that an appropriate door from gold be built for it.

After a while, the artisans melted the gold and built a new door. Then the swords were hung from the two sides of the doors.

They said, "The first person to decorate the doors of the Ka'ba with gold was Abd al-Mottaleb. Before him, no one had used gold to decorate the Ka'ba."

These gifts of my husband opened the mouths of the Qureish and the other people of Mecca admirably and raised his stature among them. But the knot closing down his work did not unravel. I myself was a daughter of the desert and knew the Arab well. Time revolved around the pivot of power. The Arab killed weaklings. He loved good and great acts, and he valued them. But that which made him submissive and cheerful was capability. When Abd al-Mottaleb was feeding those without anything and putting clothes on the naked, and forewent his right to the profit of others, they respected him. Then, though, when he insisted on his right and stood firm in that against them, the story changed.

The next day, as I began to excavate Zamzam again, I was very sad and depressed. My heart was heavy and something had closed my throat.

Certainly, just as it is not a shame for a man to weep, perhaps until that hour, Abd al-Mottaleb let go of the reins of the eye and heart and permitted the torrent of tears that were imprisoned behind the dam of his will and self-control to break the wall and pour out.

Now, it was only him and solitariness; he and the well, far from the eyes of friend and stranger.

A tear in the corner of his eye stung. He put the pickaxe aside and knelt down on the soft ground of the hole. He raised his hands toward the sky and with a voice that was jerky from the abundance of feelings, he said, "O' God, You witness that nothing like You walks vainly on your earth nor wants superiority over your servants. You know that my figure does not do other than what pleases You. But the thinking of these people is such that they bow to nothing save power and glory."

"O' God of the Ka'ba! Look upon this broken-hearted servant of yours with mercy! I made a contract with you that if you give me ten sons, I will sacrifice the best of them once he reaches maturity."

He had been unburdened. He felt calmness and comfort. With the back of his hand he wiped away the tears that he had not realized had fallen on his cheeks. Then he stood up, picked up the pickaxe from off of the ground, and continued digging the well.

"My children, the time has come to be faithful to that contract. One of you has to be sacrificed today! All of you go now to your homes and bid farewell to your mothers and sisters. Then wash your heads and bodies, put on your best clothes, and make yourself fragrant with perfume, rose-water, and amber. We will go to the Ka'ba in an hour to learn what fate has in store."

We, the people of Mecca, were more or less informed of his commitment a few decades ago, but no one took that contract seriously. What person believed that one of the Arab nobles would sacrifice his best son with his own hand? It had been known that some of the poor people had buried their daughters alive because of the fear of having nothing or of being taken prisoner and being dishonored. But never sons! In the eyes of the Arab, the son was the possessor of greatness, the substance of the support and ability of the father, and his walking stick in old age. He was also considered the protector of the life, property, and honor of the family. Thus, what person would contemplate doing such an unthinkable thing?!"

When I learned of it, I went crying to Abd al-Mottaleb and said to him, "What an ill-omened thing this is that you are going to do."

But he, with his usual habit of sticking to his decision once he had made it, answered by saying, "This is a contract between me and God."

I said, "But when you made this contract, my Hares already existed. So your contract does not apply to him."

He hesitated and seemed to be thinking. Then he said, "At that moment, though, I did not distinguish Hares in my own mind."

Abd al-Mottaleb breaking the contract, that with the God of the Ka'ba! Never!

It was for that same reason that Meccans, upon hearing the news, all dropped what they were doing and waited, stupefied.

Those who had stayed in the city until that hour gathered together every where and were heatedly talking about it. The wives of Abd al-Mottaleb, after failing to dissuade their husband from that task, appealed to their relatives and tribal elders to prevent this catastrophe. But no one placed any hope in those requests. Based on the tradition of the Arabs, the father, like his other possessions, also possessed the choice over the lives of his children. Thus, no one was able to prevent him from killing his child. Especially a leading person from the Qureish, and his children, those children obeying the order of their father, like the sons of Abd al-Mottaleb!

The sun little by little raised its head and approached the middle of the sky, and the time of the ceremony of sacrifice had arrived. Suddenly, the people who had gathered around the Bani Hashem door ended the uproar with screams of a black-faced and barefoot child.

The young boy, clothed in rags, and wearing a *dishdasha* with wide stripes of blue and pink, wiped his nose with his sleeve and with a voice like that of a baby crow cried out, "They have come!"

All heads turned toward the eastern side of the sanctuary.

Amidst the thick dust that had arisen with the coming of a group, Abd al-Mottaleb, with a black turban of muslin on his head, a black silken shawl around his waist, and a black cotton cloak on his shoulders, was entering. His sons Hares, Bu Lahab, Aqabeh, Zobayr, Abd Manāf, Abdullah, Abbas, Ghaydāq, Qotam, and Zerār[1], clean, with faces smelling of amber, bodies sprinkled with perfume, in fine clothes, and thinking, were following him. Samra, Fatimah, Omm Jamil, and Natilah, the wives of Abd al-Muttaleb, and Safiyyeh, ʿĀtekeh, Borreh, Haymeh[2], Orwā, and Mozāyereh, his daughters, had encircled them like the band of a ring, and they were coming, most barefoot and wailing. The mothers, with broken figures, having given up their last bit of life, and dejected, and the daughters, like restless grains of wheat roasting on a frying pan, were constantly running in this direction and that. Sometimes they hung themselves around the neck of

1. The names of the sons of Abd al-Mottaleb in some sources are different from this one. For example, in some histories, Abd al-Ka'abah, Abdu, and Hejl are some of the names mentioned. But all are in accordance on the names of Hares, Abd Manaf, (Abu Taleb), Abbas, Abu Lahab, Abdullah, and, later, Hamzeh.

2. Or, according to one tradition, Omaymeh.

a youth or their brother and drowned his head and face with kisses. Some looked around themselves in the hope of a helping hand and assistance, or turned their heads toward the Ka'ba. But Abd al-Mottaleb, grave and magnificent, tall and a little plump, and with a face whose hardness and attractiveness brought to mind the magnificent Roman statues of stone, kept going. In this situation, such uprightness and determination could be seen in his wide, pleasant eyes that even the highest individuals of Mecca refrained from approaching him.

Most of the sons of Abd al-Mottaleb were calmer than the other people. They realized that that sacrifice had to be the best and most desirable son of their father, they and their mothers and sisters calmed down some, because they more or less knew that he had to be the youngest and most handsome brother of theirs, Abdullah. If there was any doubt or worry, it was for fear of a mistake in the divination and that because of a bad occurrence their name would come up by mistake. The secret of the impatience of the mother of Abdullah and his sisters over the other wives and daughters of Abd al-Mottaleb was being aware of that situation.

Abdullah was the best of the young men of Mecca. A special brightness that could be discerned on his wide, smooth forehead from childhood made him stand out from his other brothers and his peers. At times when drought made people anxious and they followed Abd al-Mottaleb in heading for the plains around Mecca for a blessing of rain, out in front of the seekers of a blessing Abd al-Mottaleb would grasp the hand of Abdullah, and with his head toward the sky, would designate him the intercessor. On the many days when Abd al-Mottaleb was thinking about his faithfulness to the contract, he had narrowed down the actions and characters of his sons, and in the end he could think of none but Abdullah! On many nights, when imagining the day of fulfilling the oath, he could see the scene of sacrificing Abdullah before his face and it had brought moisture to his eyes! How many days he had kissed him many, many times, and smelled him, and taken him in his arms and caressed him. And how many hours had he spent beside him in order to satiate his eyes and heart! But he could see that, on the contrary, those expressions of closeness and affection had made him greedier for this unique child.

Abdullah, however, come forward with his father step by step, calm and accepting, and he struggled to calm his mother and sisters. On the other hand, his brother Abd Manaf tried to distance his mother from Abdullah and himself, and implored her to calm down and be patient.

As soon as Abd al-Mottaleb and his sons stepped into the Ka'ba, the door was closed, and the crowd of people stood expectantly in the sanctuary along with Abd al-Mottaleb's wives and daughters.

The Ka'ba, as it is now, was a rectangular structure. All around it was covered in black Yemeni velvet. Its structure was of stone, and its roof was of wooden beams and mud.

The door of the Ka'ba was situated at the end of its eastern wall, which was known as the "Syrian column." An old man said, "Earlier, this door was even with the ground. When keeping the Ka'ba fell to the Qureish, they built it higher than the ground so that entering it would not be easy and they could throw down from the stairs anyone they did not want to go inside.

We, according to the tradition Walid Moghayneh had established, at the bottom of the stairs, would take off our shoes at the door and leave them there. Once we had gone up the stairs, there were the double doors of the Ka'ba. These were the same doors that, by father's order, had been covered in gold, and the ancient swords were its decoration.

Inside, we went down several stone steps until we reached the floor of the Ka'ba.

Inside the Ka'ba stood six wooden columns in two rows. The roof rested on them. On the first column was a drawing of Maryam Omrān, painted in the likeness of an Arab woman. On her lap rested her child, Jesus. The drawing was decorated with gilt and had very beautiful colors. On the second column was a drawing of Abraham, the "friend" of God, in the likeness of an aged man who was busy divining with arrows. In this same manner, on the other columns and walls were drawings of Ismail and the other prophets or angels. The angels had been drawn like human beings with wings.

On the right side of the door there was a well-like hole into which people would drop their offerings to the Ka'ba. Behind it stood the idol Hobal, towering, thick and fat. Its body was of one piece of purple Yemeni agate. Its left hand, however, had been broken and in its place they had built a hand of gold for it. Opposite Hobal was a wooden ladder that reached to its belly.

The roof was covered in hanging decorations that people had given to the Ka'ba. On the western wall were two ram horns. The people believed that those were the horns of the same ram that Gabriel had brought for Abraham to sacrifice in place of Ismail.

On the south wall were iron rings. Any weakling who was fearful of a powerful person went there and clutched them. In that way, they sought the protection of the Ka'ba. No one dared to hurt or threaten them then.

After we had all gone inside the Ka'ba, father said to me, "Hares, close the door and stand behind it. Don't let anyone in until the divining has finished."

I did what he said and stood behind the door at the top of the stone steps. Then father told the arrow-keeper of the Ka'ba to get ready to do the divination.

The arrow-keeper, with what he knew of the

process from long before, asked in the usual tradition of divining, "The divination should be between what persons or things and for what?"

Abd al-Mottaleb said, "Between ten of my sons so I can know which one must be sacrificed in allegiance to my oath."

Then he gave a bag full of coins to the arrow-keeper and said, "There are one hundred coins in dirhams. My slave will bring the rest of the fee, a camel, when the herd returns from grazing."

The arrow-keeper took the bag of money and placed it in the fold of his gold thread shawl. Then he went around the hole for offerings and toward the platform opposite Hobal. With his hand, he dug into the silver vessel specially for divining that was situated on the platform. Then he bent down beside the leathern, saffron-colored bag hanging on the right side of the platform. He removed the bag from the nail and withdrew the wooden arrows from inside it. The divination this time differed from earlier ones. The seven wooden arrows used for 'blood-money,' 'yes,' 'no,' 'it is you,' 'it is from others,' 'it is stuck,' and 'waters' were of no use.

The arrow-keeper took a pen and inkwell from a corner and wrote the names of Abd al-Mottaleb's sons on ten new arrows. Then he threw the arrows into the divination vessel and mixed them up. In this state, his expensive gold-weave silk cloak waved in the light under the lights of the torches that were placed on the columns, and took on a special shine. Its very wide sleeves resembled dark, deep caves in that dim and secretive light whose termination was hidden from the eye.

After the arrow-keeper had finished mixing up the arrows, he replaced the lid of the bowl[1]. At this time, Abd al-Mottaleb raised his head to the sky, lifted his hands in supplication, and in a voice that more or less reached his sons' ears, said, "O' God! You are the decider, praiseworthy. You are my god. You create and you take away. You bestow and you take away. Every new and old thing is from your presence. O' God, reveal your will to us in these arrows of divination!"

The arrow-keeper, with his face toward Hobal, with a rough voice that he tried to bestow with a varying, amazing, and spiritual cadence, said, "O' our gods! O' great Hobal! You who are near the superior god, the god of gods, you are our intercessor! Now, Abd al-Mottaleb, the son of Hashem, a great man of the Qureish, has resolved to sacrifice one of his children at the foot of the Ka'ba. As the creator, the highest god, guide him in this matter and manifest the truth to him in these arrows."

He closed his tiny, sagacious eyes and recited, "O' Hobal! O' Lāt! O' Manāt! O' 'Uzzā! O' Great God! The possessor of the greatest glory and the highest place!"

He then turned the outside cylinder of the vessel, which was the same shape as the one inside except that it was a little larger, several times.

The vessel rotated with a dry sound and then stood still. The arrow-keeper removed the lid, which was a

---

1. The special container for casting lots.

thin, small plate on the surface of the vessel. The he made a strike on the body of the arrow shaft with a narrow stick he had in his left hand.

One of the arrows fell out through the small slit on the surface of the vessel.

All breathing stopped. Abd al-Mottaleb felt he was choking amid the heavy air filled with the smoke of the torches and candles and the perfume from Taif and the smell coming from the burning of aloeswood, Indian frankincense, and Roman resin. Hobal, though, with that sparse beard and the different hands of stone and gold stood looking on this scene with his large eyes, cold and emotionless.

"Abdullah! The gods have selected Abdullah, O' Abd al-Mottaleb!"

Abd al-Mottaleb, in a voice difficult to hear, said, "I know."

All heads turned toward Abdullah. Abd Manaf, tears running, held his brother tightly in an embrace.

Abd al-Mottaleb, in private, felt he had been released. But he quickly restrained the spread and advance of this feeling with the power of his will and suggestion.

The god of the Ka'ba granted my desire, and after years of waiting, he gave me nine other sons. Now, it is time for me to be faithful to my contract.

There was nothing else to do in the Ka'ba. Abd al-Mottaleb headed for the door. Abdullah followed him. Then, Abu Lahab, who until that moment had been leaning his plump and large body against one of the columns of aloeswood, roused himself and heavily and languorously started moving.

Hares opened the door and stood to one side.

First Abd al-Mottaleb, then Hares, and then the other sons, through the crack in the door, placed their feet on the wooden steps.

The people opened a path, and, amidst their silence, the great man of the Qureish and his sons placed their feet on the sandy soil of the sanctuary. For fear of the answer they thought they might hear, however, no one dared to open their mouth. All stared at Abd al-Mottaleb's young men in case they could discern from their countenances which person the gods had chosen for the sacrifice. The silence was so intense that it had even compelled Fatemeh to cease her wailing.

Abd al-Mottaleb, and behind him his sons, set out for the place of sacrifice in the direction of the Zamzam well. Abd al-Mottaleb stopped beside the rock of the place of sacrifice, which was covered with clots of dried blood. The people, who were like a wave that had unthinkingly moved behind them, formed a circle around the place of sacrifice.

Abd al-Mottaleb called Abdullah forward. He clearly struggled not to let his gaze meet his and have his determination waiver in this situation.

Upon hearing the name of Abdullah from the mouth of Abd al-Mottaleb, a sigh arose from the hearts of the men and women.

"He has perhaps not even seen twenty-four springs!"

"Abdullah is the most beloved and best son of Abd al-Mottaleb!"

"How well the gods have chosen!"

In a trembling voice whose shaking the excitement had increased, a stooped old man said, "We must not let him be sacrificed!"

Fatemeh leaped to Abdullah's side, hung herself around his neck, and wailed.

I yelled, "Abd al-Mottaleb, I will not allow it, unless you first kill me…!"

Then her knees bent and she fainted in the embrace of her son.

I most certainly liked Abdullah. I liked him just like the other wives of Abd al-Mottaleb, even though I was not his mother. There was something in the stature and being of that youth that pulled hearts toward him. In that case, now that the falcon of death had departed the shoulder of my Hares, unwillingly, I felt a lightness in my heart. The other wives of Abd al-Mottaleb were more or less like that too.

That day, when Fatemeh lost consciousness, I hurried to her side. I placed her head on my knee and asked for water from the others. Then I took her golden earring from her ear and placed in under her tongue so her heart would strengthen.

Even though I was engrossed in myself, I suddenly realized that the people were surging and ill at ease.

There was fear of a revolt, especially given that Moghayreh Abdullah Makhzumi, one of the uncles of Abdullah, was among them.

Thus, in order to thwart any unwanted event, and so all could hear, I faced my sons and yelled, "Don't allow anyone to come near until the task is finished!"

My sons formed a circle around me and their brother, Abdullah. The onlookers had no choice but to take a step backwards, and the circle became a little larger.

Abdullah hugged his brothers one by one and bid them farewell. Tears had formed around the eyes of the ten brothers. But the awe of their father and seeing his patience stopped them from allowing the tears to flow.

Abd al-Mottaleb called Abdullah forward. His soft, expressive voice was now broken.

Abdullah quickly finished his farewells and went toward his father. He was contemplating. In this way, he tried to take the lead so as to follow his father in his own desire for life. Centuries before, if Ismail, at the last minute, had been saved from being sacrificed, for what reason could that occurrence not be repeated for him?

Thus, submitting to the desires of the god of the Ka'ba and his father was better! If salvation and granting salvation awaited, it was best that he face his own test with a high head. Too, there was no way of escaping his death if it was to happen that way. Hence, accepting it as a man was many times better!

What was this voiceless feeling inside him though?! What had happened that with that measure of hope in life and tomorrow, that now that death was one step away from him, there was not one iota of fear in his heart?! Was it that he could not show it because…?

Abd al-Mottaleb, with a signal of his head, called his slave forward. 'Āmer, with fear hidden in his old eyes, placed the straw basket he had on his shoulder in front of his master. Abd al-Mottaleb picked up a piece of rope from inside of the basket. Abdullah, without saying a word, clasped his hands together and approached. Abd al-Mottaleb, gently turned the boy around and tied his hands from behind him. At that time, he took his turban off his head and removed the cloak from his body and gave them to 'Amer, and he led Abdullah to the stone at the place of sacrifice. Abdullah, accepting and calm, went with his father.

Beside the stone, Abd al-Mottaleb took the *kafiyyeh* and *aqal* from the head of the boy and gave them to 'Amer, who was quietly crying. Abdullah's long and voluptuous locks, which on their ends had beautiful wrinkles and curls, were spread over his shoulders and moonlike forehead.

Upon seeing this scene, the wailing of the women watching rose to the sky, and the sisters of Abdullah threw themselves onto the ground. Several of the women who could not find it in them to watch that spectacle, turned their heads away, wailing and seeking shelter behind the onlookers.

Abd al-Mottaleb, though, without paying attention to what was happening around him, with a sign of his hand, wanted Abdullah to kneel down beside the stone of the place of sacrifice. Abdullah did that and in one movement placed his face on the stone. Abd al-Mottaleb, with one knee on the stone and the other in the air, in a state of half sitting, withdrew the Syrian dagger with a steel blade from the scabbard under the shawl about his waist.

The wide blade of the dagger glistened under the light of the sun and its reflection settled on the eyes of Abdullah. Abdullah blinked with his long, beautiful eyelashes and for an instant closed his deer-like eyes.

Abd al-Mottaleb took his eyes away. He raised his head skyward and slowly said, "O' God of the Ka'ba, this is now me and my favorite son, Abdullah! You granted my desire, and I am now being faithful to my contract. Grant me and his mother patience, and grant heaven to him who is giving his head for your desire and his father's order!"

At that time, and with the intention that weakness not appear in his will, he quickly placed his left hand under Abdullah's chin, which his soft, fine hair had covered, and bent his head backwards.

The appearance of the throat of the young boy, and the appearance of the white of the neck took away the tolerance of those watching.

Abd al-Mottaleb's hand prepared to introduce the blade of the dagger to the throat of the boy when suddenly from behind a strong hand grabbed his wrist away from the throat of Abdullah.

Abd al-Mottaleb, in the midst of waves of diverse feelings, turned around and saw Moghayreh Abdullah

Makhzumi.

Moghayreh, with a mixture of anger and request said, "Sometimes, instead of a sacrifice, one can be faithful to one's contract by paying money. This is a tradition that has been accepted by the Arabs for a long time. Why can this tradition not be implemented for your son?"

Unhappy, Abd al-Mottaleb said, "But I am not one of those who substitutes the desire of the heart for his contract with his god."

An old man from among the crowd said, "O' son of Hashem! What inauspicious tradition is this is that you are starting among the Arabs? For us, the son is the substance for opening the day and the wellspring of power and greatness. The pride and powerfulness of the Qureish comes from its many and experienced men. If you sacrifice your own son, this act will henceforth become a tradition. Others, following you, will sacrifice their own sons whenever anything happens, and little by little it will extinguish a generation of our men. No! I swear to the gods that as long as there is any other option, you must not taint your hand with this disagreeable action!"

'Akrameh 'Āmer, the senior man of one of the clans of the Qureish, said, "Abd al-Mottaleb, you have always been the example of considered opinion and intelligence among us! But now I see that your contract with the gods has made you blind and deaf, and you have become incapable of accepting another reason or way! How did you arrive at this belief that the gods are not happy with this substitute?! Did not the Arabs establish the paying of blood-money to compensate the shedding of a person's blood among themselves centuries ago?! Is your god more hardhearted and less forgiving than we humans?!"

Abdullah's uncle said, "Yes, Abd al-Mottaleb! Swearing to the same god of the Ka'ba that you believe in is a grave matter. If money can be given to the Ka'ba in the place of killing Abdullah, I and my kinsmen are prepared to give all of what we have for that cause."

Abd al-Mottaleb, of two minds and confused, said, "But…!"

Moghayreh did not give him the opportunity and said, "Put aside the 'ifs' and 'buts'…! Let that go. Did you stipulate the time for your allegiance to your oath today?! Certainly not! So forego this act for several more days. Perhaps a better way will be found for it."

A man from among the crowd yelled, "Why don't you turn it over to the Jewish priests? In this respect, they do not take anyone's side!"

Another said, "Sajāh, the wife of the priest from Yathrib, is the best person for this."

No excuse was left for not accepting. Abd al-Mottaleb did not say anything else. The onlookers began to trill their voices out of happiness. The young men threw their hands around each other's waists and sang and danced together and stamped their feet around the place of sacrifice. The women ululated. A group of the children who had become enraptured by the happiness of the adults became busy among themselves and had fun and played.

When the ceremony of sacrifice was finished, I circumambulated the Ka'ba seven times in thanks, and I told my sons and slaves that no one was to refrain from taking and eating meat, even the birds in the sky or the wild animals of the desert. I wanted all living things to share in our happiness on that day and to give thanks to the god of the Ka'ba.

It was just one day since I had returned from Yathrib. I had gone there with a group of my people to ask the view of a woman priestess of Yathrib about sacrificing Abdullah.

Our going and coming had taken almost twenty days. In Yathrib, I went to see my mother's relatives, my uncles and cousins.

Sajāh first told us to visit her the next day so that with this opportunity she could summon the spirit serving her and ask its opinion on this matter.

The next day, we went to see her again.

The old woman, whose intelligence and shrewdness was obvious from her old yellow eyes, had placed the Torah she had to one side. She had prepared the round plate of copper with four parts and the other tools for necromancy and the astrolabe. Then she asked, "Among your people, what is the blood-money for killing a person?"

"Ten camels."

"Cast lots for your companion and ten camels. If the lots come up in the name of the 'camels,' sacrifice ten camels instead of him. If they come up in your companion's name, add ten camels to the previous ones and cast again."

"And if it came up 'Abdullah' again…?"

Add ten every time to the number of camels and cast the lots until it finally lands on 'camels.'"

"But…!"

"Have no doubt in what I said, and know that your gods will be happy with you."

After we returned to Mecca and cast lots the way that woman had said, the lots came up on one hundred camels. Since I was of two minds, however, I then asked for the casting of lots to be repeated.

The lots came up on one hundred camels again.

So that the certainty be unblemished, I wanted the casting of lots to be repeated for a third time.

When the lots came up on one hundred camels once again, I was certain that the god of the Ka'ba was pleased with this change.

Thus, the next day, I took one hundred of my camels to the place of sacrifice and sacrificed them there.

The people, who had been awaiting this moment since the early morning, rushed toward the carcasses of the camels.

Abd al-Mottaleb cast a final glance toward them as they were loudly, encouragingly, and actively going about skinning and cutting up the carcasses of the camels. The knives, daggers, axes, were repeatedly rising and falling. The bags and straw baskets quickly filled up and were carried out of the sanctuary on the backs of donkeys or on the shoulders and backs of men and the heads of women and children.

Abd al-Mottaleb, happy, warmly grasped the young hand of Abdullah and gently pressed it.

"Let's go son!"

Abdullah answered by affectionately squeezing his father's hand and acceptingly took off.

As they were leaving the sanctuary, Abd al-Mottaleb, unburdened, and with a tone he tried to make sound serious, said, "Do you see how expensive your price has become?"

Abdullah, with the air of a sinner, said, "So it is father! On hundred camels is one man's salary for fifty years! You have given up a large portion of your wealth with this.

Abd al-Mottaleb, this time seriously, said, "I swear to the greatness in whose hands is your father's soul, that if the lots had all come up for all that I own, I would have gladly given it. There is no sorrow now. That which had given has now taken. My rightful possessions are you, my children. The one apprehension of I had was that something would go wrong and I would not be able to fulfill my obligation."

There was no need to repeat this point. Not just Abdullah, but all of the Meccans were certain of Abd al-Mottaleb's firm belief in his contract. Seeing for years his pure life had made it clear to them that when belief and faithfulness to a contract and the next world were concerned, Abd al-Mottaleb would not refrain from sacrificing dearest thing he had.

Abd al-Mottaleb, who did not consider it proper to darken those pleasant moments with any disturbing words or memories, said, "My son, whatever happened has passed. Your father has no other feeling in his heart save happiness and gratitude. You think now about the pleasant moments you have ahead, about Ameneh, and about marrying her! Earlier I sent a messenger to Wahab. "He, his wife Borreh, and the elders of the Bani Zohreh clan are waiting for us. Your brothers will quickly prepare the Hashem valley for the celebration of your wedding as soon as they finish the sacrificing."

Blood rushed into the young, fresh cheeks of Abdullah. Abd al-Mottaleb rubbed a hand on his back and a brilliant smile flashed across his face.

I had wanted that Abdullah to postpone his going on a trading journey to Syria. I said that I did not know why I was not satisfied with that journey. I didn't have a good feeling about it! But Abdullah smiled and said, "Don't be nervous! The people of the Qureish have been passing a large part of their lives in these kinds of journeys for years. The possessions, the abundance, and the happiness of days of the people of Mecca has come from this commerce. Without journeying and trade, Mecca would not be able to continue for one month."

I said, "At least wait a little while! Not even a few months have passed since our marriage!"

He said, "Being far from you is difficult for me as well. You know, however, that one has to struggle to live. The lands around Mecca are so stingy that they don't even allow wheat to grow. One can not even live in this parched city by having livestock, because there is no water or grass for them here. With this situation, if we ignore trading, life will be very hard for us."

What he said was true. In that respect, our ancestor, Hashem, had made those same yearly trading expeditions to Yemen and Syria. Twice each year, in the summer and winter, a trading caravan would set out from Mecca. In the event that Abdullah did not go with that caravan, he would have to wait for months until the winter caravan set out. That time would last so long that the bazaar would become empty of goods from Syria. Losing that opportunity meant that he had to rely on his own fortune.

In the end, the last words of Abdullah shut me up. He said, "I desire very much to be at your side when our children open their eyes to the world in Mecca. But if I leave with the winter caravan, that will not be possible."

Then he encouraged me to be patient and calm. Instead of being anxious and dejected about that, he wanted me to pray that he return soon and with full hands. I accepted and did not say anything else.

Almost half of the men of the city had been standing outside Mecca for an hour under the hot sun and on the last days of summer looking down the road.

Since the evening of the previous day when a rider, tired and dusty, had entered the city and had brought the news that the caravan was near, the city had become completely enveloped by a great deal of excitement. The women, joyful and vocal, had begun cleaning the houses. They had quickly washed their young children and dressed them in clean clothes. They had touched up their own faces and had put on their best clothes. Then they went to bed early and got up at dawn. Then, either riding or on foot, they picked up their children and went outside the city to greet their husbands or brothers. A group of men that had gone to intercept their goods and to quickly determine their profit and loss had also attached themselves to this horde and a large crowd had formed.

Some had built a light shade with legs and had laid out a rug of camel's wool or goat's hair and were sitting on it. Another group was carrying a small umbrella-like shade from several pieces of thin wood and cloths with bright colors. In the midst of this, and in the dauntless warmth of the sun, children were jumping and running and causing an uproar or they were playing hide-and-go-seek among the boulders and calling out to one another.

Several of the youths had gone on top of one of the highest boulders beside the path and were standing facing the place where the dry plain spread out and the road extended like a faint line along its chest. Sometimes they would look at the road using their hands as shades over their eyes so they could inform the people about the approach of the caravan before others.

In front of those who had come stood Abd al-Mottaleb, eyes toward the road, amid several of the great men of the Qureish and two of his sons, Hares and Abd Manaf. A little farther back Fatemeh, Ameneh, and her mother, Borreh, Samra, Haleh, the daughter of Ameneh's aunt who, at the time of her marriage to Abdullah had become Abd al-Mottaleb's wife, and several other women of the Qureish were sitting and had their eyes toward the road.

The women were all busy talking with one another. Ameneh, though, was waiting, quiet, with nervous and happy eyes.

Suddenly, the voices of the youths standing on top of the boulder rose in a scream together, "They have come! The caravan has come!"

A lane opened up in the middle of those waiting. Those sitting stood up. Those standing straightened up to see better. The children stopped playing and surged to the front. The hearts of Ameneh and Abd al-Mottaleb began to beat faster.

Some of the men went atop the stone slabs so as to see the coming of the caravan with their own eyes.

When the large cloud of dust arising from the coming of the caravan was seen, men, women, and children began to move slowly towards it.

Little by little, the leading camel of the caravan, which had a bell larger than the others camels, and whose head and neck were decorated with many red, yellow, black, green, and white tassels, could be seen. Then, the ambiguous tumult of the caravan, along with the faraway sound and sad little bells of the camels, reached the ears.

Thanks! Finally it has ended! The long days of waiting have ended.

The caravan came forward calmly and unhurriedly. It was as if the camels were too tired for even the tempting enthusiasm of arriving at the end of the journey to be able to breathe new life into their weary bodies and increase the speed of their steps. With their own particular dignity, they took easy, though long, steps. And with every step, the bundles of heavy loads on their backs swung like cradles. The soft and pleasing sound of the small bells accompanied by the staccato grunting and drawn out braying of several of them was mixed with the short but audible calls of the camel drivers and they dispersed a pleasing sensation to those who had come to greet them.

By the time the crowd of well-wishers reached the caravan, the pace of the camels had decreased and they slowly came to a halt. The people and the members of the caravan, like two streams of water, converged, waves rose up, and then, little by little, they stopped. All of them sought out their relatives. The voices were all mixed together. Everyone was hanging on someone's neck. The mixture of fine, clean, pressed, and perfumed clothes with those that were rough and dirty, and faces that were tired and sun-burned, had created a surprising scene. The older children were hanging on to their fathers, and the smaller ones were being embraced by them and were saying pleasant things.

Questions and complaints. Weeping and laughing. Kisses and kindness…voices lost amidst one another and unheard.

Astonished and uneasy, we searched for our traveler, but there was no sign of him.

Abd Manaf went up and down the caravan several times on horseback and scanned the crowd with his eyes, but he could not see any sign of his brother. Finally, he came to us nervous and tired and said to his father, "There is not sign of Abdullah."

Upon hearing that, a short, sharp scream jumped out of my throat unwillingly, and I took shelter in my mother's arms.

Abd al-Mottaleb said, "Are you sure?"

He himself knew that it was an inappropriate question. How could Abdullah be in the caravan and not have seen his father, brothers, mother or wife by then? And not have hurried towards them?

Earlier, before Abd al-Mottaleb could give another order, Heshām, one of his slaves who had gone with the caravan to Syria, came to us and, after conveying his greetings, added, "Do not be worried master! Abdullah is in Yathrib with your uncles."

Abd al-Mottaleb asked, "For what reason?! Why did he not come with the caravan?"

Hesham said, "He became ill after returning from Syria, and by the time we reached Yahtrib his fever intensified and he could not continue traveling. I took him to a Christian physician in Yathrib. After seeing my master and giving him some medicine, the physician said that he had to rest for a while. Abdullah is now in the quarter of Bani Qaylah with his uncles and your mother's relatives. He said to tell you and his wife that he will come to Mecca when he gets well."

Abd al-Mottaleb asked, "How many days ago was it that he said that?"

Hesham said, "Almost ten days ago, master."

Apprehension caste a shadow over the faces. Ameneh and Abd al-Mottaleb became more anxious. Fatemeh was, in any case, a mother, and loved Abdullah like her own soul, and this news had upset her, but it did not cause her to feel bad. Sickness was not a serious threat for a young man like Abdullah. Mecca, with its dirty air in the summer, brought a steady variety of illnesses as gifts for its inhabitants. And a Meccan, taken ill, especially in this season, had an old familiarity. Only hearing the news of one sickness on this basis could not make Abd al-Mottaleb and Ameneh very fearful. But that inner call and that worry before Abdullah's journey had made them nervous about this journey. Combined with this news, it brought considerable apprehension to their two hearts.

At that time I unconsciously thought about the death of my father Hashem. Did he not also become sick on the road in the middle of a journey to Syria and thereafter pass out of this world? Did Abdullah not also...?

I thought about those apprehensions I had before my husband's journey, that unfamiliar worry and that fearful doubt. Did they have any connection to that illness? Did that illness cause the death of my Abdullah?

Abd al-Mottaleb remembered the sorrow of years long gone by. The memory of that unfamiliar feeling that continuously spoke to him until his heart and eye could have enough of Abdullah. The memory of those inner commands, one after another, that he would not have Abdullah beside him much....

Until the matter of the sacrifice, Abd al-Mottaleb always thought that Abdullah was that same one whom he was to have sacrificed with his own hand. He was certain that that unfamiliar and tragic feeling issued from this same affair. It was for that reason that, for a while, after sacrificing one hundred camels in the place of Abdullah, that former inner apprehension departed from him. From that same moment, though, when he had told Abdullah to establish his life and to prepare for a trip to Syria, those same anxieties and apprehensions, he did not know from where, returned.

He felt that he would not see Abdullah again. He tried to overcome that unfounded nervousness.

For the men of the Qureish, going on long journeys was a commonplace thing. Abd al-Mottaleb himself had gone on these summer and winter journeys, and he had sometimes brought back a great deal of profit from them. So how could he prevent his own children from going on journeys for business with the excuse that it was not necessary for them? He felt now, however, that it seemed that that apprehension was not so baseless.

That old worry and anxiety; that feeling of foreknowledge of a calamity. Were they related to this journey? If he were to see his Abdullah again….

On the other hand, Ameneh believing the call in her heart, had the same feeling as Abd al-Mottaleb. But this feeling, because it was not old and rooted like Abd al-Mottaleb's apprehension, gave her more reason for hope.

Abdullah was a healthy and fresh youth. In that respect, there was no cause to worry that a sickness would indispose him. Besides that, it had been some time that Ameneh was no longer just one body. The fetus that was being nurtured inside her and that had begun to move around was another part of her. She had to take better care of herself so that she did become injured.

I convinced myself that there was no cause for worry! Abdullah would come back healthy.

She tried to think about the future rather than those painful temptations; about the time when Abdullah would come back from the journey. She tried to remove the long hard suffering on the road and the affliction of the illness with her own treatment and to return the lost power to her darling husband's body once again. Then, as always, and in a tone that should not reveal how disturbed she was within, she said to Abd al-Mottaleb, "Father, what solution should we contemplate now?"

I said, "Tomorrow morning I will send Hares to Yathrib on the fastest camel in Mecca in order to bring Abdullah back with him. By the time Hares gets to Yathrib, he will have certainly regained his health. Don't worry. Life is brief! The life of man was always accompanied by suffering, sickness, and those sorts of hardships. We must be thankful that Abdullah has made it to Yathrib in such a condition!

On father's order, I set out for Yathrib on his fast camel.

I went so fast that the time was shortened by three days.

When I reached Yathrib after five days of traveling, nothing was left of the camel except skin and bones. On the road, I pushed the animal so much sometimes that I feared that it would fall under it own weight. For that reason, despite my anxiety and haste, I had to stop and let it rest.

In Yathrib, I went to the quarter of Bani Qilah and the fortress of the khans of Bani Najar. When I reached the house of my father's oldest uncle, however, there was no sign of my brother. Father's uncle was not in the house either. Only his elderly wife was there. She took me inside and wanted me to rest a while, but I was worried and in a hurry to know where Abdullah had been taken.

The old woman, with an agility that was slightly surprising for her age, went into one of the rooms. She brought out a weaving made from the leaves of date palm trees and she spread it out on the porch opposite the room. On that and with her back to the wall, she leaned against a pillow made of skin and the hair of camel and said, "Sit down, son. Sit down until I bring you a cup of sherbet."

"Thank you. I am not thirsty."

Hares caste a glance mixed with doubt at the room and said, "I don't see any sign of Abdullah. It looks as if he recovered and left the house."

The old woman's grief burst out.

Hares, nervous, rose from his place.

"Has something happened to Abdullah?"

The old woman leaned her heavy body back against the wooden column, relaxed her knees, and amid the sniffles of crying said, "Abdullah was, but is no more!"

Hares, incredulous, took her by the shoulders and looked into her eyes and said, "You mean Abdullah… left the world?"

"Yes, son. Two days ago…! We even brought the Jewish physician of the city to his bedside, but it was no use. Abdullah's fragrant flower lost its petals. Abdullah died…!"

How thirsty his eyes were to see him!

The signs, they were all there. There was a state of anticipation everywhere.  It was as if the world, the earth, time all had a feeling of restlessness. It was as if life was wearied and dispirited. It seemed the weak and the good were tired and impatient. Being, like a field overcome by dust and thirst and heat, it had opened it own thirsty furrow toward the sky. It was pleading for the dampness of the rain of mercy so it could find life and moisture once again.

Corruption and oppression, even inside Mecca, the city of God and the mother of all cities of the world, poured down from its roofs and doors and walls. When he pitched his black tent in the city, the day of libertine pleasure seekers had begun. The fast and sensual playing of the tambourine, the lute, the flute, and the bagpipes filled the alleys and byways of the city of Ismail and Abraham. The alleys of the city of faith in God were reserved in the middle of the night for carousers and the ugly and reckless curses of drunkards.

The days were not very different from the nights. Of that wealth and blessing from God, the intersection and the heart of commerce in the Arabian Peninsula, only a small group benefited. The others were entirely poor, and they thanked the times. So much so that sometimes they buried their daughters alive for fear of hunger and abjectness and shame.

In the meantime, someone like Abd al-Mottaleb was a blessing and an opening to salvation for the destitute and oppressed. The existence of such a man was the last place of refuge for the helpless and the oppressed. The situation was more complicated than what on person alone, no matter how pure, great, or capable, could fix and set right. It was for this reason that the tired and dust-filled eyes and the ears tired of the fear and hope, were to the sky and ground so as to find that savior to set them free no matter when or from where that heavenly call rose up.

Except for Abd al-Mottaleb and some others who were *hanīfs*[1], and others who were idol-worshippers and pagans, a few Meccans had given their hearts to the Christ. One of those was me.

Every year when the days of the pilgrimage arrived, and while people from every region headed toward Mecca and its seasonal bazaars, we went to the 'Ukkāz bazaar to hear the words of the priests and monks who had come there.

Some time before the year of the elephant came, one day in this bazaar I saw a monk. He had gone atop a platform and a crowd had gathered around him. He was a middle-aged man with a slim figure, a thin beard, and long locks. He spoke Arabic with the accent of the Romans of Syria. In his mien and the tone of his voice he possessed a quality that attracted me to him.

---

1. Hanif: Refers to those individuals in Arabia prior to Islam who were believers in monotheism.

Like others, I entered that circle and listened to what he had to say. The monk, with a special enthusiasm, was saying, "O' people! I have read seventy-two books, all of which have come down from heaven. In many of those books, the signs of the last prophet who will come have been written about.

"In the *Zabūr* of David has come, 'O' God! Encourage those who adhere to the tradition so that the people know that Jesus, peace be upon him, is a man and not a god.'

"In the New Testament has come, 'Christ said to his disciples, "I am going, and the day will come when Farqelit will come to you with the Holy Spirit. He will not speak for himself. He will only do what inspires him.

"Farqelit witnesses my prophethood just as I confirm his prophethood, and he reproaches the world for its sins."

"He will revive the people of God, reveal the secrets to you, and interpret the complicated points. I brought examples for you, and he will bring their interpretations."

Meanwhile, a man asked, "What about the Torah? Is there a reference to him there too?"

The monk said, "Yes! In the fifth book of the Torah has come, 'In the same manner, I will inspire a prophet for them from among the brothers of the people of Israel, and I will put my own words in his mouth.'" (Their "brothers" are the children of Ismail.)

"In the book of *Hayquq*, the book of David, and the book of Ash'iyā words like this have come about him."

I asked, "O' man of God, have they written about his signs?"

He said, "Yes! He is from the land of *Tehāmah*[1]. The Arabs call him Ahmad. He had other names besides that, such as Muhammad and Yāsin."

"He is the opener of eyes and the connector of eyebrows. Between his two shoulders is a sign like fur whose color tends toward black."

"He is the most beloved creature close to God."

"It has been said in the Book of Daniel that when born, the angels did not descend for any prophet save Jesus and Ahmad, and neither will they come."

"The night he is born, they will adorn heaven from end to end. At that time, they will call out to them, 'Rejoice and be proud that the master and leader of your friends has been born.'"

"Thus, heaven will laugh, and it will keep laughing until resurrection day."

My husband, Sorāqah Jo'shan, who is a merchant of Mecca, one day told me in confidence, "Keep this secret hidden. On this trip to Syria, I saw a monk who was in retreat in a cave in a mountain, and he was busy praising his own god. When the caravan stopped by the side of the mountain, I went with three of my companions to see him and to ask him to relate a story to us."

"When the monk learned what we wanted, he asked us, 'What land are you from?'

"We said, 'Mecca.'

---

1. *Tehāmah*: Mecca and the lands that are adjacent to it.

"He said, 'It has not been long since God inspired a prophet among you to call the people to the straight past. As he invites clearly, hurry to accept him and follow his path.'

"I asked, 'What is his name?'

"He said, 'Muhammad.'

Then he left us and went to his place of prayer."

"Since that night, we four decided that if we had a son, we would name him Muhammad. It may happen that that messenger will come from our generation."

When I was carrying him, one night someone came to me in a dream and said, "Know that you are pregnant with the great man and lord of this people. Thus, after you gave birth to him, say, 'I give him to the one God to protect from the evil of every envious person, and name him Muhammad."

One day, I was asleep at the wall of Ismail in the Ka'ba. While sleeping, I saw a sprout grow from me. The tree grew so tall that its top brushed the sky and its branches stretched to the east and the west. A bright light began to shine from it, and the Arabs and others prostrated themselves towards it."

Thus, a group of the Qureish came, and they were determined to uproot that tree. But when they approached it, a youth with a beautiful face and presence, prevented them from doing it.

I reached my hand out to pick some fruit from that tree, but I could not. That youth called to me, "You can not have a share in that."

I said, "The tree is from me and I can not have a part?"

He said, "Benefit belongs to that group which they hang from it."

Thus, I awoke from sleep, fearful.

On the road, a priest saw how I was shaking and had become pale. He said, "What has happened to this great woman of the Arabs to cause her countenance to become transformed like this?"

As I told him the story, his look changed, and he said, "O' lord of the Qureish, know that if it is a true dream, a child will rise from you who will become the possessor of the east and the west of the world, and the people will enter his religion."

I rejoiced and thought that that child might be from my son's generation, Abu Taleb!

One night, I had a dream in which I gave birth to the child I was carrying. The women who saw me when I gave birth said, "For women, giving birth to a child is a very hard and painful thing. Why did it not happen like that for Ameneh?"

I awoke at that point.

On another evening, during a dream, they called to me, "O' Ameneh! You have the best of creatures inside you. So, when you give birth, name him Muhammad, and don't tell anyone about this secret.

At that point, I awoke with a start, and that voice was still with me.

There were none of the signs of a pregnant woman

in my mistress, such as heaviness, tightness of breath, pain in the waist, heart burn, or lack of appetite.

She was continuously depressed over her young husband. One night, though, her state suddenly transformed. A special radiance appeared in her eyes, and her sadness decreased considerably.

It was the first of Rabi' ol-avval. I was alone late at night in the room. That room was such that when you came through the door, it was at the end of the courtyard on the left. Suddenly, I felt birth pangs. Then I heard some voices that did not resemble those of worldly people.[1]

An intense fear grabbed me. In that state, I saw a white bird that brushed its swings against my chest and the fear departed from me. Next, I saw three women so tall that they resembled date palm trees. Their countenances were so bright that one might have supposed that the sun shone from their faces. They entered the room, and upon their entering, the space filled with the smell of musk and amber.

The women were wearing colorful and quite beautiful clothes, with a beauty I had never seen before. In the hands of one was a crystal bowl full of white sherbet. She held the goblet toward me and I drank from it. It had the taste and scent of heaven.

Suddenly, a strong light appeared in front of me and encompassed me from head to toe.

At that moment, it was not clear to me whether

---

1. Shaykh Kolayni, the writer of *Osul-e Kāfi*, which, after the Koran and *Nahj ol-balāgheh*, is one of the four basic sources for Shiites, considered the birth of Muhammad to be during the "days of *Tashriq*" (the 12th, 13th, and 14th of that month). Other Shiite scholars, however, consider the 17th of Rabi' ol-avval to be the day on which he was born. The Sunnites consider the 12th of that month to be the birthday of the Prophet.

I was asleep or awake. I felt as if those women were sleeping in my bed and congratulating me.

At first, I thought they were the women of Hashem! Except that they resembled specters from another world. Therefore, it occurred to me that they were perhaps Maryam, the daughter of Umran, Asiyeh, the wife of pharaoh, and Hajer, the mother of Ismail!

One day, Hassān Thābet said to me, "When I was seven years old in Yahtrib one night I saw one of the Jews who had gone atop a roof and in a strident voice was saying, "O' Jewish people! Arise, for the star of Ahmad has appeared!"

The Jews of Yahtrib had earlier told us, the Arabs of the city, that we should be in wait of a prophet who was coming. They also said, "You are one of the first groups that will be drawn to him and that will accept him among you. For that same reason, you will be superior to all the other Arabs."

That night, I had left Taif to do something. I spent many nights in the desert. I do not recall, though, earlier or later, at no time the stars shined so brightly as that. It seemed they had come to the earth and were descending towards it. Being, everything, was wrapped in the silk of heavenly light. A surprising whisper filled the air. It was as if the rocks, clods, thorns, and stalks, those things that were in both the earth and the sky, were murmuring secrets in each other's ears.

I was at that time engaged in business in the land

of the Persians. I heard that on that same night, the large portico of Chosroes shook and fourteen of its crenellations had fallen down. News also came from Fars that the fire temple of the Magi had gone out after being alight for one hundred years.

A great fear had overtaken Chosroes Anushirvan. He immediately sent a messenger to the ruler of Yemen to ask the Arab priests about the secret of his dream.

At that time, there were two priests in Yamāmeh[1] superior to all the other priests. One was Rabi' bin Mazen, whom, because of his miracles, they called Satih. The other was Washaq bin Bāheleh Yemeni. Satih was more knowledgeable than Wathaq. Satih had amazing miracles, and they told stories about him.

He was a naked priest of meat who, except in his head, had few bones.

For this same reason, he kept falling on his back and nothing of him moved except his eyes and tongue.

When they decided to take him some place, they wound him in some clothes. When he reached their destination, they would lay him on a straw mat or basket.

He only slept a little at night, and he was continuously thinking and watching the sky.

The shah and rulers, when they were unable to do something, they summoned Satih so he could inform them about its future, what was hidden, and secrets. The ruler of Yemen saw no choice but to ask Satih about Chosroes' dream.

---

1. Yamāmah: Refers to an area in Arabia that is located in the north of its southern plains. It consisted of Najd, Tahāmah, Bahrain, and 'Oman.

But Satih was in Syria at that time. So a fast courier had set out to him so he could tell the dream and ask him about its interpretation.

Without having heard the story, Satih told the courier why he had come to him. Then, interpreting that dream, he had said, "Time has some surprising events ahead. The kings and queens, according to the number of crenellations, will pass away from the world. When the sound of recitation rises in the land, the people of the Magi will fall from prominence.

Seven days after Ameneh gave birth, Abd al-Mottaleb, as was the custom of the Arabs, sacrificed a number of camels and rams, and cooked a great deal of food. Then he invited the leaders of the Qureish and members of the tribes to a feast. On that same day, the name of the newborn infant became known though his name had been determined earlier and those close had known it.

At dawn of the night Muhammad was born, my wife said to me, "Baraka, go and tell the story to Abd al-Mottaleb."

I found my master in the sanctuary. He was circumambulating the Ka'ba.

When he heard the news, he gave me a gold coin for the good news and he hurried toward my mistress' house.

There, he picked the new-born up with much enthusiasm and smelled and kissed him. Then he wiped a tear from his eye and said, "Thanks be to the god of the Ka'ba that Abdullah will not be without a descendant. Oh how lovely this infant is!"

He said to my mistress, "Name him Qotam."

It was clear as to why he wanted that. Abd al-Mottaleb had had a son by the name of Qotam whom he liked very much. Qotam, however, had died at six years of age, and father had been greatly disturbed by his death. Now my master wished to revive his name.

My mistress, so he would not become upset, softly said, "But in a dream they told me to name him Muhammad."

Abd al-Mottaleb took the infant in his hands. He stared gently at him for a while. Then he pressed him to his breast and said, "I hope that this name will bring a great station along for the memory of my Abdullah."

Now, after seven days, the time had arrived to give the infant to others and have his name become known among them. Thus, after eating food and drinking sherbet, Abd al-Mottaleb asked for Muhammad. Baraka brought him.

Abd al-Mottaleb took the infant all around the assembly and showed him to those present. All looked affectionately at him.

Meanwhile, an old man asked, "What did you name him Abd al-Mottaleb?"

"Muhammad."

"Why did you name him Muhammad, since that name was not used earlier by your fathers or relatives?"

Abd al-Mottaleb had decided to tell the story of his daughter-in-law's dream, but then he quickly remembered that that secret had to remain concealed. So, he thought for a moment and then said, "So he could thank God in heaven and be the lover of His servants on earth."

Our tribe, in the talk of the Arabs in terms of speech and bravery. For that same reason, the great men of the Qureish liked to hand over their children at a young age to us. That was also a boon for us.

That year the sky had been stingy, and it had not rained. The clan had set up camp in a quarter beside Taif – its place every spring and summer. Every day at dawn, the herd would go to the tribe's pasture in hopes of finding grass, and in the evening come back to Taif foaming at the mouth, gaunt, and with dry udders. Finally, some of them swelled up and died. Many of them were killed for fear that they too would die.

It was a dark year. The storage bins of wheat, barley, and other grains were empty. Many days, no smoke rose from the fireplaces of Taif. Many of the young children and some of the elderly were close to death. The rest were no more than skin and bones.

Our Zamareh was still nursing. But I did not have any milk in my breasts to give her. So we took her with some other women of the tribe and went to Mecca. My husband Hares went with us.

Halimeh and Zamareh were sitting on our white donkey and I was riding on our old she-camel. We had set out for Mecca to get an infant from the great families of the Qureish.

After that dry year, Halimeh had suffered greatly

and had become thin. The donkey on which she was riding was no more than skin and bones. So much so that its bones were visible under it skin. On the road, the animal kept weaving to the right and left because it was so weak. It sometimes also became entangled in its own feet and stumbled and came close to falling.

That was our story. How we hoped raise a spoiled infant in that condition and those times and give it milk, we did not know. We were only thinking about how to get through one day.

It was spring time, and the nighttime air was cool. When night came, we decamped beside the road.

The long evening passed dark and bitter for us. Zamareh's hunger had become intense, such that she was continuously crying. But Halimeh's breasts were dry and small and produced no milk.

Zamareh, for one or two days, was not calm during the day and did not sleep at night. That night she wailed so much that first Halimeh, and then I, and finally all of the women, started to cry.

By dawn, sleep and us were like two tribes that were blood enemies of one another. Zamareh was yelling and crying, and I, tired and shedding tears, circled around her and Halimeh and sighed.

At dawn, having tied down the loads, we set off. By now, Zamareh was in her mother's arms, asleep. But Halimeh's donkey acted up. After a while, it laid down from extreme hunger and refused to get up. When it rose again, it could not go on. Therefore, we kept falling father behind the others.

Finally, all of the others went on and we stayed

behind.

We were going home from the sanctuary when, at the passageway of the bazaar toward the Bani Hashem door, we saw several nomad women from the desert. The shopkeepers said they were from the Bani Sa'd Bakr clan who ad come to find an infant to care for. When we heard that, I thought about my grandson, Muhammad.

Spring was coming to an end, and as the heat became more intense, the weather of Mecca would become more strenuous. On the other hand, being given to a clan like the Bani Sa'd would give Muhammad the benefit of strong support in adulthood.

I went to those women and said, "I have a grandchild whose father died. Which one of you will take care of him?"

All of the eyelids were closed in sleep. One of them said, "There is hope of getting something from the father of a child. What hope is there from a child whose father is dead?"

At this time, I saw a woman of tall stature and thin who had a light brown face. Although she was wearing decrepit clothes, in her demeanor were the signs of purity and greatness. He resembled someone of nobility or high stature whom fate had thrown to the ground and made destitute. She was of pleasant character and temperament, with limpid eyes in which kindness surged.

She was riding the white donkey and had a small infant in her arms.

When she came closer, I told her those same words. She said the same thing the other women had said. Then she added, "Good sir, the family of a dervish is enough!"

That is the way it was. Fate determined that he would come to me and that it would become clear to us that we were mistaken.

By the time we reached Mecca with our exhausted and lifeless donkey, it was more than an hour after noon. Within that hour, most of the women had succeeded in finding infants.

After another hour had passed and the shadows had begun to lengthen, each one of them had obtained a new-born child, except for me, who remained empty-handed as before.

The women of the tribe had begun to prepare to return when I told my husband, "Abu Zamareh, is it not a shame that all of the women are going back to the quarter with a child and we are not? Will not the people of the tribe say, 'Why didn't anyone give Halimeh a child?'"

Hares said, "So it is! But what can we do?"

I said, "What would you say if we took that fatherless child?"

Hares sympathized with her and said, "At least it is better than nothing."

Asking, we found the infant's house. We placed Zamareh in a box on the saddle of the donkey and I gave the reins to my husband. Then, still of two minds, I knocked on the door.

A plump slave girl opened the door. I told her what I wanted. She went inside. She returned after a while and said, "Come inside."

I did that, and I saw before me a beautiful and clean house.

The house that Ameneh had received from Abdullah was not very large. It was almost twenty meters in length and twelve wide. The courtyard was covered in even black and grey stones, and its walls had recently been whitewashed.

The house had two rooms. Both of their doors were opposite its door and faced the Ka'ba. That which was on the left side of the house was the larger and had a dome-shaped roof. The roof of the other, which was on the right side, had wooden beams. Both had wooden windows opening to ward the courtyard. The larger one had three double-shuttered windows and the other had two of the same kind. The doors and windows had green paint like the leaves of date palms.

Halimeh went down the two short steps and entered the smaller of the two rooms.

The interior of the room was more beautiful than its exterior. Tow Arabian carpets with broad paintings in yellow, red, and black colors was spread on its floor, and one of the walls was covered in white plaster. In one corner of the room a leathern cradle was gently swinging with a soft squeak. Hanging above it from the ceiling was a small blanket with flowers on it. With each swing, the blanket, like a fan, would fan the sleeping infant lying in the cradle.

A woman of medium height, and smiling, came to greet Halimeh. Her attire was appropriate and her forehead bright. Her cheeks were slightly pronounced and her lips thin. She had delicate, white skin. In her sheep-like large and kind eyes an old sadness resided.

I said, it at a good time and received an answer.

So I sat down and that young slave girl brought a goblet of sherbet for me. After I drank the sherbet, the woman took me to the cradle. A new-born infant covered in clothes whiter than milk was sleeping on its chest, and half of its face was visible. It had full cheeks and thick, black hair.

I turned him over face up. I saw a face like the sun that appears after a hard rain and after thick clouds. Upon seeing that, my heart suddenly began to beat faster, and every vein in my body popped out.

The side of the infant's that was on the pillow had wrinkles on it and had become red. His skin was whitish like his mother's skin, but his was more florid. And too, his lips had the thinness of his mother's.

My heart wanted to hug him and kiss him, but I did not consider it proper to wake him.

I placed my hand on his chest. A sweet smile came across his face and his large eyes opened. A light like lightening that flashes from a cloud jumped from his eyes. With that look of his, my heart warmed, and overflowed with kindness. And it seemed that he had realized my condition and laughed out loud and moved his small arms and feet in my direction.

I placed a kiss between his eyebrows and asked, "How long has he been nursing until now?"

With a pleasant voice the woman said, "For the first seven days from me. Now it has been a while that Thowaybah, his uncle's slave girl, has been giving him milk."

(A while later, Ameneh's slave girl, Baraka, told me that Thowaybah had also given milk to Muhammad's other uncle, Hamzeh, but Umm Jamil, the wife of Abu Taleb, did not like that and had stopped it.)

I picked him up from the cradle and hugged him.

After the grandfather of the new-born infant gave us dirhams and dinars, we headed for the bazaar and bought some wheat, dates, and other things we needed. In the afternoon, we set off for the quarter with the other women.

The beginning of the road from Mecca to Taif is on a plain, and has several twists. Then mountains appear one at a time and then several. The road becomes rocky, full of turns, and inclines. So much so that traversing them is difficult. Surprisingly, though, although we had not given our animals much to eat, Halimeh's donkey went so fast that it caused the other women of Taif to look toward heaven. One of them said, "Halimeh! Isn't that the same female donkey that couldn't walk when we were coming?"

Another said, "O' daughter of Abu Du'ayb, a little shower! Go so our animals can keep up with yours!"

Stranger than that was supper that day.

We had prepared ourselves to tolerate the tears and

sighs of that Meccan new-born along with the hunger and wailing of Zamareh.

Thinking that, at nightfall we stopped beside the road.

Not an hour had gone by when Zamareh's crying arose. I placed a nipple in her mouth. She was deceived and became quiet. I was surprised to see that that milk boiled so much in her that she became short of breath.

I was dumbfounded by that until I informed Hares. But his scream arose before mine when he said, "Halimeh, a miracle! The udders of our camels are full of milk!"

For that reason he then came to me with a bowl overflowing with milk like ivory and I drank it. I believed what he said was true.

I had told Halimeh that I could not stand being far from my grandson. Ameneh was the same. After the death of Abdullah, she was sorrowful and mostly crying, even though she would hear about her child in dreams and get some rest. So, when Muhammad was born, her intense sorrow, like ice that touches fire, seemed to suddenly melt and disappear. The next time, however, after entrusting her infant to Halimeh, her heartache gradually intensified again.

When Halimeh came to more or less learn about these circumstances, she promised to take Muhammad to Mecca every month for a while.

I was not unhappy about entrusting my child in Halimeh. Taif of the Bani Sa'd in eloquence and bravery, was famous among the Arabs. Its people spoke in the purest and most eloquent accent and used the most correct expressions in their speech. The weather of the desert, though it was dry and its days were warm, was nevertheless healthier than Mecca.

Mecca, as you know, is a city that sits in a depression that is surrounded by low-lying hills. In that respect, when the heat became hard, the air became dirty, which was dangerous for newborns and young children. On the other hand, in the desert the children's courage and strength increased.

There were all true, but the story of the heart was

something else....

My master, Abdulmuttaleb, wanted Halimeh, her husband, and his tribe very much.

I remember well when Halimeh came to get Muhammad. My master said to her, "Now, tell me my daughter, what is your name and who is your husband?"

She said, "Halimeh Sa'diyeh, the daughter of Abu Du'ayb. My husband is Hares, the son of Abd al-'Uzzā, the son of Refa'ah Sa'di."

My master smiled with kindness mixed with good naturedness, and said, "From the brave clan of Bani Sa'd Bakr Havāzen!"

Then he added, "Patience and happiness are blessed qualities. That must be considered a good sign. May my child also benefit from your good habits."

Subsequently, I heard from a Meccan woman that Halimeh has a noble lineage and that in her own tribe she is well-known for her intelligence, purity, and eloquence.

Until that time, I had given milk to several of the great persons of Mecca and had raised them. Even earlier I had loved the suckling infants and young children. But this nursing child opened another place in my heart from the time he opened his eyes and smiled at me. I don't know what happened that my heart was taken with his kindness. When I saw his grace and auspiciousness, that compassion grew in me, so much that sometimes I became afraid least my compassion towards him be the cause of less affection for Zamareh.

Not just me alone, but my husband, Hares, and most of the women and children of the tribe were fond of his kindness. My older daughter, Khadāmeh, whom I called Shimā, and who at that time had seen no more than eight or nine springs, was very fond of the child. That is perhaps why she was the best helper for me in caring for and raising Muhammad.

It was difficult for mother with her own two hands to cook, wash, milk, spin wool, weave carpets, sweep the **then**, and to also nurse and care for two infants.

Our Qureishi brother was not a troublesome child, and caring for him was pleasant for me. For that reason, I usually took him from mother whenever I wanted.

To tell you the truth, I had less trouble raising Muhammad than my own children.

He grew bigger every day, so much so that he was notably taller than children his own age. For that reason, the mother and her grandfather were quite satisfied with me. From the time he was nursing, he was so clean that I had never seen an infant as clean as him, and I did not afterwards.

No matter how much we exerted ourselves in Muhammad's care and cleanliness, he differed from the other nursing infants. His body always had a pleasant scent. Whenever I took him in my arms, I would first kiss him for a while and my mind seemed to be refreshed by that.

After he became a bit bigger and began to walk, he stayed clean in that same manner. In the clan, small children like him, when they awoke from sleep, usually had sleepy in their eyes. I do not recall Muhammad ever having had it in his, however.

I remember well when one day Shima said to me about this, "It seems that our Qureishi brother wakes up with his face already washed."

Early every morning, when they put food on the table for the children, they normally took food from one another. But Muhammad never reached for the food of any other child.

When he went toward the desert, I looked out for him. Our Qureishi brother never talked very much, and whenever he opened his mouth to speak, his speech was deliberate and with hesitation, and in the desert he became even less talkative.

At first he played with us enthusiastically. Then he would go aside and stare into the distance or, more often, at the sky. In the quarter as well as on nights when we slept outside the tents, he would constantly stare at the sky, the moon, and the stars until bedtime.

One day in the desert, and without telling the others, he went up a mountain alone. Zamareh, thinking he had become lost, hurried back to the quarter and related the story.

Mother headed for the pasture right away. There, she saw Muhammad sitting at a high point on the mountain looking at the sky.

Mother immediately went to him and took him in her arms and kissed him between the eyes. Without saying any harsh words to him, she took him back to her quarter.

I was not happy about giving Muhammad back to his mother. With Halimeh, we were always recounting the good things about him to our relatives. For, from the time he came to us, our lives changed. Our livestock increased in number, and the milk of our female goats and camels became more. It was as if hardness and misfortune had fled from our black tents, and the sun of good fortune had started to shine upon us.

What is the use, though, for time does not always turn on one axis!

Hares himself knows well that my enthusiasm in caring for Muhammad was more than his. But it seemed our benefit from him was not more than that.

For his fourth birthday, I washed him one day and clothed him in a white dishdasha. I then rubbed oil on his face and put collyrium on his eyes. Then I tied sandals on his feet and took him to his mother's house, to his Mecca.

When the time to return came, Ameneh said to me not to take Muhammad with me anymore.

Suddenly, my face lost its color, and tears came to my eyes. Distressed, I gave the excuse of the cholera that had just arrived and of which all were talking. When she remembered that event, Ameneh did not insist on what she had said.

Joyful, I brought Muhammad back to the quarter

with me, and he was with us for a while longer, until the time when one or two startling events took place and frightened us.

By the time Zamareh began to stand up, sometimes my sister, Onaysa, and sometimes I, would take the goats to the pasture. Zamareh was with us most of the time. During those hours, mother put the Qureishi brother with the other children so she could do her work.

Muhammad would stand watching the play of the other children, but he would not play with them. He seemed to search for me, Onaysa, and Zamareh without finding us. One day at sundown, when we returned to the quarter and were busy playing with him, he said, "Mother, why do I not see my brother and sisters during the day?"

Mother said, "May my mother and father be sacrifices for you! Because they are in the desert."

Muhammad said, "You are not sending me with them?"

Mother said, "If we sent you with them, the sun would burn you to a crisp."

With a sweet frown Muhammad said, "The sun doesn't burn my brothers and sisters?"

Mother hugged him, squeezed him to her chest, and kissed his cheeks.

From then on, whenever I was the shepherd of the flock, mother would rub oil on Muhammad's face and send him with me. Our Qureishi brother was also quite pleased. At sunset, he would return happy from the desert with us.

One day, I came back to the quarter to do something while Muhammad had stayed in the desert with Onaysa.

I was just going back to the desert when Onaysa, frightened, arrived. She was eight years old at the time, and she kept screaming, "Mother, help us! They have killed our Qureishi brother!"

When mother heard that, she let out a scream and asked, "When? Where? What were you doing?"

Onaysa could not speak. She was sobbing, and we gave her some water to drink. After she calmed down some, she said, "Two men wearing white clothes and quite large like no one I had ever seen before. We were in the desert sitting under the shade of a bush when all of the sudden, they appeared. Without saying a word, they took our Qureishi brother to the top of a hill. Frightened, I stayed where I was and could not do anything to help. From afar, I saw one of those two make him lie down and the other, it seemed, split his chest with a knife and took out his heart. He appeared to split it, and he took a piece out of it and threw it away. Then I saw that he seemed to wash it in a pan full of something white, as they say about snow, and he put it back in its place. In the meantime, I came, let out a long scream, and hurried to the quarter."

We had just come from Taif when from our black tent the sound of wailing arose. Anxious, I rushed over there and saw my wife, Halimeh, who had rent her collar and disheveled her hair. She was throwing dirt on her head and racing toward the desert. She had scratched her cheeks so much with her fingernails that blood was running from them. She was crying and screaming, "My dear child, light of my eyes, fruit of my heart, O' Muhammad, where are you?! Why don't you show your face to your suffering mother dear child?"

Several women of the tribe, tears streaming down and wailing, were following her into the desert.

When we reached the place where the herd was, I saw Muhammad. He was calm, standing with his hand on a white kid and watching us come.

Astounded, I ran towards him and took him in my arms and kissed him. Then, I immediately looked at his chest and belly. There was not the slightest sign of any blood or a bruise on him.

Angry, I said to Onaysa, "So what was it you told me?!"

She swore that she had seen what she said.[1]

I took Muhammad on my shoulders and went back to the quarter. The people of the clan had gathered there, and they asked about that amazing occurrence. When I told them the story, one of the old men said,

---

1. Some of the Shiite scholars have expressed doubt about this event. But it has appeared in most of the histories of the Sunnites and the Shiites. Similarly, it has come in one of those histories that at the time of his prophethood, one of his friends asked about the secrets of that event. He answered by saying, "Those two figures clad in white were Gabriel and Michael. That basin was full of the snow of mercy, and they washed my heart in the water of mercy. That black speck that they removed from my heart and cast away was the crevice where Satan resided. It is in the hearts of others, but not in mine, because I was never a nonbeliever, and doubt and temptation were never in me."

"This young boy has been overtaken by spirits and he will soon become crazy. Take him to a Jewish priest so he can see him and give him medicine."

Several other persons spoke up in confirmation of his view.

At this point the grandson of Abd al-Muttaleb spoke up and said softly, "Sir, what you say is not correct. I am healthy, and I do not have the slightest pain or injury."

And I said, "If sympathy for him is proper, I represent his father in this affair and have precedence over all of you. How is it that you don't see that his mind and body are healthy and that he speaks competently?"

Most of them were in agreement with that old man, however.

With no choice, we set out for the 'Ukkaz bazaar with Halimeh and some of the elders.

'Ukkaz was one of the seasonal bazaars of the Arabian Peninsula and was held every year in the month of Zi Qa'deh. It was the most magnificent of those bazaars. Persons who intended to go on pilgrimage first went to the bazaar. They then went to the bazaar of Zu al-Majāz until the arrival of the month of pilgrimage, when they went to Mecca.

'Ukkaz, in addition to its activity, had a good location as well, because it was in the wide plain of Athidā along side a small village with a flowing river, date palms, and a mild climate. The Arabs liked that very much.

The humble merchants from every corner of the Arabian Peninsula and sometimes from Iran and

Syria brought them various goods and sold them is this bazaar or traded them for other goods. 'Ukkaz, though, was not the only place for trading. The briskness in the market of eloquence and boasting, and their poetry, was no less than its business. Every corner of that market was busy and something was supplied that had something for its own particular customers. A group gathered around several persons who knew the lineage of their various tribes and listened to their words about the pride of their leaders and ancestors. An assembly of men formed a large circle around the beautiful and singular tent to hear the newest refrains of the Arab poets from the mouths of their reciters and to become informed about those poems from the perspective of precociousness. Some also came to this bazaar to see the Jewish priests and soothsayers in order to learn about their and their children's future.

In the bazaar, I saw a very old soothsayer from the Hodayl tribe. He had braided hair and a long, hanging beard, entirely white. The hair above his lips was so long that when he spoke, his mouth could not be seen. His eyebrows were so curly and long that they caste a shadow over his eyes.

One of our companions told the story to him.

The old soothsayer, when he heard what he said, lifted his eyebrows with his hand, stared at Muhammad's figure with his tiny grey eyes, and said, "He is certainly not your son."

I said, "What you say in true."

Thus, with a quickness that was surprising for

a man as old as him, he sprang from his place and grabbed Muhammad's collar and pulled him toward him and hugged him tightly and growled, "Kill this child and me with him! I swear to Lat and 'Uzza that if you let him live, by the time he grows up, he will denigrate your relatives and your fathers' customs. He will rise in opposition to you and bring new traditions that you have never even seen or heard of before!"

Muhammad was calm, but an intense anger overcame me because the blood of the people had been defiled. But before I could recover and think what to do, I saw Halimeh suddenly grab and take Muhammad out of the clutches of that old jackal. Then she very vociferously said, "You ignorant old man, it seems your long life has diminished your intelligence! What kind of behavior is this that you are showing toward this child? What is this that you are saying about him? You are more disturbed and crazy than any of the people! If I had known you would say this kind of nonsense about him, I would never have brought him to you. We will never kill this child. If you yourself are anxious for death, find someone else who will kill you and relieve yourself of life's suffering!"

Then, in the blink of an eye, Halimeh and Muhammad, like drops of water seeping into the ground, disappeared into the bazaar.

All of these things happened, but we still did not want to return Muhammad to his mother, until that day when I washed and perfumed him before taking him to see his mother in Mecca.

On the road, we descended from our camels several parasangs outside Mecca in order to relieve some of the tiredness.

Several Ethiopian Christians had started a fire beside the road and were cooking food.

When they saw Muhammad, they asked about him and how he was doing. At that time, I thought that since they had found us alone, a child and a woman, they were thinking about stealing Muhammad.

From where I was sitting, with my back against the camel on the ground, I heard with my own ear when they whispered to one another, "If we take him for the king of Ethiopia, he will give us whatever we want."

When I heard that, my knees began to shake from fear. While there was still an opportunity, I placed Muhammad on the camel and quickly headed for Mecca.

It was the month of the pilgrimage, and people had crammed into Mecca and its environs. When we drew near to the city, I descended from the camel and drank some sherbet and removed the dust of the road from my face and clothes. I did not know then what happened when, in an instant, I was overtaken by heedlessness, and when I turned my head, I did not see Muhammad.

A tremendous anxiety over came me, and I thought, "You see, your heedlessness overtook you, Halimeh, and those Ethiopians succeeded!"

So I screamed at the top of my voice, "O' people of Mecca! O' Qureish! Why are you sitting down when they have stolen the grandchild of your great man?!"

And I sobbed.

We were returning to Mecca with various people. On the side of the Tahāmah desert, in the shade of a Moghaylan thorn bush, I saw a small boy who was standing alone watching the passing of the people.

When I went near him, I saw the signs of greatness in his demeanor and it seemed to me that I knew him. I stroked his head and said to him, "Whose child are you, son?"

Shyly, he lowered his eyes and answered, "I am Muhammad, the son of Abdullah, the son of Abd al-Muttaleb, the son of Hashem."

When I realized he had become lost, I took him with me to the city.

I was sitting along the edge of the sanctuary under a shade woven of strands from palm leaves and was conversing with several persons of the Qureish leaders when I heard that news through the cry of the crier from the direction of the Bani Hashem gate.

Instantly, I sent my slave Amer to find my grandson and I nervously ran toward the Ka'ba and clung to the Yemeni cloth on its wall and asked the gods of the Ka'ba for him.

I was like that for a while, weeping and asking for assistance, when they came and said they had found my grandson. Waraqa Nawfel had found him and brought him to me.

I hugged Muhammad and kissed him. Then I sat him on my shoulder and went around the Ka'ba seven times thanking the gods of the Ka'ba.

That time, Halimeh brought Muhammad one week late to Mecca. Annoyed, I told her, "What happened that you did not bring him on time Halimeh? It is surprising how covetous you are of him!"

But she, sad, said to me, "He has now left my hands!"

I said, "What happened for you to say something like that?"

Halimeh explained the reason.

I said, "Tell me what you are thinking, Halimeh. Is the devil frightening you?"

She said, "I do not know, but I do know I fear him."

I said, "No! I swear to god that the devil has no influence over my child! He has a story that must stay hidden until its time comes."

That is why Muhammad stayed with me from then on. He was five years old at the time.

Finally, after seven days and nights of traveling, the blackness of the city appeared in the distance.

Muhammad loved his grandfather, Abd al-Muttaleb, deeply. Every day at dusk, when he set out for the sanctuary, Muhammad was also with him. At the time of the crowning of Sayf, the son of Zi Yazan was the governor of Yemen. After a long period of time during which the Ethiopians ruled over Yemen, Sayf, who was the descendant of the former kings of that land, and with the assistance of the shah of Iran, overcame them and became the ruler of Yemen. Thus, Abd al-Muttaleb set out for his land with a group of the leaders of Qureish in order to congratulate him.

Muhammad was also very attached to me. But he also longed for Halimeh, her children, and the desert. It was clear that after more than five years living in the desert, staying in the city very much was difficult for him.

As long as his grandfather was in Mecca, that longing was not so evident. When he was gone, however, Muhammad sometimes became homesick and he used his father as an excuse.

One day he told me, "Where is my father's resting place?"

When I said to him "in the House of Nābegheh in Yathrib," he said, "Will you take me there?"

I was myself despondent over the separation from Abdullah. When that happened, I decided to go to Yathrib with Muhammad and Baraka, to have my child see his uncles and cousins and so I could go visit the resting place of my young husband too.

So we waited until the time the caravan was leaving for Yathrib and we joined it.

When the day of departure came, I first hurried to visit the Ka'ba. There, we collected supplies for the road and went to the caravan.

At dawn of the tenth day of traveling, the outline of Yathrib appeared in the distance.

My mistress had relatives in Yathrib. She had gone to Yathrib two or three times before and had seen the resting place of her husband. This was the first time, however, that Muhammad had gone there.

It was springtime, and the heat was not very intense. Surprisingly, on the road, wherever Muhammad did not have any shade, a cloud would appear over his head and cast a shadow over him!

Muhammad was in the pannier near his mother when he heard the trilling of voices. He cast the curtain of the pannier to one side and gazed outside from atop the camel. The caravaneers were overjoyed and congratulated one another.

Muhammad was casting glances this way and that in search of the cause of his companions' joy when Baraka saw the young boy. Baraka, sitting on a black-haired camel, was traveling beside them. When she saw Muhammad's expression, she said, "The outline of Yathrib has appeared. It is not much father to the city."

Muhammad looked ahead. At the end of the road, where it went between two mountains, a green and luscious point like an emerald shone on the surface of the plain. Behind the city, a mountain resembling a low, short wall was standing. Not much of the barren plain behind it could be seen from this direction.

Amaneh said to Muhammad, "They call this range of mountains that is on the right So'ayr, and that that is on the left Ohod. That green point that keeps expanding is Yathrib and it is adjacent to the al-Saylah mountains."

Happy at seeing all of that pleasing greenery, Muhammad said, "Those green things must be the date palm groves of Yathrib."

"Yes, my child. Those are the orchards and groves of the city. Yathrib has more water than Mecca. Its weather is also cooler."

After the caravan had gone a bit farther, the camels seemed to intuit that they had arrived at the end of their long journey and that a place to rest was near. They grunted for joy and increased their pace. The gentle slope of the road helped quicken their steps.

A little earlier, the mud buildings of Yathrib with their dome-shaped roofs rose above the palm trees, and the crow of a rooster could be heard. So this was Yathrib, with its wide dirt lanes. The caravan, which had succumbed to the soft spring breeze, was moving along with its previous unhurriedness.

The caravaneers, content with walking in that pleasant air without the tumult of a sand storm or running out of water, the annoyance of the heat, or the innervating fatigue of the journey, had loosened the reins of their camels and were in step with them while going toward the city's bazaar. The hope of resting in that pleasant atmosphere and that kind city after ten days of traveling without comfort had stimulated a particular happiness in their hearts. It seemed that, still not having arrived, upon seeing that different space, the gentle habits of the people of Yathrib had spread to them too.

At mid-day, we were in the quarter of the Bani Qaylah of Yathrib in the fortress of the Najār khans.

The Najar khans were capable and noble people. Their fortress was a long and stout structure. All around it were very tall ramparts. Inside the fortress, in the first room, was that **Nabegheh person**, their chief.

He was an old man, tall and white-haired. The signs of chivalry and good habits were apparent in his countenance. He and his wives, the mother of Samāk and the mother of Amineh, came to greet us and were glad to see us. Then the people, one by one and in groups, hurried to see Muhammad and my mistress in that same room.

When that was finished, we rested for a while and relieved some of the fatigue from the road. Then we washed away the dirt and grime of the road from our bodies with water and went to the **House of**

Nabegheh, which was a cemetery near the fortress.

The House of Nabegheh, quiet and calm, sitting on the edge of the slaughter grounds and a small date grove at the edge of the city, had a sad air about it. In the middle of it, the resting place of Abdullah lay alone, covered with weeds, lilies of the valley, and anemones.

At that time of day when every person had gone to the fields, the orchards, or the bazaar, a heavy silence hung over that tent. Only the occasional sound of several sparrows or nightingales disrupted the silence.

Amaneh had not wanted to go with them, save with one person. He was one of the young cousins of Muhammad who had come along to show them the way.

The desolateness and silence was so profound that it provoked a feeling of timelessness in Amaneh.

Rest calmly Abdullah, without any unease or worry. Relax to the extent of that eternity in which you are now submerged.

After that suffering, you have become so relaxed that no storm can disturb the limitless ocean of your calmness. Death has made you in need of nothing, and thus you need fear nothing.

Be calm, for no one will ever think of sacrificing you any more, and you will never have any illness or other agony.

Truly, what humbling and illuminating greatness does death have.

How and on what feet Amaneh reached the side of her beloved husband's resting place she did not know. She only came to when she realized she was kneeling down on the ground and digging her hands into the soft soil of his grave.

"Is this you, Abdullah, who, like this, confined and helpless, have become the prisoner of this dark soil?

"So what happened to that youthful freshness and strength? You lacked nothing for your dear body to join the earth like this so soon."

Ameneh, unwillingly, had returned to the past, to the evening of her wedding. O' what good fortune she had come upon! The most well-disposed and handsomest young man in Mecca, who had stolen the hearts of all the young girls, had become hers. She had stolen that amazing light that shone on Abdullah's forehead and for which girls such as Fatemah Khath'amiyah were prepared to give everything they had to make him theirs.

Ameneh was herself worthy of that union. She was also one of the most beautiful and chaste girls in Mecca. In spite of that, even though she had never mentioned it, being married to Abdullah was a distant desire of hers.

It was a strenuous struggle. There was one Abdullah and more than two hundred young girls of Mecca who wanted him, and they did not refrain from using anything for that purpose.

Many of them, in terms of the beauty of their

faces and figures, were the most outstanding of their families and clans. The best of them was Fatemeh Khath'amiyah, who in terms of knowledge had no equal among the young girls of the city. These, those many possessions and that life like princes, were enough for Fatemeh to steal the mind of any man and throw him to her feet like a slave. With that, what hope could Ameneh have in her own good fortune? She neither had many possessions among her relatives nor did she like those kinds of reckless things of the other girls. She was so virtuous and chaste that she did not consider it proper to attract Abdullah's eye towards herself or even to show herself to him.

Ameneh recalled the tears and jealous looks of the young girls of Mecca on the night of her marriage to Abdullah.

"What happened that the bird of happiness, after making circles in the sky, alit on your shoulder amidst all of those hopeful competitors?! What came up that this surprisingly good fortune, which resembled more a sweet dream, came to be only yours?! Among all of those, did you have anything other than patience and self-restraint?! You, who had not even told your own mother!"

She could not! She could not do what she did until this good fortune had taken place, and the unseen had been digested! Sometimes she was even afflicted with doubt about whether this was not a dream in which she was writhing. Was this really that same

Abdullah, the darling of all the young girls of the city who was now hers and beside her?! Had these now become hers? This balanced form of loneliness? These voluptuous locks that taunted the night? These black, seditious eyes?! More than that, this incomparably amazing brilliance that caused the splendid secret of the mixture of the heart to shudder? And willingly cast fear in the heart with those predictions…?!

Ah! Thinking about the greatness of that good fortune was beyond Ameneh's capability, and sometimes it awakened an unfamiliar fear in her heart. "Will this happiness last a long time? Will Abdullah always remain mine? Will a hand—a hand I don't recognize, but whose nerve-wracking presence I feel every moment—one day take him away from me?"

Ameneh, now at the side of Abdullah's resting place, remembered clearly that, at that time, imagining this day would dry up the blood in her veins, and her heart came close to stopping.

"Mistress, if you give your permission, Muhammad will go back to the fortress with his cousin."

Baraka was kind and sad when, tears streaming from her eyes, she placed her hand on her shoulder and spoke. She then brought her head near so Muhammad would not hear, and said, "I dare say, mistress, that it is better that he not see you in this condition."

Ameneh, agitated and gloomy, said, "Let them go back. You are right, Baraka. His small heart may not be able to withstand this much sorrow."

What there was became even heavier with the

departure of the two children. What village-like calm this Yathrib has! What stillness and loneliness! What remorse from being alone this prostration at Abdullah's grave placed on Ameneh's heart!

I know what you are going through, my Abdullah, because of this distance and loneliness. Earlier, I endured the despair of exile. Oh, Abdullah, if you only knew what Ameneh went through during that journey you took to Syria!

My mouth had a bitter taste because of your being away. Mecca seemed empty because of you not being there. The city seemed to be dead. It was as if it was not the birthplace and land I had known earlier. I felt as if in exile day and night. It was as if I had set foot in a strange city gripped with sadness, where no one looked for me in any of its alleys or houses, and no heart yearned for me. My mother came often to see me. Whenever your father was in the city, he would remember me at every opportunity. But not one of them could fill your empty place or settle the depression from loneliness inside me.

It may seem surprising to you, but with all of that sense of loneliness, I sometimes deeply desired that no one be near me so I could think about you without any hindrance.

When I decided to eat something, before placing the first bite in my mouth, I would remember you. That piece would stay in my throat with the thought of where you were at that moment and what you were eating. When I wanted to take a drink of cool water, overwhelming feelings would close my throat and the water would not go down easily with the thought of you in that dry desert and drinking nothing but warm, undrinkable water.

Ah! If I had only known that this would be your end!

That year, we were in Yathrib for thirty days. During those days, my mistress would go alone to the House of the Nabegheh and mourn and weep over the grave of my master, Abdullah. Those who did not know the love my mistress had for her husband were surprised at why there was still sadness and lamentation that after six years. But I, who knew well that wife and husband, and the attachment and faithfulness of the Bani Zohreh to her husband, I was not surprised at this affair. For that reason, I was always afraid that this sadness would kill my mistress. And for that reason, I made sure that Muhammad did not learn of this story and not worry more than that.

The Hashemi master went far away from the caravan,
    And fate deceived him,
    And death called him to him,
    And took him from me.
    His relatives took his litter on their shoulders,
    And his friends cried blood mourning for him.
    Woe is me, who gave up the dearest of my dear ones!
    Regret for him, who, in seeking to be free of being sacrificed,
    In youth, went to the mouth of death!
    Poor me,

Who in the springtime of my life
Became your widow and mourner!
Woe is me, Abdullah!
Woe to those long and painful nights of mine…!

The uncles and cousins liked Muhammad very much. He had two cousins in particular who were always with him. Onaysa was a kind girl with black hair and long eyelashes from one of the neighbors of the Najar family and the same age as Muhammad. These four played with one another every day. The cousins sometimes took Muhammad to the date palm groves and the orchards, and they sometimes went together to swim at the pools and ponds. But they were mostly in the pools of the 'Adi Najar spring. Sometimes they also went to the towers of the fortress where the cousins would put the birds to flight and he would watch.

During these days, Muhammad played in the water so much that he learned how to swim, and those things made him quite happy, because there were no pools or water in Mecca for the children to play in so as to learn how to swim.

Yathrib had moderate weather and fresh and drinkable water. In those date groves and orchards were tangerine, lemon, peach, apricot, grape, pomegranate, and fig trees. There were also many green and summer melons. For that reason, the inhabitants raised in this moderate and generous climate had gentler characters than the people of Mecca.

The forts and buildings made mainly of mud in Yathrib gave a softer appearance to the city in comparison with the dry, rock houses of Mecca. The sloping lanes of Mecca were the source of some of the special games and pastimes of its children, whereas the wide, smooth passageways and the small squares of Yathrib provided many opportunities for running and jumping and various other games of the children of this city that Mecca lacked for its own children.

What a pleasure it was to live in this green and kind city! The pleasing aroma of the date palms, that cool, moist breeze that blew among the date groves and above the green summer expanse and the summer crops between the date palms, along with the melodious songs of the date nightingales, the sharp chirps of the green parrots, and the flights of flocks of sparrows plunged Muhammad into a heavenly world.

I also liked Yathrib. But when I saw the physical decline and the affliction of my mistress, I decided to take her away from Yathrib. To be far away from the grave of her husband to relieve her remorse. So I told her, "Mistress, my master, Abd al-Muttaleb, has probably come back from Yemen now. I fear that if we are late, he will become worried."

My mistress agreed.

We then packed our luggage and prepared things for the road so we could set out for Mecca at dawn the next day.

It was summer, but the heat was not very uncomfortable there.

The caravan took the southerly route. At the end of the long line of the caravan was Ameneh's yellow-haired camel on top of which was a wooden pannier with curtains of the same color. Muhammad was inside the pannier with his head on his mother's knee. A black-haired camel was moving along beside them. The young Baraka was seated on it.

The middle-aged singer of the caravan was singing with a pleasant tune now, and the camels, intoxicated by his singing, hurried in their movement. His singing affected the souls of the travelers, and a shadow of distant sorrows, though deep and sweet, was cast over their eyes. Some of them were so engrossed in their own thoughts that tears welled up like springs in their eyes and rolled down their cheeks.

"Ring, ring, ring!"

Praise the dear city that kills the stranger!
Praise the silent House of Nabegheh!
Praise my Abdullah who has no one!

Ameneh closed her eyes, leaned back against the small pillow of palm leaves, and with her hand on Muhammad's shoulder, sank into a sweet sorrow. It seemed like just yesterday that she was in her home when her mother came into her room and told her, "Daughter, get ready. A suitor is coming for you in the evening."

Borreh remained quiet and gazed at the figure of her daughter. Ameneh, blushing from shame, cast her eyes downwards.

"You did not ask who the suitor is!"

Ameneh still did not say anything.

"Okay, I will tell you. Abdullah."

"Which Abdullah?"

"The son of Abd al-Muttaleb."

Ameneh's heart began beating faster, and blood rushed into her face. So as to keep the secret hidden, she turned her face away.

Borreh went into the courtyard before her daughter had an opportunity to find herself. Ameneh then sat in a corner to give her heart an opportunity to calm down.

The rest passed like lightening. Before she could realize what she had said or what she had heard, Ameneh was in the valley of Bani Hashem and on the wedding platform.

Crowds of people filled the valley. So many torches, candles, and fires were alight that the space was as bright as day. On the north side of the valley, several platforms were placed beside one another and a large surface had been formed. At the forefront of this surface was a small platform a little lower. It was covered in green silk, and Abdullah was on that seat in a milk-white *dishdasha*, and with a cloak of camel's hair on his shoulder.

Abdullah was wearing a small green turban that enhanced his beauty and dignity. He, with that bright wide forehead and that demeanor of a young man, was sitting shoulder to shoulder with her, and the shadow of her large curly eyelashes fell on her protruding cheeks.

His mother, the mother of Abdullah, and his sisters, like a half circle, were behind them. On the other platforms, like this one, Arabian carpets were spread out. On them, Abd al-Muttaleb and others of the leaders of the Qureish and others were sitting, talking and laughing.

The sandy courtyard in the middle was covered with the brittle branches and leaves of eucalyptus trees, as well as vines and tamarisk. Every now and then a nice breeze blew gently and brought the pleasing and fresh smell of plants, so much so that it seemed that they were sitting in the gardens of Taif. At every step were tall silver and bronze incense burners. In them were aloes-wood, sandalwood, frankincense, Arabian gum, and Yemeni incense were burning and their aromatic smoke was wafting in the air. On the short four-legged stool of granite at the edge of the platform there were glowing pieces of fire, and wild rue and alum were burning to ward off the evil eye from Abdullah and her.

Around the middle courtyard, from one end to the other, women and men, large and small, were sitting and standing. At the end of the courtyard and opposite the platforms, the players of *sornās* and kettledrums were playing fast, epic songs from atop a large rock. In the middle, two nomads of medium height and slender as sticks were doing the sword dance. Each one had a helmet on his head and a pair of curved swords from India in their hands, and they were enacting a lively battle. Sometimes, opposite one another, and with even steps, they turned around in opposite directions. Then they twirled the swords in the air around their wrists and came to each other's side. Sometimes, like two symmetrical parts, face to face or back to back, they did surprising things. One would circle around the other. The one would stand while the other went around him. As the *sorna* and drum sped up, their turning and show would also go faster. Back to back, and swords in hand, they would jump in the air. When they came down, they turned like lightening, squatted on the ground face to face, and in that position, with a loud cry, they hit their swords together, so hard at times that a spark would fly into the heart of the night. (At the same time, the people trilled their tongues and the young people whistled.) Sometimes, one would back off and the other would follow him. Then, the second would scream and jump up in the air and the other would sit down. At that point, one would kneel and the other one would stand and both of them would hit their swords together.

At the edge of the platform, two small children, each with a wooden sword in his hand, were imitating the sword dance. Suddenly, a young girl became scared and screamed, and her mother took her in her arms and away from the spectacle.

The sons of Abd al- Muttaleb were busy helping the slaves and servants and attending to the various tasks. Meanwhile, Abu Taleb, Hamza, and Zobayr were mainly talking excitedly.

In a corner far from the excitement, the cooking fires were blazing. Large pots of food were boiling and large pieces of meat were grilling over fires. In the crossroad, there were four pools of stone filled with sherbets from the juice of grapes from Taif, dates, and vinegar-honey, and all around them a number of children, women, and men were drinking.

She was sitting behind the green veil hanging over her face, shoulder to shoulder with her Abdullah, and she was gulping down that great happiness. Abdullah, too, with a sweet smile on his lips, was looking alternately at her and at the dance of the two nomads.

The long bellow of a camel brought Ameneh out of that state of mind.

"Mistress, the caravan is going to stop at this place so we can rest awhile and refresh ourselves by washing our hands and faces.

Ameneh signaled her agreement to Baraka with a kind gesture. Thus, they turned the heads of the camels to the left and alighted at the edge of the date grove far from the others. Muhammad awoke with the movement of the pannier when the camel knelt down on the ground, and he got out.

Ameneh wiped the large drops of dewdrop-like sweat from the forehead of her small boy with a handkerchief of white silk. With a smile on her face, she smoothed away the hairs that had fallen on his forehead and squeezed him.

While Baraka was busy adjusting the pannier on the back of the camel by fastening its ropes, Ameneh took a water-skin from the camel's load and said, "My darling, wash your face and hands so that you become refreshed."

Muhammad, drunken from sleep, lifted up the hem of his striped *dishdasha* and followed his mother.

They sat beside a dried up stream. With the water his mother poured from the water-skin, Muhammad began to wash his face and hands. At this time, Baraka finished the work with the pannier of her mistress' camel and went over to her own camel's saddle.

The young woman and the young girl poured water on one another's hands and washed their faces and hands. Then Baraka took the camels over to a well that was farther away so as to give them water to drink.

The sun had reached the middle of the sky. The melodies of some birds that seemed to have sought shelter in the grove from the noonday heat, like a sad lullaby, lulled Ameneh's tired eyes to sleep.

Baraka came with the camels and brought with her a white blanket. Ameneh took the blanket from her and spread it out in the shade of a date tree. Then she brought some bread and a small copper pot from the saddlebag on the back of Baraka's camel.

Farther away, Muhammad seemed to be looking for something among the short green plants under the date tree. Baraka called out to him to come. Muhammad came. He had his small hands behind his back and had a smirk on his face. Then, with a quick movement, he extended his two hands together and said, "For you!"

In his right hand was a stalk of desert narcissus and in his left was one of anemone.

Ameneh and Baraka happily took the flowers from him. Baraka gently kissed Muhammad's soft hand

and said, "A flower was not necessary my dear. You yourself are a flower!"

Ameneh took some halvah from the copper pot and placed it in front of Muhammad with a piece of bread. Then she put some on her bread and gave the pot to Baraka.

Baraka and Muhammad began to eat, but Ameneh could not eat more than two or three bites. Baraka looked at her worriedly. Ameneh had no color in her face.

"Are you not feeling well Mistress?"

"No. I just don't have any appetite. Perhaps it is the heat."

Baraka did not say anything else. With her back against the trunk of the date tree, Ameneh stared ahead, and her look gradually became far-off.

The land and its people have changed.
And the world is dark and ugly.
All of the colors and tastes have changed,
And the people, in place of large orchards,
Have thorny trees and lotus.
An enemy that never forgets
And an entity that never disappears
Has come near to us.
Woe for that pleasant figure
That is sleeping in the earthen grave!
....

The sun was setting at the end of the plain. The caravan, as before, was going towards Mecca, so as to travel to a safe place before night arrived. Muhammad, sitting on the saddlebag of the camel in front of Baraka said to her, "So when will we reach Mecca nanny?"

Kindly, Baraka said, "We have only been on the road for two days now. If it continues like this, we will be in Mecca in eight more days."

Muhammad yawned and said, "When we get to Mecca, will my grandfather be back from Yemen?"

"Yes. He may have already come back."

"Nanny…when do people leave the world?"

"When they grow very old. But why do you ask?"

"Did my father leave the world when he was old?"

"What things you ask my dear!"

"Was he old?"

"Okay…no….He was young. He became ill. Then…."

"In Yathrib?"

"Okay. …Yes."

"Did he leave the world after having a fever?"

"Yes. That is what they say."

"Mother also became sick after we entered Yathrib. She also contracted a fever. Will she too?"

Crying interrupted Muhammad's repose, and he could not say more than that. Baraka pressed him to her gently and said, "Relax my little one. Who told you that everyone who gets a fever will leave the world?"

So as to change the course of the conversation, she said, "Do you miss your grandfather very much?"

Muhammad did not answer. Musing, he quietly cried and watched the blood-red globe of the sun go down in the east.

"Do you know how many springs your grandfather has seen until now? More than one hundred! Do you think that your grandfather has never been afflicted by a fever until now? No, my dear!

"Man exists from breath to breath. Sometimes a sickness overcomes him, and the next day he rises, healthy."

Baraka said these things, but she thought to herself that her mistress' illness might be more than just sorrow over the death of her husband.

"Did I tell you what courageous things your grandfather did in the year of the elephant and what happened?"

Muhammad wiped the tears from his eyes with his right hand and said, "What year?"

"At the time when Abraha, who had the cut nose,[1] came toward Mecca with his army and elephants to destroy the Ka'ba."

"What did my grandfather do at that time?"

"That is a strange story. Let it be until a day or night when there is an opportunity, and I will tell it to you from beginning to end."

At this time, several date tress, and then mud huts, came into view.

The leader of the caravan called out to the people in the caravan that the place was the village of Abwā'[2], and he had decided they would stay there for the night.

---

1. Abraha's nickname was *ashram*, which means "cut nose" in Arabic.
2. A village that is twenty-three miles, or approximately sixty kilometers, from Medina.

Night. That night was a long night. Every moment seemed an hour! The sun seemed to have drowned in the eastern well and had stayed there and did not have the ability to rise. Sometimes fever would come and, like a red hot furnace, would consume the afflicted body of Ameneh, and sweat like narrow rivulets of water would roll down the crevices of her body. Then her breathing would slow so much that one thought there was no air to breathe. She then tossed the curtain aside and tried to rise to go outside, but her hands and feet did not have the strength to help her do that. So that her child and Baraka would not wake up, and unable to do anything, she would fall back on her bed, bite her lip, and quietly sob.

Sometimes a shaking would overtake her. At those times, she would gather all her energy in her arms, pull the blanket over her, and curl up, and sweat would cover her entire body from one end to the other. Then a strange slackness would overcome her. For a while, she would forget herself and not be aware of anything. But the suffering from the nausea and the headache was more than any of those. It was as if a hammer inside was continuously striking her brain. Her brain seemed to have swollen and was pressing on her skull and seeking a way out. Her stomach became unsettled and suddenly a wave came up from it to her throat and mouth. Yet, she was so empty that nothing came up, other than Ameneh's desire that, "O' how I wish I had all these pains, but not this one!"

Amidst the fever and the shaking and the nausea and headache, sometimes, for just a little while, the suffering would diminish. Repose. Then Ameneh would think about human frailty and the unreliability of life, and she would remember her husband.

You were also overtaken by this condition Abdullah. The body is like a flower, and your freshness wilted like that. May Ameneh be a sacrifice for your loveliness and sickness in those moments! I wish that I had been there to care for you!

Weakness, numbness, and fatigue. The joints of her body seemed to have come apart and no longer had that connection they always had before. Ameneh no longer seemed to have control over her limbs. Going. Coming. Struggling between death and life.

"Where are you death…?"

During these three nights, and with a continuous fever until morning, Ameneh suffered so much that she now longed for death. No matter how bitter her life had been earlier, she had never considered death so sweet as now. The intensity of the pain, the remorse, and the despair had brought her to here where she found death to be a relief for her.

Earlier, one thought constantly made her terrified. "What will happen to Muhammad without me? For this fatherless six year-old child, will the former orphan be able to accept being an orphan? In this time full of merciless turmoil, what will he do?" Now, no matter how preoccupied she was with this thought, the pain and agony was such that she could not stand to think about it much.

What benefit is there in thinking about that from which there is no escape?!

Then, unwillingly, that surprising vision from before Muhammad was born entered her mind, and those visions from the unseen about her orphan. Then she murmured to herself, "I entrust him to that self-sufficient One from the evil of every jealous person seeking to harm."

Surely, if Muhammad, without the kindness and support of a father, had gotten through those years full of emotion and danger such as that, he could also survive without his mother. If neither Abdullah nor Ameneh were around, at least their god and he were. The same one who had protected her child during those dangers and hardships can also protect him from then on.

The first white rays had begun to appear. The milky-white lightness of morning shining through the cracks in the door of the room brought with it a strange calmness to Ameneh, like the person who stands atop the roof of the world and from that vantage point looks upon the creatures and what they do.

With the start of day, the pain and fever subsided. In addition to that, even, Ameneh found herself more able than in those last two days. So she half rose up and stayed with her back against the pillow, half sitting up.

The small village of Abwa also awoke now from last night's slumber. The sound of life could be heard from the mud huts; its narrow, twisting lanes. A cow lowed in the stable. Then the squeaking of the well wheel came, followed by the rushing of water into the animal's water trough.

Ameneh heard from the lane behind the hut the sound of a small herd of goats and kids and the calls of the young goatherd. Following that, the smell of the herd filled the room and dust wafted in through the cracks between the double doors. At that same moment, several sparrows–probably looking for food–sat loudly in the courtyard.

Baraka awoke from sleep with their chirping. She quickly looked around at her surroundings. She seemed to be afraid of something. But when her gaze fell on her mistress, she suddenly became both happy and ashamed.

"Forgive me mistress that tiredness and sleep caused me to neglect you."

"Be calm, Baraka. Calm! In these few days, you have gone to so much trouble for me and my child that such negligence should not be the cause of your shame. You deserve sleep and relaxation. Have peace of mind, long time companion of Ameneh's grief! Calm, patient sympathizer of Abdullah's orphan!"

These words were spoken without the exchange of words and with only a few looks. Ameneh and Baraka had become so close in these seven years that many words were conveyed from one to the other without a word, and with only a look.

"May life be better for you mistress! It seems you are better."

With a look from Muhammad, who got up from his bed, Ameneh suppressed her response.

"Good morning my son! Did you sleep well last night?"

With a sweet smile, Muhammad answered his mother, and then he hugged her.

"Don't worry like this, mother's little companion! If I am not around, your protector will be."

When I arose from sleep that day, I saw my mistress sitting up on the bed. She seemed to be better than before. I became happy and went outside to get her a cup of milk.

But my mistress only drank a few gulps of that milk.

After Muhammad and I ate breakfast, my mistress took Muhammad in her arms. She kissed him, smelled him, and shed a few tears. Muhammad leaned his head against her chest and cried a lot. I could not stand it, and I wept. Then mistress sent Muhammad to do something in the courtyard and called me to her.

She held my hands between her own feverish hands and kissed me on the face.

I began to weep profusely and kissed her flower-like hands. She placed her weak hand on my hair and caressed it. Then, with that sweet and comforting voice of hers, she requested that I deliver Muhammad to his grandfather after she was gone, and until that time, while possible, not leave her for a moment.

My mistress said to me, "Baraka, you know well that Muhammad is no more than six years old. From the beginning, he never saw his father, and he only saw a little of his mother's kindness. He does not have a brother or sister. For that reason, after me, he will be quite alone. In the meantime, he has a special affinity for you. Your being at his side should bring him comfort and peace of mind."

I wept bitterly again. Then I tried to console her, saying she could survive the illness. But she said, "No, Baraka! Every new thing becomes old, and every living thing dies. I will die too. You can see this right now. It is the calm before the storm. I am very familiar with my own condition. Last night, during those few moments when I could not sleep, I saw Abdullah. He was worried about Muhammad, but he told me that I had to go with him….I am leaving, Baraka."

Including that day, it had been three days and three nights that we had been in the village of Abwa. On the second day of our stay, the caravan had left, and we had to stay. We went to the house of an old woman who was blind and alone, and we rented a room from her.

During those two days, my mistress' condition sometimes became so bad that it frightened Muhammad and me. At first, I fed her whatever medicinal plants I knew of and that were available. But it was to no effect. So I resorted to the old women of the village and I provided whatever she needed for treatment and I fed them to her. But still it had no effect. That day when I heard those words from my mistress, I went crying to the old woman of the house and asked for help. She told me that there was a knowledgeable Jewish priestess who lived on top of a hill far from the village and who had come there from Mecca some years ago. I should go to her and bring her to my mistress' side. Maybe relief would be found.

I told Muhammad not to go outside, and I went to that priestess. But when I reached her home, her servant woman said, "My mistress went to her shrine on the mountain of Abwa, and she will not return for three days."

Discouraged, I returned to the village. Before reaching the room, I heard Muhammad's wailing. I rushed to the room. I saw that Muhammad had placed his face on that of his mother. He was sobbing and moaned, "Mother, what happened to you? Why don't you say something to me? Why don't you get up so we can go to Mecca? Don't you know I don't have anyone but you?"

I cried from the bottom of my heart and went to my mistress. Her eyes were closed and her moon-like and weak figure resembled that of a suffering angel that was in a deep sleep.

Scared, I put my ear to her chest. Her heart was not beating. I raised my two hands as if to beat my head and dishevel my hair and tear my collar. But when I saw the scared and sad figure of Muhammad, I became afraid lest he die from excessive remorse. I was terrified. "Be calm Baraka! Now it is only you and this memory of happiness and your mistress! Understand that!"

Thus, with much effort, I separated Muhammad from his mother and said to him, "My dear, she is no longer able to speak to you."

When I saw the perplexity in his innocent person, I added, "May Baraka be a sacrifice for you. The name of this condition is death. Mother…is dead!"

It is daytime again now. Again, the light and radiance of the sun. Another day in the long life of the old world. Another uncomfortable period in the cycle of life. Lives. Death. Building to be destroyed. Destruction for the sake of building. Deaths and lives. Birth, for death!

O' sun, earth, mountains, plains, and sky, how many deaths you have seen, and yet you are still in your places, with such lack feeling, and such hardheartedness! Those, who were tied to you like that for a long time and so fond, and who had their feelings of relationship and acquaintance, are now no longer. You, however, without any alteration, remain, and, inattentive, pursue your own existence. It's as if you never knew them and there was never any affinity between them and you! As if their being or not-being was the same for you!

Oh, what an untrustworthy companion you are!

The small mourning caravan, with an empty pannier, cut through the breast of the dry plain and headed toward Mecca. The empty and quiet plain ahead seemed to stretch on forever, from one end to the other, flat, monotonous, and soft. Its sands seemed baked by the merciless sun of the desert and had become purple.

The dull, deep clanging of the large bell on the camel empty of the traveler Ameneh, mixed with the shrill and memorable sound of the small bells of that other camel and awakened the dumb sleeping memories in the minds of Muhammad and Baraka. At that moment, it filled the bitter sadness of their hearts and from the gravelly road poured its poison into their souls and encircled all of their two existences.

Baraka preferred that this quiet linger and leave her to herself so she could look into the mirror of her soul and journey in the secret layers and folds of life until she discovered the secret of her being. But only the silence of the young orphan who was now sitting with his back against her chest on this saddle of the black-haired camel and looking far away did not allow doing more than that. In addition to that, since she was deep in thought, the companionship of this kind sweet child was of immense value to her.

It was true that in that strangely dry and rough life of hers, this young beautiful object of desire was like a spring with cool, refreshing, and ebullient water that had produced flowers and plants along with it.

When Muhammad stepped into the world, it was as if Baraka herself had borne a child. The world was transformed. It was as if a rain of mercy had fallen and washed away all of the darkness in her despairing life that had collected the dust of exile. Thus, life had found a surprising transparency and glimmer. Being became kind. The dour figure of life opened up and a pleasant smile appeared on it.

How the young heart of Baraka opened up when

she hugged that dear child, and how sad it became when he was taken to the desert as an infant. Now, though, this blooming blossom, the scent of whose body intoxicated Baraka, had been entrusted to her.

For Baraka, Muhammad was also a memorial to her master Abdullah and her mistress Ameneh. At the time of her death, had her mistress not entrusted Muhammad to her and made requests?! Thus, Baraka was responsible for keeping this dear trust and caring for him.

A sad smile came over Muhammad's face. Then, staring ahead like before, he said, "Is much left until Mecca?"

Baraka said, "It's not more than a few days."

Then, before Muhammad's thought switched to something else, she said, "Shall I tell you about the adventures of Abraha and his elephants?"

Flashes of enthusiasm flew from Muhammad's big eyes and he said, "Yes. Tell it! Tell it nanny!"

Baraka, happy at his attitude, said, "With pleasure my dear!"

She then adjusted her seat on the saddle. She straightened her back. She placed a gentle hand on Muhammad's shoulder and softly said, "This story is famous among both the Arabs and the non-Arabs. So much so that the year this event took place came to be called 'the year of the elephant," and it became the beginning of a new history of the Arabs."

"You know that gate of Mecca that they call 'elephant'? It acquired that name because Abraha's army entered Mecca by that gate. Along the road, too, that spring whence the elephants drank water was given the name 'the elephant spring.' The road that Abraha followed from San'a to Mecca became known as 'the elephant trek.' In short, every place where that army did something was given the name of elephant."

Muhammad adjusted himself a little on the camel's saddle. Then he asked, "Where is San'a? In which direction is it located?"

"San'a is in Yemen, and Yemen is south of Mecca."

"It is not in this direction from where we are coming?"

"No, my dear. Yathrib is on this side of Mecca, to the north. Yemen is on that side of Mecca, to the south. Yemen is a large land and quite developed. The Yemenis are speakers of Arabic and are distant relatives of the Qureish."

"On the trip Halimeh and I made to Mecca, I saw some Yemenis and they were quite white in complexion."

"Yes, the skin of the Yemenis is whiter than that of the Arabs of Mecca, Yathrib, or the desert. But their land is in the Arabian Peninsula, and all of them speak Arabic."

"Didn't you say earlier that Abraha, the king of Yemen, was black?! Was he not from Yemen?"

Baraka kissed Muhammad on the head through her white shawl and said, "How smart you are! No, Abraha was from Ethiopia. Ethiopia is a large land on the other side of the Red Sea. Yemen is on this side of that sea."

"So what did Abraha do in Yemen?"

"The story about that is a long one, my dear. I fear that if I tell it from the beginning, you will lose patience. Anyhow, Abraha was the leader of the Ethiopian army. When the king of Ethiopia, Najāshi, raised an army to go to Yemen, he placed Ariāt in command of it, and Abraha was with that army. Zu Nowās, the king of Yemen, lacked the capacity to confront the Ethiopian army, so they came to govern Yemen. At that time, Najashi made Ariat the governor of that land."

"Are you of the people of Ethiopia, nanny?"

"Yes, my dear! They brought me from that side of the sea to this side as a concubine."

"How did Abraha become the king of Yemen?"

"Abraha was one of Ariat's commanders. After Ariat had ruled over Yemen for some years (one group says two years), Abraha became covetous of the crown of that land and some in the army joined him. At that time, Ariat was in San'a and around it and Abraha was in Janad and around it."

"Where is Janad?"

"Janad is a city in Yemen, forty parasangs from San'a. It is an unpleasant place and has distasteful water. Anyhow, when Ariat saw that, he decided to put Abraha in his place. So they met one another, and they and their supporters had a battle."

Groups from the two sides fought one another until Abraha sent Ariat a message saying, "This war has occurred because of me and you in the army of

Ethiopia. But it is not sensible for our armies, which are from one land and of one people, to be wasted. So you come and fight me now alone. Then, once one of us is killed, the other will become king."

Ariat agreed to that suggestion, for he was a brave man, with a pleasing figure, tall, stout, and quite powerful. Abraha, no matter how able, warlike, and agile he was, was short and fat, and his back was a little bent.

So, Ariat said, "This is quite fair. Now that he is in bad straights and wants to confront me, why should I not accept?"

Abraha knew very well that he was no match for Ariat. So before the battle took place, he thought about a trick. He told his slave, 'Atowda, before the fight between him and Ariat, to be ready in the first row of the army. When he saw things become difficult, come onto the field of battle and kill Ariat with a spear.

The next day, the armies watched the battle between their two famous commanders.

The kettledrums of war began to beat. Ariat came out from among his army with armor of red leather on his body and a long spear in his hand. Abraha did the same. Once face to face, Ariat first attacked with his spear and left a mark on Abraha's head. Abraha nimbly ducked his head, but Ariat's spear ripped his forehead, eyebrow, and eyelashes and cut his nose and upper lip.

When Abraha's slave saw that, he rushed forward and assaulted Ariat from behind and plunged his spear into his heart.

In short, Ariat died. When the soldiers saw it was like that, all of them went over to Abraha and gave their allegiance to him.

They say that when Najashi heard that story, he was very surprised that Abraha had done that with his appointed commander. So, he immediately swore on Jesus Christ that he would not sit still until he himself had gone to Yemen and pulled out Abraha's hair and beard, spilt his blood on the ground, and stomped on the soil of the land of his rule.

They took that news to Abraha. Abraha was a sly man, and he had a great deal of patience. When he learned of that oath, he began to think about what to do in order to deflect that evil.

So, he plucked out some hairs from his head and beard and placed them on a piece of leather. He also filled a bag with dirt. Then he told a cupper to take a cup of his blood. He also wrote a letter and therein he maintained his allegiance to the Christian faith and loyalty to Najashi. He wrote in that letter, "Ariat was your slave and servant, and I am one of your slaves and servants. What I did was not for my own sake, but for yours, for Ariat did not lead the army and he did not know how to rule.

"All of the army complained of him. I was afraid that a dispute would occur among the Ethiopians, and we would lose Yemen. And you know what happened after that. Now I swear upon the Christian religion and the Father, the Son, and the Holy Ghost, that Yemen belongs to you, and that I am still your appointee over it. I am, however, more able than Ariat in the affairs of the Ethiopians, more politically astute than him, and a better administrator. Thus, is it prudent for the king to come here with his army and endure such hardship for such a minor affair?

"They say, though, that the king had sworn a serious oath concerning this servant. So that your oath is fulfilled, here is the hair from my head and beard! Pluck those with your hand. And this is my blood. Pour it on the dirt. And this is dirt from Yemen that I have sent for you. Have them put it under your feet and stomp it."

Then, along with large gifts of money, he sent those to Najashi's court in Ethiopia.

They say that Najashi, when he saw those, he calmed down. He smiled and said, "How clever he is, that man with a cut nose and no lip!"

So he turned over the governance of Yemen to him.

In that way, my dear, Abraha became the king of Yemen.

The day was now getting close to its hottest time. So that the sun did not bother Muhammad, Baraka wanted to tell him to go and sit in the pannier. She quickly remembered, however, that in these three or four days, she had told him that several times, and yet each time Muhammad had declined to sit in the pannier. It seemed he did not want to sit in a pannier in which his mother had earlier sat and on the small pillow in it she had leaned on. So she placed his head on her knees and caressed his hair with her long thin fingers.

Baraka also did not consider it proper for her to sit in the place of her mistress whom she held so dear. Thus, with a hidden compromise, the youthful Ethiopian concubine and the noble Qureishi orphan had accepted that Ameneh's pannier, empty, and on the back of her white camel, be their companion from Abwa to Mecca.

It was very hard for both of them to believe that Ameneh was no longer with them, that joyful figure whose happiness was obvious and whose sadness was concealed. Now, in an unfamiliar corner of the village of Part, she was sleeping on a dark bed of dirt. Those eyes full of beautiful shyness that took away all of the sorrows of the world from their hearts had now become dull and had dried up in the skull. They no longer heard that soft pleasant and kind voice.

In these few days since leaving Abwa, Muhammad had cried so much that Baraka had become afraid that his delicate spirit would break the brittle form of his body and unite with the spirit of his mother. So, even though she was weeping bitterly in her heart, she always resolved not to let him have a moment alone so that he did not think more than that and not be sad. For her mistress' spirit would be happy if her orphan mourned less and reached his grandfather healthy, no matter how much the question of Ameneh's relatives—how she had left with her and come back without her—went unanswered!

"Are you thirsty my dear?"

"No…. Aren't you going to continue with Abraha's adventures?"

"Aren't you tired? If you want, we will rest a little under the shade of these rocks, and then resume our traveling."

"Did you not say it was better that we get to Mecca soon? Let's go now and rest at night."

Earlier, before the sun began to bother them, Baraka had seen a cloud that had slowly come over their heads and cast a shadow over them. Baraka gave a cup of water to Muhammad from the bottle hanging on the side of the camel and said, "Drink! Drink even if you are not thirsty! The heat is intense. Don't let it get to you."

Muhammad took the cup from Baraka. So that the water did not spill because of the camel's swaying, he put it to his lips and quietly drank. Then he gave Baraka the cup.

Baraka put the cup back in the saddlebag behind the saddle and with a sad smile on her face said, "Yemen had many cities and the happiest population on earth. Its cities are both in the plains and in the mountains; both in dry places and beside the sea. Aden and Hadramawt are beside the sea. San'a, the city where the king resides, is in the dry area. Yemen has a lot of water and its agriculture flourishes. It has innumerable orchards and forests, like heaven. Its trade also flourishes. You know that the winter trade of the Qureish is connected to that land."

Anyhow, after a while passed, Abraha knew that every year at the time of the pilgrimage, groups of people go to Mecca from every corner of the Arabian Peninsula. Thus, he decided to learn the reason. They told him, "In Mecca, there is a building they call the Ka'ba. The Arabs go every year to visit it and circumambulate it. Before and after this custom there are also bazaars in that city and around it, and in them a lot of trading takes place."

Abraha asked, "What kind of place is this Ka'ba for which the Arabs have so much regard?"

From that day, Abraha resolved to build a temple in San'a, magnificent, beautiful, and without equal in the world. So he announced that in the Arabian Peninsula and people were called to come on pilgrimage. He thought that with that trickery he could diminish the brilliance of the Ka'ba and Mecca and increase that of Yemen and San'a.

So he sent letters to Caesar in Rome and Najashi

and other Christians and explained his plan to them.

All of them congratulated him and sent assistance to him. Of those, the king of Rome sent Abraha engineers and experienced sculptors with blocks of marble of various colors.

On the other hand, the queen of Sheba, who was at one time in the city of Ma'āreb—some say Sheba—and ruled in Yemen, had a very large and magnificent palace. Ma'areb was to the west of San'a, three and a half parasangs away. (This Sheba was the same woman who became the wife of Solomon.)

At the time of Abraha, some of that place still remained. Abraha ordered the blocks of marbles, multicolored stones with paintings, and other decorations that still remained of that palace, be taken to San'a.

He told all of the people they had to work on building it in turn. So they cleared a high place beside his palace on an extensive plain. Then they built the foundation of a building with four corners, of which all the sides were equal.

By the time this temple was built, several years transpired. During that time, Abraha oppressed the Yemenis harshly and forced them to work hard without wages. He ordered that any person who appeared for work after sunup must have his hand cut off, and many of the men and youths of Yemen in this way lost their hands.

The temple, once it was built and opened, was a great structure without equal. All around it was a rampart that had a length of one hundred meters on every side. The bottom of that area was covered with engraved stones with pictures from end to end. They say that the slabs were so even that a pin could not fit in between them.

The wall of the rampart was built with those same stones, and it was ten meters high and three meters thick. The crenellations of the rampart was made of three-cornered stones of green, red, yellow, white, and black. At the four corners of the rampart were four towers, with walls and made of white marble on top of each one of which was a small tower one meter tall. Every row of stones in those towers was of one color. The first row was a shiny black marble that they had brought from the mountain of Naqm. (This mountain was on the edge of San'a, on the western side of that temple.) The next row was of yellow marble. Above it was a row of white marble, bright like silver.

In the middle was a square structure that was thirty meters high, so high that they say the Sea of Aden could be seen from it height. Its stairs were also of marble. This building had three levels, and every level was of one color. Its walls were decorated in wood with pictures. Marble had been used in every place along the wall that had an entrance. Above the marble there was shiny black marble, and on top of them were white stones.

This building had a door of copper, painted with very beautiful drawings. On it sheets of silver and gold had been provided and jewels were apparent at various places on it. This door was five meters high and two wide.

When you entered that building, there was a white hall, forty meters long and twenty wide. In it were columns of teakwood, decorated with gold and silver nails. There was a portico there twenty meters on each side. The portico had windows on whose glass were figures of trees and various designs. Then there was a courtyard that was fifteen meters long and fifteen wide. The walls of that courtyard were covered with tiles of azure. On the tiles, crosses or stars of silver shone. Inside that hall were two columns of teakwood. Quite surprising pictures had been carved on them of humans. (As time passed, people came to call one of them "Ka'ib" and the other "the wife of Ka'ib," and they sought blessings from them.) In the middle of the roof of the courtyard were two doors. The ceiling was covered with tiles with pictures of gold crosses. On the eastern side of the dome was a marble, transparent like glass, so much so that the light of the sun and the moon passed through it into the courtyard. Underneath the dome was a pulpit of ebony. The steps of the pulpit were of teakwood, decorated with gold and silver. On its two sides were embedded white pieces of ivory.

Golden chains hung from the dome, and bronze Syrian chandeliers were attached to them. In every corner of the courtyard brass incense burners were alight and disseminated a pleasant scent into the air.

They named that temple "Qolays." (One group says they called it that because of the great height of its dome.) Abraha put nice coverings on it and designated people to serve it. Then he ordered that they build churches in other cities as well, and he invited the people to become Christians, and he imposed a tax on anyone who did not accept that religion.

Abraha spread the news of the Qolays temple in the world. For example, he sent a letter to Najashi that "I built a temple in your name of which there nothing like it in the world."

He also ordered the painters to draw the pictures of that building on a skin and sent it with the letter.

Talk about Qolays came up everywhere. Wherever there was a road, they hurried to see it, and they all made sacrifices there and composed eulogies to him for building that temple. Then the news reached the king of Rome, Caesar. This time, he sent colors for Abraha along with pictures of Jesus, Mary, and the other holy persons of that religion so they could be used in that temple. Caesar also wrote a letter for Najashi, saying, "That official of yours in Yemen did something that no king in the world has ever seen or heard of. With that, he has elevated your and his name so high that higher than that can't…."

Najashi was elated, and he wrote a letter to Abraha and congratulated him.

Then Abraha wrote to Najashi, "Here, in Mecca, the Arabs have a house of stone which they call the Ka'ba, and they circumambulate it and make pilgrimages to it. But this temple you built is better than that. From now on, order the Arabs to stop making pilgrimages to that house and instead make them to this temple so your pride and glory will increase and be eternal."

Najashi was also gladdened by that, and he gave him permission.

Abraha first ordered the people of Yemen, all of the Christians and Jews, to go on pilgrimage and circumambulate Qolays. After a while, he also sent a message to the other peoples of the Arabian Peninsula telling them to make pilgrimages to it. Therefore, in the month of the pilgrimage, he sent officials to the beginning of the roads to Mecca to call and direct the travelers to Mecca toward Qolays.

Baraka whetted her lips with her tongue and said, "Now it is time to eat and to rest a while. You have most certainly become tired from listening. You can listen to the rest when we start traveling again."

So they drove all three of the camels to the side of the road to where several old date palms were grouped together.

Abraha was firmly committed to the Christian religion, and he had tied his hopes to Qolays. But what he envisioned did not happen, and every year when the time of the pilgrimage came, the Arabs would again come to Mecca in droves from every corner.

They informed Abraha that during these days people from the cities of Yemen were heading to Mecca in groups or one by one, clandestinely or openly. Abraha became angry and issued harsh orders against them. Yet, the situation was more complex than that.

The situation was such that Abraha grew angrier by the day until he decided to take the Ka'ba.

The people became very amazed about the reason for that decision. Some said it was to repay what that man of the Bani Foqim had done. This Bani Foqim was one of the branches of the Bani Kenāneh tribe that lived along the path between Mecca and Yemen. They said that Abraha's order and actions upset a man of that clan. So he dressed up like a Christian priest and went to San'a. There, he claimed that he had come a long way on pilgrimage to Qolays. He went inside the temple and performed the pilgrimage and sat there until nightfall.

The caretakers came and told him to get up and leave because no one was permitted to sleep inside the temple at night.

The man of the Bani Foqim said, "I have traveled

a long distance and borne many hardhsips in order to worship in this place and to perform a pilgrimage as it should be done. Now, how do you consider it proper that my suffering be for nothing and that I not achieve my intention from this magnificent place!"

He said that and pleaded and lamented a great deal, so much so that the key holder felt pity for him and granted him permission.

So they closed the doors and left.

When day neared, that man did a large amount of damage in that place and fouled the doors, walls, and decorations of that building. Then he hid in a corner.

At dawn, when the keeper of the key came and opened the door, than man, without him knowing, quickly ran to the door of Qolays and fled.

Abraha heard the news of that. He became very upset and on the spot swore that he would not rest until he had gone to Mecca, destroyed the Ka'ba, and brought its stones to Yemen.

He then ordered them to wash Qolays with water and rosewater from Iran, and they covered its doors and walls with musk from Khotan and amber. They also made a thousand censers full of aloeswood and burned them in that place until the bad smell had left. He then sent a letter to Najashi asking that he send that large white elephant to him. (That elephant was the vanguard of the Ethiopian army, and they said that it was in every battle that the Ethiopians had won.)

Some, however, related another story. Their claim was that one night a caravan of Arab merchants made a fire near the walls of Qolays in order to prepare some food and to keep warm from the night's cold. In the middle of the night, however, a strong wind came up and blew that fire onto the walls of Qolays and burned parts of it.

At first, some were gladdened by this occurrence and said, "The respect for Abraha, the Ethiopian king, and their temple has been lost among the Arabs and others." But some of the old people believed that this story was propagated by Abraha. For, by means of that pretext, he decided to destroy the Ka'ba so there would not be another place of worship in Mecca for the Arabs, and they would have to look to Qolays.

At that time, news came that Abraha had assembled an army of sixty thousand, black as sparrows, terrifying like demons, and as agile as lizards, and they intended to advance on Mecca with eight elephants.

Then they said, "Zu Nafr is responsible for raising an army to confront that of Abraha on the road. (This Zu Nafr was originally from Hadramawt and before Ariat had ruled in Yemen.) Men joined him from around Mecca as well in order to help him in that cause. They said Zu Nafr raised an army of ten thousand men.

But Abraha defeated Zu Nafr, who was taken prisoner.

Abraha wanted to take Zu Nafr's life, but Zu Nafr said to Abraha, "O' king, if you don't kill me, a large portion of the Yemenis will become indebted to you because of that. Doubtless, I am more useful to you alive than dead."

Abraha was a clever and patient man, and that is

what he did. Zu Nafr joined him as a prisoner.

When Abraha's army reached the land of Khoth'am, they say that Nofayl, the chief of the Khoth'am tribe, blocked his way. (The Khoth'am had two clans, the Shahrān and the Nāhes, and there were fifty thousand families in those two clans.) But the Khoth'amis were also defeated by Abraha, and Nofayl was taken prisoner.

Abraha wanted to kill Nofayl. Nofayl told Abraha, "Abraha, you know what my position is among the Arabs. There are fifty thousand families behind me. You can make them all obligated to you by forgiving me. Set me free so I can join you and guide your army, which can not proceed though Arab lands without knowing the way."

"I myself had seen an elephant. Every elephant drinks as much as a hundred camels. For that reason, on that long road from Yemen to Mecca, the guide has to be familiar with the springs and ponds and show them to Abraha so that the army and its elephants are not beset by thirst and don't collapse. With that in mind, Abraha did what Nofayl had wanted and refrained from killing him, and Nofayl guided him as far as Taif."

At this time, a sad smile came across Muhammad's face, and he said, "When I was in the desert with my nanny, every spring her clan would camp near Taif. During that time, Halimeh's husband would sometimes go to Taif and bring different kinds of fruit for us."

Baraka lovingly stroked his head and said, "I was in Taif for a while too. It is quite a large town, on high ground, and in a valley. It has clean air and so much water that it resembles one of the towns of Syria."

Anyhow, the people of Taif decided to get along with Abraha. Their leader, Mas'ud Mo'tab, went to greet him with a group of the town's elders and said, "O' king, we are all your slaves and servants, and none of us has any quarrel with you, because the king has not come to destroy our town and temple." (They meant their idol temple to Lāt, whose location was in Taif, and the Arabs honored it.)

Abraha was satisfied. His army stayed a while in Taif and rested from their trek, and the people of Taif treated them well and they provided all they needed with respect to food for the army and forage and water for the animals and elephants. Besides that, when Abraha decided to head for Mecca, they sent one of their men by the name of Abu Raghal to show him the way.

The people of Mecca became very frightened because the distance from Taif to Mecca was no more than twelve parasangs.

A group of Arabs hurried to Abraha and said to him, "Take our animals, livestock, and all of our other belongings, but do not destroy the Ka'ba."

But Abraha did not agree.

More than any was the talk of the elephants. Most of the Arabs had never seen an elephant until that time. For that reason, it was very surprising for them.

One said, "Its body is like a hill, and its height is that of several buildings." A second one said, "Its feet resemble enormous columns." Another said, "They say that its nose is like a thick pipe and so large that it reaches to the ground. When it is angered, it rips large trees out of the ground with it and flings them away." Or, "It has two teeth that are the size of two swords." Some also said of its scream that men's hearts stopped from fright.

To be brief, they said so much about the awesomeness of the elephant that what remained of the men's courage vanished and all of them lost hope, and became fearful and distressed. So most of them took their livestock and other means of livelihood and set out for the mountains around Mecca.

The time for a difficult test had arrived. You grandfather, Abd al-Muttaleb, appealed to the people to seek refuge in the Ka'ba. In order to remove the fear from their hearts, he told the story of those three former kings of Yemen who had also had designs against the Ka'ba, but they did not attain them. In that confusion of terror and danger, no one lent an ear to that kind of talk. Some even answered him by saying, "Whatever happened, those kings were Arabs and of us. But this one is black and an Ethiopian, and he has no affinity for the Arabs. Another thing is that they did not have an elephant. Abraha has frightful elephants like enormous battering rams, and we have no protection against them."

So he gathered the leaders of the city in the assembly building in order to determine their opinion.

They all said, "We haven't the ability to stand up and fight an army with elephants. It is best that we evacuate the city and save ourselves."

At that time, news arrived that Abraha's army had reached Moghammas and had set up camp there. At that locale, some Arab men, seeing an opportunity, assaulted Abu Raghāl and killed him. (Moghammas is two stages from Mecca.)

When your grandfather learned of that, his eyes watered up and he considered it a good omen. The people of Mecca also became happy at that news, and they praised the killers of Abu Raghal. (After that, whenever an Arab passes by that place, he curses Abu Raghal and throws stones on his grave. For that reason, that grave has become a hill from all of the stones they have thrown on it.)

On that day, a messenger sent by Abraha came to Mecca and got a view of the large city. They took the messenger to Abd al-Muttaleb.

He said to your grandfather, "Abraha, the ruler of Yemen, has sent me to give you the message that he has no quarrel with the people of Mecca. Thus, if they do not oppose him, he will be satisfied with the destruction of the Ka'ba."

Your grandfather said, "Tell him we are incapable of confronting or doing battle with you. This holy structure is God's house and was built by His true friend Abraham. The God of the house can protect His own house if he wants. If it is leveled, we can not do anything."

The messenger returned and those people who

were there also left Mecca. Only your grandfather remained, and the city.

All of the people left. Mecca remained, empty, silent, and gloomy, with Abd al-Muttaleb and his choking feelings.

Abd al-Muttaleb went to the Ka'ba. He clasped the black cloth faded by the sun and prayed intensely.

"O' God, your servants have taken their possessions in order to keep them out of the enemy's reach. You, too, keep the enemy from your house!"

"O' God, now all of the doors are closed, and all of the lights of hope have been extinguished. No hope remains for us save You. O' God, do not allow their cross to overcome Your house and their glory and power to excel Your glory and strength!"

"O' Answerer of Requests and Eliminator of Sorrows! O' Knower of Secrets and the Destroyer of Oppressors! Fortify us against this onslaught and support us!"

"O' Lord! These who have chosen to live with dignity, even with all of their sins, are Your slaves and servants. If You now allow the enemy to destroy Your house and sanctuary, tell us, where will we worship You thereafter?"

Your grandfather wept so much on that day that an hour later when his wife Samra saw him, his eyes were still red and bulging.

At sundown, they informed Abd al-Muttaleb that a group of Abraha's army had taken away two hundred camels from his herd.

The next day, your grandfather went to Abraha's

army camp with some of his children and relatives. There, he went to Zu Nafr, with whom he was previously friends. He said to Zu Nafr, "Can you do anything about this predicament that we are in now?"

Zu Nafr said, "Uncle, I am myself like a prisoner, and I fear every instant that in the morning or evening they will kill me. What can I do?"

Abd al-Muttaleb said, "Give me some guidance right now."

Zu Nafr said, "The elephant driver who rides the large elephant has information about Abraha. His name is Anays, and every day he takes news about the army to Abraha. We used to be friends before. It is better that we send him ahead."

Zu Nafr went to Anays and told him the story. Then he added, "Anays, we are distant relatives with the Qureish, and this Abd al-Muttaleb is one of the headmen of the Meccans and is the leader of their caravan in the mountains and plains. There is no one more beneficent than him among the Arabs. He is equal to the north wind in generosity. He always gives food to the needy, and what is left over he sends to the wild animals and birds of the mountains and plains. See whether you can get his camels back."

Anays said, "I will tell these things about him to Abraha, and I will get permission for him to see Abraha. He can tell Abraha himself about the affair of the camels."

On a high point in the middle of the army camp, a tent with a dome of red brocade stood, and above it the flag of battle waved in the breeze. That flag was red as well, and in the middle of it was the drawing of a yellow cross. Inside the tent, Abraha was sitting on a golden and bejeweled throne, and he was lying on a pillow of swan feathers. When news of the arrival of the headman from Mecca reached him, he stood, placed the crown on his head, and put the royal robe over his shoulders so Abd al-Muttaleb would perceive his awesomeness. At that point, he permitted the court to be convened.

Your grandfather, as you know, is noble, stout, and dignified, and he had a very pleasant figure and appearance.

When your grandfather entered the tent, Abraha realized his gravity and magnanimity, such that he descended from the throne and greeted him. He did not return to the throne, but sat with him on a cushion on the carpet.

Abraha honored your grandfather very much. He told his translator to ask what he wanted.

Abd al-Muttaleb wanted his camels.

When the translator related what he said, Abraha's attitude changed. In a very different tone, he said, "Tell him, that when I first saw you, I was impressed by your dignity and pride. Now, though, after I heard this small request from you, I had another thought about you, and that magnificence and greatness diminished in my view. I was thinking that you had come to me to mediate for you and your people's temple. But I now see that you have abandoned the fundamental thing for your people, your ancestors, and the pride of the Arabs, and you are only concerned about some camels!"

Abd al-Muttaleb, in answer, said to him, "I should intercede for the house of God? I should mediate for his Creator, to a slave? I? Who am I? A small slave like myself has no such presumption! The divine Ka'ba has. If it wants, it is not incapable. I am only the owner of my camels."

Abraha ordered that those camels be given back to your grandfather. Then that army with elephants advanced a little ways and set up its tents and camp at Abta. (Abta is on the edge of Mecca.)

On the next day, after the sun came up from behind the black mountains of Mecca, Abraha ordered an attack. The drums and horns of battle roared like thunder, and the army, with surprising discipline, headed out for Mecca.

The Meccans, who were sitting in the mountains, when they saw that, began to shudder, and they went up higher from where they were.

Your grandfather had placed several of his slaves and sons as lookouts at several high points, and they brought him news every moment. He himself was at the mountain of Hirā, praying and weeping.

When he saw Abraha's army advance toward Mecca, the veins in his neck bulged from anger and blood rushed into his face. In that condition, he said, "Abraha is acting arrogantly toward the sanctuary. Soon, though, he will see the reward for his impudence."

The white elephant was larger than the other elephants. It went ahead of the army like a mountain, and behind it came the rest of the vanguard sitting atop the other elephants and fast horses. Hey had decorated the two tusks of the white elephant with different jewels and on its forehead a rather large ruby shone. Bells of different colors, and coins of gold and silver were hanging from around its neck. On its back a beautiful and small carpet was spread out. The other parts of its body were covered by large sheets of armor.

On top of the heads of the other elephants, two horns of iron and on their tusks swords made in India were attached. All of the army had helmets and armor of iron on their bodies. On the hands of every person was a large shield and in the middle of it a large sword hung. Aside from those, the vanguard had large spears in their hands.

Once the sun had risen in the sky, the glitter of the metal and iron from the armor and weapons of the army was so much that, even from those heights where the Meccans were, their eyes were irritated by it and became watery.

The Meccans watched the army with its elephants, speechless and scared. The soldiers advanced unhurriedly and without fanfare, all of them together with the sound of firm steps and the clanging of their weapons against one another, and it made an ominous and frightening tune until it doubled the terror in the hearts of the people of Mecca.

The air was heavy, without any breeze. It was motionless. The dust from the mass of the army very slowly rose in the air like a large cloud and hung over them.

Abraha's army, from that same gate that today they call the Elephant Gate, entered Mecca.

All were thinking that the affair had come to an end, that soon Abraha's elephants, like enormous battering rams, would level the Ka'ba and the houses of Mecca to the ground.

The large white elephant, however, stopped when it reached the edge of the sanctuary. The elephant driver hit its head with wood, iron, and his hooked stick, and he scratched the skin on its side, but the elephant would not step forward. It knelt down right there and, like the mother of a dead child, let out a loud wail.

Anays, familiar with the character of his elephant, said, "There is some secret concealed in this situation!"

The commander of the army said, "Perhaps this is the work of sorcery!"

The other elephants, when they saw this, did not put another foot forward.

Abraha, angry, said, "These are groundless thoughts."

Anays, the elephant driver, before he could correctly convey his words to the king, turned the white elephant's head toward Yemen. The elephant stood up and quickly began to move. He brought it to a halt and again directed it toward the Ka'ba. When it reached the edge of the sanctuary, it knelt again and did not get up. He beat it so much that he cut its head and blood flowed onto its white skin. But it moaned and did not go forward.

Anays turned the elephant's head toward Syria. The animal stood up and began to run.

To make a long story short, in whatever direction he turned its head, it went, except for the direction of the sanctuary. The other elephants did not take a step toward the compound of the sanctuary either.

The army became perplexed and its discipline disintegrated. A group of Meccans on top of the hills sobbed bitterly from delight and remorse when they saw that scene. Having lost heart, the people now found joy. In the meantime, your grandfather had so immersed himself in weeping that it seemed his soul might depart his body. He kept moving his head and weeping bitterly, and saying "God is Great!" Several of the people also shouted out "God is Great!"

At this time, Nofayl and Zu Nafr fled and headed in the direction of the people on the heights of the hills.

Suddenly, in the sky towards the port of Jidda, a redness appeared. (You know that Jidda is to the west of Mecca along the Red Sea coast.) And that red thing headed in the direction of Mecca. Then it first became somewhat black and finally grayish in color. The globe of the sun lost its tint and looked like a circle of blood. At first a breeze wafted, and then ever so slowly a strong wind picked up. The wind became a gale that swept through the plain and mountains, and the people became terrified. Sand enveloped everything, and the people in the mountains crouched in crevices and under rocks and pulled whatever they had over the top of them. Breathing became difficult. Eyes and lips became parched. Inside the people a strange burning sensation arose that was unbearable.

In the plain, all of the animals began to run as if they had gone mad. Some of the camels stayed where they were and placed their heads under the sand and gravel, and rubbed their noses on the ground. It was as if all of the creatures had lost their senses. Neither human nor animal had any sense of itself. That confusion increased. The air became hot. Heads began to spin and hands and feet lost their sense of feeling and would not move. The people had no choice but to hug the ground.

After the storm passed, the Meccans saw Abraha's army broken up and prostrate on the ground. Cries and laments were going up from the army. Then those who were nearer said, "Birds that looked like sparrows have come from the direction of the sea. They are circling above the army. It is not clear what they are doing, but the soldiers are writhing on the ground and not getting up."

A while later it became clear that each bird had three things resembling tiny stones, each one like several chickpeas, two in its talons and one in its beak. The birds dropped the stones on the head and body of each one of the soldiers. Those stones were like fire that they had brought from hell, and when they fell on a soldier, it was as if fire had fallen on him. His flesh blistered, his ears burst, and his limbs separated one from another. Some of the army fled toward Yemen. Most of them, however, died someplace. A few of them were overpowered and taken prisoner and became slaves of the people of Mecca. (Of those prisoners, the elephant driver, Anays, became blind.

He is now crippled in Mecca. He sits beside streets and people help him with food.)

Abraha himself was not spared. A stone fell on his body and stayed there. Surprisingly, he did not die quickly. They say that by the time they took him to San'a, he had suffered tremendously. His flesh had fallen off of his body, and he had come to resemble a duckling just out of the shell, small and ugly. Most of the skin came off his body. Every little while one of his joints would separate and blood and puss would seep out of it. His body came to smell so badly that even his sons could not stand it. He was constantly moaning, and he pleaded for God to kill him. Finally, he accepted death as if it were a satisfying sherbet.

Baraka, worn out from the long story, stopped speaking. Muhammad said, "Is the story of Abraha at and end?"

"Yes, my dear. Abraha left this world like that. And yet his story remains for posterity and is a lesson for people. I heard that in Yemen slates still exist on which he talked about himself and boasted. Now, though, people look on those like cold and bitter bantering."

Muhammad yawned and said, "Did Sayf Zi Yazan become king then?"

"No, my dear. After Abraha, his sons Yaksum and Masruq ruled over Yemen. During the time of Masruq, the Iranians came to the aid of Sayf. Thus, Masruq was defeated and Sayf became king. That happened not long ago. Your grandfather also went to Yemen to offer his congratulations for that event."

The nanny did not say anything more to the child. They both stared at the blood-red sun that was setting on the horizon.

The camels of the lone small caravan, now tired from a long day, had slowed their pace. But with patience, like strange travelers, they had their eyes on the blood-red horizon. Then a soft murmuring from Baraka reached Muhammad's ears.

What a sorrowful thing that was, the voice of that black Ethiopian concubine!

San'a was baking in the heat of the sun and the last days of spring. The Samum wind was also blowing from the plain and intensified the hotness of the air. At that time of midday, the streets and thoroughfares of the city were empty of people. In the meantime, the small caravan of Qureish leaders, dusty and tired, every so slowing headed for the Palace of Ghamdān.

An hour earlier the caravan had completed its long journey and had entered the city. The caravaneers had at first intended to go to the Wardi Palace. But they had been told that it was now the flower season, and the amir was spending time in the Ghamdan Palace now. An old person had advised them that Sayf, fatigued by years of peregrinations and that trying battle with Marsuq, the son of Abraha, was now relaxing. Thus, it was not unlikely that he would agree to receive them.

Abd al-Muttaleb, however, told his companions, "The amir is a distant relative of ours. When he knows that it is us, and what our intention is with seeing him, he will certainly accept us."

They had decorated Sana very beautifully. They had

hung pieces of cloth and other colorful decorations in the alleys, thoroughfares, squares, and bazaars. The sound of a *sorna* and kettledrum could be heard from a place far away. The city was happily prepared to have one of its own rulers sit on the throne after decades of violence by the oppressive Ethiopians.

A wide and quite clean thoroughfare appeared before them. Its surface was covered in black and white stones and an intense heat radiated from them. On both sides of the thoroughfare, sour orange trees stood in a row, even and of the same height, like a battalion of guards. At the end of that, on the highest point of the capital, an amazing palace scraped the sky. Therein, the sun was shining so brightly that the eye could not look at it for long.

The garden in which Sayf was spending time that day was on the left side of the Ghamdan Palace, and it had a door to the plain. When we arrived at the gate of the palace, the guard, who had a spear in his hand, told us that we must enter the garden through that door. So we went back and proceeded  in that direction.

Two guards wearing armor and with long spears in their hands were standing on either side of the rather large and pleasantly painted door of the garden. When they understood what we wanted, one of them went inside the garden to ask Sayf about what to do. He then returned and opened the door for us.

We, who were ten persons, entrusted our camels

and their loads to our slaves and entered the garden.

The air of the garden was cool and pleasant. Once we entered it, the scent of its flowers and plants intoxicated us.

The flowerbeds were covered with flowers and plants from one end to the other. Flowers of various colors were so wonderfully mixed together that the soul was immersed in joy upon seeing them.

In front of us was a narrow path paved with square bricks in whose cracks grew tender and short green plants. On both sides of that path very shady plane trees stood in rows. On either side, there was also a stream with water like crystal flowing and making a soft sound.

Inside the garden, a number of birds were singing with pleasant songs that someone who had just entered might imagine that he had perhaps stepped into heaven.

In the middle of the garden was a structure of one storey with porticos on each side and white all over. Sayf, the son of Zi Yazan, was sitting facing the doors of the garden with that noble and erect stature and wearing a white Arab cloak. In age, he appeared to be forty or fifty, with a neat beard that had a lot of white streaks growing in it. He had white skin and a bright countenance. He was sitting on a large carpet, and behind him was a pillow with the same picture as that carpet. In front of him were large goblets of fruit and sweets, and pitchers of various kinds of sherbets. Several persons from among the important men of Yemen were sitting on either side of him, and concubines and slaves were constantly attending to them.

Upon seeing us, Sayf, appearing happy, got up from his place and took several steps in our direction. He hugged each one of us one by one and greeted us and said friendly things.

I said to him, "We are the neighbors of God and the servants of His house. We passed through our own dry deserts and your green pastures and deep valleys and came to Sana. We have travelled a long way and have seen clouds bearing rain and lightening one after another until we reached your court."

With a sweet smile, Sayf permitted us to sit down. Then he sat in his own place and said, "The guard of my palace said who you were and from which land. Welcome now to your second homeland, family of God![1] May your camel, migration, and where you decamp be pleasant! You are held dear in this place where you are, and when you decide to return, you will receive a gift."

I said, "We are grateful, O' amir! May the people of the desert and other people all be sacrifices for you! Abraha the Ethiopian oppressed your land and people for a long time. Then, with an excuse, he set his sights on the sanctuary, the Ka'ba, and our city. But in the end, he was afflicted with that calamity, and his fate for has since become a proverb among the people, and

---

1. After that calamity that descended on Abraha and his army during the attack on Mecca took place, the people of the Arabian Peninsula believed that the tribe of Qureish was the special recipient of God's attention. For that reason, they referred to it as "the family of God."

a lesson."

After him, his sons Yakum and Masruq followed the path of their father and added to his oppression. Now, in thanks for your victory over Masruq and the delivery of Yemen from the clutches of the Ethiopians, we have travelled this long distance in order to congratulate you and your people."

Sayf said, "May God be thanked for having humiliated your and our enemies. Now, until the day of the crowning arrives, stay in the guesthouse of the palace. Right this minute I will command that you be entertained in the very best manner."

We expressed our appreciation to him.

Then he ordered his slaves to attend to us.

After the group had become busy eating and drinking, Sayf called me to him and said, "Are you the son of our sister, the son of Hashem?"

I said, "Yes, amir."

(Because Sayf was one of the descendants of Qahtān,[1] and we were from the family of Ismail. The descendants of Qahtan were from his brother and those of Ismail from his sister.)

In a way so that the others would not hear, Sayf said, "I have a great secret in my heart that I must tell to you at the proper opportunity."

I said, "I am very grateful, amir."

From that moment, my mind began to think.

"What is the secret the amir of Yemen has for me?

---

1. Qahtān was the name of the first father of the tribe from the Arabs, and thus they are referred to as the Qahtani Arabs. He is considered the father of the families of Himyar, Kahlān, the clans of Yemen, and the Ghassanids of Syria.

Which secret is it? And whom does it concern? What secret is it that only I should know about it?"

We were with Sayf for a while longer that day. The slaves and concubines continued to serve us, and Sayf asked us about Mecca, the Ka'ba, Abraha's going there, and we answered him. Then we took leave of him and went to the palace's guesthouse.

During the day, we were in the guesthouse of the Ghamdan Palace. During this period, I was constantly waiting for that opportunity that Sayf had mentioned and when it would come about. I was also thinking about what kind of secret it was that he was so enthusiastic to talk about. Furthermore, what was my relation to it?

Ghamdan was one of the amazing palaces of the world. It had a square structure of stone. Every side was one color. One of its sides was white. Another was red. Another yellow and another side green. Heads of lions or falcons were covered in plaster on its innumerable columns.

The palace had seven storeys. A Yemeni poet told us, "On cloudy days, it appears as if the Ghamdan Palace has a turban of cloud on its head."

The guesthouse where we were was on the first floor. After us, other guests from near and far in the Arabian Peninsula came and stayed in other rooms in it.

At dawn, the fifteenth day we were busy preparing ourselves to go to Sayf's crowning. For on the pervious day, after days of having no news from Sayf, a slave came from him and said to us that, "Tomorrow is the crowning." Then he gave me a small purse and said, "The hot springs is ready. This henna is from the amir, so you can color the hair on your head and face with it while in the hot springs."

I was previously familiar with henna. When I was middle-aged, once when I was coming to Yemen to do trade, I knew what it was and what it was used for. I took a lot of henna with me to Mecca on that trip, and I made a ot of profit from it. I was also happy on realizing that Sayf had remembered me. I told the slave to convey our thanks to him. Then we went to the guesthouse's hot pool and all of us put henna on our hair, but I did not.

We slept early that night and rose the next morning. By the time the sun appeared, we were wearing our special clothes and ready to be called to the celebration.


The crowning was held on the seventh storey of the palace, in a very spacious hall the size of several squares.

On every side of the hall were a large number of windows of ebony wood polished with lacquer were outward. When you looked out of them, Sana and its gardens were in your view from one end to the other. In the middle of the ceiling was a large stone, smooth and clear like glass, such that from this side you could see the sky very well, and you could tell the difference between a crow and a raven.

There was a crystal chandelier hanging from the ceiling, and on the walls were brass or silver lamps. Our slave said, "At night, when the lights in the hall are lighted, their light seems like that of day."

In every corner of the hall there was a copper

statue of a lion with a thick body and hollow inside. They said, "When the wind blows from a particular direction, it goes inside one of them and a sound like the roar of a predator can be heard."

The slaves, all wearing identical clothes, were going and coming in every direction and attending to the guests.

We were in the hall for a while when on its north side a commotion erupted. All heads turned to that side. Then one by one they stood up, for the amir had come into the hall.

Sayf was more magnificent than on the day we saw him in the garden. He was accompanied by several important men from Iran and Yemen. He had a black turban with gold thread in his head and a dishdasha and cloak on his body that were as white as ivory. On the top of his turban a large ruby glittered. In his right hand was a bejeweled cane and on his waist a sword with emeralds. He came, grave, and with his head and eyes he welcomed those present. All of the hair on his head and face was now entirely black. It seemed that he had used that same henna that he had sent for us.

Sayf went toward the royal throne, which was on that same north side of the hall. He stood there for a while facing the audience. He smiled and with a sign from his hand allowed us to sit down. Then he sat down on the throne. We sat on both sides of the throne, on a carpet, and leaned back against pillows. But the important men from Iran and Yemen and their sons stood on both sides of the throne, except for Nahriz, the Iranian army commander.

In the hall, I was on the right side near Sayf. And I was still thinking of that day and whether the opportunity would arise for him to tell me that great secret and whether, during this event, Sayf still remembered what he had told me or not.

Sayf had covered his body with amber and the blackness of musk. That was clear from his hair and beard. On the right side of his throne there was a narrow stand of red agate that rose to the level of his chest. On top of that, there was a small cup of ruby full of pure musk. On the left side of the throne, on top of a stand the same as that other one, except of silver, there was a cup of red gold.

On the right side of Sayf there was a shorter throne. On it was sitting like a mountain an aged man with long hair and beard. He appeared to be close to seventy years old. The signs of greatness were obvious in his face and behavior. He had a countenance and form like that of great commanders. His body was covered in armor. (After a while, I realized that he was Vahriz, the Iranian commander.)

The first person seated on the carpet was our caravan leader Abd al-Muttaleb. He was more noticeable than the others, tall, stout, and handsome. The hair on his head and face was white as silver, and his high forehead had a special shine to it. In truth, the grandeur of the prophets and the magnificence of the kings had come together in him.

Sayf began to speak. First, he praised the Creator.

He welcomed those present and thanked them.

After him, Vahriz stood and praised God. Then a large platter was brought in which were a royal crown, a coat of mail, and a cloak. He said that those were gifts from Anushirvan, the shah of Iran.

At that time, Sayf took the turban from his head. Then Vahriz went forward and placed the crown on his head and put the cloak on him and present him with the silver chain mail to him as a gift. Then he praised Sayf for his bravery, his manliness, and his love of homeland. And on behalf of Anushirvan, he read the royal sermon for Yemen in his name.

When the time of the guests to offer their congratulations arrived, Abd al-Muttaleb was asked to begin. Easily and gravely, he stood. The other leaders of the Qureish rose with him. All eyes were now focused on him. Some asked others who that good-looking and dignified old man was.

Abd al-Muttaleb took a step forward and began to speak.


O' king, our dear and great Creator has granted you a high position and stature. He has brought you from a family that is pure, shining, dignified, and numerous.

You were raised in a dear, pure, and good house.

May harm remain far from you, for you are the amir of the Arabs and their joyous springtime. From that spring, all derive their verdance and prosperity.

O' amir! You are the leader of the Arabs to whom they bow. You are the column against which they lean. You are the high place where the people seek refuge.

Your fathers were the best fathers, and you are their best successor. May he who follows you not be unknown. And may those, like you, who have descendants, never be forgotten.

O' amir! We are the inhabitants of God's sanctuary and the curtain keepers of his house. Happiness at the repelling of that calamity that afflicted all of us compelled us to come to your court. We have now come to you as a group in order to congratulate you. Therefore, please accept our good works. May you be healthy and live long so that your people, following that period of suffering and sorrow, so they can have you beside the like a kind and capable father.

The sign of happiness appeared in the intelligent eyes and joyful figure of Sayf, and he congratulated Abd al-Muttaleb. Then the others stood, one by one, and praised Sayf on behalf of their people and tribe and congratulated him.

When midday arrived, and it came time to eat, they spread out the colorful tablecloths. After the meal had finished, Sayf's court minister told those present to all assemble at night in the garden of the palace.

Then Sayf stood up, as did everyone else.

In the sky, the moon rose like an Arab sword. The stars were twinkling like diamonds sewn into the dark overcoat of the night sky. The soft breeze with its gentle blowing was playing with the branches of the willow and aspen.

Sana, with its torches and lights, shone like an island of light in the darkness of the night. People, feeling a lightness, were enjoying themselves and happy in every alley, quarter, and square. The sounds of *sornas*, drums, ululating, and feet stomping rose up from every direction. But in the Ghamdan Palace, something was going on.

In front of the staircase at the beginning of the palace was a large round pool with a small fountain that gently went up and down. Several small ducks bounced on the water like skiffs and went from side to side. All around the pool many platforms had been erected, on them small carpets with the same picture had been spread, and pillows with that same picture had been placed.

The platform of Sayf, Vahriz, and the other important persons was larger than the others. Sayf was reclining on the middle of it and with his head on the pillow he had made a column. He was wearing fine white clothes and had a white and emerald turban on his head. Vahriz, however, since daytime, was wearing armor and sitting beside him like a mountain with his wrists on either knee, which were parted. The other important Arabs from Yemen and elsewhere were on the other platforms and busy talking and laughing. A torch holder of copper was on a stand between the two platform, and in it a torch was burning. Yet, there was not so much light that the imagination could not take flight.

On the other side of the pool, facing the side of Sayf's platform, there was an open space with lighted torches around it and bright as day. At the end of it, there was a large curtain hanging. The night, with the soft and pleasant sound of a lute, which rose from an unknown course of the garden, had taken on an imaginative attractiveness.

On the right side of the platform on which Sayf was sitting was one platform of the Qureish. The slaves and concubines were constantly coming and going, and they attended to the guests with politeness and kindness.

I was again thinking about whether it was time to hear that secret from the mouth of Sayf; whether that opportunity that Sayf wanted had come. And essentially whether he remembered the pledge he had made to me.

Suddenly, Sayf clapped his hands. All of the talk and laughter came to a halt and the lute player stopped playing. I don't know from which direction the old man entered the party. He was of medium height and the hair on his head and face was entirely white and resembled camel's milk. His locks fell on his shoulders and back, and he had a cane with a round head, like a small mace, in his hand. He was wearing clothes that were all white, and he had fastened it with a black shawl around his body. The men watched him in silence.

The old man obtained leave from the king. Then he began to speak. First he remembered God. Then he began to talk with a warm and deep voice.

After he spoke for a while, we knew his story is the adventure of the manliness of Sayf, from the beginning until the defeat of Masruq, the son of Abraha. We knew about the story of the coming of the Ethiopians to Yemen and their victory over the last king of that land. He started his own story from when Abraha had died and Sayf set about taking Yemen back from the Ethiopians.

What happened was like this, that many years earlier, the rulers of Yemen were kings from the family of Himyar. For several centuries they had ruled over Yemen for generations until the time of Zor'eh Zu Nawas arrived.

Zor'eh accepted Judaism and took the name of Yusuf. At that time, there was a group of Christians in Najran, one of the cities of Yemen, believing in the New Testament. They were good and pious people. But the other people of Najran were idol-worshippers.

Yusuf Zu Nawas had taken solemn vows that he would not sleep or rest until he had spread the Jewish religion throughout all of Yemen ad had enforced the Torah in the land.

He assembled an army and headed toward Najran. When he arrived there, he told the people that they had to either accept the Jewish religion or lose their lives. The Christians had to choose death. Zu Nawas ordered several pits to be dug and enormous fires were lit in them. Then, one by one, they threw the Christians into those pits and they burned, more than eighty persons. They killed the rest, up to two thousand, by sword. (They have also said twenty thousand.) But no one foreswore his own religion. (Those who were burned are the same ones who became known as "the helpers of Ohdud," [1] and their story became well-known.)

Of those believers, however, one mounted a horse and fled from that debacle. Zu Nawas's soldiers could not catch him, and he survived.

That man went to seek help from Caesar in Rome, for the Romans were themselves Christians. Caesar sent him to Najashi, the king of Ethiopia, with a letter. For the Ethiopians were Christians too, and Ethiopia was nearer Yemen than Rome.

When Najashi learned of the fate of those who were burned in the pits of fire, he swore that until he got revenge for those innocent victims of oppression from Zu Nawas, he would deny himself comfort and solace.

So that occurred which you all know about. Zu Nawas was badly defeated by Riat the Ethiopian and died. The kingship left the family of Himyar, and the Ethiopians came to rule over Yemen.

---

1. "The helpers of Ohdud": This is the name that is used in the Koran to refer to those people.

Yet, when Abraha the Ethiopian became the king of Yemen, the oppression of us Yemenis increased. Until this brave man, whom they call Sayf, the son of Yazan, emerged, and removed the humiliation from the Yemenis and returned their previous greatness to them.

We had seen many story-tellers before and had heard many stories. On that night, though, the style we saw and heard was strange for us. For one man alone did not tell the story. For a while, that old man was telling the story. Then, from behind a curtain, men, in the guises and clothes of Sayf, Caesar, Chosroes, Vahriz, or others would come out and speak with one another in their voices.

"Caesar! I am Sayf, the son of Zi Yazan, from the Himyaris of Yemen. The kingship of Yemen was in our family, but the Ethiopian army attacked from that side of the sea and took our country from us."

"The Ethiopians vanquished us and oppressed our people very much. We endured that humiliation with patience for several decades, but now the people of Yemen can not stand any more."

"O' Caesar! Transgressions have been committed against us, of blood, property, and honor, and acts so obscene have been endured that I am ashamed to repeat them here in your presence."

"We have heard what you have said, young man. But you know that Yemen is far away from Rome, and our soldiers do not have much desire to go there."

"O' Caesar! I am not thinking about myself. What

has brought me here is sorrow for my oppressed people. If Caesar knew what we have experienced, his position and greatness among the kings of the world was such that, without the help of our wanting it, he would rush to assist us. I have now come to this court with the hope that God will defeat our enemy and exact revenge for us with the hand of Caesar."

"It seems your youth prevented you from knowing at one time what one of these did with our co-religionists in Najran! Do you not think that what you have experienced over those years is revenge for those Christian believers whose only sin was remaining steadfast in their belief in their own God?"

"That was a mistake that happened, and we are always ashamed of it. He who ordered that oppressive act received what he deserved. Now, though, if our people were guilty of any sin, they have been forgiven and they have been cleared of it."

"It any case, these Ethiopians who were ruling over you, like us, are Christians, and you are of another religion. This will not allow us to help others to defeat our co-religionists. Now, for you, if cruelty has gone, say it again so we can write a letter and remove oppression from you."

When Sayf gave up hope in the court of Heraclius, he turned to the court of Chosroes Anushirvan, the shah of Iran, and he told his story to him in detail.

"O' shah of shahs! My land is very blessed and productive, and is not like the other Arab lands. And for this reason, the Greeks and Romans considered Arabia blessed because it was famous for abundance, civilization, and the abundance of rain and foliage. In addition to that, Yemen is where the important men of India pass, and merchants from everywhere are constantly going to and coming from there. They are bringing incense, leather, cloth, valuable stones, and other minerals from Yemen and taking them to the farthest reaches of the world. They first bring pearls from the Persian Gulf, silk from China, slaves, ivory, and gold from Ethiopia to my land, and then they are taken to other markets in the world. Now, if the shah comes to my aid with some of his soldiers to take Yemen from the grasp of the Ethiopians, a country such as this will be added to your other lands."

"I am aware that you have been oppressed and that you are saying those things from your heart. The requirements for justice and diplomacy, however, is that the shah first protect his own country and then deal with other lands.

"Your country is very far away from mine. Also, on the other side of that sea there is a desert without water or grass. To send an army to such a desert would be to decimate it, and waiting on that side of the sea are other dangers. This is something that requires patience and thought."

Chosroes ordered them to give Sayf a nice house and to treat him with great respect. After a while had passed, however, he became preoccupied with the Romans, and he forgot about Sayf. Ten years passed in that manner with our amir there. Then, when Sayf wrote him a letter and reminded him of that commitment, Chosroes ordered him to be given ten thousand dirhams and a fine cloak.

That affair bothered Sayf very much, and he distributed those dirhams among the servants at Anushirvan's court.

Informers—who were the eyes and ears of the shah—relayed that to Chosroes.

"What you have done with our dirhams should not be done by courtiers with what shahs bestow. What was the reason for that?"

"My distributing in his house what the shah had granted me was not done out of impoliteness or because I did not recognize your beneficence. Rather, I did that in thanks for God's blessing and what, after a long period of time, He did for me with the shah and His having him hear my voice.

"The shah knows that I did not come to his court looking for gold and silver, because all of the soil of the mountains and plains of my land are themselves gold and silver. And taking gold and silver to its mineral mines is proper for neither me nor the shah.

"I had set out for the shah's court with the objective of removing the oppression from my people and lifting the humiliation from us, not for him to bestow dirhams on me. I had hoped that the shah would send an army with me so as to rescue the oppressed from the oppressor, and to also do a service for the shah so that he could come to possess that prosperous realm without difficulty or suffering."

When Chosroes saw that it was like that, his anger subsided and he said, "Let it be until I have looked into your affair."

He then dismissed Sayf and summoned his vizier and related the matter to him.

"This man's ambition is very high, but my view is that if we do not help him, it will be embarrassing for us. And if we send an army with him, it will be decimated, which will not be good. What do you think about this issue?"

"O' shah! We have an obligation to this man because he has been waiting tent years for us. The shah had a great many prisoners. Of those, some are cavalry and several persons are experienced soldiers. You threw all of them into prison with the aim that they die there. I think you should send those of them who are able with this prince. They will either be victorious over the Ethiopian army and will add Yemen to our domains, or they will be killed, which is what the shah had in mind."

"You said it well vizier! Do it!"

They brought the people from the prisons and selected the agile men from among them. They also included warriors from the Turkish and Daylam tribes with them. The Chosroes Anushirvan put one of his great commanders over them. He was from the people of Daylaman and his name was Vahriz. Vahriz was from a great family, he was a relative of the shah, and he was very manly. Although he was up in years, for Chosroes he was equal to a thousand cavalrymen. Once he had sent him off to the side, he said, "I have sent one thousand soldiers."

Vahriz ordered that eight ships be built on the shore

of the Persian Sea[1], one ship for every one hundred men. Then, until the ships were built, he taught those men how to fight in every way.

They then went from Ctesiphon to the Persian Sea at the mouth of the Euphrates River. They boarded the ships there and set out for Yemen. Along the way, however, they encountered a storm, and two of the ships sank.

When they reached the coast of Hadramawt, they disembarked at Mathub, a place on that coast.

"Now, here we are in Yemen."

"Yes. Sometimes there is a battle! We can not stand up to the Ethiopians with this number of men."

"Do not worry. A lot of firewood and a little fire will suffice. Sayf, what do you have and what will you do?"

"Whatever you want of Arab men and Arab horses! I will put my men with yours, and we will be together, step by step, until we all either taste death or drink the sweet sherbet of victory together."

"You have said it well and honestly. Now step forward and bring with you whatever you have of men, equipment, and weapons."

Sayf went to his own tribe and the others of Yemen looking for assistance. Several thousand warriors gathered around him.

On the other hand, the informers reported the story to Masruq, and Masruq rode toward them with thirty thousand Ethiopian and Arab soldiers.

When the two armies lined up facing one another,

---

1. i.e. Persian Gulf.

the two edges of Masruq's army could not be seen. On this side, however, the cavalry was less than four thousand men.

When Masruq saw the fewness of that group, he considered it small. So he sent a message to Vahriz. "Why did you intend to attack us with this small number of men? If you are serious about attacking us with these, you are endangering your own life. It is embarrassing for me to do battle with you with this small number of men that you have."

"Now, consider well. If you want to return to your own land, I will not bother you or your army. Consider that and return! But if you are set upon fighting, I will fight you."

Vahriz wanted a while to think about that. He hoped, however, that in that period, a larger group of men from Yemen would join up with him.

But none did, except for a small number.

A day remained until the end of the period and Vahriz ordered the army to assemble and prepare to do battle. He reviewed them and spoke to the army of Iranians and Arabs. One by one, he checked their armor, helmets, swords, shields, and belts. Then he ordered all of the ships, which kept alive the memory of friends and homeland in the hearts of the Iranians, to be burned. He also ordered all of the tents and supplies that they had to be thrown into the sea, except for the clothes on their bodies, their weapons, the materials of the army, and a small amount of food.

"The reason I burned the ships was so you would believe that you have no way back to your homeland.

I caste your supplies in the sea so you can not flee into the desert, and with the intention that you would not have anything of value or property that the Ethiopians can take as booty.

"Now you only have two choices before you. Victory or death! If you are victorious, you can expect to get whatever you want. And if you are killed, a dead man has no need for property.

"If you are that group of men who will fight hand in hand with me, and you are steadfast, tell me. As for me, I will neither turn my back to the enemy, nor accept a shameful fate, nor will I give my self to them alive.

We will fight alongside you until death or victory!"

"We Yemenis are also with you! We and our swords. We will be right beside you until we are killed or become victorious."

The next morning, Vahriz the Persian ordered his army to prepare for battle. They had their backs to the sea and face to the enemy, and he said, "Be brave and manly until one of those two fates arrives: with you are victorious over the enemy or you die with a good name.

"Now, string your bows. When I order you to shoot, launch your arrows all together at once and keep barraging the enemy with arrows. And the Yemenis, one of you who knows Masruq well come to me."

"I know Masruq, commander."

"Very well. Now show him to me."

"He is the one sitting on the elephant, with a crown of gold, and who is wearing a large helmet. That one from whose crown a bright ruby the size of several eggs hangs on his forehead."

"Well done! The elephant is the mount of kings."

"He now seems to have decided to dismount from the elephant! Yes, he came down from the elephant and has now mounted a horse."

"That is fine. The horse is also a prestigious mount. But why did he do that? What was his reason for doing so?"

"It seems that he did not because he despises us. So that he can tell the people that we are not worthy of needing an elephant to fight with us."

"Commander, now I see that he has come down from his horse and intends to sit on a mule! It seems…!"

"On…that which is born of an ass?!"

"Yes, commander!"

"His kingship is now lost, since he has gone from a great mount to a lesser one. Bring me my bow and an arrow so I can take aim at that rider of an ass and let fly an arrow at him. Pay attention. If his mount moves, you know that it missed and did not hit its target. If it jumped, however, and they gathered around him, the arrow has found its mark. The all of you start to shoot arrows all at once."

Masruq the Ethiopian was drunk from victory, but Vahriz the Persian had seen a lot of battles and had experienced the vicissitudes of time. He was a famous archer, and unequalled in the strength of his arm. His life had been long, but his eyes could still see well.

When Vahriz began to prepare to shoot his arrow,

he ordered that his white eyebrows, which had fallen down over his eyes, be raised and bound with a white strip of cloth across his forehead. Then he picked up his bow, which no one but he could draw. He placed a poisoned arrow in his bow and aimed for the ruby that was on Masruq's forehead. Then, as was the custom of the Iranians, he called upon Yazdan the Pure and pulled back his bow. The arrow flew like a burning meteor and landed in Masruq's brain.

All at once, the Ethiopians gathered around him. The Iranians, as their commander had ordered, began to shower their arrows down upon them.

The People of Ethiopia and Yemen had never seen that kind of fighting with arrows before, because their battles were face to face with swords, spears, and axes. The Iranians, however, were famous from ancient times for shooting arrows in battles.

Masruq's army fell apart. At that time, the agile cavalry of the Iranians and Arabs attacked them, and each one captured four or five prisoners and took them away in lines.

Our amir, Sayf, in the meantime, acted like a hero and interceded so that the Yemenis in Masruq's army would join him. When Vahriz saw that, he ordered his own soldiers not to attack the Arabs and only pursue the Ethiopians and capture or kill them. You know very well what happened after that, and you have assembled in this place to offer congratulations for it.

May all of you have a good night, and may the amir's rule be firm!

When the old storyteller stopped speaking, the audience said bravo to him and his assistants.

Then, Omayyeh, the son of Abi Sallat, a well-known poet of the Arabs, stood up and recited a poem in praise of Sayf, Vahriz, and their army.

"No one has exacted vengeance like the son of Zi Yazan.

He, who gave his life and property for years on land and sea!

And no one has fought like the freedmen of Iran.

You would think that those on land are like their mountains,

The white-faced border guards and the victorious cavalry,

Who at the time of battle, fight like a lion in the underbrush,

You have not seen anyone like them among any people.

When their armor is torn, they are not discouraged,

And they do not move from their place for thrusting their spears.

Yes, our brave amir, Sayf!

You brought the lions to the dogs, many groups of whom were very many among the people.

May victory taste sweet to you, and may the crown on your head be raised!"

All of those in attendance congratulated the son of Abi Sallat, and Sayf granted good gifts to him, the storyteller, and those players. Then, he stood up from his place, and the others stood as well.

That night did not present the opportunity either for Sayf to tell me that secret.

For that reason, when I went to bed, I was still thinking about that, and sleep did not come to my eyes until part of the night had passed. For we had stayed in Sana a long time, and Sayf had now placed the crown on his head. The next day, all of the guests left for their own lands. So there was no reason for me to stay any longer.

The next day at dawn, I awoke to sounds. My companions were ready too go. I began to make my own preparations.

We were eating a mid-morning meal when a slave called out to me and I went to him. He said the amir wanted me, and he took me to Sayf.

Sayf was sitting alone in a simple room. He greeted me and had me sit beside him. Then he said, "The large amount of work did not allow me an opportunity to sit with you in private for even a moment. Now I have heard that you are preparing to leave. Before it became drawn out any longer, I told them to summon you so I could say what I needed to you."

I said, "I am grateful. Your command is correct amir! Now I am all ears."

He said, "This is a very great secret, and it must remain concealed until the time when it is fulfilled."

I said, "So it shall be."

He said, "I have a book on the secrets of the world that only the great and spiritual men of the Jews know about. What I am about to tell you comes from that book.

"During these days, in the land of the Hejaz, a child lives, of beautiful appearance and mind, singular in the world in terms of beauty and goodness. Between his shoulders is a mark like a piece of fur that tends toward blackness. His mother and father departed this world when he was young, or will, and his grandfather and uncle will be his guardians. He is the same one who is the prophet of God. He will be inspired in Mecca or other cities of the southern Hejaz, and he is the one who will be the great intercessor on the Day of Resurrection.

"Once he is inspired, God will have a group of us Yemenis assist him, and his friends will consider him dear, while his enemies will despise him.

"He will break the idols and extinguish the fire temples. What he says is wisdom, and his actions are justice. He will command good acts to be done and prevent bad and incorrect acts."

Sayf stopped speaking for a while and became immersed in thought. Then his eyes became watery, and he said, "O' that Sayf were there at that time so that with all that he has, he could bow his head to his orders and assist him! Even now, if there was not the fear that his enemies would harm him, I would reveal it and invite all of the Arabs to him.

"But nephew, you take care if him everywhere, on land, on sea, and in secret, especially from the Jews, who are his greatest enemies."

I became fearful for Ameneh and said to Sayf, "I thank you, amir, for having informed me of this secret. With those signs that I saw earlier, I believe that he is that same Muhammad, my grandson, even though his mother has still not left this world."

Sayf said, "It is a good fortune for you if that is how it is. Good for you, son of Hashem! Good for you!

"May it be confirmed now that I believe in him and

what he had brought form the God of the people of this world."

Then, with much sorrow and pain, he sighed and said, "What will happen when I realize that moment and die helping him!"

He kept that feeling for a time. Then he took me in his arms, kissed me on the face, and gave me leave to go.

Once we had set out for Mecca, he gave me nine hundred ounces of gold, nine hundred ounces of silver, and a pouch full of amber. And, as is customary in the giving of gifts, he bestowed upon my companions something more or less like that.

It was sundown, and like every day, Muhammad was going to the sanctuary. He was tired, but happy. In his shining countenance happiness overcame tiredness. He had spent that day in the service of a helpless person, and that had made him happy.

The sloped alleys of Mecca were passing under the small feet of Muhammad as he quickly went to his grandfather. The slope of the path, for those feet that were covering the flat ground seemed to be going over a sloped surface, doubled the tension. His knees bent slightly under the weight of his body and the upper half of his body would bend a little with every step forward.

Under his gaze, Mecca, like a pool of water in which a large black stone was suddenly thrown into its center, had spread out its dress in circles of waves. At the heart of that valley, sitting in the embrace of the bare black, red, and purple mountains, stood the Ka'ba, four-sided, tall, and covered with a black Yemeni cloth. Then there was the square, sandy courtyard of the sanctuary, and the porticoes around the sanctuary at the level of a man of medium height. All around that were the houses of the city, with high roofs and the short walls of their courtyards, of stones, either shaped or not, and clay bricks, baked or unbaked. All were rectangular, with windows and doors like eyes and mouths open toward the Ka'ba.

The houses formed a ring of circular rows surrounding all of the sanctuary. The first circles were smaller. Then they gradually sent out rays and became more expansive. The first circle was composed of the houses of Qosay and his sons and grandchildren because of their longer precedence in residence and their higher lineage and position. Then there were the houses of the other clans of the Qureish and the other tribes, those also according to each one's precedence and position. Of them all, that of Qosay was larger and more magnificent. For that reason, after his death, and according to his instructions, they had made that the assembly building[1] of the city.

In every alley and quarter, the freshness of the houses was of one sort. Some were larger; others were smaller. A few had been decorated with marble or other colorful stones, and several had been decorated in unusual ways, with colorful seashells. Here and there, a lone palm tree had risen from the courtyard of a house and its fall leaves could be seen moving slightly in the gentle afternoon breeze.

Muhammad wiped the sweat remaining on his face with his white *kafiyyeh* and adjusted the small green *aqal* around his head. The moderate breeze that had begun to blow with the setting of the sun smoothly caressed his face, which was blushed from his fast and unceasing movement.

Muhammad took a deep breathe and joyfully took the light fall air into his lungs.

With the diminishment of the heat, the city

---

1. *Dār al-nadwa*: The advisory council of the Qureish used for administering Mecca and the Ka'ba.

seemed to have regained life again, and people were going up an down the alleys and passageways. In the length of the narrow street which Muhammad was passing through, in the shops and huts, merchants were selling spices, perfumes, cloth, clothes, shoes, leather bags, stone containers, and pot of honey. Also, peddlers, here and there, on platforms or the ground, had spread their cloths and offered their goods to passersby. In one corner, around an old seller of halva, young tatterdemalions were gathered about and exchanging their small change for pieces of halva. Further over there, at the edge of the street, a woman selling milk in clay pots was giving milk to some Arab nomads. The pleasant and sweet smell of the camel's milk involuntarily attracted every passerby in that direction.

Beside the seller of milk was a black slave girl announcing her handmade and colorful fans. In the middle of the street, small and barefooted children were playing loudly. Their playing attracted the large eyes of Muhammad in their direction for a moment, but he quickly continued his course.

Muhammad, like others his age, did not have much desire to play and banter. That yearning had diminished a great deal, especially since the time that his mother Ameneh left the world in her youth and he became an orphan on both sides.

Although he was only eight years old, a profound sadness cast a shadow over his demeanor. He was mostly focused inward, and seldom did his narrow lips open into a smile. For that reason, he was very patient, and tenderhearted and of pleasant personality. In play and other things, he never had a tendency toward interesting and force. There was not an iota of selfishness in him. Usually, he gave others precedence over himself. He was always ready to forego his own right in the interests of friends.

These, along with his correctness in speaking and action, made other children, his relatives and strangers, to want very much to be friends and play with him. Muhammad, however, liked being alone and seclusion more than any kind of play. He wanted to relax with himself in some corner so he could think about existence, life, and the past. It may be that he had forgotten the heartrending sorrow of being an orphan with the memory of that short, pleasurable time that he spent with his mother.

During this period, Muhammad's young nanny was a good nurse for him. Baraka, for fear that the poison of sorrow would wilt this newly blossoming, fragile and delicate flower, would talk and be with him at every moment there was an opportunity. That young slave girl tried not to let Muhammad be by himself, no matter how brief. She encouraged Muhammad to go the street and play with the young boys his own age. Sometimes she also told the children to go to Muhammad and ask him to play with them, and they happily and enthusiastically did that. Hamzeh, the son of Abd al-Muttaleb, was also with him many hours.

Hamzeh was from Haleh, and Haleh was the last wife of Abd al-Muttaleb and the daughter of Ameneh's uncle. In terms of age, too, Hamzeh was more or less the same as Muhammad, and those two were friends. Especially from that day when Muhammad returned from that sorrowful trip to Yathrib, he was usually in Hamzeh's house, and their friendship became stronger each day.

In addition to the important people of the neighborhood who had heartfelt affection for this likeable child, children, relatives, and strangers also liked him very much. Sometimes his uncle, Zobayr, who was a handsome youth, and joyful, whenever he passed Muhammad, he would play with him for a while and try to make him laugh. The other uncle of Muhammad, Bu Taleb, sometimes took him to his humble dwelling and did not refrain from expressing any kindness towards him. In the meantime, however, Muhammad had a different relationship toward Abd al-Muttaleb. He gave off the scent of his unseen father and revived the memory of his mother's kindness. It was also for that reason that Muhammad loved his grandfather from the bottom of his heart, and he continually sought to see him and be with him.

At the mouth of the bazaar that was connected to the door of the sons of Hashem, Muhammad saw Hafas, the so of Morreh. Hafas was sitting on a chair in one of the shops selling perfumes, and he was talking with the owner of the shop. Muhammad wished him a good afternoon with a sweet smile.

Hafas was a man with a grimacing appearance and bitter tongue. But with Muhammad he had different manner. At this instant as well, at first he answered Muhammad as if he were a stranger. Then, since he knew who he was, he cleared the wrinkles from his brow, and with a loud voice said, "May all of your hours be pleasant ones, my beautiful boy! May good fortune always be with you!"

Muhammad softly said to him, "I am grateful uncle. May you also always be happy."

Then he went on his way. At this time, the affair he had with Hafas some time before came to his mind.

His grandfather was the chief of the Qureish and the head of Mecca. So that delivering food and water to the pilgrims could be done well and the city could be taken care of, all of the property owners in Mecca would give part of their earnings to him every year. Hafas also had a great deal of wealth. In Taif, he had a very productive farm. Aside from that, he was the owner of much property and many camels. But he was very stingy when it came to giving his part to Muhammad's grandfather. It was like that this year as well. Several times Abd al-Muttaleb sent someone to him to get that money from him, but each time Hafas would not give it under some excuse.

The month of the pilgrimage was near. Abd al-Muttaleb had gone to the assembly house to look at the accounts again and to give any needed instructions to his workers. This assembly house was the center for the council of the great men and all of the important affairs and discussions of Mecca. But only the children and grandchildren of Qosa and their confederates had permission to enter it. The other people did not receive that permission until they reached forty years of age, except for girls on the day they had to wear the dress for their coming of age, or women at the time of marriage, or boys at the time of their circumcision.

On that day, Muhammad was with his grandfather inside the assembly house when the subject of Hafas came up. The men who were there said that they did not have solution for Hafas, because in addition to stinginess, he also had a very hot temper and was always angry with the people they sent. So much so that no one wanted to go to him again.

His grandfather smiled and said, "What will happen if we send my son Muhammad this time?"

All of those present warned him about doing that, but he said, "This will be a test for both us and Muhammad."

Muhammad was eight and a half years old at that time.

He followed his grandfather's instructions and went to Hafas' house.

When he reached there, the door was open. In spite of that, Muhammad did not enter. He waited. He knocked on the door several times and politely called for Hafas. After a little while, Hafas answered.

"Come inside, whoever you are!"

After Muhammad entered the house, he saw Hafas sitting on a chair at the beginning of the garden.

Muhammad wished him a good day him, but Hafas did not answer him. The he asked, "Who are you, and what do you have to say?"

"I am Muhammad, the son of Abdullah, the son of Abd al-Muttaleb."

Hafas' tension subsided a bit. This time, and more softly, he said, "You did not say what your business with me is."

Before Muhammad could answer, Hafas' camel-driver cheerfully brought the news that his female camel had given birth to its baby.

At that time when the grandson of Abd al-Muttaleb came, I was very angry and preoccupied. I had a very valuable female camel that I wanted very much. That camel was with foal, and her time for foaling had come. But she was in pain and could not give birth. Hours had passed in that condition, so much that there was fear that she and her foal would both die.

I was sitting in my courtyard, enveloped with my own affairs when that sweet voice came from the street and called to me politely.

Until that time, it was not customary among the Arabs that when someone wanted to go to someone's house, they would call out to the people of the house and request permission to enter. We had suffered a lot from that bad custom. But since the guest was considered dear by us, for that reason no one considered it proper to reprimand the visitor or to keep him from doing that. For that reason, when I saw that stature and those manners from a child of that age, I became quite glad. Also, when he stepped into my house and

I saw that beautiful face and good speech of his, my gladness increased even more.

I had just begun to speak with him when my camel-driver brought that good news that my female camel had given birth and that both she and her foal were healthy.

I became very happy, and I was certain that that occurred on account of the good fortune brought by that child. Thus, I at once made a promise to myself that whatever he wanted, I would grant him in total.

He said, "My grandfather, Abd al-Muttaleb, sends his greetings and asks that you fulfill your promise to him."

Happy, I said, "May the gods protect you. How well you say your message and how softly and gently you explain your intention! Since it is like that, I will fulfill all of my commitment, and I will even add something to it. If the person making the request is someone like you, someone like me as the granter will not be illiberal."

He, like a man, thanked me. Then I asked, "Is anyone with you?"

He said, "No."

I told one of my slaves to send five camels with him and to seat him on the sixth one, and that that would be my gift to him.

Hafas' servants and slaves were amazed, because, until then, they had never seen that kind of generosity, let alone excess, in munificence from him.

When my grandson returned with those camels, all of those present in the assembly hall were so astounded that they could not speak for a time. Finally, one of them said, "Is it not unfortunate that a child of this age gets that stingy person to open up and become generous? Until this day, he always gave less than he was supposed to. And that with that kind of difficulty and at times following many quarrels and much harsh talk! But now…!"

Another asked, "Did Hafas give these to you himself? Was he drunk or distracted?"

Muhammad smiled and did not answer them. Then all of them praised him.

Now the sanctuary. The sandy soil of the courtyard. Large and small idols. Of various sexes and colors and with different attire. Some were standing in the center of the courtyard. Several were also sitting along the walls of the Ka'ba. Then, the Ka'ba. Beside it, on the eastern side, under a large and broad black cover of goat hair. Above it a man dressed in white with white hair and beard resembling a lion was leaning on a cushion of camel's hair. Of thick stature, magnificent, and proud. However much he was also a little broken. Abd al-Muttaleb, the kind and dear grandfather of the young Muhammad.

A smile overflowing with kindness. Recognized from two sides, an old man on the threshold of the sunset of life and a child at the dawn of life. Grandfather and grandson.

Muhammad passed by several of the persons

forming a circle around Abd al-Muttaleb and went straight to the front of the carpet. The grandfather gladly made space for him. This had now been a special place for Muhammad for a long time, during the first days following Ameneh's departure from this world, at the time Abd al-Muttaleb had just taken Muhammad under the tent of his guardianship, because he had decided to sit beside his grandfather, sons of the uncles prevented him. However, one day Abd al-Muttaleb had told them not to bother him, so he could sit anywhere he wanted. Then he said, "From now on he can choose his own place to sit. Leave this light of my eyes alone because he is the source of my happiness and peace of mind."

Abd al-Muttaleb gently stroked the head and back of his grandchild and kissed his face with enthusiasm. From that kiss, a hidden flow of fatherly love ran through his heart and his pained face brightened. Muhammad, happy, leaned against his elderly grandfather and threw the weight of his small body against him.

The Qureish chief seemed to forget about his previous discussion with the important men of the city upon seeing his dear grandchild and straight away began talking with him.

"I have not seen you since morning, my son! Where were you?"

Building a house. I, my uncle Hamzeh, and several other children."

"Building? Where? For whom?"

"In Kalbeh 'Odhayb, the son of Mahdal."

"That blind dervish?"

"Yes."

"Wonderful, son. Good for you. Now explain to your grandfather what you did there."

"I was with a group of children from the Qureish and we were playing together. Hamzeh was with us too. When we saw that 'Odhayb was busy building the fence of his house, I said to my playmates, 'Why don't we help him, because 'Odhayb does not have any money to pay a worker to help him do that?'"

Everyone agreed. So we started bringing stones and dirt for him. First I, like my friends, placed rocks inside my *dishdasha*. When I wanted to straighten up and stand, it seemed…!"

"It seemed what, son?"

Muhammad, ashamed, moved his head close to his grandfather's ear and quietly said, "It seemed someone—I did not see him—hit the back of my hand. Although he did not strike hard, my cloak fell from my hand and all of the rocks fell to the ground. Then I thought I heard a voice say to me, 'Put down your cloak! Although you are a child too, you are not like them. No one should see you naked!'"

"So I put my dress down, covered my feet very carefully, and carried the dirt and rocks with a basket that 'Odhayb had given to me. My friends, however, all carried the rocks in that same manner."

Abd al-Muttaleb placed a kiss on the head of his young grandchild. Then he gently patted his shoulder with his had and said, "Good for you! Good! But you did not tell your grandfather what you did about eating lunch or what you ate."

"I told Baraka, and she faithfully brought food. 'Odhayb also are with us, and he praised us very much."

"What did he say my child?"

"He praised us and our clan. He said, 'May Lat and 'Uzza be your protectors. You have rebuilt my wall, and you also brought me food. Truly bread for the mouth, clothes, builders, and helpers were always from your family.' He said, 'I swear to Lat that I had not eaten such food for several months.'"

Abd al-Muttaleb's countenance opened up from happiness. Then he said, "You spoke well and did well my son."

At that time, he made a painful sigh from despair and under his breath said, "It is unfortunate that the sun of my life is close to setting. O' how I wish that I could have you under my wing until the end and see you grow up and you honorable life with my own eyes!"

"My young son, go to the street and play with the other children like your uncle Hamzeh. Staying in the house will only sour your mood."

Sad, Muhammad looked at his grandfather and said, "I am happier at home if you are here."

Understanding, a smile crossed Abd al-Muttaleb's face, and he did not say anything else. But that smile did not last long. Like a flash of lightening, in an instant, it brightened that aged and hurting figure, and then vanished. The next moment only he and the pain remained.

Haleh entered the room. She adjusted the cushion behind Abd al-Muttaleb. She put a small pillow for he rill husband to rest his elbow on and said, "The concoction is ready. Should I bring some for you?"

Abd al-Muttaleb looked at his wife softly and said, "I told you earlier that it is too late for medicine. This time it is a different matter. This is old age. Pain from old age has only one cure...."

He was about to say "death" when a sign from Haleh reminded him that Muhammad was in the room.

Abd al-Muttaleb was well aware of the extent of the love his young grandson had for him. From the time Muhammad returned motherless from Yathrib and clung to him as his last place of refuge, until now, he was always with him. They lived together in one room and they slept on one bed. They could not tolerate being far from one another. Abd al-Muttaleb would not begin to eat until Muhammad was present. As long as Muhammad was there, he did not allow anyone to bring water or food for his grandfather, or to give him his bamboo cane, or to place his slippers in front of his feet. Now, though, fate had another game hidden in its sleeve. A premonition had warned Abd al-Muttaleb that he would not get up from this sickness. It was very clear for him that no more than a few days remained until the end of his life.

Abd al-Muttaleb did not fear death, because he had lived a full life and in his long life he had received many blessings from the world. Like many other Arabs, he did not believe death to be the end of life so as to have regret or fear in his heart. For, although he had no pride for what he had done, he had lived clean and good so he would not be anxious about the record of his actions. Now he was only worried about one thing: "What will happen to Muhammad after I have died? Will this sensitive and loveable orphan be able to accept this new sorrow?"

No place, even in his thoughts, did Abd al-Muttaleb intend to get involved in the why and how of creation, because he had lived that long and had seen lives and conclusions to know that existence has secrets and truths that the small intellect of man can not delve into. Many of the events and conditions were burdensome for men in his own time and their acceptance was difficult, but after some time has passed for them, he realized in his heart what delectable hidden fruit those bitter seeds had borne. For this reason, the heart had another story. That kindness and attachment he had to the memory of his Abdullah, he was willing to lay down, with the dread of intellect.

"Ah! My young grandson. Apologies for these sorrows that have come to you one after another! I am amazed at what wisdom this is that with every person you like, you are quickly faced with eternal separation from them. I now humbly ask the god of the Ka'ba that for this sorrow that weighs on your small body, to at least bestow on you a large heart and broad breast so that bearing those hardships will be easy!"

Saddened, Abd al-Muttaleb came out of his reflections. Quickly, and hidden from Muhammad, he wanted to wipe away tear drops at the edge of his eyes with his thumb. But he saw Muhammad sitting at the side of the room on a carpet, his feet pulled up to his chest, chin resting on his knees, staring sadly with his sheepish eyes.

How sharp this child was, and how knowledgeable! Abd al-Muttaleb knew well that keeping this story from him, if not impossible, was quite hard. When he thought deeply, he found keeping it hidden to be nonsense. Now that death was inevitable and waiting to pounce on him, and that which was probable would happen sooner or later, it was therefore better to slowly prepare him beforehand so that the tragic event not hit him all at once and knock him down.

"Haleh!"

Haleh, who was in the room at this moment to do

housework, turned her head.

"Tell my son Bu Taleb to come and see me in the evening. Tell my daughters to come too."

Fearful, Haleh, because of the unpleasant sense she derived from these words, she tried not to take her husband's remarks seriously. But Abd al-Muttaleb with his penetrating look at her made her aware that this time the matter was of a different sort.

Before Haleh could go to do what he had said, Abd al-Muttaleb looked at Muhammad and said, "How are you doing son?"

Muhammad, choked up, said, "Assure me that you will get better grandfather."

Abd al-Muttaleb tried to show himself to be healthy, an unsuccessful struggle because he was incapable of accomplishing that task.

"Did you know, my son, that I, like you, did not have a father?"

Muhammad pulled himself forward. He sat beside his grandfather and said enthusiastically, "You had not told me that story."

"Yes, my child. It was like you. I never saw my father. In addition to that, in age, I was the same age as you right now when I was separated from my mother."

"Amazing! So you were like me?!"

A spark that passed quickly to the joking jumped in Abd al-Muttaleb's tired eyes. He said, "You are like me, not I like you!"

A pale smile parted Muhammad's small mouth and the shine of his two rows of white teeth could be seen by Abd al-Muttaleb. Gently, he took the two warm hands of his sweet grandson in his wrinkled, cold hands and squeezed.

"Yes, my dear child! I had a childhood more or less like yours. My father too became ill on a trading trip to Syria and then left this world. Additional to that, you are in your own hometown. I, though, at the same age you are, became separated all at once from all of my relatives for whom I had affection."

He sighed and added, "For that reason, like a man, I surrendered myself to my fate. I struggled with difficulty and sadness until I threw them to the ground and subdued them."

At first, it was not as easy as I am saying. I became very depressed and saw a lot of hardship. But in the end, it was I who won out. Thus, in adulthood, when I looked at that bitter period of my life, I realized that there had not been those sufferings, that young child would not have become Abd al-Muttaleb, the leader of the Qureish and Mecca in adulthood. Yes, my son. The story of sorrows in the life of man is the story of winter in nature. If there is not winter, there will be no spring. The harsher it is, the more beautiful and fruitful the spring that follows it will be."

"My mother told me, 'You were born in Yathrib.' But she did not tell me anything more.

"My mother, the daughter of 'Amru, the son of 'Āned Makhzumi, was himself from the people of Yathrib. That I was also born in Yathrib was for that reason. He is from a noble family of Yathribis known as the Bani Najjār. Yathrib—as you saw on your journey—is filled with the fortress. In the quarter of the Bani Qaylah there was a very large fortress and the Najjar family lived in it. I was also born in that fortress and I spent my early childhood in it.

"My mother was a generous woman with good habits. When she became my father's wife, she obtained a promise from him that he would not take her to Mecca, and that a separate choice be hers. Father relented. They say that after two or three months had passed after their wedding, the time for the trading trip from Mecca to Syria came up. My father had planned this journey two times every year: summer in Syria and winter in Yemen. In addition to leadership of the Qureish and supervisor of Mecca, he was also the leader of these caravans. So he told his new wife farewell and set out for Syria with the caravan.

"In Syria became ill. His companions returned, but he was bedfast and he stayed there with several relatives. He instructed that if my mother gave birth to a son, she should be with him in Yathrib during his childhood. Then he should be turned over to his father's relatives in Mecca.

"That is how your grandfather came into the world without seeing his father and grew up until he reached eight years of age.

"During this period, as requested by father, the guardianship of the sanctuary and leadership of the people was with my uncle, Muttaleb. During my youth, he also told me, "One day I was in the assembly house in Mecca. A Meccan man from the Bani Hares clan approached me and said, 'I came from Yathrib, and an amazing thing happened there that I must tell you about.'

"I said, 'Whatever it is, tell it.'

"He said, 'I was going through Yathrib. In one street, my gaze fell upon a child whose appearance and behavior differed from that of the others. He was playing with a group of other children. Immersed in his good looks and charm, I stopped for a while and forgot myself while watching him. The child hit a target with an arrow. Then, just like men on the battlefield, he began to sing, praising his own family. I went up and asked him, 'What is your name young hero?' He said, 'I am Shibah, the son of Hashem, the son of Abd Manaf.' I asked him, 'Was Hashem a Meccan? What is his child doing here?' He said, 'When my father left this world, my uncles forgot about his request and treated me badly. So, I, a stranger, stayed with my mother in Yathrib.'

"Then that man of Bani Hares said, 'O' child of Abd Manaf, what had happened that you have forgotten about your glory and have placed the lamp of your greatness in another house?"

I remember very well that when he reached Yathrib, I saw him first. He was wearing a cloak the color of saffron. Around it he had fastened a purple belt, the sign of being highborn from the Qureish. At that hour, I was in a contest with children of the family on the ground in front of the fortress of Bani Najjar. I had lifted a stone larger than any of the others my age and I said, "I am the son of Hashem, the pride of Mecca, the great man of the Qureish."

At that moment, I saw that man who had dismounted from his camel. I seemed to know him.

He had the camel lay down and then came to me. Then, weeping, he said, "Come closer to me, for you remind me of my brother!"

Then he hugged me and kissed me and wept again.

Once he had recovered, he said, "O' son of my brother, would you like for me to take you to the city of your father and your uncles?"

Happy, yet nervous, I said, "Yes."

Mother, however, when she learned of what had happened, said to him, "How is it that you want to separate a small child from his mother?!"

My uncle said, "I want to increase his and your honor and greatness. I intend to give the guardianship of the sanctuary and leadership of the people to him after me."

Then he reminded my mother of father's request. In that way, with tears, sighs, and regret, my mother relented to my coming to Mecca."

Abd al-Muttaleb stopped speaking. Muhammad, amazed at his grandfather's story, kept staring at a far-away point in the garden. Then, like a person who has awakened from a deep sleep, he blinked and excitedly said, "Was your name Shibah in Yathrib? Did your uncle name you Abd al-Muttaleb?"

Abd al-Muttaleb stared at his young grandchild with his old eyes and smiled faintly. He pointed to his dry mouth and said, "If you offer your grandfather a glass of water, I will tell you that story too."

Muhammad went in to the courtyard. He picked

up a clay cup that was upside down on the jug. He filled it with water from the jug, and, so the water would not spill, carefully carried it to the room.

Abd al-Muttaleb drank the water.

"So now, the story about the name! They say that when I was born, I had silvery hair on the front of my head. For that reason, they named me Shibah. When I arrived in Mecca with my uncle, I was riding on the camel behind him. He was wearing that same expensive cloak. I was wearing simple traveling clothes.

"When the Meccans saw me looking like that, they asked about me. My uncle kept my affair hidden from the people for a while. They thought I was his slave. So, they named me Abd al-Muttaleb, and that name stayed with me."

After Hamzeh had taken Muhammad to the alley as his father instructed, Abd al-Muttaleb turned to his daughters, Safiyyeh, Borreh, 'Atekeh, Arwā, Bayzā, and his sons Abbās, Bu Tāleb, Zobayr, Hāres, Hajl, Mozayyan, Zerār, and Abu Labāb, and said, "My children, I brought you together on this dark evening and in this place in order to  tell you my last requests."

The daughters began to weep. Tears also came to the eyes of Abu Taleb and Zobayr, and lumps came into their throats as they stared at their father.

"…I am now certain that my life is coming to an end, and due to that, only a short time is left."

Bu Taleb choked up, said, "Father, you…."

Abd al-Muttaleb interrupted his child, "This is a conclusion form which no one can escape. The time when what I say will become apparent is near, and nothing can be done for that inevitable matter. So, while there is still an opportunity, listen to me while I talk, so that I don't leave anything unclear behind me.

"My first words are for you Haleh.

Yes. I entrust Muhammad to you after I go. Realize that he is your nephew. Be a loving mother to him, and take him in your arms often. Pay attention to his food and clothing. Strive in taking care of him, for he is the single point of hope for the children of Abd Manaf and the beloved, not just of the Qureish, but for all of the Arabs."

Abd al-Muttaleb looked over his children with is dim eyes and said, "And you, my children! You are the best part of the children of Ismail. Those same ones who the god of the Ka'ba selected for his own, and made the inhabitants of the sanctuary and the neighbors of his house, I, who am your leader and elder, now turn over the guardianship of the Ka'ba and the banner of our forefather, Nazār, and the leadership of Mecca to my son Zobayr, and the security of Zamzam and delivering its water to the pilgrims and the peoples and the care of my grandchild Muhammad to my other son Bu Taleb. Listen carefully to these requests of mine and don't oppose them. Also, I entrust you to the son of your brother, Muhammad, for he holds a high and distinguished position."

The sons, whether happy or not, united called out, "May you live long father. We have heard your instructions and we will follow them through."

Bu Taleb added, "But you have broken our hearts with these words."

"But you, Bu Taleb, after me, I entrust you to the orphan who has become separated from his father, mother, and grandfather! He is from your brother, for you are both from one mother. As much as you have been until now, even more for Muhammad, be like a loving mother who takes her child tightly in her arms! Don't let his small heart suffer any more than this!"

Then he asked for Baraka. When she came, he said to her, "You are a virtuous and trustworthy girl. Muhammad is also very attached to you. So, you will be responsible for watching out for and consoling him."

"Most certainly master."

Abd al-Muttaleb wiped away the tears from his eyes with his white kerchief and did not say anything else.

Then a sad voice arose from Safiyyeh:

"If someone remains eternal in this world,

"Even though no one is eternal,

"Like him, you will, father!

"Because of your magnanimity and the greatness of your ancestors,

"You are worthy of eternity!

Abd al-Muttaleb, in a weak voice, said, "Bravo daughter! You composed and recited it well. For an old man who has had a long life and done few merit able deeds, it is the best comfort."

At that moment, the voice of Bayza,[1] the white-faced daughter of Abd al-Muttaleb, arose. Weeping, she recited,

"You are the abode where the lost person found refuge.

"You were a threshold where the hungry person was satisfied.

"You were a spring whence the thirsty person drank water.

"And you were the refuge when the oppressed person found safety.

"After you, from whom shall the needy and humiliated

"Seek recourse and with whom seek shelter?"

---

1. Her name was derived from the word *bayzā*', which means "white" in Arabic.

All of the daughters and son of Abd al-Muttaleb and his wife wept loudly.

Abd al-Muttaleb, with a voice so low that it was difficult for those sitting to hear it, said, "Wipe the tears from your eyes and don't mourn any more. For the place of return for the children of Adam is nothing other than this. Return now to your houses, as your children and spouses are expecting you."

One by one, and weeping, they went to their father and kissed his hand and face. As they were leaving, they saw Muhammad, who was hurrying to the room. He opened a path through his aunts and uncles and went to his grandfather. He put his hands around his neck and placed his head on his chest and cried so much that everyone started to weep again.

It was nighttime, and quiet. The night was a dark and gloomy. A black cloud had obscured the face of the moon. The air was heavy and still. Mecca was asleep, from one end to the other. The daughters and sons of Abd al-Muttaleb were in their houses and asleep. Haleh and Abbas were asleep in the room where Abd al-Muttaleb was, but they did not allow Muhammad to sleep there. They had sent Hamzeh and him to a room beside that of Abd al-Muttaleb to sleep. Hamzeh, like Muhammad, was worried about his father's condition.

Those two had wept in the darkness of the silent room until sleep overcame Hamzeh. Now it was Muhammad and the night. Muhammad and the darkness. He and sleep, like two strangers....

Muhammad could not stay in the room more

than lost. His breathing was heavy. Something was changing him. He was afraid that if that condition continued, he would not be able to take a breath and he would begin to choke. There was no water in his eyes so that he could open his throat by crying. So, without a sound, he rose from his bed and went to the courtyard. He stopped opposite the room where his grandfather was sleeping. He looked inside for a while. An oil lamp was burning with little light on the shelf. His grandfather, calmly, like a child, was sleeping on his side with one hand under his cheeks. Far away, a screech owl called sadly.

Muhammad sighed and looked toward the sky. The clouds became denser by the moment. Suddenly a drop of rain fell in his cheek and Muhammad recalled the day his grandfather had left Mecca to pray for rain.

On that day, all of the great men of the Qureish came to Abd al-Muttaleb and said, "O' you who excavated the Zamzam and who satisfied the pilgrims, you know that for three straight years Mecca has been beset by a drought. The milk of our animals had dried up, and grass can not be found on the plains. The sky, by means of you, has satiated us. Now ask the gods to have mercy on us."

His grandfather came to the house. He washed his head and body, and perfumed himself. Then he took him with him.

Where they reached the street, a large crowd of people was behind them heading for the Abu Qobays mountains.

On top of the mountain, his grandfather placed

him on his shoulder, took his hands, and with his own, raised them to the sky and recited,

"O' protector of the poor and remover of sorrow!

"You are knowing without a teacher and munificent without selfishness!

"Now your slaves and concubines who surround your honor,

"Have brought complaints of drought to you.

"The drought that dried out your land extremely,

"That time among the feet of the camels and hooves of the sleep,

Desiccated their udders,

"And decimated the fields.

"O' God! Hear our desperate place,

"And bring down rain filled with blessings!"

Then he wept bitterly, and the people wept along with him.

I was in that mood for awhile. As they were returning, Muhammad felt the first raindrops when it fell on his cheek.

Muhammad looked at the tar-colored night sky. It seemed that something moved amidst the extensive darkness. He remembered the desert sky that time when he was with Hamileh…. He liked the sky very much, especially at night, for when he looked at the substance of the days and nights with that surprising vastness, he would become immersed in thought.

Whence did these innumerable stars come? Had they existed from the beginning? Was that possible? If that was not possible, then when had they appeared? Had they created themselves? Was it possible that someone or something, when there was not anything, to create itself? So these heavenly bodies—the moon, the sun, the earth, the mountains, the camels, the sheep, the animals and people—who had created them? What was that creator itself like? However it was, it was certain that it had to be superior, more capable, and more knowledgeable than all of what it had created.

One day, he had asked his grandfather,

"Where are my mother and father now?"

"They are now in another world my child."

"How do people live in that world?"

"If they did good acts in this world, they will live well there. If they were oppressive and did bad actions, they will be punished for those deeds, my small child."

One day, they were going down a road. When they reached the plain, they saw a man wearing tattered clothes and digging in the ground. A few steps farther on, a woman with a newborn infant in her arms was sitting on the ground and quietly weeping.

Abd al-Muttaleb took Muhammad in that direction.

"Good morning."

"And good morning to you."

"What are you doing sir? Would you like for us to help you?"

"I am grateful to you. I am busy warding off more poverty than what I already have."

Muhammad did not catch the intention of the man from that allusion. His grandfather, however, nodded his head and did not say anything for a while.

Once the man had finished digging the hole, he shouted to the woman, "Bring the little girl!"

Muhammad thought that woman and man had a baby girl who had died and that they had come to bury her. He then became sad, and tears came to his eyes. At that moment,, however, the infant began to cry. With its crying, the woman also started to cry out loud. Her crying was strange. Incapability, fatigue, requesting, anger, repressed malice, complaining of fate, all could be heard together from her.

"Did I not tell you to bring that baby? Quickly, because I did not go to work today either!"

The woman held the child tighter and wept more loudly. Saddened, Muhammad said to his grandfather, "What does this man want that baby for?"

When the man heard Muhammad's voice, he seemed to have just noticed him, and he softly said, "So I can bury her."

Muhammad, surprised, asked, "You want to bury her alive?"

"Yes my son."

"For what reason?"

"Because she is a girl. You have not seen people doing such a thing before?"

"Why are you doing such a thing?"

"Because girls increase our indigence when they are young, and in adulthood, they may become the cause of our disgrace and loss of face."

Muhammad could not say any more because of his anger and sorrow. At this point, his grandfather spoke up.

"But they also bring honor and ability for us."

The man appeared not to be expecting this remark, and he hesitated for a while and refrained from answering. His grandfather did not give him another opportunity to speak.

"Did you yourself not have a mother?"

The man, his head lowered, said, "I did."

"This, your wife, was she not once a little girl?"

"She was."

"Is it possible for men to exist without women? Is it possible for men to live without women?"

"This…is the custom of the Arabs. I am one of them."

Muhammad thought to himself, "In answering, he clings to his ancestors. If our predecessors were in error, is it proper that we follow them?"

His grandfather said, "I think that your life has become very strenuous. But time does not remain the same al the time. Instead of this, go to the sanctuary and ask the god of the Ka'ba for assistance and relief in your life."

When he saw vacillation in the man, he said, "Refrain from this reproachable deed. Go back to the city with me so I can see what I can do for you."

Lightening jumped through the dark night sky, and the courtyard was lit up by a sharp light from end to end. Thunder then roared. Then a hard rain began to fall.

Muhammad's eyes had become heavy. So he got up to go to the room and to sleep a little while.

At the time when Abd al-Muttaleb left this world, he was more than one hundred years old. The people believed that he was twenty years more than one hundred. Some even said his age was one hundred and forty. In any case, on that morning, when the sound of working arose from the home of Haleh, first in the houses of the neighbors, and then in other houses in the quarter, and then in all of the houses and streets of Mecca, the people began to weep. This, in the sanctuary, the town crier went to a high place and called out while weeping, "O' people! A great and generous man has left the world!"

Sorrow sat up a tent over Mecca, All of the people stopped what they were doing and, with tears in their eyes, hurried to Haleh's house.

Inside Haleh's house, Zobayr and Bu Taleb washed the body of their father with water and lotus, in the custom of the Qureish. They then wrapped it in two pieces of Yemeni cotton and sprinkled it with some musk, which filled the entire neighborhood with perfume. Then they placed the corpse on a large board and took it out.

There was a remarkable commotion in Mecca that day. Several of them together formed a circle and sang poems of mourning in unison. Men too wept out loud like children. I did not see anyone among them, however, more mournful than his orphaned grandchild,

Muhammad. I saw him that day, bareheaded, his hair falling loose on his shoulders, his shoulders sagging, following behind his grandfather's body and weeping violently. He was so sad and depressed that I feared that mourning might make him senseless.

What is existence? For what reason do we one day step into this world filled with suffering and on another day have to leave it? What is the cause of this unwanted coming and compulsory departure? Is there some purpose hidden behind this coming and going? What is that purpose? In what way must one live so as to reach that goal?

Meanwhile, though, what enmity does death have toward me? For what reason does it take away those whom I need? Why does every person for whom I have affection quickly disappear and leave me afflicted with the pain of separation?

Muhammad, immersed in his sorrowful world, mourning, followed the corpse of Abd al-Muttaleb. His eyes and nose had become red from so much crying, and were swollen. He moved in that surprising procession stunned and like a stranger. It seemed no one felt his sadness. And it was for that reason that when he came to himself, he realized this profound aloneness with all his being.

They had arrived at the graveyard of Bani Hashem. The grave had been prepared ahead of time. Hey placed the corpse on the ground beside it, and the people sat around in a circle. They were so pressed together that

Muhammad had no way to go toward the front. So he sat down on a rock.

Hodayfah, the son of Ghanem, stood up an recited a poem in praise of Abd al-Muttaleb. Then Matrud, the son of Ka'b Khoza'i, recited an elegy for him. After him, Zobayr rose and said, "Our father always encouraged us to respect the sanctuary. He said to is, 'The Ka'ba has been honored since long ago. Take note and protect its honor!'"

Bu Taleb then stood and said, "The leader of the Qureish, in his own lifetime, left five of his own good habits for posterity. May those habits remain in place after him and be valued.

"The first is that he forbade the women of the fathers to their children. Two, he discovered a treasure and gave one fifth of it to the Ka'ba. Three, he excavated the Zamzam well so that its waters could satisfy the pilgrims. Four, he stipulated the blood-money for a person at one hundred camels. The fifth of those customs was that the circumambulation of the Ka'ba had no limit, and he designated it be seven times.

"You are all also aware that he did not drink wine, and he was disgusted with it. He considered indecency and the corruption of women and men prohibited. He cautioned against betting on arrows and circumambulating the Ka'ba naked. You are yourselves aware of most of these things."

Then Zobayr entered the grave and Bu Taleb and Hares gave him their father's body. At this time, the entire crowd stood up. Muhammad wanted to go to the grave of his loving grandfather for the last farewell, but the people had so blocked his way that he could not go forward.

Suddenly, a warm hand touched his shoulder and a soothing voice spoke into his ear, "Where were you my dear? I have been looking for you for a long time."

It was Baraka, his kind and compassionate nanny; the single remaining reminder of his mother and father.

After Muhammad was in her embrace, in the overcast sky of his heart, it seemed the dark clouds of sorrow went aside and the sun of life began to shine for a few moments.

The last stars of the night floating in the milky sky of morning lost their color one by one. The houses of Mecca and of the Ka'ba gradually took on clearer shapes behind the veil every moment as the darkness became thinner. A gentle breeze, with a bit of coolness, blew from the north and lessened what was left of sleep in the eyes of those who had risen at dawn. Far away, a rooster crowed, and its voice broke the silence sitting over the city.

Muhammad was hurrying and was immersed in deep thought. At dawn, at the time of rising from sleep, he did not find his uncle in the bed beside him. He was not in the small courtyard beside the house either. His uncle's wife had reminded Muhammad that that day was when the caravan was going to Syria, and Bu Taleb had gone to the caravan.

Fatemeh knew very well that Muhammad had so much affection for Bu Taleb that he could not endure being far from him. So, in those first hours of the day, when she saw the longing and anxiety in his small figure, she allowed him to hurry to see his uncle for the last time before the journey.

My husband, Bu Taleb, was also very fond of Muhammad. During these four years that Muhammad was with us, he took him with him everywhere he went. It seemed he had always been the guardian of this orphan of his brother, and he never forgot him for a moment. Even though he had Taleb, 'Aqil, Ja'far and a daughter, he put Muhammad to bed in his own bed until morning so he would not think himself alone, without a refuge, or get up in the middle of the night and become frightened because of the darkness.

Muhammad, as before, also had his nanny, Baraka. Fatemeh, the spouse of his uncle, was also quite noble and magnanimous. She was one of the Hashemite women and had an unusual affection for this single reminder of her husband's brother, so much that one time some stranger said dismissively of him, "He shows more affection for Abdullah's orphan than for his own children."

Muhammad never forgot that day when he was very depressed. Thus, so others would not ask about his mood, he had crouched in a corner and wept bitterly at the thought of his mother. His weeping was not like that of other children, out loud, so that someone could understand where he was and what he was doing. And, too, no one was in the house other than his aunt. He was also busy washing and separating camel wool in the roof. Suddenly, however, Muhammad felt a warm hand on his shoulder and a kind voice spoke in his ear, "Why are you crying my dear?"

Muhammad tried to stop crying because he did not like for his sorrow to be conveyed to others. But he did not know what happened that, a soon as his uncle's wife embraced him and wiped away the tears from his eyes with her large, thin fingers, the feeling in his throat suddenly burst out loudly and tears began streaming down his cheeks.

"I am crying for the memory of my mother auntie."

"My dear child, don't be sad. Fatemeh will stand in for your mother."

Truly, Fatemeh was like a caring and kind mother to him. With that, Bu Taleb had a different place in Muhammad's small heart. He had his grandfather's scent, smell, and habits. Also, although Muhammad had never seen his own father, he always thought of Bu Taleb as his father. In that way, he sought his father, mother, and grandfather in the person of this frugal, though very sensitive, uncle of his, and at his side he could bear the extreme suffering of an orphan. Now, though, Bu Taleb had decided to leave him and to go on a long trading trip to Syria.

Being a father for our cousin had gone beyond kindness. He had a kind of obsession with Muhammad. Surprisingly, for this reason our cousin also liked our father as he did his own dear soul. Stranger still was that, even though younger than all the other sons of my father, I was smaller than Muhammad in age, I loved him very, very much and I was never jealous of him. My sisters and brothers were like that too, for he was very different from all of the other children whom we knew. Although he had a lovely appearance and was quite good looking, Muhammad was never concerned with food or his stomach. I never saw nor heard talk that he was ever greedy when it came to food.

When our grandfather, Abd al-Muttaleb, had just passed away, and he had come to our house, father was so sparing that we sometimes did not have enough to satisfy all of us. For that reason, father would not start eating until Muhammad was at the table. He also stopped us from eating and would say, "Wait until your cousin comes."

Once Muhammad came, it seemed that upon seeing the amount of food, he did not want to eat much. But father always encouraged him to eat, and he insisted quite a lot in that matter.

Muhammad had told Bu Taleb one day, "Uncle, what will happen if you set the table and I am not there? Will you keep my cousins from eating?"

Bu Taleb had said with a smile, "That is the way it is while we are responsible for you my child. You are an auspicious boy for us! Even though we do not have much money, know that from that day you came to us, our poverty clearly has diminished. So much so that it has not missed the eye of your little cousin, Ja'far."

Then, when the sign of a question could be seen in Muhammad's face, he said, "One night you were in your own father's house with your nanny, Baraka. (Muhammad sometimes liked to spend a night in his father's house.) As we were eating supper, Ja'far said, 'I wish our cousin was here too!'

"In order to understand his thoughts, I asked, 'For what reason?'

"With that own childish lilt of his, he said, 'Whenever he is not at the table, we never become full. Now that he is here, we will eat until we get full, and there will still be food on the table.'

"And that night our food was not less than any other night."

Muhammad had known for a while that his single steadiest refuge was making preparations for a trip to Syria. When he learned of that that day, the world seemed to lose its color in his eyes and a heavy dust of loneliness settled over the city and all of its inhabitants. The firmament of his soul was covered entirely by black clouds of grief, and the horizons of his life became extremely dark and gloomy. Thus, every day, he cried his heart out, but he did not have the courage to tell his uncle to forget about that trip and not leave him alone. And he did not have in him to tell Bu Taleb to take him with him, because it was not the custom of the Arabs to take pre-adolescent children with them on those kinds of journeys.

Muhammad put several openings to the bazaar behind him and passed through a number of side streets. The lowest point in the city was where all of the water in Mecca collected. It was the place of small dilapidated mud huts; the quarter of the city's destitute and the exiled tribes who had no one and who had sought refuge with the Qureish.

Farther away, there was some open ground, quite extensive, that was a pass between two mountains and faced the plain, and covered with camels, more than a thousand in number. On the backs of the camels were large bundles of goods. On the backs of some of them were also wooden saddles covered with skins of sheep or small quilts filled with wool. Men were working all around. One was adjusting the saddle on a camel's back. Another was straightening the load on the camels. Still another one was putting a bit of food in a camel's mouth. Several men were talking with one another or saying farewell to their families. Several of the cameleers had spread out cloths and were eating their mid-morning meal among the camels and loads.

On the edges, on the roofs of the small, short mud huts small bare-foot children, some with their mothers, stood watching. The sounds and voices from camels and people were mixed together such that from far away no word could be discerned.

Muhammad, in order to find his uncle in of all that commotion, went atop a stone base and looked all about. When he did not find him there, he went to the front of the caravan and stood at the side of the road so that he might happen to see Bu Taleb as he passed.

Finally, the drum of departure was pounded and the time of the caravan's leaving had arrived. Hence, the camels, which had been lying down, stood up and began to move.

Nearly two hundred men and more than two thousand camels turned toward the pass between the two mountains and the plain. At first, movements occurred in all directions. Then, as the first camel began to move out, the bustle of the caravan being mixed slowly unraveled and gradually, like a long line, the camels lined up behind one another.

The sound of the camels' bells, which were jumbled and irregular at the beginning, gradually developed a regular cadence; a cadence that was pleasant and awakened the sleeping dusty memories of the mind, and infused deep sadness into the soul. Meanwhile, that gift it brought for Muhammad was a profound sorrow and tear drops that sprang from his eyes, despite his attempts at self-control, flowed until they stung the corners of his eyes.

The sun had now risen, and its golden rays had made the peaks of the mountains to glisten. At the same time, although it was the last month of spring, and more than an hour of the day had not passed, the air was quickly warming up.

His uncle caught sight of Muhammad. Bu Taleb, with that masculine and stout figure, wearing a thin cloak of muslin of saffron-color over a dishdasha of striped Yemeni cotton and a kafiyyeh of that same cotton with a black aqal on his head, was coming at the forefront of the caravan. He was riding a fast camel with a narrow waist and a small head and ears and with lots of hair, and the long line of camels was behind him.


I was also very upset at being separated from the only reminder of my brother, but I could see no other solution. My life was hard. I thought to myself that with the small amount of possessions I had, to go to Syria so that things could open up for me.

I had just set my mind on the trip and rang the bell of departure when I saw my nephew. He was standing like a stranger at the side of the road, and sadly watching the caravan. When he saw me, he quickly ran up to me and grabbed the reins of my camel, and crying from the bottom of his heart, he said, "What will happen if you take me with you uncle?"

Bu Taleb's mood changed completely upon seeing that condition and action of his nephew. Thus, with tears in his eyes, he dismounted from his camel and took him to one side and said, "You are right, my dear, that I am not comfortable one moment without you being present!"

He immediately turned to one of the slaves in the caravan and said, "Get on horse right now and hurry to our house. Tell the mother of Taleb to put some clothes in a satchel and give them to you. And too, tell her that Muhammad is going with us to Syria."

Then he wiped away the tears from Muhammad's eyes with his thumb and put him on the camel saddle behind him.

In an instant, all of the dark clouds of sadness departed the sky of Muhammad's heart, and his loving figure began to shine like the sun.

The caravan, upon passing through the pass, put the barren mountains north of Mecca behind it, and like a narrow stream, flowed across the surface of the burnt and barren plain.

Six years separated the first and last of Muhammad's journeys. During those years, save for a few times when he had gone to the plain to let the animals graze with his uncles, he had not placed a foot outside of Mecca. That trip had been to Yathrib. This one, though it would pass by Yathrib, was going much further on past it.

Muhammad had heard things earlier about Syria and its cities. Now, this trip made it possible for him to see those things he had heard about, and even more that that, and to experience them.

On that trip, he had taken to Yathrib with his mother and Baraka, they had also been with a caravan. That caravan, however, did not go farther than Yathrib, and it was not a trading caravan. For that reason, when he now saw some of the men had, in addition to swords, bows and quivers on their backs, he asked his uncle about the reason.

"These men whom you see are all experienced fighters from the battlefield who have been hired to protect the goods from the rapine of bandits. The Qureish most certainly have trustworthy alliances with the tribes along the route. We give something of our merchandise and property to them every year. In exchange, upon entering the territory of each one, we are under their protection, and their warriors accompany us through that land. Nonetheless, logic and experience tell us not to be careless and to always be cognizant of our own affairs."

The sun was slowly rising in the sky, and the desert was warming in its heat little by little. The camels moved forward with long strides and very briskly. With every step, the rear knees would bend a little under the heavy bodies, and along with that, their hairy heads bounced up and down while facing the ground.

Mecca slowly became hidden from Muhammad's

sight. Only the glistening black mountains at the end of it could be seen. And those had changed to dark shapes behind the purple dust from the camels' feet.

It was at this time that the pleasant song arose from a man singing the camel-driver's song. The voice was a little high, and that is what gave it pleasant softness. There was also a sadness in it that cast a shadow of mild sorrow over the heart.

"Go! Go!

"O' noble camel of mine!

"Do not be burdened by your heavy load!

" …."

The man's song was in rhythm with the steps of the camels and the constant movements of their heads at every step. Upon hearing that, a strange enthusiasm gripped the camels, as if they had completely forgotten about their tiredness, the heat, thirst, and hunger. And they stepped with greater quickness.

Muhammad, having turned in on himself, sometimes looked ahead and sometimes looked around him. A bit further, on his left side, was Qarārit, that same pasture where he had gone several times to graze the cattle. A little further on were a group of mountains, not very high, but numerous, resembling dragons with open mouths so they could swallow the road and caravan all at once and carry them down its black throat. Then there was another group of mountains, black and white, and sometimes purple, full of twists, without any sign of the plain for thirty parasangs further on….

"I desperately long to see my people, O' gods of the Arabs and non-Arabs.

"For the times did not let them unite the night with the dawn.

"Yes,

"Fate is piercing me with arrows,

"And I am helpless against it.

"Since my error has no effect on it, I wish I had a horn

"So I could fight with it.

"Or I could tell it, 'You have taken your own portion, so leave my part.'

"It screamed and consented.

"O' fate!

"You have killed a great many of those dear to me

"And you have broken their bones.

"You have taken away whatever I had,

"And you have not left anything.

"What injustices you have inflicted on me!

"...."

He was a black slave who, with sadness, sang a poem by Zohayr with a sweet voice. Though Muhammad was self-involved, that voice was so pleasant and doleful that he entrusted his ear and mind to it, and perhaps because he had also given up many of his dear ones.

Further ahead, there was a graveyard, small, covered

in dust, distant, at the side of a small and dry village.

When Muhammad looked closely, he recognized it. Then, in his mind the veils seemed to draw aside one by one and he saw Abwa, and himself, at six years of age, and his mother Ameneh.

How simple and easy his life was when young, and how beautiful the world at his mother's side!

The memory of that pleasant and short time came alive in Muhammad's mind: those days when he would return home and see mother who had prepared food and who was sitting waiting for him. Then mother, on seeing him, would brush his head with a hand out of kindness and kiss him warmly on the cheek. Then she would wash his hands, feet, and face, place the food in front of him, and encourage him to eat. But now…!

"A thorn has gone in the eye, or does he see it backwards?

"…Or when the land becomes empty of the friend, it overflows with tears?

"Whenever I remember

"My eyes on the face

"Become like clouds with a hard rain.

"My eyes are filled with tears

"—And it must be so—

"For that dear one,

"Whom they have concealed in the ground…."

It was now another slave who, with a choking voice and with a touching voice, was reciting a poem by Khansā.[1]

Tears welled up in Muhammad's eyes with the

---

1. Tumadir bint ʻAmr al-Khansā (575-646) was a famous Arab poetess who lived during the pre-Islamic period.

memory of his mother.

How seeming strange his mother was and how much alone! Even seeing her grave—which could have been a comfort for him—had been refused him.

Muhammad's condition did not go unnoticed by Bu Taleb. Kindly, he brushed his hand over his head and with a cold sigh said, "Do you know where your mother's grave is?"

"Yes."

Bu Taleb told the caravan to continue on its course. Then he turned the camel's head toward the graveyard so as to take his brother's orphan to see the grave of his mother.

Much was left until the end of the long journey of the caravan. Now, after nearly a month of traveling, they were at the end of the Arabian Peninsula and near Syria.

On the road, as was the ancient custom, they camped for three days at the southern edge of Yathrib. There, the Yathribis and the people around it, such as the Aws and Khazraj tribes and the Jews of the Bani Qorayzah, the Bani Nazir, and rhe Bani Qaynoqā', came to the caravan and had bought some goods from them and had sold some things to them. Too, for Muhammad, an opportunity arose to go with his uncle to see his father's relatives, the grave of his father, and the Dar on-Nabegheh.

Finally, they put behind them the plain covered by black sharp volcanic stones at the southern and eastern edges of Yathrib and had also passed near the water-filled plain of Khaybar. Thus, once again the vegetation tended toward dryness and roughness, for they had penetrated the borders of the scorched wide and long desert.

A few days after passing that valley of death, the land became a bit more colorful. It was the land of the Bani Solaym. In order to compensate for those hard and strenuous days, the caravan stopped traveling for a day and rested awhile with the hospitality of the Solaymis, as well as to pay them the annual tribute from the Qureish and to refill their empty water-skins. Therefore, they had started off again, and after a day and a night, they entered the lands of the Bani Ghaytān tribe, and they had camped half of a day and a night next to that tribe.

From then on, the plain had come to an end. On the right side of the caravan there was now a line of mountains connected together and somewhat high. In the other direction there were also at times scattered mountains and sometimes attached, such that, the caravan seemed to be passing through a long valley much of the time.

That region had air that was noticeably more moderate than most of that road that they had traversed. On either side of it were springs. As a consequence, bushes and lone trees were growing there, and large and small birds, singly or in groups, were unhurriedly and smoothly flying above the valley or mountains. Here and there, the remains of a campfire of stone or the ashes of a fire and the dung of camels showed that caravans had camped in that valley. For that reason, a mysterious and profound silence had been cast over it, such that, in its amazing emptiness, every loud sound bit the mountains and came back, repeated several times, and gradually lessened and disappeared.

Muhammad liked the silence and being alone very much, and following that long passing of those dry and grim valleys, this mildly transformed nature must have pleased him. He saw, however, that in the depths of his soul, a strange fear had cast a shadow. It was as if in his soul he could smell an ominous odor in that air. An unusual feeling told him that an eternal smell of damnation was rising up from that beautiful empty land. For that reason, and unwillingly, a veil of sadness was pulled over his large black eyes.

He wanted to ask his uncle the name of that valley, when the warm, masculine voice of Bu Taleb arose in sad murmur,

"These are lessons for us to learn from people who have passed away.

"When I saw them go to a drinking place that had no way back,

"And I saw relatives, young and old,

"Going in that direction

"Whence those going did not return and the living did not stay,

"I became certain that I was going down that same road."

"Who is this poem by uncle?"

From Qoss Sā'edeh, my child."

Muhammad conjectured that Bu Taleb did not say that poem off-handedly, because he knew that even though his uncle had a strong liking for poetry and eloquent speaking, and that he had recited a lot of poetry, he nevertheless never engaged in idle talk.

Bu Taleb, it seemed, was aware of what was passing through Muhammad's little mind, and he said to him, "They call here the Valley of Hejr. More than two thousand years ago, before the time of Abraham, this was a settled and bountiful land. A capable people were here who lived well and comfortably. The name of that people was Thamud. All of them perished in their houses after a tremendous catastrophe afflicted them."

Then he pointed with his hand to the cracks in the mountains on the right side and said, "Their city was in this place. They had built very stout houses and structures of stone or had carved and drilled into the mountain. If you look closely, you can still see the signs of those buildings."

Muhammad looked where Bu Taleb was pointing. On the side of the mountain, on a gentle slope beside the peak, were diggings like button holes with dark openings. The structures were so strong that after all those years they were still more or less in place. Detritus from the mountain and the growth of bushes and plants had covered them all over or the openings of some. From the distance they were at, the ruins of those houses on the mountain looked like the dark, empty eye sockets in the heads of men that were looking at them dispassionately.

"Earlier, on another journey, I had gone to see those houses, because the caravans would continually camp for a few hours in these valleys. The buildings that were the dwellings of that powerful and wealthy people for a long time have now been transformed into very depressing ruins and is a place for hyenas, jackals, vultures, owls, and other animals of the desert. On the surface of some, however, there remain still etched writings on stone. On some of the walls of the houses or the walls of the mountains too there are still paintings of birds or idols. If it was not close to sundown now, I would take you to see them."

That is what Bu Taleb had said. In that valley where the mountains were such that the aurora of the sun shined its light later on them, and the time of sunset lifted up its rays quickly, a quickly arriving sunset was coming on. The shadows gradually lengthened and cast a dark shadow over the remaining diggings of the city of the Thamudians. Then the single sad sound of an owl issued up and echoed several times in the emptiness of the mountains. Then the other owls seemed to slowly come to life and began their dolorous voices, the inauspiciousness of that calamity-stricken and abandoned city became two-fold in the minds of the people of the caravan.

Muhammad, depressed by that fast-arriving sundown in that strange and frightening land, desired in his heart that they could pass more quickly through those valleys and at night stop at another valley.

Muhammad, sitting on a bundle at the edge of the Duma al-Jandal bazaar watching the traffic, the talk, and the trading of the people. Merchants from Iraq, Syria, and the Hejaz were many in that bazaar that was full of merchandise and very large and lively. Everyone with his own particular goods, all engaged in trading.

It had now been three days that the Qureish caravan had camped here and the caravaneers had unloaded their cargo and were offering and trading their goods with the merchants from Syria and Iraq. In that time, the people of the city were busy watching and sometimes buying different goods from the merchants.

After they had passed by the Valley of Hejr and the dwellings of the people of Thamud, and after traveling another day, they had entered the land of Syria. They had also then spent a day on the road to the east until they arrived at Dumah al-Jandal, a very green and verdant town with much water and abundant groves of date palms, like an emerald sitting in the middle of the plain of Setarun. There where the roads from Hejaz, Syria, and Iraq came together.

Staying three days in that crowded city, aside from selling and trading merchandise, had brought respite for the men and camels of the Qureish caravan so they could rest their bodies and souls after the hardships of the long journey and wash the dust of the road from their clothes and bodies. Besides that, Muhammad had seen a new city and people that were different in their figures, clothes, talk, and behavior from those of the Hejaz. Therefore, when he looked acutely, he found that the merchants of every people and nation were very much alike. All were quite greedy for wealth, and they were prepared to use any deceit or lie to get more profit.

No matter how exhausted his body had become during this journey, and how many hardships he had made for himself, Muhammad was still happy in the depths of his heart. He had above all devoted himself this journey full of suffering so as not to remain far from his uncle. Now he saw himself longing for Mecca, his uncle's wife, his kind cousins, and his nanny, Baraka, and he realized anew how attached he was to that rough city and the desiccated environment around it. For that reason, seeing those lands and cities, and their multitudinous peoples and special customs, setting out in those open plains and mountains, traversing valleys and the multicolored environment and the nights, and sleeping under desert sky full of stars, was itself a lengthy book that had many lessons for him.

"Muhammad, you are not going to go on pilgrimage to Vad?"

The voice was that of Zyad 'Amr. Zayd was a man from the Bani 'Adi, who was with the caravan from Mecca. He did not have very many goods. And too, Muhammad realized from his childish sentence that his behavior was not like that of the other merchants.

On the journey, Zayd kept trying to be alone. Most of the time he was thinking, and he did not speak unless it was necessary. Muhammad had seen him sometimes earlier in Mecca. He made the pilgrimage to Mecca in a different manner, and he did not have anything to do with the idols. For that reason, the idol-worshippers of Mecca had turned their backs on him. They said sarcastically to one another that he considered himself searching for the truth. How surprising it was than that he had asked Muhammad to make a pilgrimage to an idol!

Muhammad was so disgusted at hearing those words that he could not answer. Zayd, thinking that Muhammad had not heard him, asked his question again.

Muhammad, in a disapproving voice, said, "I am not going."

"But a number of out companions are going to visit it today as soon as they tie down their loads."

Muhammad was aware of that, because for an hour he had seen a number of the men of the caravan who had finished trading had tied up their loads, placed them in a corner, and, with gifts, had set out for the side of a hill or the edge of the city.

His uncle had told him that the place of worship for the idol Vad was in that fortress. Thus, a child of the people of Duma al-Jandal had given the description,

"It is an idol carved out of stone and resembling a warrior. It is quite tall and thick. It stands with a straight neck. A sword hangs from its neck, and around its shoulders are a bow and quiver. In its right hand is a spear. On its head a banner was waving. A container full of ricks is on the ground beside it. All of those are completely of stone."

Muhammad had a lot of questions about this subject. For what reason had people built with their own hands statues of stone, clay, plaster, dates, or things such as those and then set about worshipping them, was an insoluble problem for him. He also wanted to know what had caused the people to deviate from the traditions of the Abraham and thus had transformed it? What was the original religion of Abraham and its traditions?

"Why are you not going on the pilgrimage like the others?"

"Because I don't like it."

"Good for you my son! I wish the adults of this people had your intelligence."

"Is it true that for some time you have given up worshipping the idols?"

"Yes, that is right, my son."

"What caused you to do that?"

"Thinking! I thought and reached here with my own intellect. Also, it is many years that I have been going in every direction at every opportunity, ad asking questions about this subject from men who know and the elders of every people."

Zayd sat down on a bundle of merchandise facing Muhammad and said, "What I realized about the idols and the idol-worship of the people was that every awakened heart that realized did not do other than what I am doing."

When he saw Muhammad listening intently to his words, like an old man whose enthusiasm for teaching his abundant experiences and what he knew to others had made him impatient, he said, "Our people were the followers of the divine and virtuous religion of Abraham and his son, Ismail, peace be upon them. The Ka'ba was clear of the idols and their ornaments that have now polluted it. Every year during the month of the pilgrimage, the Arab people would descend on Mecca from every corner of the peninsula and perform the pilgrimage to God's house in the manner of Abraham, until 'Amru Lahayy, may he be eternally damned, came to rule over Mecca.

"He was from the Khoza'is, and it was he who altered the traditions of Abraham. 'Amru was not like that at first. He was respected and liked by the people. He gave food to the people and took on the burden of paying the loans of borrowers who could not pay. The people wanted him, and they obeyed every command he issued. Gradually, however, Satan suggested things to him that were contrary to Abraham's traditions, and those appealed to 'Amru. He brought the idol Hobal to Mecca and placed it in the Ka'ba. Then he placed seven other idols n the place of Mani. Also, at the time of the hajj, he changed the 'labayk' of Abraham[1] and added things to it of his own. They say that the devil inspired him to do that when, during a pilgrimage,

---

1. The "*labayk* of Abraham" is that same phrase ("I have come") that the Moslem Hajjis say on certain days of the hajj ("I have come to you, O' God, I have come. You have no partner. I have come"). 'Amru Lahayy, inspired by the devil, changed that to this: "I have come, O' God, I have come. You have no partner, I have come, save for a partner that he is for You. He and whatever he has is Yours."

in the guise of an old man, a rider on a camel with red and white hair appeared to him. Thus, other Arab tribes gravitated to idol-worship as well, and 'Amru gave an idol to every chief of every tribe so he could take it to his people and set it up as a partner with God."

The sun was setting. In the Dumah al-Jandal bazaar, the former commotion and crowding had diminished. The stalls closed one by one, and the foreign merchants were collecting their goods. Bu Taleb was also packing up his goods with some hired workers and preparing for the next day's journey.

Zayd cast a glance over the bazaar and said to Muhammad, "Yes, my son, that is how the people worshipping one god turned to the worshipping of many gods, and thus, in that way, were overtaken by black days and error by their own hands."

Then, when he saw the signs of unease in Muhammad, he said, "I know that you want to help your uncle. Get up, my son. Get up and go help him. May God give you a reward for it."

After Dumah al-Jandal, that former poisonous heat slowly diminished. Along with that, the scenery also changed and started to become softer and more moderate. Therein, gradually, the signs of life became much more. Little by little the land emerged out of its previous deathliness, barrenness, and dryness, and had taken on the smell and tone of life. Thus, there were villages and large herds of cattle and sheep and goats and sometimes camels. Fields, orchards, and gardens. Springs and streams. The white-faced people of Syria with bodies and figures a little thicker and chubbier than the people of Hejaz, no matter how much they were not as agile, experienced, or shrewd as those people. Their clothes were also finer, more colorful, and more varied than their attire.

During those few days the caravan was traveling through the Syrian valley, Muhammad had noticed form the few people of that land he had seen that besides their appearance and stature and clothing, they were also different in their temperament and behavior form the Arabs of the Hejaz. These people, though they lacked the simplicity, forthrightness, and honesty of the desert Arabs of the Hejaz, they nevertheless were more cool-tempered, more civil, and more patient than them.

With his intelligence and perspicacity, Muhammad saw, weighed, and committed them to memory. The joy from these experiences decreased the fatigue in his body from the road. Being at the side of his uncle was for him the greatest pleasure.

Muhammad was now sitting atop the load of one of the camels, with out and fear of the burning heat of the sun. He had taken his kafiyyeh off of his head and had given his black hair to the moist breeze of the green plain. He had come atop his uncle's camel, and was thinking about what he had seen on that journey. However much on the road in Hejaz the sun had its usual intensity, it had not bothered him. But a purple hue showed on his red cheeks.

The camels of the caravan were like a moving chain of seeds, patient, and had their heads down following one another. Following that long journey, now the indications of fatigue were obvious in the appearances of all of the caravaneers. The steps of the camels were also clearly slower than in the days at the beginning of the trip. Every now and then a single loud and long cry of complaint of the fatigue of the long road would rise up from the voice of one of them and break the silence of the plain.

At this time, the voice of the leader of the caravan could be heard.

"Now Bosri."

Then Bu Taleb, atop his camel, turned his upper body around toward Muhammad and said, "This is a big city of the Syrian valley, on its eastern side, and had an active bazaar."

Muhammad looked at his uncle kindly and with thanks.

Some way was still left until the city. The signs of the gardens and the blackness of the buildings surrounding it had just appeared.

After they had gone a bit further, there was a copse of trees on the right side of the road. In the middle of it was a stream that went to the fields below. At the edge of the trees, toward Bosra, there was a rocky hill. On top of it was a large, simple, and beautiful building and all white. On top of it was a small turret with a sloping roof. All of its windows on the side from which the caravan was coming were open. The black wooden windows in the middle of bright white walls resembled eyes looking toward the road to see the coming of travelers form far away.

Bu Taleb gave the order to halt. The camel-drivers turned the heads of the camels toward the open plain at the end of the small copse. The large skein of camels slowly turned and gathered together in that open space and mixed together. Then the camels of each caravan knelt down some place.

The building that was on that hill was a monastery. It had not been there very long, thirty or forty years. They say that the monk Bohayra, who was its head monk, had built it. Bohayra had stayed there since that time and had isolated himself from the people and spent his life in worship with several of his pupils.

At that time when we settled at the foot of that hill, Bohayra and his monastery were very famous. The people of that region related a lot of storied about the magnificence and wonderment of his work, and they came from near and far to see and ask for his blessings and prayers. But Bohayra demonstrated no desire to see others unless necessary. He liked solitude.

The caravan had just settled in when the door of the monastery opened and a young, slim monk came out. He went to the copse and the place where the leaders of the caravan from Mecca had decamped. He greeted and welcomed them and asked to see the caravan's leader. They directed him to Bu Taleb. The young monk said to him, "My lord, Bohayra asked me to convey his greetings to you and to invite all of the leaders of the caravan for supper in the monastery. Once you have rested for a while and washed the dirt form the road from your heads, please honor us and come to the monastery."

Bu Taleb and everyone around him were very surprised. One of them then said, "This is an auspicious occurrence. The sun must be shining from another direction today for the great monk to deign to look upon some poor men."

"Yes. That must be the way it is, because it has been a long time that every year we have been camping here day and night in this location, but I don't recall his honor Bohayra ever paying any attention to us."

The young monk was staring at the ground with his honey-colored eyes and did not say anything in response. Bu Taleb, in order to correct the course of the conversation and to secure the young monk from that situation that was bothering him, said to him in a gentle tone, "This is an honor for us, and for that reason we are grateful to his honor Bohayra. What surprised my friends was the lack of any precedence for this generosity."

The young monk, pleased by the courtesy and gentleness of Bu Taleb's words, said, "I was also shocked at this action by my master. But in these years I have been his pupil, I realized that nothing he does is without wisdom, even though that wisdom may not be apparent to others at first."

Bu Taleb, in confirmation, said, "Yes. We have also heard much talk in praise of him."

The young monk seemed to find an opportunity to explain the hidden and unsaid things in his heart said, "Do not think that because I am a Christian and a student of Bohayra that I have his fervor. But never in my life have I seen someone at this level in knowledge and abstention as he has among monks or others."

This is what that young monk said. Bohayra had reached a high station in knowledge and abstention. He knew secrets about the Torah, the New Testament, and what the predecessors had said, that few persons have access to.

Bu Taleb, more or less aware of those points, told the monk, "Convey my appreciation to father Bohayra. I will do what he says."

In a large hall, a large table was prepared. On it were a variety of foods such as yoghurt, cheese, olives, lemons, and grilled meat.

Once the senior men of the caravan were seated around the table, Bohayra stood up and welcomed them. All of them thanked him.

The aromatic smell of the food intensified the hungry men's appetite. More than that, however, seeing the famous Syrian monk was a privilege for them. Even though none of them were Christian, the considered being the guest of a man like Bohayra to be reason for honor. For that reason, all of them were gazing intently at him so as to remember him well so they could describe him to others after they returned home.

Bohayra was tall. He was wearing a long gown of the priests, black in color. The gown fit the outline of his thin body, but it had quite wide sleeves. He seemed to have a white blouse on under that, and on his waist he had tied a band as a belt.

His locks and long beard were entirely white. His appearance was so light and calm that, upon seeing him, the observer got a strange sense of tranquility. His profound gaze penetrated to the depths of the soul, so much that you felt yourself naked before him.

Bohayra looked upon the group of those who had come. Then he said to himself, "The extraneous ones have come. There is no sign of the essential one."

Then, facing them, he said, "O' distinguished gentlemen. It seems you have left someone and did not bring him with you."

"We all came except for a child, whom we left to look after our clothes and things."

Bohayra said under his breathe, "He is not a child, but an adult more mature intellectually and more knowledgeable than all of us."

This whisper did not go unnoticed by Bu Taleb who was sitting beside him. So, when Bohayra told that young monk to summon Muhammad as well, he became quite glad.

When my nephew came, Bohayra looked at him intently. Then he brought him to hi side and was very affectionate towards him. Everyone then ate, and we thanked Bohayra and the other monks and headed back to the caravan. But Bohayra kept Muhammad and me.

At this time, I realized that he wanted to have a word with us, and inviting us to supper was for that same reason. Thus, we waited for him to begin speaking.

Once the others of the caravan had gone, Bohayra took us to a room where we sat down. Bohayra began to speak and asked me, "Do you have any relationship with this boy?"

I said, "Yes. He is my child."

With an indication of disbelief, his thick eyebrows knit together, and he said, "He should not have a father! He should have lost his father as well as his mother when he was small."

Surprised, I said, "You are right. I am his uncle, but he is dearer to me than my own children."

"What is your name?"

"Muhammad."

"Yes. That is right. Muhammad or Ahmad. My son, I swear to Lat and 'Uzza…."

"Do not talk to me about Lat and 'Uzza because there is nothing on earth with which I am against more than them."

"Yes, yes. It should be exactly like that. Now, I ask you in the name of your god to answer my questions honestly."

"Rest assured honorable monk that until now, no one has heard a dishonest answer from my nephew. He is disgusted with lying. Now go ahead and ask your questions."

"What you say in the way it is sir. Do not be offended, because I have a purpose in the words I use. Okay, Muhammad, tell me, what do you like the most?"

"To be alone."

"What do you think when you are alone?"

"About creation, existence, life, death, the other world, and those kinds of things."

"And what other things?"

"…."

"What do you like the most of those things you see
I the world?"

"Nature."

"And within nature?"

"The sky and the stars."

"Do you have dreams very often?"

"Yes."

"And so?"

"I see those same things when I am awake."

"What do you see when you are asleep?"

"...."

Bu Taleb's eyes unconsciously fell on the eyes of
the old monk. In those sad blue eyes a light from life
seemed to now issue. Then he anxiously said, "Only
one matter is left for me. Let me now look between
the shoulders of the boy. Will you let me do that?"

Bu Taleb looked at Muhammad. When he did not
see any opposition from him, he opened the band of
the shirt in the dishdasha and pulled back his shirt so
that the back of his shoulders could be seen, Bohayra
quickly looked at Muhammad's two shoulders. When
he saw that blackish furry sign, tears began to well up
in his eyes. Then, like a child, he began to cry loudly.
Crying, he kissed that sign and said, "O' secret of the
heavenly books! O' expected promise! O' subtlest of
spirits! O' place where God's kindness is shown! I
swear to God, in whose hands Bohayra's life is, that
he is that same one. He is that one the Torah, the
Gospels, have foretold his coming and earlier prophets
have explained his signs. O' how fortunate I am that
I finally saw it! What a good day to day was for me."

He then prostrated and said, "O' God, thank that you have brought my years of waiting to an end and opened my eyes with seeing him!"

Bu Taleb recalled the visions of Ameneh when pregnant, and his father, Abd al-Muttaleb, before Muhammad was born, and those inspiring things that Halimeh had related about the orphan of his brother, and he fell into deep reflection.

Bohayra began to speak again. This time he was speaking to Bu Taleb.

"All of his signs are exactly those ones that have come in the heavenly books and the stories of our predecessors. He is Ahmad, Muhammad, and that same Farqelit. "Fortunate man, know that this son of your brother has very great adventures in store. The keys of heaven and hell are with him, and he has a great advantage. He will eliminate the idols and will cast aside the evil of disbelief and blasphemy form the eyes of men.

"He is the best son of man, the last of the prophets, and the leader of the virtuous. It is related that when he is born of hi smother, the earth will smile, and it will continue to smile for joy from his existence until the day of resurrection. And the devils, the idols, and their followers will weep at his coming into the world, and they will weep until resurrection day."

He sighed and added, "I am seventy years old and I have been waiting for a long time for a prophet and his invitation, because I read on what the predecessors have related and have heard form the great men of religion that he would pass through this land one day.

I came here and settled down beside this road. After that, my eyes have been upon this road until the time he arrived and visit him, until yesterday when my patience bore fruit. I then wept much for God and asked to see him from Him. I had a surprising dream last night. Its meaning was that the end of waiting is near.

"Today, since morning, my eyes have been on the white road, until, suddenly, I saw dust from afar. Then your caravan appeared, and above it was a white cloud like a dove. After the caravan had come nearer, I saw that cloud coming with it, and it was casting a shadow over the head of this dear one.

"At first, I thought I had perhaps made a mistake. When I looked closely, however, I saw that it was that same one. I was certain that my vision was true and that good tidings it had brought about his coming was in this caravan."

Bohayra heaved a sigh from the bottom of his heart and said to Muhammad, "I wish my life could endure long enough to see your message and give my life for you."

When he saw Bu Taleb deep in thought, he said, "This news has not remained hidden. Some others of the Jews and monks are also aware of it. It is not unlikely that, if they recognize you, they will seize him and cause him harm. Even though they can not kill him—as some one on whom God has looked can not be destroyed—nonetheless, it is possible they will injure an foot or another part of his body."

At the time, when we were starting back to the caravan, Bohayra gave us a package of biscuits and a jug of olives as a gift for my nephew.

Muhammad was preparing to go with the herd when Bu Taleb said to him, "Son, Khadijeh, the daughter of Khowaylad has sent you a message."

"Khadijeh the Virtuous?"

"Yes, son. You know that it has been some time that her husband died and a lot of wealth was left by him. Khadijeh does business with that money and sends goods to Yemen and Syria every year and brings merchandise to Mecca from those lands. Previously, she would send her merchandise with her slave, Maysara. Now, though, she has decided to give them to you. Yesterday when you were with the herd in the desert, Maysara brought this message."

Muhammad thought for a while and did not say anything. He had heard different things about Khadijeh, because she was a lady to well-known for anyone in Mecca not to know her. The merchants of the city said that most of the merchants in Yathrib, Syria, and Yemen also knew her. More than that, Khadijeh was one of the good persons of Mecca. Many of the small businessmen who, in their own trips, became partners with her in investments, or who essentially traded with her money. Too, many persons when they were not well off, got loans from her. But at that time when giving a loan with interest was a common matter, and was itself a kind of business, this lady did not want interest from anyone, and except for her original sum.

Muhammad also knew Marsara more less. That middle-aged stout and tall black-complexioned slave in whose broad figure were clear signs of virtue and purity and magnanimity truly had the worthiness of credibility for such a lady. But it was not clear what had happened that Khadijeh now decided to give Maysara's task to him.

For that reason, these things did not preoccupy Muhammad's mind and heart much. That which had caused him to start thinking was his own story with his uncle. Bu Taleb's life was quite difficult. Although he was usually frugal, for a while now his poverty had become more intense because his age had reached more than fifty and he had five children. And since that journey when Muhammad as a child had gone with him to Syria, he could not go on another trip to trade. Of his sons, Taleb still did not have much property or business to where he could help his father. "Aqil did not have the foresight to have any hope in him. Ja'far was no more that a small child. The rest were two daughters. In the meanwhile, Muhammad had tried hard not to be a burden to his uncle. At first, he would take several goats and camels of Bu Taleb to graze in the desert. After a period of time had elapsed, the other uncles and relatives had also given him their herds to him to take to graze. But now that his age had reached twenty-five, he needed to take another job so that with that he could perhaps free himself from his uncle and help him. For that reason, with his hand bowed, he said to his uncle, "What do you say?"

Bu Taleb, with that magnanimity and seriousness he always had, said, "Although you are now a fortunate youth and in terms of intellect, you have the maturity of older men, for me you are still that same son Muhammad and I can not bear being far from you for a day. But when I look closely, the time has arrived for you to chose a wife and settle down in your life. Even though it will always be a source of shame for your uncle that he did not have enough money to help you in that, now I hope that with the profit from this trip, I will be able to help in this matter. For that reason, the decision is yours. I will accept whatever you desire."

Muhammad's appearance, which was always flushed, became more blushed by what Bu Taleb said. Thus, with his head down, he said, "Give me some time uncle so I can think about this matter."

"Think about it, son. And if you decide to go, begin to make preparations. Today, I will tell Taleb to take the herd to the desert."

Muhammad said, "Thank you, uncle."

He then left Bu Taleb and went out of the house. This was a serious matter, and he had to think about it. Thus, a sin the past, when he needed to be alone, he headed for the Mountain of Nur[1] and the cave of Hirā.

---

1. The word *nur* means "light" in Arabic.

He stopped at the foot of the Nur mountain after going two parasangs very quickly—as was his manner—in that hot weather, now it was time to rest a while. So he sat on a stone slab at the edge of the road.

This was the same place where they said that their ancestor, Abraham, had decided to sacrifice his son for his god.

Behind him was the mountain of Tabir, pyramid-shaped and high. Opposite was Nur Mountain, the beloved place of his longing and solitariness. The same place that, when he became depressed inside Mecca, when he looked at its sharp peak and triangular shape, his sadness dissipated some.

The heat of the first month of summer was baking the rocks of the mountain. Sweat was rolling down the temples of the young Muhammad to the side of his well-proportioned cheeks like small streams, and diminished amidst his thick, black beard. In spite of that, the weather there was more moderate, as it was lower than Mecca, in a depression among the mountains. A soft breeze sometimes also blew, gently rustling the thorn bushes amid the rocks.

Muhammad took the aqal and kafiyyeh off of his head. His black hair fell on both sides of his face. Then he turned toward the plain north of Mecca. There, the way to Yathrib resembled a dry and narrow river in the desert, and in the end disappeared amid the crowds of dark mountains.

How varied was the nature of the Creator! On the side of it was the grim and dry valley of Satarwan, and on the other side were the fields, orchards, and gardens, and bountiful springs of Syria full of water!

Muhammad wiped the sweat from his brow. He got up from his place in order to say the first farewell with his likeable companion and the keeper of the secrets of hours spent alone. He started up the road toward the peak of Mount Nur.

Although the light was no higher than two hundred meters, its pathway was uneven and steep. Its surface was covered with rocks and thorn bushes that were difficult to go over. Nevertheless, Muhammad, during the long years of childhood and youth, has climbed it so much that climbing over the now was not difficult. I particular  walking in the plain and mountains following the herds had trained his feet and strengthened them that paths much harder than this did not tire him or make him short of breathe.

Muhammad turned his head around, under his feet, in the direction of the city, was the gorge of Mani. Silent and empty. Devoid of any passerby. Further in that direction, Mecca, from which nothing could be heard save the dumb and distant commotion.

Suddenly, the memory of Abd al-Muttaleb came to Muhammad, and his heart became tight form sorrow. Abd al-Muttaleb, like Muhammad, sometimes came to this mountain alone and sought reclusion for part of a day in the cave of Hira. Every year when

Ramazan came, Hira was where he passed the days and nights for the whole month. During that period, his old slave, 'Amer, brought him food and water. When Muhammad was small, he sometimes came with 'Amer in order to see his grandfather again.

Muhammad stepped onto the peak. A scene more or less clear, spread out, nearly forty meters. In every direction, all around him, a clear sky and blue without blemish. A slight breeze was blowing, and for the hot body of Muhammad, it brought a heavenly sensation as a gift.

As was his former habit, Muhammad lingered for a while on that height and looked around. On the eastern side of the mountain was a road that went to 'Arafat. Mecca was to the southeast of the mountain crouching on the low mountain sides. In the center of it the Ka'ba stood like a black gen amidst the circle within circle of the city, sorrowful. A thin and pale mass of purple dust was moving in the sky above the city, stationary like a large piece of cloud.

Inside the city, the houses, more or less like before, opened out like rays in a circle around the sanctuary. Now, however, in that section of the city toward the north of the city that was on a height and which could not be reached by floods, the wealthy of Mecca, from every clan, had built dwellings. For that reason, that quarter had been named Batha'.

The houses of Batha' were large and elegant. They had walls of stone, and most were of two storeys. Among them, still, the large two-storeyed house of Khadijeh, with that green silk canvas like a dome above its roof had a different splendor.

When someone stood on the roof of Khadijeh's house, the road to Yathrib and Syria were easily within their view. Khadijeh sat under that dome-like canvas every afternoon and guests went to see her there.

They said many things about Khadijeh, and some, as was the habit of the Arabs, engaged in exaggeration.

A very beautiful woman, even if she is forty years old and had had two husbands and had three children from them. Still, she has many suitors. Aside from some of the wealthy of Qureish such as Bu Lahab and 'Amru Hesham, all of the kings of the Arab Peninsula would like to marry her.

Muhammad had  heard that some of the youth of Mecca too, who were many years younger than Khadijeh, were thinking abut her great wealth—or for other reasons—wanted to be her husband very much. But Khadijeh had rejected the proposals of all of them.
Until that time, Muhammad had never seen Khadijeh. He had heard talk this way and that. He also knew that she is without doubt one of the wealthiest women in the land of Hejaz, without having the bad habits of the wealthy.

In generosity and helping the needy, no one could equal her.

It was also for this reason that some of the ladies of the Qureish had given her a title. She had lived in such a way that one group had named her "Khadijeh the Viruous."

Muhammad sat down on the ground facing Mecca. How much he liked this city, and how disgusted and saddened he was wit the bad behavior and customs of the people!

In the days when his grandfather, Abd al-Muttaleb, was alive, even though the people were the same way, the city was in a better situation because his influence and magnanimity were such that, more or less, it prevented the strong people from oppressing the weak. After he left this world, ad his son, Zobayr, took his father's place, little by little the situation changed, because even though Zobayr was a good man and a courageous one, he did not have his father's greatness or splendor in the eyes of the people.

Muhammad's gaze was pulled toward the Ka'ba and the account of a strange man came to his mind.

It was in the afternoon and he was going to circumambulate the Ka'ba when he saw people in the sanctuary. They were gathered around a middle-aged and slender man. The man had gone atop the platform on which the idol Asaf was situated and he was crying out in a loud voice.

When Muhammad went closer, he realized he was a man from the Bani Zobayd. The man of Bani Zobayd brought some goods to Mecca and 'Ās Wā'el of the Bani Sahm clan had said he would buy those goods. He had taken them from him, and now he was refusing to pay for them.

The man form the Bani Zobayd cried out painfully, "O' men of the Qureish, come to the aid of a wronged man far from his tribe and people, for they have oppressed him in this safe city."

Upon hearing these words. Muhammad's heart began to hurt. He thought for a while about how he could get back the right of that man far away from his country.

Then he found the solution was to relate this story of this affair to his uncle, Zobayr, so he could think of a solution for this situation.

When Zobayr was informed of the different aspects of the story, he summoned that wronged man and told him to have patience for a day. Then he sent a messenger to the leaders of the two clans of the Qureish to assemble in the council building.

At night, some came and several—each with an excuse—remained absent. Muhammad went there with his uncle Zobayr.

Zobayr repeated that story to those present. Then he added, "This affair has two aspects and both are ugly and damaging for the Qureish and Mecca. The first is that, when this news is propagated, all of the people of the Arabs and others will say that the honor of the sanctuary has been violated and Mecca is no longer a safe and secure city.

Thus, the merchants of the other lands will suffer loss and decline. The other is that the greatness and high position of the Qureish will be broken for the Arabs, because both the administration of the city is in their hands and the oppressor is from it."

Upon hearing these words, uneasiness arose within the group and every person said something. Then Zobayr said, "So that this does not happen again, we have to think of a plan."

One said, "What plan? Mecca needs to be managed with an imposing presence like Hashem of Abd al-Muttaleb so no one dares oppress the stranger or weak person. It is now bereft of such a person."

Zobayr, without taking that allusion to heart, said, "Yes. That is how it is. I have, however, been thinking about this matter for a long time. Since we do not have such dignified men, we should not sit and watch the boasting of bullies. My view is that the brave and chivalrous men should volunteer to come forward from the various clans of the Qureish and make an agreement among themselves to support the weak and oppressed after this and to help them to banish oppression."

Muhammad approved of this suggestion by his uncle very much. Among that group, the view of the other men was mostly the same as that. Thus, Zobayr said, "Think about this matter tonight. Also deliver this message to the other men of your people so whoever wants can join this agreement. Tomorrow afternoon come to this same place."

At this time, Abdullah Jad'ān said, "I accept those brave young men. I like that this auspicious contract will be made in my house."

All accepted, and they congratulated him.

The next day, several of the men of the Bani

Hashem, Bani Asad, Bani Zohrah, Bani Taym, and Hares, the son of Fahr of the Bani Nazir were all present at the appointed place. Muhammad and Zobayr were there too. They killed a cow and poured its blood in a copper pail. Then the mother of Hakim Bayzā, one of Muhammad's aunts, brought that pail of blood, and one by one they placed their hands in the blood and swore that they would support one another in that endeavor as long as the mountains of Tabir and Nur were in their place and until some water moistened some wool.

News of that contract quickly spread through Mecca and became known as "the contract of the young men." The people also considered those young men who had made the contract great and they praised them.

On the following day, they sent a message to 'As to pay the cost of the goods to that man form the Bani Zobayd. 'As, because he had earlier heard the story of the contract, became frightened and did just that.

A smile of satisfaction came across Muhammad's red lips. He heaved a sigh of relief and rose from his place.

This was the only group with which Muhammad was attached until that day, and he was so glad about it that one day in talking, he had said to Bu Taleb, "This is a contract that, if they were to give in exchange for it red-haired camels, I would not be content."

Muhammad descended the south side of the Mountain of Nur toward the cave of Hira. Hira was on a height of forty meters from the ground at the foot of the mountain. It was not a cave like the others, a digging that appeared in the side of the mountain. It seemed to be several stones lying on top of one another and underneath them a cave-like space could be found.

He passed with difficulty between two boulders that had fallen in front of the cave and entered Hira, a small cave-like place with smooth walls and ceiling. Its height was several times the height of an average man. Its floor was soft and covered with purple and glistening sand.

Muhammad had a great deal of affection for this cave because, aside from it being his companion and retreat, it protected him from the effects of wind, rain, and the hot sun. Too, Hira was such that when he stood or sat in it, or lay down, he saw his beloved Ka'ba.

He sat on the surface of the cave and put his back to its wall. The air here was lighter than outside.

He stared at the plain between the mountains Nur and Tabir. The plain was covered in thorn bushes. Then the barren desert spread out. The familiar plain of Muhammad. The passing and the grazing place during many days and nights for the herd for which he was the shepherd.

The caravan needed to start off before the sun had risen in the sky. Although Muhammad had not gone for trading, except for one trip as a child, he had heard and had seen many things about that.

From there where the houses of the city came to an end, a little way from the pass whence the road to Yathrib began, the caravan was now prepared to go. Muhammad, with Maysara and other slaves of Khadijeh, had earlier spent several days binding the loads. Very large loads of skins, leather, and wool from Taif, water skins and wild and salutary plants from Mecca, ivory from Ethiopia; coconuts, spices, aromatic incense, valuable ebony, and steel swords from India; pistachios, beautiful carpets, fine muslin, fine gold and silver ornaments from Persia; varied-colored silk cloths and muck from China; ambergris and pearls from Bahrain and Oman; gun Arabic, collyrium, henna, firmly-woven cloth, simple and striped cottons from Yemen.... Aside from those, there were several boxes of wood, iron, and leather full of gold and silver coins from Rome and Persia. All of the gold and silver— coins and ornaments—were in those boxes, and in Khadijeh's house, with the understanding that once the loads had been fastened on the camels, Maysara would go back to the house and bring them.

Muhammad had earlier put his things for the journey in a leathern sack. Two sets of clothes. One simple and for the road; the other better to be worn in the city. Also a wooden comb, a small container with stones of collyrium, a bronze container of musk, several pieces of wood for cleaning teeth, a small goblet of bronze for drinking water, an oil container with violet oil, a needle with thread, and a pair of scissors.

At dawn, 'Aqil and Taleb had gone with the herd to the plain. His uncle, Bu Taleb, had earlier left his house to do some work, but he had said that he would go to the caravan to say farewell to him.

Muhammad said farewell to his uncle's wife. Then he gently stroked the head of his uncle's small daughter and said good-bye to her too. Fatemeh was anxious, like a mother who was sending her own dear child on journey. But she did not want to disturb Muhammad by crying at this, the last moment. So with a lump in her throat she put a smile on her face to conceal her feelings and followed him to the door.

Muhammad came out of the small wooden house and headed off.


Creator, I rely on your support on this trip. I look to you and cling to your mercy. You are behind me, and I have hope in You.

O' God, notice me during difficulties. And in those things I ignorantly do not consider important, and yet they are important, support me!

O' God, make cleanliness and correctness my provisions, and forgive my sins, and make me aware of goodness and rightness wherever I look!

On the road, he saw Abi al-Hamaysā. He seemed to also have an acquaintance in that caravan and had come to tell them farewell. Abi al-Hamaysa, laughing, said "Good day!" to Muhammad, and Muhammad, with a smile on hi slips, answered him. Then they set off together.

One day, I had sold something to Muhammad. Then I could pay the rest of the cost of it, it was agreed to meet the next morning at the beginning of the bazaar beside the sanctuary.

This transpired, and I forgot about my agreement. Then I left Mecca for some work and did not come back for three days.

On the third day, when I returned, I did not remember that appointment, and I passed by that same pace and saw Muhammad. He was sitting on a bench and looking down the road. Then I remembered that appointment.

When I went up to him and talked with him, I realized that that forthright youth came there every day and waited on me until evening.

I was very surprised at his faithfulness, and I was ashamed of my own forgetfulness. It was then that I realized why the people had given him the title of "Amin" and they respected that young man so much.

When the bazaar ended, the door of Bani Hashem appeared. At this point, Muhammad said farewell to Abi al-Hamaysa and entered the sanctuary through that door.

The sanctuary was empty in that milky-white air of dawn. The idols, with their rough, severe, and cold figures around the courtyard, were without any visitors.

Muhammad, angry and sad, looked away from them and headed for the Ka'ba.

First, he touched the black stone with his hand. Then he wanted to circumambulate the Ka'ba when he heard a voice. A man was crying and murmuring some words. There was an ache in his voice that drew Muhammad towards him.

"O' God, if I had known which was you want them to worship You, I would worship You like that. Forgive me that I do not know that way."

When M heard those words, he knew who the speaker was, because he had seen him several times in that situation. He was 'Amru Zayd, one of the four monotheists of Mecca of whom people spoke. He was the same one who was with the Qureish caravan on that journey going to Syria during M's youth.

The other three persons were Waraqa Nawfel, 'Obaydollah Jahshu, and 'Othman Huyareth.

Of them, Waraqa and Othman had accepted the Christian customs. Obaydollah had not accepted any particular religion. Zayd told the Qureish that he worshipped the god of Abraham, even though he had not received anything from the customs of that people.

After a little hesitation, Muhammad began to

circumambulate the Ka'ba.

On the other side of the Ka'ba's wall, he saw Zayd facing the Ka'ba with his forehead on the ground and self-absorbed. However much Muhammad had affection for Zayd, he did not consider it proper to disturb his pleasurable state by speaking. Thus, he silently circled the Ka'ba seven times as a farewell and left.

Five hundred loaded camels and several camel riders of Khadijeh's caravan, with small red woolen tassels around the ears, head, and neck, visible among the other camels of the caravan, were preparing to go. Aside from Maysara, there were fifty capable and experienced slaves and hired workers who had seen many journeys riding with Muhammad.

I had instructed all of them to follow Amin's orders and not oppose him. I had also told Amin to make Maysara his advisor in this journey because Maysara had been my caravan leader before, and although he was a slave, he was nevertheless a good man with experience on trips, and he had a lot of experience in this field.

Muhammad divided the camels and entrusted every ten camels to one man. He entrusted those five camels that had the loads with coins, pearls, gold, and silver to Maysara.

With the appearance of the first rays of the sun from behind the mountains east of Mecca, the drum of departure began to beat.

Bang, bang, bang....
It is time to move out....
Those who are sitting, stand up!

Those standing, make the camels get up!
Bang, bang, bang….
Now the last farewell!
Bannng….
Put the camels in a line one behind another.
Bang, bang….
Prepare to go!

It was the Qureish custom that when a trading caravan was heading somewhere, they would select one among them to be the leader of the whole caravan. Thus, on the road, the caravaneers would obey him. On this trip, great men from several clans of the Qureish were accompanying the caravan.

As far as I can recall, "Amru Hashem from the Bani Makhzum, and from the Bani 'Ada, Mot'am, and from Bani Nazir, Nasr Hares, and from the Bani Zahra, Ahja Halaj, and from the Bani Banulawi, Bu Sofian, and from the Bani Hashem there was Amin, our caravan leader.

The caravan of which Muhammad was its leader was larger then all the other caravans. Several from Bani Hashem were with us with their merchandise.

I and all the Bani Hashem said that Amin should be the caravan leader. 'Amru Hashem, however, did not agree. Hamzeh, Muhammad's uncle, the bravest and strongest man of Mecca, was with us too. When he heard that, he became angry. He pulled his sword from it sheath and went toward 'Amru. Muhammad quickly stepped forward and said to him, "Uncle, sheath your sword. They will be in front on going and we on returning. In any case, we are both from one tribe, and whatever the situation, the Qureish are in front."

Then the caravan started off.

The road and the caravan. Men and camels. The camels with heavy loads of goods from China, India, Persia, Ethiopia, Yemen, Bahrain, Oman, and the Hejaz. The men, with swords and daggers on their waists, and some with quivers and bows on their backs and shoulders. On the lookout. Ready to stand up to any danger.

The long train of the caravan's camels was marching forward with long steps on the dry bed of the Yathrib road. More than three thousand camels had goods on their backs, and nearly three hundred men were there to take care of and protect those goods.

The initial sorrow of the beginning of the journey had still not lifted off the chests of the men and camels. This was clearly visible in the silence and lack of talk of the men and those human-like looks of the camels that were continually distant.

The point man of the caravan and camels was 'Amru Hashem. He was also the first person to mount a camel. His helper in this journey was the youth 'Amār, that same one whose father, Yāser, took refuge with the Bani Makhzum. Both he and his mother, Safiyyeh, were slaves of Abu Hodayfa.

Thus was Khadijeh's caravan. So long that the Arabs had never seen a caravan as long as it before belonging to one person. At the very front of it, Muhammad was sitting astride a fast, yellow camel.

Behind this caravan were those of the Bani Hashem, and following them were caravans of other clans of the Qureish.

The cradle-like rocking of the camels plunged the men, who were tired after waking up early, into a pleasant state between wakefulness and sleep. The most pleasant of states spent while in it, dreams or distant memories of the deepest layers of the mind, gain strength before the eyes.

Muhammad, however, with eyes and heart that were awake, sometimes looked ahead and sometimes around him, at the familiar plain and the soil that was his companion day and night.

Qarārit was to the left side of the caravan, in the place Muhammad took most of the herd to graze. His expansive and endless thoughts about many days and nights.

"Good day Amin!"

M looked ahead. It was 'Amār, who had now come to the end of Abu Hodhayfa's caravan in order to guard it.

"And good day to you brother!"

Upon hearing those words, blood rushed into 'Amar's face, so much so that the redness could be seen under his young brown skin.

A youth with a source of greatness, from the highest clan of the Qureish and the grandson of their most honorable person, and too the leader of the largest caravan of Mecca, had called him "brother." For him, who was no more than a slave and the son of a slave, with the value and worth of a single camel, nothing could be greater.

'Amar, overjoyed and also ashamed of that address, put all of his feelings into one short phrase and said, "I am grateful master."

Muhammad, with a smile and mixed with kindness answered him. Then, when he saw his displeasure at his camel being situated in front of his camel, he said,

"Do not worry 'Amar. These manners do not exist between friends."

Another source of shame for 'Amar. Muhammad Amin had addresses him, who was unworthy, as his friend! This kind and likeable youth truly had a great character and was humble!

Aside from the free men, all of the slaves whom Muhammad knew, like me, also liked him very much, because, even though he was an aristocrat who possessed dignity, nonetheless he had a life and behavior that was very simple and humble. He wore clothes that were simple, but clean. When he walked, he did not strut like those who considered themselves great, and he did not hold his head high. He kept his steps a little apart from one another and walked in the manner of someone who was going down a slope. When sitting, he did not lean. He sat on the ground like us slaves, and he ate on the ground. He slept on the ground, and he patched his own shoes and clothes. And like the slaves, he sat cross-legged, or he put his arms around his knees. No one had ever seen him to sit with his legs crossed.

Aside from these, his good works were the talk of the people of Mecca. I, who was the shepherd of the Bani Makhzum, saw Muhammad a great deal in the desert. One day, I said to him, "Amin, I heard that there is a good pasture in Fah. What do you say that we take the herds there tomorrow?"

He said, "That will be good."

The next day when we went there, I saw Amin, who

had arrived there before me. But he had firmly kept his herd from entering that pasture.

Surprised, I said to him, "Why did you do that Amin?"

He said, "We had agreed to come to this pasture together. Therefore, I did not want to get ahead of you in this."

Along the edge of the caravan's path, a herd was waiting to go to the other side. Its shepherd, upon seeing Muhammad, made a gesture with his hand in recognition. So, as was the custom of shepherds, he wished him a good journey in a loud voice, and Muhammad answered him warmly.

The young shepherd seemed familiar to him. After staring at him for a while, he remembered. This youth, dusty and with disheveled hair, was the same young Hoshām of a few years before. He was not a slave. At that time, he also did not like shepherding, but his father compelled him to do that. Finally, Hosham quit shepherding, and Muhammad did not know what he was doing. Now, after some years, it seemed he had come back to shepherding.

Upon seeing Hosham, M remembered the incident that had happened at the beginning of his youth. It was springtime, and the grass was abundant in the plain. At that time, the shepherds stayed with the herd in the plain at night. When night came, several of the shepherds would gather their herds together in one place and stay together until morning. At times, one of them would entrust his herd to the others and go to the city to wander around and watch or do something else.

They were with Muhammad, four shepherds. All of them had gone to the city in turn for one night, except for Muhammad. On the night his turn came, Hosham and the other two shepherds asked whether he was going to the city.

Muhammad said, "No, because there is nothing for me to do at night in the city."

Hosham said, "You have never gone to Mecca late at night?"

Muhammad said, "No."

"It is a surprising world, and worth seeing!"

One of the other shepherds said, "Most of the other young people of the city are awake at these hours of the night, and they go to the alleys and gatherings that are occurring in the city."

Muhammad said, "I don't care for those gatherings."

Hosham said, "What about the weddings and the conversation parties? Most of those are happening at night. You don't have any desire to see those either?"

They said a lot of things like that to Muhammad, until Hosham said, "You need to see those at least once. It is, in any case, worth seeing once."

In the end, Muhammad agreed, and he went to the city.

When he reached Mecca, he headed into the alleys and was wandering around. He wanted to understand what kept those night people of the city awake until late at night, and what the source of their efforts and enthusiasm in that matter were for.

Along the way, in a passageway, he heard the sound of a tambourine and flute. He asked, "What is happening there?"

They said there was a wedding celebration.

He went on and sat in a corner of the assembly, but sleep quickly overcame him, and he woke up with the heat of the daytime sun.

When he returned to the plain the next day, Hosham said, "Now tell us, what did you see?"

Muhammad repeated the story. They laughed in jest.

When night came that day, that same talk came up again, and Muhammad again agreed to go to the city, but sleep once again overtook him, and he did not see anything. So he returned to the plain again in the morning and related the story. Then he added, "I don't think it is in my interest to go to those assemblies."

So he never went to those kinds of places again.

The flat and naked plain had come to an end. The caravan now slowly entered a narrow road through an opening between the mountains scorched by the heat of the sun.

A little while later, there was no sign of the plains and mountains of Mecca. Mountains were in every direction, naked, without any covering of plants. And there were large and small stones scattered this way and that.

At this point, a heavy sadness settled over Muhammad's heart with the memory of his uncle, aunt, and cousins.

The night before, Bu Taleb was very restless, such

that the thought occurred to Muhammad that he had regretted his decision about sending him on this journey.

"Son, I wish I had not spoken and agreed to your going."

"For what reason uncle?"

"I am afraid for your life form the Jews and some of the Christians. Do you remember what Bohayra the monk said on that matter? Even though thirteen years have passed since that time and you are now a successful youth, in those lands you are an alien, and the deceitfulness of the Jews is considerable."

A large lizard darted out from under the foot of Muhammad's camel. After a short hesitation, the camel continued. The lizard, moving quickly but in jumps and starts, reached some purple rocks. It stayed for a moment and turned its trapezoid head toward the caravan. There, it disappeared among the rocks. Meanwhile, Maysara arrived astride a camel. Large drops of sweat were sitting on his black masculine features.

He came so far forward that his camel's nose touched that of Muhammad's camel. With a smile mixed with respect, he said, "It is as if fire is raining down from the sky."

Muhammad said, "Yes. It is a very warm day, and the air is hotter in the middle of all these rocks because the rocks hold in the heat and radiate it. Behind and among these mountains stops any breeze from blowing."

"That is the way it is master. This group of

mountains, however, at one time was the cause for saving the leaders of the Qureish from death."

When he saw the questioning signs in Muhammad's eyes, he added, "This event goes back to the beginning of the Fejār wars. I think that was nine years ago, in the month of Rajab. On that day, I, like many other Meccans, was in the "Ukkaz bazaar trading when I suddenly saw a ruckus among the Qureish. I asked the reason. I knew that at the time they had secretly brought news to them that Barrāz Qays Kanāni had killed 'Orwa Rahhāl of the Hawāzan. Since in that bazaar, the Qureish were fewer in number than men from the Hawazan, it was feared that when the Hawazan attacked, they would all be decimated. So the leaders of the Qureish considered it prudent to present an excuse and quickly go toward Mecca. I came with them too.

"We came quickly, and we were afraid. When we got near these mountains, we saw them far away and pursuing us.

"Seeing that, we became more afraid because they were twice as many as us.

"By afternoon, there was hardly any distance left between them and us. Thus, a battle ensued. By fighting and retreating, we kept them busy until we reached these mountains. Darkness also came to our aid, and we survived.

"We did not sleep that night, and we traveled continuously among these mountains until we reached the security of Mecca and found safety from their evil."

Muhammad shook his head out of sadness. Although he had more or less heard about that event, every time he thought about it, he became sad, because it had am illogical quarrelsomeness that did not need to happen so that these men on both sides die. A stupid rogue like Barraz had, out of jealously, killed a brave man like 'Urwa in a cowardly manner and in a month when quarreling was forbidden by the custom of the Arabs. He had earlier committed many other excessive violations that caused his tribe, the Kanana, to expel him. So he had gone to Mecca and sought refuge with the Harb Omayyeh with the Qureish. But he did not stop his corrupted ways there either. Harb had decided to revoke his right to refuge. Although it was agreed Barraz would leave Mecca, he decided to come back. Barraz went to the territory of the Hireh and started that resurrection, until finally the 'Urwa tribe attacked the Qureish and Kanana because of his revenge. Because, although Barraz was from the Kanana, he was also protected by one of the leaders of the Qureish.

All of the Qureish believed that a quarrelsome man like Barraz was not valuable enough to cause that long four year war and spill the blood of that many men from both sides. What the solution, however, of running out a refuge when he was in danger was a great shame for a tribe. And too, it had along been the custom of the Arabs that when a person of one tribe spilled the blood of the people of another tribe, all of the people of his tribe would calculate the blood, and when the tribe of the victim attacked them, they considered the spilling of the blood of each one of them to be permissible for them. Thus, every person killed by one side, brought the killing of someone by the other side. In that way, revenge became deep and the killing sometimes went on for decades. As the wheel of war turned, each death seemed to make it go ever faster. So much so that stopping it from turning became more difficult every moment. Then, there was no escape for anyone except to be either the prey or the hunter; the killed of the killer.

Muhammad's silence had become long, and the signs of sorrow were becoming more evident each moment in his countenance. So as not to allow an opportunity for this mood to advance in his nature, Maysara said, "I do not think you were in the Fejar wars yourself were you master?"

"I was not at first as you have described it. The next year, though, when the Qureish and Kanana went to do battle with the Havāzan, my uncle took me along."

"Was Bu Taleb in that war too?"

"My uncle disliked that conflict. He said, 'I and my family will not be tainted by it.' But the people of the tribe said to him, 'This is something that has taken place, and the Qureish were not the ones who started it.' They also said that if he was with the Qureish, they would be victorious. My uncle went with them with the understanding that they would not, by any means, conduct oppression. That year they were victorious. I was also at my uncle's side in that battle, and I deflected the arrows that came toward him with my shield. When my uncles' arrows ran out, I went around the battlefield and picked up any arrow I found and gave it to them."

"You were not at all afraid in that situation?"

"No, because I was certain that if my life was in the world, I would not die. If it was not to be like that, there was no escaping from the inevitability of death."

At this moment, a large shadow passed over the caravan. Muhammad and Maysara caste their eyes toward the sky. A portion of a black cloud had blocked the view of the sun.

"Master, they call this 'The Valley of Floods.'"

It was three days that they had been going between that range of mountains.

From atop the camel, Muhammad looked around him. Then, in answer to Maysara, he said, "Yes. The existence of detritus everywhere tells of the passing of many floods. For that reason, it is better we not stop in this place.

Maysara, with that same maturity and softness he always had when speaking, said, "This valley, however, is a narrow and long passage between these two mountain ranges and does not end soon. Also, night is now here, and I am afraid that on the road it will harm the camels or that several of them will become lost.

"In any case, these black clouds that have appeared beside Mecca are not a good sign."

Maysara was well aware that in the summer, whenever the heat becomes very intense, if rain comes, there is a real threat of a flood. The threat of that doubles in that valley. Thus, acceptingly, he said, "The decision is yours master. We will do whatever you order."

"Now that we have no choice but to halt, we must settle down in a high place where there is no sign of debris."

"That is what we will do, even though it will be twice as difficult."

Muhammad, while passing through the dim darkness of the early evening, scanned in every direction. Then, a little later, he indicated a point on the side of the mountain with several large boulders and said, "What do you think about here Maysara?"

Maysara said, "It is good. The boulders can be steadfast places of safety when a flood comes."

Then, facing toward the front of the caravan, he shouted, "Prepare to halt! Follow me. Prepare to halt!"

The camel-drivers of the caravan of Khadijeh and Bani Hashem, happy or not, turned the heads of their camels toward the mountainside and followed the camels of Muhammad and Maysara.

Muhammad went up the mountain as far as the fatigue and heavy loads of the camels allowed. The other camels followed behind him. He then ordered them to take the loads off of the camels and to water and feed them.

When the other caravans saw what was happening, they unloaded their loads on the heights, except for the caravan of Mos‘ab of the Bani Jomah clan.

His caravan had stayed behind on the road. When they arrived, he told his men to unload the camels in the middle of the valley on the open ground beside the road.

When Maysara saw that, with good intentions, he told him not to do that, but Mos‘ab mockingly answered, "Tell your master that great fear is the same as death! If we are afraid of a few clouds, we would not be on this journey."

When Maysara heard that, he did not say anymore.

The night had now set up it black tent over that valley. In the sky, a black cloud had obscured the light of the dagger-shaped moon. The darkness was more depressing in the long shadows of the mountains. In every place, the camels folded their front feet under their bodies and were chewing their cud or sleeping. Every man was also busy doing something. One was putting pieces of food in a camel's mouth. In order to keep away snakes, scorpions, and tarantulas, others were gathering up bushes with thorns and twigs and lighting small fires here and there with flints. Several had set out their small cloths and were eating that night's meal. Because of fatigue, a group were sleeping without having eaten, leaning against the saddle of a camel or with their head on their shoes or a bag among the goods of the caravan. The older men, however, had assembled together and were telling stories about their pervious journeys. In the caravan of Bani Makhzum, an old story-teller was setting on a small rock and relating the story of Sayf Zi Yazan to those around him.

Meanwhile, Muhammad, after finishing settling in the caravan, was now setting on a rock on top of the mountain and watching the sky and the movement of the clouds, moon, and stars.

At this time, in the northern sky, Canis Major came out from behind a cloud and in its nose, the Dog Star, the brightest star in the sky, appeared, the sign of the beginning of the month of Jowza[1] and the intensification of heat....

---

1. The last month of spring.

The night slowly lengthened. The moon, now freed from the grasp of the clouds, rose in the sly from the side of the range of mountains in the direction of the road. But the clouds gradually got thicker, and the valley was immersed in a deep darkness. Mos'ab and his caravan could not be seen at all now. The other caravaneers were slowly falling asleep. The flames in the small stone fireplaces were going out. The bustle of voices, near and far, were dying down. That gentle evening breeze, however, had turned into a wind. The howling of hungry hyenas and jackals came from far away. M, distanced from all of these things that were happening, and was starting at the night sky as before and absorbed in his own secret world.

They did not move that valley for four days.

At the beginning of the night, I started from my sleep with the large drops of rain. Cries arose from every direction. I started to search for my master, Amin. Then I saw him busy waking the others and directing them. Fearful, I joined him.

It rained harder than I had ever seen before. After a short while, a torrent of water, resembling large rivers, were coming down from the mountain. They joined together and created a small river in the valley, fast and strong. I myself saw how that torrent knocked down the men, camels, and all of Mos'ab's goods and carried them away. Fearful and helpless, Mos'ab and his men screamed and sought help, but the other caravans were so frightened and busy trying to protect their own goods from the flood that no one had the opportunity to help them. Only Muhammad, at the same time that he was busy protecting his friends, was constantly yelling to them to leave the goods and camels and save themselves. But they did not seem to hear him. In the meantime, the darkness added to the fear and confusion, so much so that the eye could not see. And the camels, with all their patience and courage, gave up and fled this way and that while screaming.

In the end, that dark night turned to day. By midday, the dark clouds had gone away and the rain had stopped. So the men began to look for the camels that had become scattered. They were lucky that the camels by instinct in that darkness and fear had headed toward the high places, and the flood had not taken a single one of them. Maysara had tied up the loads in such a way that the water had not done much damage to Khadijeh's goods.

The same was more of less true for the other caravans, except for the caravan of Mos'ab.

Once the darkness had gone away, I knew that we were all okay. Only one of 'Amru Hesham's camels that seemed to have gone searching for grass during the night, went down into the valley and was then swept away by the flood. Of Mos'ab, however, twenty men had died, and he had died with them. Only five of his slaves had survived, and that was because they had disobeyed his command. On the third day, we saw them coming over the mountains, and they told us about that. Thus, my master, Amin, told me, "Maysara, give them some food to eat and clothes to wear. When they decide to return to Mecca, give them water and provisions so they do not go without on the road."

I did that. Then they took off for Mecca on foot to relate the news to the Bani Jomah.

We now dried off the merchandise and got it ready so we could go. In front of us, however, was a narrow and deep passage where a lot of water had gathered. The caravan could not pass through it because no one knew how deep it was. The beginning of it was also muddy and we were afraid the camels would sink into the mud and get stuck. On both sides of the passage, the mountains had such steep and slippery slopes that no camel would be able to get past it.

It was such a surprising situation that we who had done much traveling before had never seen anything like it.

At dawn of the fourth day, after I had woken up, I saw the caravan of Bani Makhzum preparing to return to Mecca, for the road was open in that direction.

When I saw that, I went to my master to find a solution. Amin said, "Tell the men of the caravan to tie down the loads on the backs of the camels and to prepare to move out."

That is what we did, and we all thought that we would return to Mecca with the Bani Makhzum.

So my master sat on his fast camel, gave thanks to God, and turned to face in the direction of Syria.

When 'Amru Hesham saw that, he derisively said, "Do you have business in sailing, son of Abdullah?"

Muhammad did not say anything to him. When I saw the uncertainty and fear in the men of the caravan, I said to my master, "What caused you to decide that today? The flood has now blocked the road in front of us."

He said, "Last night I saw in a dream that they told me to load up the caravan at dawn. When a white bird appears in the sky, and marks a path on the water with it wing, I should remember God and enter the water at that spot. I just saw that bird come and do that."

With a sweet smile, he added, "Be strong of heart Maysara! God does not leave His friends alone or without protection."

That day, we of the Bani Zohreh were confused about whether to return to Mecca like the Bani Makhzum or to wait. After the sun had risen, I saw that Amin was at the head of the caravan of Khadijeh and facing the flooded area.

We all waited and stared at him. Amin entered the water at one place and slowly went forward. The other camels of his caravan began to move after him.

Once they had safely passed through the water, the other caravans cried out in happiness and followed them. The caravans of 'Amru Hesham also did it. So the caravan of Khadijeh was as far ahead as Bosrā.

Maysara, after taking care of the caravan, sat under an olive tree and let out a sigh from tiredness and gladness. He remembered that every year following the month of traveling from Mecca to Bosra, this dual feeling would come over him when they stopped here. This certainty that there was no longer any fear of bandits, thirst, or getting lost gave him deep satisfaction.

Maysara leaned against the olive tree and took off his shoes. A cool breeze blew softly through the grove of trees around the spring and renewed his soul.

This was one of those hours when the caravaneers more or less all had the same feeling. That former haste dissipated. Looks became friendlier and behavior more gentle. By no means was a voice raised in anger. It seemed even the camels of the caravan decided not to waste those pleasant hours at any price.

Every caravan had gathered its own goods in some place. The leaders of every people were sitting of reclining on the short wild grass under the trees and were busy talking or listening. One group was occupied washing their bodies or clothes around the spring. A few of the slaves had lighted a fire here and there and were cooking food over it. Large pieces of meat on long skewers were grilling over a stone fireplace, and their aroma wafted in every direction. The camels, pleased and lightened, were grazing on the plain on the other side of the road.

Mayasara relaxed for a while and put his shoes under his head and lay on his side. In that position, he was situated facing that stone hill on which the monastery of the monk Bohayra was located. The monastery, with those high stone walls, stood wrapped around the hill, and a narrow road like a white strip went from it to the grove of trees where the caravan was and connected them.

At the beginning of that road, a man, tall and thin, was facing the grove. He was wearing a long black robe like that of a priest, and, on his head, a tall hat without a bill, also like a priest's. The long golden locks, which fell on both sides of his face bounced with each step he took on the sloping road.

When the man reached the edge of the grove, he hesitated for a little bit and stood to one side. Maysara half rose from his place and looked in that same direction. There, under a lotus tree, Muhammad was sleeping, tired from work.

When that man's hesitation went on, Maysara began to have doubts. So he got up from his place and went toward him barefoot.

He had a white face and was close to fifty years old. He had golden hair that in some places had streaks of white.

When the middle-aged monk saw Maysara looking at him like that he said, "Good day," in order to alleviate his doubt and fear.

"And good day to you."

"Welcome to our land. I hope your journey is going

well."

"Thank you."

The monk came a little closer, and after a short pause, said, "I have a question for you brother."

"Ask it, what ever it is."

"That handsome youth who is sleeping under that lotus tree, who is he?"

"He is a man from the Qureish. His name is Muhammad. He is the leader of our caravan."

"What kind of a man is he among hi sown people?"

"He is a poor boy, but quite noble. He is so insistent on truthfulness and correctness that the Meccans have given him the nickname of 'Amin.' Now, sir, what is your reason for asking these questions?"

"He must be that same Farqelit whose name has appeared in the Gospels."

"Farqelit? Who is Farqelit?"

"In the language of the Arabs it is the same Ahmad or Muhammad. He is the last prophet and the final dispensation of God's guidance to man, and the time of the revealing of his affairs is near."

"Whence are you saying these things sir?"

"From his signs and manner in which they are revealed that have come in the Zabur, the Torah, the Gospels, and other great books of our people. He must be that same one who passed by here when he was a child. At that time, Bohayra the wise informed us about him. Today, when you were coming in this direction, I saw a cloud in the sky that was casting a shadow over part of your caravan and it was coming along with it. Once you had come closer, I saw that the shade of that cloud was over the head of this young man. Also, this lotus tree under which he is sleeping has been dried up for a long time. Now, however, look at how it has come alive and put out branches and leaves. It is as if its branches are bowing toward him so the sun does not bother him. These are other signs of his prophethood that have come in our books."

The monk was talking like that. Maysara, however, did not hear anything anymore. His look had become distant, and he was thinking about what he himself had seen of Muhammad during this journey. Those astonishing nights of staying awake and periods of solitude; those true insights and prognostications; that correct dream that he has seen after that flood; that magnanimous behavior; that virtuous attitude and good…. Maysara now saw that on the road, when the heat became intense, he could feel that two ethereal entities, like shining beings that were there and also not there, were hanging over Muhammad's head. Maysara did not realize that those two were casting a shadow over Muhammad or that their invisible wings were fanning him. In order to know whether the other carvaneers also saw them, he had asked them, but no one except him had seen them. Then he had had doubts and thought he was seeing things. So that none of the others would think him crazy, he had remained silent and had not told anyone about this story. But now, with this that this monk was saying….

Maysara wanted to tell the monk about what he had in his heart, but when he came to, he could not see it in himself.

Maysara looked around. Muhammad was now sitting up under that lotus tree, and the monk was standing beside him and talking with him. Then the monk fell on the ground in front of Muhammad and wanted to kiss his feet, but Muhammad did not let him. Then he took him by his wrists and had him go beside him.

Upon seeing this scene, tears began to well up in Maysara's eyes. At this instant, he saw the monk take Muhammad in a tight embrace and, like an orphan who had found his father, placed his head on his shoulder. He then released the lump in his throat and, from the intensity of his weeping, his shoulder began to shake.

The bride of the cities of Syria, its back to the high mountains beside Lebanon and lying amidst groves of figs and orchards of apricots, pomegranates, hazelnuts, and olives, lifted it head from last night's sleep. The sun bit by bit rose up from behind the thick groves of trees in the east and with its rays cast color over the high mountain peaks. And in those rays, the large palaces sitting among the gardens of flowers, with their tall columns and wide porticos on four sides, took on an imaginary splendor.

Damascus, with those large bazaars and well-known merchants and new possessors immersed in wealth, for all trading caravans, was both the end point and beginning of the journey. In this city and its brilliant bazaar, with the enormous profits easily made, for several days, the hardships of the long and dangerous trip had gone had gone from the caravaneers bodies, and they, with full hands and new goods, were starting out again toward their own country. This time, however, it seemed that another adventure was in store for Khadijeh's caravan.

The caravan had entered the city the previous night and had set down its loads in a space at the beginning of the bazaar. The caravaneers, as was the habit of the Arabs, had risen from sleep at dawn. Thus, they had washed their heads and faces with cold water from the Bardi river, whose source was the snows from the mountains. Then they had opened the loads and prepared for the acceptance of the buyers. Although the caravan of Khadijeh had arrived at the Damascus bazaar late by two days, and the other merchants from Mecca had filled the bazaar with many of the same goods as theirs, they did not have much hope of finding good buyers.

The reason for being late was that on the road between Bosra and Damascus, some of the men in our caravan experienced an intense agitation in their breath, so much that traveling for them became very strenuous. Once my master became aware of that situation, he said to me, "What do you think of this matter Maysara?"

I said that the bazaar at Damascus now has none of our goods, and if we reach there in time, we can find good customers for our merchandise just like every year. If we arrive late, however, even by one day, we will suffer a tremendous loss."

In that situation, he did not accept that for that reason that those sick and suffering man bear more. So we stopped at a village along the road and treated the sick persons. For that reason, we fell behind our rivals by two days, and when we arrived in Damascus, the other merchants from Mecca had sold most of their merchandise and were buying Roman, Palestinian, Lebanese, and Syrian goods.

The sun now lessened the coolness of the early morning from the city's body and picked up the dew setting on the doors, walls, and gardens. And that time, the big bazaar also began to flourish and the commotion and traffic therein increased.

With some anxiety in his heart, Maysara said, "Master, on earlier trips, our caravan had mutual trade with several of the Damascus merchants. If you allow me, I will now go find them and offer our merchandise to them. Perhaps something will open up for us."

Muhammad, with a calm relaxation in his clear eyes, said, "Do what you think is right."

Thus, they handed over their goods to their men, and the two of them headed off for the city's covered bazaar.

That day with my master, we walked through the Damascus bazaar from one end to the other, and we went to very place in it, from the section of the cloth-sellers until the section of the sellers of skins, leather, and shoes, and gold, jewelry, metal workers, glass workers, spice and perfume sellers. I offered the goods that we had to all of the merchants I knew. Though they expressed their sympathy for us, nonetheless, they were intent on buying the goods for a very low price with the excuse that the bazaar was full of our goods.

Finally, except for almost half of the goods which the other merchants from Mecca did not have, we were left with what was left.

After the mid-day break, the bazaar had now regained its activity. The people of the city, after a short nap, were now heading to the bazaar one by one or in groups. Except for slaves, most were light-complexioned. Some also had blond hair and green or blue eyes.

The Syrian merchants, behind the counters of their stalls filled with goods were busy ordering slaves, slave boys, or hired workers about and putting their stalls in order or selling their goods. Some that did not have any customers, sitting on high stools, seemed to be continuing their mid-day nap.

Muhammad and Maysara were sitting in the green space at the first of the bazaar beside their remaining goods and without any obvious customers. The merchants of the other caravans of Mecca now began to mock Muhammad. They also belittled Khadijeh as well for having entrusted a caravan of that size to a young sensitive man like him. Maysara was offended by hearing those remarks, but he did not respond to them because he had also become very anxious. Muhammad, however, was so calm that he seemed to have no worry at all.

At this moment, an uproar and voices could suddenly be heard from a street that was connected to the beginning of the bazaar.

All of the people who heard those voices stopped their discussions and transactions and turned their heads in that direction. A few moments later it became clear what the story was. A large caravan of goods from Palestine had come to Damascus at that hour and was heading for the bazaar.

This was a new splendor for the market of goods from Mecca, but among them only Muhammad's caravan had goods to offer them. Thus, Maysara's despair and anxiety ended. And also the removal of doubts about Muhammad's worthiness in administering the caravan and trading….because it had now become very clear that they, if they had arrived in Damascus on the first day like their competitors, they would not have benefitted from this good fortune that was now awaiting them.

…It was one evening, and Khadijeh was sitting behind the window in the room facing the large courtyard of her house. It was half night or the beginning of the night. It was not clear to her. In any case, she was alone and looking at the sky and thinking about fate and her own loneliness.

Suddenly, in the dark night sky of the city, a bright point appeared near the horizon. That point slowly approached and neared the earth. In this state, its light increased each moment until it looked like the shining sun.

Khadijeh was startled by that sudden phenomenon and staring at the light of that sun when suddenly an even stranger happening occurred. That sun stopped above her house. Then it slowly went down into the courtyard and all of the house was bathed in its light.

At this moment, Khadijeh awoke with a start. She sat up on the bed and looked out of the window toward the courtyard. The light of dawn was beginning to appear, and in its milky-white brightness the bunches of goods that were lined up in rows on every side of the courtyard could be clearly seen.

Khadijeh, happy, thought about what was in that dream.

What was its interpretation?

Without a doubt, a great good fortune was coming to her. But what was that good fortune? Perhaps it was that amazing profit and those fine goods that Amin had brought her from Syria.

No. That could not be the interpretation of such a dream. The profit that Muhammad brought Khadijeh was more than she had ever conceived from any earlier trip. It had also been apparent for Khadijeh in these three days that the goods Amin had brought from Syria were worth more that what he had taken to Syria. For that reason, the meaning of that dream had to be much beyond those.

So what could the interpretation of that be? What good fortune was it that was coming to her?

She wished she could learn something about it before hand.

Khadijeh came down from the bed, opened the door and called her servant. Nafisa came with a ewer and a basin made in Syria in her hands.

"Good morning mistress."

"Good morning to you too."

Nafisa placed the basin on the mantle in the room. Khadijeh was sitting on the floor facing her, and she washed her hands and face with the water Nafisa poured on her hands.

"Mistress, several merchants from the markets of Mecca and Taif are coming today to see and buy the merchandise. We also told Amin to come see you and get his payment."

Khadijeh froze on hearing the name of Muhammad. Then she remembered what she had seen several days before....

It was the time of sunset, and I, like every day at sundown, was sitting under the canvas above the roof of my house. The time for the arrival of the caravan from Syria was now near, and I had an eye toward the road in order to see the sign of it vanguard.

All of the sudden, it was as if the curtain in front of my eyes had been pulled aside, and I saw a bright light coming down the road and coming toward Mecca. At first I was suspicious of whether that was not my imagination that had overcome me. When I blinked and closed my eyes and opened them again, I still saw that bright light, my mood changed. It was as if then my chest expanded and joy rushed into my heart. It seemed like the mountains of Mecca also moved from delight, and every tree in the city grew taller, and every bird began singing the most beautiful melody. At that moment, the women around me, surprised, asked, "What kind of behavior is this we see from you?"

I asked, "Tell me, am I asleep or awake?"

They said, "You are awake."

I said, "Do you see those same things I am seeing?"

They said, "We see a small black thing that appears to be a rider heading toward Mecca."

I realized that they were seeing that point in a different way.

After an hour had passed, we all saw the rider come from the street


Khadijeh did not know how she ran barefoot from the canvas taking two or three stairs at a time to the courtyard. She reached the door before her maid servants and asked, "Who is knocking on the door?"

A warm voice that penetrated to the depths of Khadijeh's heart said, "Good day to you people of the house!"

It was Amin. So he was that rider covered in light!

"May you be healthy, O' light of the eyes of the Qureish!"

"May it be good tidings to you that we have delivered your possessions safe and sound."

"Your good health is the best good news for us."

"My lady, I am Amin."

Khadijeh suddenly started up in the bed. It was Nafisa.

"Why did you not eat your mid-morning meal mistress?"

"What? Mid-morning meal?"

Khadijeh looked at the large copper platter beside her with the food that had not been touched. She had completely forgotten when she had brought the food for her. When she looked outside, the sun was in the sky and its light had lit up all of the courtyard.

On seeing her mistress' hesitation, Nafisa said, "I will tell Amin to wait until you have eaten your meal."

"No. No. No! I don't feel like eating this meal today."

She then put on her scarf and black robe with gold trim over the silken cloak with various colored designs and went to the courtyard.

Her appearance was startlingly dignified with those clothes and that tall and full stature, such that only her two black stunning eyes with those shining eyelashes and full eyebrows were visible in the middle of her face.

"Good day Muhammad!"

"And good day to you cousin!"

Muhammad was seated on a chair in white and clean clothes, and the fragrant smell of his body filled the space of the large guestroom of the house.

Khadijeh sat on a seat facing Muhammad. Then Nafisa came with a goblet of honey-flavored sherbet. She placed the goblet in front of Muhammad and, with a sign from Khadijeh, sat on the corner of the seat.

Muhammad, with his eyes turned down, and his hand around his right knee said nothing. With her eyes staring at the ground, Khadijeh said, "Amin, you also have interest in these profits that have been acquired. Tell me now what you want, for I will accept whatever you want."

Muhammad said, "Whatever you received from this trip was from God. I was no more than a mediator in it."

"Since you will not say anything concerning this matter, I will stipulate a payment for you and then Maysara can pay you."

Khadijeh hesitated for a moment. Then she asked, "Now, cousin, what have you decided to do with this money you will receive?"

Unprepared for this question, Muhammad, after a short delay, said, "I am very obligated to my uncle, Bu Taleb. I intend to give all of my money to him as compensation for a small part of those obligations, but he did not agree. He has decided to use that to find me a wife."

Khadijeh looked at Nafisa for a moment. Nafisa stared in the eyes of her mistress. Then Nafisa said, "That is good Amin! Before I heard you say that, I was going to say that you, who are a handsome, strong, and upright young man, why have you not chosen a wife for yourself?"

Muhammad did not say anything in response. Thus, Khadijeh said, "Cousin, do you want me to select a wife for you whom I like?"

Shyly, Muhammad said, "Yes."

Nafisa said, "She is a woman from your tribe, who is one of the most beautiful, virtuous, wealthy, and perfect women of Mecca. Most of the men and leaders of the Arabs want her, but she only wants you. Also, she is somewhat pleased with everything about you, and, in any case, she would be your helper."

Adding to what Nafisa had said, Khadijeh said, "She has two defects, however. First, she has had two husbands before you. And the other is that she is fifteen years older than you."

Muhammad reflected for a while and did not say anything. Then he said, "You won't say what her name is?"

"My mistress, and the noble lady of the Qureish, Khadijeh!"

In an instant, Muhammad's features, always blushed, turned entirely red from shame and large drops of sweat covered his broad forehead.

As his silence lengthened, Khadijeh said, "Why

don't you say anything cousin?"

Muhammad said in a low voice, "Cousin, you are wealthy, and I am a poor man. Also, in that respect, I want a wife who is like me in terms of wealth and temperament."

"Oh Muhammad, what kind of talk is this? There is no one superior to you in terms of lineage and family. There is also no one better than you in terms of honesty and virtue. You are also aware that I have many suitors among the great and young of the Arabs. But I have heard things about you from Maysara and other, and I have seen things myself that have attracted me to you. If you are also attracted to me now, I will consider me your servant, and I will turn over all of my possessions, slaves, and servants to you."

Khadijeh became silent for a while. Now, when she saw signs of acceptance in Muhammad's countenance, said, "Think well of me cousin, just as I have good thoughts about you. Also, do not be worried about the dowry, because whatever it is, I will pay it from my own money."

Muhammad wiped the sweat from his head with his thumb and said, "Let it be so."

'Amru Nowfel, dizzy from the drunkenness of the night before, raised his head form the bed on hearing some noise. The sun had risen in the sky and its heat added to his headache. He then angrily yelled, "Jāber!"

The elderly servant quickly came inside and said, "Good day master! Were you talking to me?"

"What is that uproar?"

"What uproar master?"

"That drumming and trilling and foot-stomping?"

"It is coming from the house of your niece, Khadijeh, master."

"From Khadijeh's house? Why?"

"How do you not know master? Last night was her wedding."

"Huh? Her wedding? With whom?"

"With Amin, the son of Abdullah, the son of Abd al-Muttaleb."

"With Amin? But he is nothing more than a poor youth! How did Khadijeh do that without my permission, for I am the eldest uncle and the elder of the family?"

"Master, she did not do that without your permission. Bu Taleb and Amin's other uncles had first gone to ask her, but my mistress sent them to you. You were with your friends drinking wine when they came."

"Okay, okay! Explain to me so I know what

happened during those hours."

"Amin was bathed and wearing clean clothes. An Indian sword was hanging from his neck, and he was riding an Arabian horse. His uncles and ten persons of the leaders of the Qureish were also with him."

"Yes, now some of these things you are saying are coming back to me."

"Yes, master. When they came, you were drunk. You were happy to see them and you honored them. At that time Bu Taleb said they had come to you on behalf of their nephew. You happily said, 'Bravo for Muhammad! I swear to God, Lat, and 'Uzza that I always liked him, and today my affection has for him has increased. So whatever bequest he has is permissible in my view."

"Bu Taleb said, 'Muhammad's and our request is that you give your niece, Khadijeh, to him as a wife.'

"You, without hesitation, and in front of all of those present, said, "O' people in this assembly! You are witnesses that I have given Khadijeh, the daughter of Khāled, to Muhammad, the son of Abdullah, the son of Abd al-Muttaleb, to wed, and whatever dowry Khadijeh and Bu Taleb want.'

"Bu Taleb said the wedding vows on behalf of Muhammad, and he agreed to provide the dowry, whatever it was, from his own wealth. Then M gave you a Yemeni robe as a gift, as is custom, and you graciously accepted it."

Jaber pointed at that white cotton cloth with wide blue stripes that was beside 'Amru's pillow and said, "That is it."

'Amru looked at the robe for a few moments. Then he angrily threw it in a corner and said, "Tell Khadijeh to come and see me!"

Jaber said, "I will."

Then he quickly left.

Khadijeh's house was two houses down from 'Amru's.

Before Khadijeh arrived, got out of bed and went to the courtyard to wash his hands and face with water.

Once he had finished washing his face, Khadijeh entered with Jaber. Her head and face were covered and she was wearing a white outer garment over her clothes.

"Good day uncle!"

"What was it that you did Khadijeh?"

A dark curtain suddenly descended over Khadijeh's happy eyes. Then, with a tone that had a slight shaking from anger in it, she said, "What did I do uncle that displeased you?"

'Amru, taken aback, said, "That that you did last night!"

"Was it not with your permission uncle? And did you not yourself say the wedding vows for me?"

Tired, 'Amru was silent for a moment. Then he looked at the flap of his cloak and said, "Did you not have all of those suitors from the important men of the Qureish?"

"Uncle! Are you denying the noble lineage and high position of Muhammad among the Qureish?"

"No, but he is poor."

"Even if he is poor, I have enough wealth and possessions to suffice for you, me, and him."

Upon hearing that, 'Amru's grimace suddenly went away. Hen, with a tone devoid of any ill-will, he said, "Khadijeh, if you are happy with Muhammad being your husband, then I am happy too with this marriage. Thus, if I did not give you to him a wife yesterday, I am doing it today."

With a smile, he added, "Where is your young husband now?"

Khadijeh's black eyes took on a playful look and she said, "If I had not stopped him, he would be in the house of his uncle Bu Taleb just like before."

Pleased, 'Amru said, "Huh? Why?"

"Last night, after the banquet, and after all of the important people of the family had left, Muhammad got up to go too. I grabbed his cloak and asked, 'Where are you going?'

"He said, 'To my uncle's house.'

"Laughing, I said, 'Let your uncle be now and be with your wife.'

On hearing that, my uncle laughed so much that he became short of breathe, and tears streamed down his face.

Abu al-Qasem came out of the room and looked at the courtyard. There was not any sign of the clamor and excitement of the previous day and night. But the air had a light coolness to it. Following that hard and unrelenting downpour and that uncontrollable and heavy flood, Mecca had now been overtaken by a deep and pleasant silence. If there was a sound, it was the bubbling of life; life, the animals, and the exalting of the city after its fearful nightmare of a day and a night.

Nothing was left in the sky of those dense, dark, and depressing clouds except for several small white pieces resembling newly pounded cotton, each one of which had appeared in the shape of some creature. The sky, devoid of dust and washed by the rain, appeared so blue and deep that it seemed to have no end. Those fragments of clouds, like white skiffs, were sitting softly on its chest and sliding to the south with the invisible hand of the breeze.

The face of the sun had now appeared from behind the several cracks whose faces were hidden from the earth behind the mask of the clouds, and it shone more powerfully than before and poured its cataract of light and gentle warmth on the city and its inhabitants. Again, however, at the beginning of that dawn in the last month of fall and after that much relentless rain, the gentle northern breeze that came at the city after passing the moist mountains and plains, brought with it an unfamiliar coldness and shivering coolness.

Muhammad thanked God and sought refuge in Him from every other calamity and evil. Then he called Maysara.

Maysara was on the roof with his wife, Baraka, Halimeh, and Zayd repairing and gathering up Khadijeh's cupola-like silk canvas again. (Even though it did not have its earlier newness, splendor, or beauty, during Khadijeh's years of widowhood this canvas was her place for sitting in the afternoons and receiving familiar and unfamiliar women.) Upon hearing Muhammad's voice, Maysara quickly went to the edge of the roof and leaned over. He placed his hands on the notched short wall of the ledge around the roof and said, "I am coming master!"

He then went to the second storey of the house.

Since coming back from that trading trip to Syria ten years earlier and telling his mistress about those amazing points that he had seen or heard about Muhammad on the road, Khadijeh had removed the bonds of slavery from his and his wife's necks. Nonetheless, he had remained with his mistress. Also, just as before, and from the bottom of his heart, he always liked, just like slaves, to call Khadijeh his mistress and Abu al-Qasem his master no matter how well he knew that M was not pleased with that address.


The behavior of master, not just with us, but with all of the slaves, was the same as his behavior with free and noble men. His speech and actions were with respect and kindness with all of us. He ate the same food that we ate, and clothed us with the same clothes that he wore. He did not burden us with the difficult work beyond our abilities. And he was always easy with us.

"Good morning Maysara."

"And good morning to you master."

"I see you are very busy."

"Yes, master. We have been busy since morning inspecting the walls and ceilings and roof of the house."

Then after a short hesitation, he added, "The plaster on the roof was washed away by the rain and needs to be repaired. The ceiling of the room facing the street is wet and must be fixed. But none of the walls on the side of the street received any noticeable damage, save one channel from a large rock that hit it when it fell with the flood. My mistress' canvas fell and its ropes were torn loose at several places. We are now repairing those."

"What about the other houses of the city? Especially those in the depression beside the place the flood passed? This much rain and the flood certainly damaged them more."

"Yes. That is what probably happened. But I still have not had an opportunity to leave the house and learn about that."

On saying that, Maysara looked down. This, the last thing he said, was said with a low and guilty tone because he knew that at times like these, when a calamity strikes all of the people, his master, more than worrying about his own household, was anxious about the poor and disadvantaged of the city.

Muhammad, following a moment of hesitation, raised his head and without noticing the stare and eyes of Maysara, said, "Let the house be for now and get ready to go out. Also tell Baraka to come with us. We may well need her too."

"I will do that master."

Maysara wanted to go to the stairs when Muhammad said, "What is Halimeh doing? Has she eaten the mid-morning meal?"

Maysara, with a fond smile, as was his usual habit, said, "Yes, master. You know that the nomads rise with the birds. She ate her mid-morning meal in the morning with us. Now she is with the others on the roof, and she is helping them set up the canvas."

Abol Qasem's figure relaxed some after hearing that. Acquainted with his master's character, Maysara knew that he was angry that the guest had been put to work, because he had heard him say many times, "When someone comes to see you, honor them." Especially because that guest, like Halimeh, was someone whom Muhammad respected like his mother and he was kind to her. She, who, when she came to Mecca to see Muahmmad, his master gladdened and blossomed like a flower. We stood in her presence, and if a cloth was not handy, he would place his own cloak on the ground for Halimeh to sit on.

In order to deflect any bad thought from him, Maysara said, "She herself wanted to help us. I wanted to prevent her from doing it. I told her my master does not like this, but she persisted, and said that sitting in one place without doing would make her sick."

Abu al-Qasem did not say anything and he started up the stone stairs to the roof with Maysara behind him.

From the time that Muhammad took Khadijeh as his wife, just as before, every time I came to Mecca, I would go to see him. He also treated me very well. I was very dear to him, and every time he saw me off to my tribe in the desert, he would give me many gifts. Our life was very difficult that year, hardly any of our animals were left for so we could get by. (After that flood, there were three years of drought.) As I had heard and seen previously, M and his wife assisted the indigent and needy. I told my husband, "What will happen if we too tell my son, M, about our plight so we can also get some help?"

Hares was ashamed to do that, but he did not keep me from going. So I set off for Mecca on a donkey and went to Muhammad's house there. When that flood occurred, I was bedridden night and day like the other people.

When Abol Qasem and Maysara reached the roof, all three of the women stopped working. Abol Qasem, with a friendly smile, wished them a good morning and asked how they were doing. They answered him with that same pleasant demeanor they always had when he came to see them.

Then Abol Qasem went to Halimeh. He placed a hand on her bony shoulder and affectionately said, "How did you get through the night nanny? Could you sleep comfortably?"

A bolt of orneriness and motherly playfulness streaked through Halimeh's sunken eyes. Then she said with a laugh, "With all of that thunder and lightening and rain and flooding, if a single person in this city could sleep peacefully, then I am the second one! As long as I am in this kingly residence beside my son, I consider myself safe from any injury."

Abol Qasem said, "Will you be with us today too nanny?"

"No, no, no!"

Muhammad said with a sweet smile, "Does that mean that you are having a hard time here with us?"

Halimeh squeezed his hand with hers and said, "You know quite well my son how much I love you. But what can I do? My children and husband are waiting for me. And after this flood that occurred, they are certainly worried about me."

Abol Qasem said, "I was joking nanny. You are right."

Then he turned to Maysara's wife and said, "When my nanny decides to leave, select forty sheep and goats from the herd and send them with her so she can shepherd them and benefit from the milk and wages for caring for them. And give her whatever she needs for the journey."

The skinny and broken figure of Halimeh all at once over flowed with acknowledgement and kindness, and tears of joy came to her eyes. Her lip quivered several times before an expression of heartfelt gratitude came to her lips. Now, however, Muhammad took the opportunity away with a question. "Do you want me to send someone with you to accompany and help you?"

With a lump of happiness in her throat, Halimeh said, "Thank you so much for your faithfulness and gentlemanliness! Your nanny can still do shepherding even though she is more than fifty years old now!"

Muhammad said, "Don't say that nanny, because no matter how much good I do for you, it is not much."

He added, "I have some work to do, for which I need to leave the house soon. Other wise, I would stay with you. When you get home, convey my greetings to your husband and children. I have never forgotten their kindness, and I will not."

"I will do that. May God bless you."

Abol Qasem then bid farewell and went toward the stairs. Upon placing his foot on the first step, however, he turned around and said, "Zayd!"

The big-boned youth who was busy fastening the silken ropes of the canvas with iron nails, raised his head and answered, "Yes, father?"

"Come with us son."

"I will father."

He then stopped his work and followed him.


This Zayd was my master's step-son. He was not his son. Zayd's family lived in Syria. When he was small—when Zayd was no more than eight years old—bandits had stolen him in order to sell him in slavery. Hakim Hezām Khowaylad, who was a slave merchant, had bought him.

When Hakim returned from his trip to Syria, and his aunt—my mistress—went to see him, he said to her, "You can have whichever one you chose of these slaves I bought."

My mistress chose Zayd, who was a brown, sweet child.

After a while, my mistress gave Zayd to my master, and he freed the young boy. Then be took him to the sanctuary, and as was the custom, he accepted him as his step-son in front of the black stone.

By this time, three years had passed since the union of my master and mistress, and their son, Qasem, was an infant. In spite of that, my master held Zayd very dear and was very kind to him. He tried with all his effort not to let him be sad about being away from his mother and father.

It was like that until two years had passed and Qasem left this world. Affection for Zayd then increased in Abol Qasem's heart so much that he would not let him get far from him, and he had put him in his own bed.

When they reached the house for the second time, Abol Qasem sent Zayd to the courtyard while he himself went to the room on the right of the hallway facing the courtyard. He then opened the double flaps of it and looked inside. Zaynab, his eldest daughter, awoke from sleep and sat up on her bed.

Muhammad caste a deep and loving look at her attractive eyes and her lovely white figure and showed her a smile. With that look, he remembered his mind was again filled with memories of Qasem. And with that, a shadow of sorrow fell over his eyes.

…Oh how quickly Qasem's wings had folded, and how much sorrow it had put on the sensitive and young father's heart!

It had been five years since he left the world, but his memory had not left the father for even a day. However much Abol Qasem now looked to the past and thought about his past and the deaths of his dear ones, for himself he found no escape but willing surrender to the will of the Creator.

With a short sigh, Abol Qasem caste a passing glance at his other young daughters, Raqiyyeh and Om Kolthum. Both were in the bed sleeping soundly. He then asked Zaynab, "Where is your mother my daughter?"

With her childish sweet and sleepy voice, Zaynab answered, "I think she went to the courtyard father."

Abol Qasem went back. He went up the high stairs and stepped into the courtyard. When he did not see his wife there either, he went toward the street. At this point, Maysara and Baraka came too.

Zayd was sitting by the large double-door of the house on a large stone platform to the left under the small arch. He stood when he saw his godfather. Muhammad took his warm masculine hand in his and all four of them headed for the middle quarters of the edge of the city.

Mecca proceeded slowly until it could regain its former state after a day and night of hard rain and the flowing of that fearful flood. That opportunity which had presented itself to the people so they could stick their heads out of their houses and see what had happened to them.

Abta and the other quarters situated on the heights of Mecca had not seen much damage because their structures were sufficiently stout. The rain and flood, however, had washed the doors, walls, and roofs of the houses of that neighborhood and had cleaned off the dust and filth from their surfaces, such that, from afar, they shone like varied colored gems in the bright light of the morning sun.

Except for that, the flood had turned the dirt courtyards of those houses upside down, and brought out the filth of the inhabitants that had been hidden under the dirt and had taken it toward the lower portions of Mecca with it, because the Meccans, like the other Arabs of the Hejaz, were not used to building cesspools in their houses. Thus, when nature called, they went to the valleys and grounds on the edges of the city. Among those paces was a steep place on the side of the mountain Abu Qobays by the name of Fazeh. Children, women, and the elderly, however, sometimes went in the dirt of courtyards of houses and covered it with dirt. For that same reason, after that flood, the quarters in the middle and on the edge of the city were now filled with the dung of those above, in addition to their own mud and filth. Especially the quarter of Ahābish, which was also on the edge of the pathway of the large flood.

In the alleyways of this quarter the mud and muck was so much that a person on foot could not pass by there with much ease. A large rock had fallen and had hit the roof of the mud hut and caved it in. An old, helpless woman was killed in it. The walls of several houses had been damaged or cracked by the strikes of rocks or the flood.

When Abol Qasem, Zayd, Maysara, and Baraka reached there, the neighbors had just pulled out the body of that old lady from under the collapsed structure. The old woman had a small and skinny body. She seemed to be a refugee in Mecca and not have any relatives there. She was one of the women without any support whom Khadijeh looked after. Muhammad had seen her once or twice before when she had come to their house for food or clothes.

Muhammad told Maysara and Baraka to make preparations to bury that old woman. He and Zayd then went to the sanctuary. After day of being away, his heart now strongly longed to see the Ka'ba. With all the signs of the flood that could be seen all around, he knew that he could not circumambulate it right now.

His thinking was not incorrect. When he saw from afar the crowds of people who were standing some distance from the Ka'ba, and heard their clamor, he knew that the water around the Ka'ba was still so much that he could not get close. When he went further, he saw the piles of mud and sediment and rocks that had piled up around the Ka'ba. At the edge of the water was the dead body of a large lizard, and the children had gathered around it. Between the idols of Asaf and Na'eleh, near the stone of the place of sacrifice, was the corpse of a black and white calf that the flood had brought.

The floodwaters had reached up as high as the black stone; as high as a man of medium height. The idols, covered in mud and sediment, quiet and helpless, were standing amidst the floodwaters. There were no signs of some of those three hundred and sixty idols. Several of them had been knocked over by the force of the water flow. Some of those that had no stand or that were short were now hidden under water. Asaf, in the meantime, was still standing as before on its high stone base close to a corner of the Ka'ba near the black stone. The water had gone no higher than its throat.

Upon seeing the large copper head of Asaf, which had a rusty shine under the brightness of the sun, Zayd remembered the events of that day when he went to circumambulate the Ka'ba with his godfather.

That day, when we arrived at the copper idol of Asaf, in the tradition of the Arabs, I touched it with my hands. When my father—I called my godfather "father"—saw me do that, he said, "Don't touch it."

I started to circumambulate the Ka'ba, and when I came to Asaf, I unthinkingly touched it again. When father, who was with me, saw that, upset, he said, "Did I not stop you from that?"

From then on, I never touched that idol or any other idol to gain a blessing.

Abol Qasem looked at the Ka'ba with regret. How polluted that simple old structure with those mortar-less stone walls had become inside and out by the floodwaters! Its building too, that earlier had been weakened by the fire from the brazier of an old woman that had fallen on its covering, was becoming decimated now by this flood. For example, sizeable cracks had appeared in its two walls that were in front of Abol Qasem, and from that distance they were quite visible.

The black cotton covering of the Ka'ba was completely soaked, although all of its sides were pulled up and held at the top of its walls by four ropes. The people, men, women, and children, were talking about the flood and the damage to the Kaba. The youth who was beside Muhammad and Zayd, so loudly that the others could hear, "The floodwaters have gone down a lot now. In the morning when I came here, nothing could be seen of Asaf or Na'eleh, may their names be glorified, for the huge amount of water."

His companion, who was older than him, said, "I heard that someone seemed to have been overcome in the sanctuary.

"I saw someone swimming around the Ka'ba, but in that twilight I did not recognize him because from this position that I was in, he did not come out of the water so I could see him."

A familiar voice from the forefront of that group said wrenchingly, "He was certainly circumambulating the Ka'ba and making a pilgrimage to the idols at that time! His faith had probably increased because of the terror of the flood, and he could not wait until the waters subsided and do the circumambulation then!"

Abol Qasem did not see the speaker of those words, but he knew from the vain tone and biting words that it had to be 'Amru Hesham.

Even though 'Amru was one of the wealthy and great men of the Qureish, he nevertheless had a mean and bad character. For that reason, the people did not like to be around him, and in order to be safe from his sarcasm and bad character, they avoided him. Abol Qasem as well, even though he had never had any acquaintance with 'Amru, he nevertheless arrived him after that trading trip to Syria and his marriage with Khadijeh, because he knew that jealousy of him had become like a blazing fire in the heart of 'Amru. For that reason, again, one day he had sought his aid. In a place, 'Amru had been deluded by his own power to combat him and to denigrate him in front of the people. Despite the fact that Abol Qasem disliked doing that, he was forced to confront him. Thus, in front of others who were satisfied, he had pounded him to the ground, and in that situation 'Amru's thigh had hit a rock and broke.

"I know who that person in to whom you refer, and I know his story. But one hour ago I saw Bu Wahab go into the water with my own eyes, and he did not come out until he had circled the Ka'ba seven times. May the gods help him, for during these long years that I have been alive, I have never seen that kind of circumambulation."

These words came from an old and stooped person who was standing heavily bent over and leaning on a twisted cane made of bamboo at the edge of that group.

Abol Qasem, his hand in that of his godson, left those people so as to pay respect to the Ka'ba from a distance. But he had still not begun to do that when he suddenly heard the angry snort of a camel.

The sound came from the direction of a bazaar that was attached to the door of Bani Hashem. All heads turned in that direction. Then, from behind the wall, a black male camel appeared which came dauntlessly toward those people.

The camel was enormous and wide, and one of those that carries loads. It was foaming at the mouth and the ground seemed to shake under its steps as it ran. It let out a long cry upon seeing the people and flung froth on the face of a man.

Upon seeing that from that animal, the people knew that it was out of control and that it was angry. It was as if it were angry because of some wrong treatment it had experienced or as if it were drunk. At that moment, it did not matter, even though the beginning of the normal period of rut for camels was in another month, during the first month of winter.

Whatever it was, a stubborn attitude had appeared in the animal, and it attacked with strength double that of a single camel and toward anyone it found in its path.

Fear gripped the crowd, and everyone fled screaming in some direction. The danger was so big that 'Amru

Hesham, with that degree of arrogance and pugilism, fled the scene without any hesitation because anyone who was familiar with that state of camels knew that standing in the way of that camel was the prelude to death.

At this time, in the beginning, it attacked its adversary by throwing saliva in his eyes. Then it started to use its powerful jaws and tore pieces of flesh from his body with its teeth. Then it would trample him with deadly blows from its front feet until it knocked him down to the ground.

Abol Qasem had decided, like the other people, to go to the side and not to place himself in danger senselessly. When he heard a scream from a woman, however, he stayed put.

In the middle of the commotion, only a few steps away from that camel, a small girl had fallen on the ground. Her mother had her back to a wall father away and was screaming uncontrollably from the bottom of her heart. Two or three steps farther back, that doubled-over old man with death in his eyes was trying vainly to get his suffering body to one side and out of the scene.

Zayd, standing to the side on a high place and scared, yelled, "Get away father!"

Farther ahead, though, before he could finish what he was saying, he saw his godfather block the camel's path. Hen, in a split second, he grabbed its hanging reins and quickly twisted them to his left side and pulled the head of the animal toward him with a hard and fast jerk.

The camel seemed to have swallowed a great deal of air, and with a loud sound it let the breath out of its throat. At the same moment, it turned half around in order to free its head, but the strength and skill of its opponent won out over its blind anger, and the animal, with a sudden slip on that slippery and muddy ground, fell down to the ground with the entire weight of its body. That gave Abol Qasem an opportunity to bolt toward the camel and firmly take its reins in his fist so that he turned the camel's head to one side and kept that position so it could not do anything else. It then submitted after one or two more efforts.

The outburst had come to an end. There was a universal sigh of relief. The mother of the child ran to her small child as if she had bee saved from a terrifying nightmare and took her in her arms and started to weep loudly. The bent-over old man was taken to one side with the help of a man. Zayd went toward his godfather and stood proudly beside him. It was clear that he wanted to tell all of those people, "This incomparably brave man is my father!" All of the children also came forward and gathered around Muhammad and looked at that newly-discovered hero of the city with awe and approval.

Was this the same Abol Qasem who had done this great deed?!

In their opinion, Mecca had heretofore had two heroes: Hamzeh, the son of Abd al-Muttaleb, and this same 'Amru, the son of Hesham, who today had run away when confronted with that mad camel. Hamzeh had a thick neck and shoulders, sturdy arms, and a broad chest. He was not seen often among the people. Sometimes, however, the children saw him going out of Mecca toward the mountains with a long bow on his shoulders, a quiver on his back, a sword at his waist, a garment from the skin of a lion, and riding his black Arabian horse.

Those things and those penetrating big eyes has created a myth of Hamzeh in the mind of the children of the city and made him untouchable. For this reason, it was the fear of him in their hearts that kept them from going near him. No matter how infatuated they were with him, and their vision, they were with him, he was an adult.

'Amru Hesham did not have the height and figure of Hamzeh, and he did not go to hunt lions and leopards. In the city, however, he had rubbed all of the strong and powerful men in the dirt. No matter how much he avoided Hamzeh, he had been humbled like that by Abol Qasem.

In terms of his figure, 'Amru was a little thicker than Abol Qasem, and the boys of Mecca, following the manner of their fathers, praised him for his strength and athletic ability.

In that regard, the sharp sparks that were constantly shooting from his eyes terrified them.

This newly-found hero of the city, however, was of a different sort. There was also an amazing penetration in his eyes too that strongly affected the onlooker, but this penetration was not from the coarseness, ill-will, and bad temper of the possessor of that look. He also liked the children very much, and when he met them, his face opened up like a flower. And then a deluge of fatherly affection would pour out of his gaze and polish their small hearts with its limpidness.

Now that kind and large spirit, since it had joined together with this strong body and arms in one body, in their mind, made Muhammad into a hero before whom those other two lost their luster.

"Congratulations to you, our hero! May Hobal give you a good reward!"

When they heard that, everyone's head turned toward the speaker. He was a middle-aged man and dark-skinned with the appearance of a nomad who had come running from the road and looked ay Abol Qasem and his camel unbelievingly.

Once he had taken the reins of his camel in his hands, the people came to their senses again and one by one or a few at a time they praised Abol Qasem and thanked him. Except for 'Amru, whose head was hanging because of his humility before him and, filled with jealousy, with his back to the people, was leaving.

"I think that this old structure of the Ka'ba needs to be cleared away and destroyed, and in its place a new building be erected. Repair won't do it any good."

"What you say is correct Walid, because it has had a long life and repair will not restore it."

"So that that larceny does not happen again, we need to build its walls higher."

The building that Abraham the prophet had built for the Ka'ba was thirty meters long and twenty-four meters wide. Its height was nine meters. It had also been a long time since it had had any roof. For that reason, going on top of it and getting inside it was easy. On the other hand, inside the Ka'ba, to the right of its entry door, in front of Hobal, there was a well-like basin. They said that this well had been there since the time of Abraham. Thus, what the people brought there as gifts—gold, silver, jewelry, and such like— they would place there.

In that year that the flood occurred in Mecca, no one knew what person or persons had entered the Ka'ba and had raided that basin. So the elders of the people considered the solution to that to be raising the height of the walls of the Ka'ba.

Muhammad was sitting in a corner of the large hall of the council house and listening silently to what the elders had to say.

In the end, after a time of commotion, his uncle, Bu Taleb, began to speak.

"Now that everyone believes that the Ka'ba should be destroyed and rebuilt, so that talk does not go too long, and so that the task does not fall behind more than this, let us talk about how to do it."

"That is good."

"That is a good and commendable idea."

"Yes. Let's not argue until the work begins. It is better that we do that."

Muhammad's other uncle, Zobayr, said, "First, for the good of this work, we should not share the work with any other tribe or groups. It should not be done from the beginning until its end except by the hand of the people of Qureish. Also, the Qureish should not use slaves or concubines in this great task."

No one was opposed to that suggestion. Thus, everyone nodded their heads in agreement. But on hearing that, Muhammad remembered his grandfather—that time when he was excavating the well of Zamzam—and his heart became heavy.

Zobayr added, "What do you say that we give the task to dividing the work to the oldest of the Qureish, Walid Moghayrah, and all of us submit to whatever he says?"

Walid, in addition to being an experienced and intelligent old man, was also the chief of the Bani Makhzum clan. In that respect, there was no reason to oppose his judgment. So everyone in some way expressed his acceptance.

Upon seeing that situation, Walid looked over the assembly. Then he faced Bu Taleb and said, "I don't think there should be any rule or agreement in the destruction of it and all should take part. In building it, however, let us have an clear understanding. Huh? What do you say sons of Abd al-Muttaleb?"

Zobayr and Bu Taleb said, "Let it be thus."

"Now that understanding…the Bani Hesham and Bani Zohreh will build the wall in which the door of the Ka'ba is."

"Very well."

"The Bani Sahm will erect the wall between the Yemeni column and the idol of Asaf."

"Most certainly."

"The building of the wall beside the stone of Ismail will be for the Bani Abd al-Dār, Bani Abd al-Ozā, and the Bani 'Adi Ka'b. And that wall that is between the black stone and the Yemeni column the Bani Makhzum, Taym, and others will build."

"You were fair, and you apportioned justly Walid."

With that deep experience and adequate familiarity with the positions and ranks of each, Walid had given each of them a proper share. Also, the agreement of the dignified elder of the Qureish—Bu Taleb—had given him strong support with his view. Thus, it happened that if anyone was not happy with that view, he swallowed his words and did not say anything.

Then Bu Taleb changed to another subject so as not to offer an opportunity to any incorrect thought or word.

"A budget is also needed for this task and each clan

needs to pay its part of it. But all of us need to watch closely so that only clean and permissible money is expended for this task."

A common call of confirmation came from the assembly. A smile opened Abol Qasem's bright countenance, and he said a prayer in his heart for his uncle. So, with the understanding that all would appear in the sanctuary the next day at dawn, they arose from their places.

Now the Ka'ba! What person could be so brave as to begin to destroy it?

That old man, no matter how much he laughed at this talk, it was clear however that he was quite frightened of this task. It seems that other men had not thought of this problem earlier. Suddenly they thought deeply.

It was not the case that until that time that whoever had thought about destroying the Ka'ba had been obliterated before he could do it, or he had refrained from doing it! In that case, what person was courageous enough to lift a hand to destroy it? For, from the time of Abraham the prophet no one had moved it at all.

Bu Tāleb,[1] knowing that what the others were thinking, said so that all of those present could hear, "Our intention in destroying it was not the destruction itself. The god of the Ka'ba is aware of our intention and what we want to do."

This talk was agreeable to reason, but it did not diminish the long-standing fear in the hearts of the

---

1. "Bu" is the abbreviated form of "Abu," which means "father" in Arabic. Hence, Abu Tāleb or Bu Tāleb means "father of Tāleb."

people.

Walid, so as to end that irritating doubt, said, "This decision either should not have been taken in the beginning or once it was taken, it must be carried out."

'Amru Heshām sarcastically said, "You are older than all of us uncle. What would happen if you begin this work? We will watch what happens. Then, if calamity does not befall you, we will take up the task."

Walid jokingly said, "May your mother mourn you 'Amru! For nothing comes from you save badness."

So he picked up a pick-axe off of the ground and headed toward the Ka'ba.

He had still not gone a few steps when he halted facing the wall. Upon seeing that, all heads turned in that direction. On the wall of the Ka'ba, a very large asp was crouching. It had a yellowish color. For that reason, it was difficult to see at first.

The asp was holding its trapezoidal head toward Walid. Its mouth, wide, was open, and its bent, needle-like teeth instilled fear in one's heart. Its reddish forked tongue constantly appeared and disappeared, like lightening, and placed a moving picture in the air.

Everyone, spell-bound, by its fearful eyes, stayed where he was and could not do anything.

Was this the same asp that their precursors had said was the guardians of the Ka'ba?

At the time of the Jorhamis—before the Qureish came into Mecca—property for some time, time after time, had been taken from the treasury of the Ka'ba. The Jorhamis had no choice but to place guardians for the Ka'ba.

But after many years, one of those guardians was tempted by the devil. Then, one day, when the heat became most intense, and all of the people had gone to their homes, he entered the Ka'ba and entered the pit of the treasury and carried off all the gold, silver, and jewels. Then, when he wanted to place the stone of the treasury in place—and this was a huge, heavy stone—he fell into the treasury and that stone blocked his path of escape.

The man stayed in there until the other guardians came and found him in that situation.

A short while after that event, a large asp appeared in that depression. It is now five hundred years that that asp is there, and no one enters the hole of the treasury without that asp threatening his life.

After the people had waited for a while, one said, "This could show that the gods are not pleased with the destruction of the Ka'ba."

The other men seemed to affirm what he said with their silence. But in the meantime, because it did not seem reasonable that the god of the building would prefer its destruction and the listeners would prevent its reconstruction. Thus, with Bu Tāleb in front and the others following him, they headed for the place of Abraham, which was several steps further on, so they could appeal to his ancestor and request the solution of the problem. Abu al-Qāsem also accompanied them.

There, Bu Tāleb removed his sandals and entered the place. Then, facing the Ka'ba, he placed his tow knees on the stone surface of the place. The other men—the older ones in front and the younger ones behind—sat down on the sandy ground behind Bu Tāleb.

Bu Tāleb unwound the wrap of his green turban from his head and let it hang on his neck and chest. Then, like a impotent or fatigued slave, he bent his head. He extended his hands in need and supplication toward the Ka'ba and began to speak to his ancestor.

I was also __ that day with my step-father, Abu al-Qāsem. Although he was __ the people, and he accompanied them in supplication, his supplication was always in his own manner.

A while passed in that way and all of the men were still supplicating, until suddenly, and no one knew from which direction, in the sky, a bird with a thick body appeared. Then, fast, like a heavy piece of rock, it descended in to the middle of the sanctuary, such that all of those present thought that a stray arrow had fallen to earth.

Quickly, though, we saw it rise into the air and something like a thick whip was in its thick talons swaying back and forth. It seemed to be an eagle that had taken that large yellow asp with it.

All of their action had taken place in a few moments, so fast that there was no time for those men to think ort do anything. But the Qureishites were pleased by this great happening, and they all shouted out in unison.

The men, happy and also grateful, picked themselves up off of the ground and went in the direction of the Ka'ba. The end of all the fears and doubts. They most certainly had a great task ahead of them.

At this time, from among the crowd, a voice said, "It seems that after centuries, another administration has come for the god of the house!"

Several of the young men stretched their necks so as to see the speaker of those surprising words.

He was Zayd 'Amru. That same monotheist searching for the truth who had spent his life and youth doing that.

When they searched the Ka'ba, Walid stepped forward. It seemed that it was him again with that clear sign of doing the right thing who had to start that work.

Walid took the cloak off his shoulders and placed it on the stone at the front of the idol Asaf. Then they brought him a wooden ladder.

Walid placed his foot on the rung of the ladder and slowly climbed up the wall of the Ka'ba with his large body. At this time, not from fear, but from a long life, in his knees a shaking could be seen.

"Now the pick-axe!"

Zobayr went up the ladder and gave him a pick-axe with a nice handle.

Walid in that situation, halted for a few moments on the wall.

All of those present held their breath and not a sound came from anyone.

"O' God, do not be afraid! O' God, we have only

good intentions."

Upon saying that, he gently brought the pick-axe down on the wall. In a moment, several of the people took a step back.

A dry voice arose and the tip of the pick-axe landed in the crack between two stones.

Walid, in a movement, separated the top stone from the wall and threw it on the ground.

Nothing at all happened. No lightening came down from the sky to incinerate him, nor was his body frozen in place.

Walid straightened up and victoriously looked at the people. Then he moved the small black turban from his head and placed it on the wall. He separated his thick legs from one another and with greater certitude began working.

He swung the pick-axe more quickly now, and the hits were more effective.

A small mound of stones that Walid had torn from the wall had accumulated on the ground. At this time, he straightened his back and looked at those gathered. His tired look, seemingly like a hint, said to me, "Is it enough for tearing down __?"

Zobayr, in answer, extended his hand. "May your life be long Walid! Now come down. You have done what you had to do."

Walid three the pick-axe on the ground and picked up his turban from off the ground and placed it on his head. He then put his foot on the ladder and slowly descended from the wall.

When he put his cloak over his shoulders, he looked

at the leaders of the Qureish and said, "You saw that nothing happened. Now the rest of the work is yours."

'Amru Heshām said from among them, "It is late in the afternoon now, and it will soon start to become dark. I think we should start to work tomorrow."

None of the other leaders objected to what 'Amru said, because they, like him, had still not been saved from their fear of engaging in that enterprise. And for that reason too, they thought like 'Amru that, "Let us wait until tonight passes and see what to Walid. Then, if he did not suffer anything, perhaps we will begin this work."

'Father! Father!"

It was Ja'far, who had entered the house panting and in a hurry from the alley. What has happened, though, to make the youngest of Bu Tāleb this disturbed?

Worried, Bu Tāleb asked, "Huh? Has something happened to Ali?"

Before Ja'far had an opportunity to answer his father, his mother, who was busy guiding wheat with a hand pestle, quickly asked, "Haydar?"

(And Fatima liked to call her young son Haydar, even though Bu Tāleb had named him Ali.)

Ja'far, after catching his breath, said, "No. Nothing has happened to Ali. He is playing in the alley with the other children."

Bu Tāleb said, "So what is wrong?"

"In the sanctuary! Now in the time when the clans of the Qureish draw their swords against one another and shed one another's blood!"

Bu Tāleb, without another question, pushed himself

up from the plaster wall of the portico and stood up. Then, quickly, he threw his cloak on his shoulder, tied his turban on his head, put on his sandals, and stepped out of the courtyard of the house.

It had been four days since he had been to the sanctuary, that same day that the walls of the Ka'ba became so high that the time of installing the black stone. And it was over that that those disagreements arose.

That is how it was when, once that night had passed, and no harm had come to Walid, the work began.

First there was the destruction of the old structure of the Ka'ba, which took half a day. Then we began to take up the foundation, and we went under the ground to the height of a man. There, some green stones were uncovered that resembled teeth connected together. When one of us pounded a crowbar among them, a quick spark erupted, and those stones began to shake. But no stone came out of place.

My father said, "This must be that same foundation that Abraham, praise be on him, had built the Ka'ba on. So do not intrude on it and do not go beyond it.

That is what we did.

Before the destruction came to an end, we began to remove stones from the Mountain of Sayada. (Sayada is situated over a valley on the edge of Mecca, and its stones are very desirable for building.)

There, some began to break the stones and a group placed them on the backs of camels, donkeys, and cows. Women, girls, and children were also involved in pouring plaster and mud on the loads and carrying it with animals to the sanctuary.

At the time of the construction, the women built mortar and the men, two by two, laid stones. Our helper in this task was Abu al-Qāsem, my cousin.

When the walls reached a height near one and a half meters, and when the time for placing the black stone came, a quarrel arose, because every clan maintained that that task had to fall to it so its name would endure.

For this reason, the work stopped and the knot was not unraveled by the efforts of the elders. Also, from that day on, Abu al-Qāsem and my father did not come to the sanctuary. However, my brother Tāleb and I went there every day with the other men. Thus, we returned at night and related what had happened there for father.

"Huh, Ja'far! You did not say how this came about."

Ja'far, while striving to keep pace with the long and quick strides of Bu Tāleb, breathlessly said, "Nothing father! Today began just like those other days. All of the men of the various clans of the Qureish sat around the black stone and talked about the past pride of their fathers and families until gradually it came to abuse and ugly words. Then the men of Bani 'Abd al-Dar and 'Adi Ka'b brought a bowl of blood and with an oath of death put their hands in it so as not to submit t being prevented from placing the black stone in its place."

"When the affair reached that point, Walid told me to quickly come to you and tell you the story."

The sound of a commotion could be heard one or two streets away from the sanctuary. Some were beginning to curse. A few, yelling, were calling and asking the aggressors to be calm and observe the right of their relatives. Several women were constantly screaming from the bottom of their hearts and their small children were accompanying their mothers and crying from fear.

When father and son reached the sanctuary, they found the space there filled with dust. There were all around the Ka'ba so many people—women, men, and children—that no one had ever seen that number before in one place outside the hajj.

In one corner, Walid was sitting on the __ of the **takht** in an angry mood and with his chin on his hand.

There were those same **takhts** that they had brought from the port of Jidda so as to build a roof for the Ka'ba.

Walid was standing atop the __ to see Bu Tāleb and yelled, "Calm down! Calm! Calm!"

A short respite came about in the action of the inciters. Walid, seeking to benefit from that opportunity, added, "Now your leader Bu Tāleb! Look to see what he has to say!"

With those words, all heads turned toward Bu Tāleb and everyone opened a path for him so he could go to the forefront.

Bu Tāleb went forward with that medium height, bulkiness, bright countenance, and dignity without saying anything. His eyebrows were knitted together, and he was thinking hard.

When he reached the side of the black stone, he stopped. Then, for a moment, deeply, he looked to both sides. On the left were those united in death—

Bani 'Abd al-Dar and 'Adi Ka'b. The handles of their bare swords in hand, ready to attack, with blood-shot eyes such that blinding anger darted out of them. Facing them, several old men and women, like a wall, had blocked their path.

To the right side, was another group of the men of Qureish, angry, bitter, and ready to defend.

Bu Tāleb, following a short hesitation, with a tone mixed with affinity and reproach, said, "I see that you have the intention of polluting a good deed with badness!"

A commotion rose up from both sides and that short silence was about to be broken.

Bu Tāleb, acquainted with the spirit of the people, without hesitation began to speak before he lost the moment.

"Be calm! Calm! Calm!"

The leaders of the Q also hurried to his side, and every one of them implored his clan to calm down. Suddenly, however, a small child hanging on its mother's shirt began to cry loudly.

All of the onlookers glued their eyes to those two in objection. Upon seeing that attitude, the woman picked up her child and left the occasion.

Bu Tāleb said in a scolding manner, "It is surprising that the Qureish understanding themselves to be the guardians of the honor and security of the sanctuary and now its men have drawn their swords in the heart of the sanctuary and are about to spill the blood of one another."

He caste a glance at the men on both sides of him.

"Don't you fear that since you have violated the honor of the sanctuary, that others will be emboldened to do the same? Then you will be deprived of repose and benefit, and calamities will bear down on you."

"What am I saying? This same flood, pestilence, ad cholera that have occurred in Mecca after that and kills our children and adults every day is not sufficient for you so that you pursue your own incorrect actions?"

Bu Tāleb's words and his calm tone seemed to awaken the sleeping and heedless consciousnesses. All at once, the blazing flames of anger in the eyes subsided and it seemed the ashes of sorrow were sprinkled over the faces. Then, the hands that were strongly squeezing the handles of the swords relaxed. Also, some of those men sheathed their swords. Then a youth of the Bani 'Abd al-Dar stepped toward Bu Tāleb and said, "Now, you who are our elder and leader, tell us what we have to do so that this conflict subsides, and no family is dishonored."

Bu Tāleb raised his hand to his firm chin and for a moment, with his head down, squeezed his thick white beard with his thick hands.

All, staring at him, remained silent. It seemed that only he had the ability to unravel that knot.

In the end, Bu Tāleb lifted his head and, facing both sides, said, "I think that no way is left but to except submission to arbitration."

"Arbitration?"

"Arbitration by whom?"

"What person can we find to whom everyone will submit?"

Abi Omayyeh, who was the oldest man of the Qureish and also an experienced ad reputable, answered those questions.

"What do you say that we turn over the arbitration to fate?"

"Arbitration by fate?"

"Yes. Fate."

"In what way?"

"Right now, everyone turn to face the four doors of the sanctuary and watch to see who enters the sanctuary first. Then let us appoint him to decide among us and whatever he says, we will do, without any objection."

"But...."

"In this situation, 'if' and 'but' need to be caste aside, because there is the fear that the strife will continue and the problem will never be resolved."

In that forum, fatigue and danger followed a reasonable course. The best method so the struggles are eliminated and the swords fall from the hands and the affair reaches a favorable conclusion.

Thus, so that no doubt or conflict remained, talk of its conditions came up. In the meanwhile, all of the talk was for Abi Omayyeh. It seemed only he was to answer any question and resolve any problem.

"That person must not be of those men who are in the sanctuary now."

"Yes! He should not know about this agreement we have made with each other."

Zobayr said, "We will place men at each of the four gates of the sanctuary right now so no one can leave here."

At that time, the people quickly left the circle of the elders.

"O' Abi Omayyeh! What if two persons enter the sanctuary together or from two or more gates?"

"There is a solution for that too. Let us agree that only one of those gates will be considered."

"What do you think about the Bani Shabeh gate?"

(This gate faced the Ka'ba and the Holy House[1]. For that reason, there was a greater likelihood that people would enter by it.)

Abi Omayyeh said, "I do not see why anyone should object to that."

Again, the leaders of this people, either with a movement of the head or with a short statement confirmed what he said.

Walid said, "That person should not be a woman or child."

Abi Omayyeh said, "Agreed. He must be a man, mature, and noble. Being dumb, ignorant, or sick is not appropriate for this affair."

"Evil-doers and infamous men are also worthy of a judgment such as this."

"God bless your soul Bu Tāleb, for you have spoken well, and you have presented the truth of the matter. Entrusting judgment to those kinds of people will bring everlasting shame of the Qureish."

"If he is from the Qureish, his claim should not be superior to the others."

"O' 'Amru, even though that word is proper, it can

---

1. *Bayt ol-moqaddas.*

however create a lot of problems. When the affair is entrusted with that substance of good qualities, questioning his opinion, whatever he says, is not appropriate."

Walid said, "Let it be so as AO has said! Let's bring the talk to an end and turn to action."

Upon hearing that, all of the mouths stopped speaking and heads turned toward the Bani Shaybeh gate.

Then, AO went atop the pile of stones and shouted so that all could hear, he said, "Now!"

All at once, every voice and murmur there was stopped and a profound silence settled over the sanctuary, such that every sound that arose in the alleys and quarters of the city could clearly be heard by the sharp ears of those people. The beats of the hearts in those breasts sped up and eyes, opened up completely, were staring at the road.

A crow, which was passing through the sky over the sanctuary, seemed surprised by the quiet and the number of people, let out a long caw. In that heavy silence and that special circumstance, that caw was so long ad discordant that suddenly the sound of a loud laugh rose up from the crowd.

Upon seeing that situation, Walid Moghayreh, laughing, said, to AO, "You forgot about the gate of the sky Abi Omayyeh!"

AO, with a smile on his face, wanted to answer Walid when a commotion arose from the direction of the Bani Shaybeh gate.

"He has come! He has come!"

All of the heads turned in that direction, and Abi Omayyeh yelled out from atop the pile of stones, "It's Amin!"

Walid, happy, said, "This Amin is honest, virtuous, and just. We of the Bani Makhzum accept his judgment."

The other heads of the Q, happy, went along with Walid.

Amin, with that proper stature, a white dishdasha of Yemeni cotton with dots the color of saffron on his body and an *abā* the color of a yellow camel of that same color on his head, arrived.

His head was down, and he was immersed in thought. Along the way, in the destroyed house of an old woman whom the flood had killed, he had seen a group gambling with knuckle-bones. A young woman, weeping, was throwing dust o her head and circling around them and yelling and damning them. Muhammad, saddened, was standing so that he might help her. Then, he realized that one of those gamblers was her husband.

That man had just lost his camel. Then his house. Finally, so that he might regain his camel and house, he had bet ten years of his own life. But he had also lost that. Now, he had lost his existence, and he had to spend ten years in slavery without wages to that winner. The woman's weeping was because of that.

Amin, with a deep hurt in his heart because of that occurrence, came forward immersed in deep thought, when suddenly, he raised his head and found the crowd of people staring at him.

Bu Tāleb, very happy from this occurrence, hurried toward his nephew and brought him out of his amazement by explaining what had passed.

Amin, head down, thought for a few moments. Then he faced the leaders of the Q and said, "Let it be so. Now prepare a little bit of cement."

Ja'far and Tāleb went to prepare the cement.

Amin went to the black stone and beside it took off his cloak and spread it on the ground.

The circle of people around had now become tight. Thos who were at the back stretched their necks and pressed in on those who were in front. All were waiting to see how that youth of thirty-five years and good reputation in the tribe with what finger of skill unraveled that hard knot.

Amin bent his back ad took hold of the black stone with both hands and placed it on his cloak. Then his pleasant voice arose with that clear explanation.

"Now, the elder of each clan take a corner of this cloak in his hand, and all together take the stone to its setting."

The elders of the clans, astonished, bent down beside the cloak. Applause and praise of him arose from the crowd.

The black stone, setting in the middle of Amin's cloak and with the hands of all the leaders of the Qureish, was carried toward the Ka'ba. The other men of each clan, pleased, followed them.

At the corner of the wall, Amin picked up the black stone from the cloak and with his own hands placed it in its empty niche. He said, "Now the clans that have built this wall pour cement around it and make it firm in its place."

The uproar had come to an end, and the quarrel had been ended. The men who an hour before had intended to kill one another, now smiled at each other.

After several days, again, all began to build the Ka'ba. Amin too placed his cloak and turban in a corner in order t accompany his uncle, Abbās, in bringing stones. At this time, Abbās heard that a man whom he had not seen before angrily said to another, "It is surprising that this people, whose leaders and elders are lazy, have designated him who is younger and poorer than all of them as their leader and judge! I swear to Lat and 'Uzzā that it will not be long until he becomes superior to them and takes their fate into his own hands."

It was dusk, and Amin, tired of the hard work of the day, was facing the sanctuary. Since the day of marrying Khadija, he had been responsible for managing all of the affairs outside the house, from trading goods to seeing off the trading caravans to Syria and Yemen, sending off the goods to the seasonal bazaars in the four forbidden months*, especially the month of the hajj, and evaluating the income and expenses and his accounting. No matter how much he had continuously tried to keep himself away from the bad attitudes of the merchants.

I, Sā'eb, the son of Abi as-Sā'eban, was a partner for a while with Amin in business dealings. In every respect, I found him to be the best of partners. I saw his attitude and behavior to be different in this matter from all the other merchants. His behavior was always accompanied by virtuousness. In trading—just as in the manner of the merchants—he was not a liar and concealer of his good's defects. He was satisfied with less, and I did not see him to be hard in bargaining. Never did he ever put his own work on may shoulders either, and I was his partner.

Muhammad liked his work very much, and he was never afraid of it, no matter how difficult. But he liked being alone more than any other activity.

How good it was being a shepherd! To have wide freedom and solitude!

Now, although he had placed his foot on the rung of forty years of life, he had still not lost that affinity he had from childhood for nature. O' that that opportunity was available again to him so he could retreat to its quiet and calm safety and be submerged in deep solitude full of his own secrets!

In the city, the talk ad traffic and crowdedness and work and everything that was good and bad, unwanted, occupied the mind. The walls and narrowness of the alleys and houses, like cages, closed off the road to the flight of thought to profound and elevated things. The view of the horizons narrowed, and the heart, hardened, became tight. Then the thoughts became small and the views narrow.

But in the plain, it was another matter. There, existence, virgin and without a blemish, stretched out in every direction. The most pleasant opportunity for Muhammad, without any impediment, sent out the high waves of his thoughts in every direction, and, with the eye of the heart, would read profoundly the amazing book of nature with a hundred pages.

O' that it was not necessary to mix with people and to live among them. Then he could be alone with himself in the safety of pure nature and his eyes, waiting and full of need, would be fixed on the sky and he would look at it so much until God receives his soul or opens the door to the treasury of the secrets of

His creation for him.

The sanctuary, like every evening, was full of people. Some were circumambulating the Ka'ba, and a group was appealing to the idol of their clan or rubbing perfume and other pleasant smelling things on its head and face. A middle-aged and fat man had taken off the earlier worn out covering from the body of the idol and put a colorful and new covering on it. On the four sides of the sanctuary, along the porticoes or in the middle of the courtyard, circles of men, every ring around a leader of a clan, had assembled and were busy talking and listening. Then, every person entered the sanctuary. After circumambulating the Ka'ba and prostrating before the idol to worship or stroke it to gain a blessing, they would join one of the circles.

Abu al-Qāsem also entered the sanctuary and went to circumambulate the Ka'ba. But as in the past, his circumambulation and supplication was in his own manner. Without looking at any idol or stroking any of them.

When I saw that, and I had seen him do that several times earlier, I said to him, "Abu al-Qāsem, why do you not worship any idol like we do and do not prostrate to any of them?"

He said, "I have no inclination Abu Bakr to prostrate to something that people have built and carved with their own hands and from which no one derives any benefit or loss."

Muhammad faced the house. But before he had

left the sanctuary, he saw Wāraqa Nowfel. He was also heading out of the sanctuary using a cane. Abu al-Qāsem knew that Wāraqa was heading back to his own house. This old and abstemious man, even though it had been many years that he had practiced the customs of the Christians, just as before, he had not forsaken circumambulating the Ka'ba. With those eyes whose light had vanished from them, every evening, with a cane, he would pass through the uneven streets of Mecca to come to circle the Ka'ba.

Muhammad, once he had gone forward, realized that Wāraqa, weeping and fluently, was reciting a poem under his breathe.

"You have become scarce cousin.

"You have become very distanced from the intense heat of the furnace.

"You observed the customs of that lord.

"For there is no creator like him,

"Anywhere,

"Day or night.

"You have passed by terrifying lands.

"You only spoke of God.

"You prayed in every place of worship,

"And you asked God to forgive you,

"And not let the unbelievers overcome you."

M knew that that poem was in mourning for Zayd 'Amru, the old friend of Wāraqa.

It had been some time without any news of Zayd. Earlier, Muhammad would sometimes see him when, old and decrepit, in the sanctuary, with his back against the Ka'ba, he would call the people to quit worshipping the idols and to turn toward the customs of Abraham the prophet. But after a while had gone by, Zayd's uncle, Khattāb, incited a group of bad and mean youths to run him out of Mecca because he was afraid that his words would weaken the people's belief in the idols and ruin their religion.

Zayd necessarily went to live on the Mt. of Light.* When he sometimes secretly entered Mecca and went to visit the Ka'ba, those mean persons would assault him again and they beat him until he was near death. Khattāb had said to Safiyyeh Hazrami, Zayd's wife, that if he decided to go on a trip, to let him know. In that way, Zayd was a vagabond who did not have permission to leave the vicinity of his city.

For that reason, one day, Khadija had brought news that it seemed Zayd, without any provisions, had set out on a journey.

Thereafter, there was no sign of him. But what had happened that his dear friend, Wāraqa, had wept like that on remembering him?

"Good afternoon!"

"Ah! It is you Abu al-Qāsem! May your afternoon be pleasant as well."

"I see that you are very sad. Is it because of your friend Zayd, or has something else happened?"

Upon hearing that, his pent up feelings burst forth and he began to weep profusely. M, sympathetic, placed his had on his bony shoulder and said, "Have you received any news from him?"

Wāraqa wiped the tears from his fatigued and wilted eyes and said with suffering, "Yes, my child.

Zayd has left this world. They killed him."

"Killed him? Where? Who?"

"Yes, my son. They killed Zayd, When returning from Syria, near Khaybar. Mean hiwaymen of the Khafājeh killed him."

Then he cried again.

Upon hearing that, Muhammad was overcome with deep sadness. Then, after a short hesitation, he said, "But what business did the hiwaymen of Khafajeh have with that bright old man? What was Zayd doing there?"

Wāraqa, seeming to have sight, turned his head to the left and right. Then he asked, "Is there anyone around us?"

Muhammad said, "There is not."

"You are not a stranger to me either. Come with me so that I can tell you the story."

Muhammad extended his hand to take Wāraqa's wrinkled hand in his own and headed toward the quarter of Abtah.

"Last night, you cousin, 'Obaydollah Jahsh, brought this news for me. (He is one of our friends too.) I don't know whether you know or not. We were three friends from long ago. 'Obaydollah, 'Uthman Howayrath, and I."

At first, like the other people, we were pagans and we worshipped idols. But then I reached adolescence, I was overcome by doubt, until, little by little, our thoughts became closer and we told each other secrets in private."

"During my middle age, one day the people of

Qureish, as was their custom every year, picked up the great idol Bavaneh and went to the place of celebration outside of the city. There, once they had made the sacrifices and had made their supplications, the time for celebration and wine drinking came. At that time, we four individuals sat alone in a corner and made a contract to search for the right religion, and we spread out in the world.

"I journeyed toward Syria and after much questioning and waiting became successful and chose Christianity. 'Uthman Howayrath did the same thing in Rum.[1] Then I returned to Mecca. But 'Uthman stayed in Rum and gained a close position to Caesar and a high position and rank. Your cousin, 'Obaydllah, could not choose a religion and he remained an idolater. The Bani Makhzum opposed Zayd, and he could not leave Mecca. But he preferred the rule of Abraham and thus made his religion clear. And from that day, he was searching to find information on the customs and secrets of that religion. But in Mecca and the rest of the Hejaz, we found no one knowledgeable about them, until one month ago when 'Obaydollah saw him in Damascus with a weak body, rough worn-out clothes, and quivering hands and feet.

There, Zayd had told him that he had traversed the Hejaz, Mosul and Syria on foot. There, the Jewish priests and the monks of the Christians had offered their religion to him. Zayd did not approve of them

---

1. The term "Rum," literally meaning "Rome," was used as a very general reference to those regions that were parts of the Byzantine Empire. It sometimes also referred more specifically to Anatolia or the ancient Asia Minor.

and had asked about the customs of Abraham, but they did not know anything about any of its details. Until they directed him to a monk in Balqā, when news and knowledge of the religion of Jesus the Messiah, praise be to him, reached him and he had all of it.

"Zayd had told 'Obaydollah, 'Once I had explained his questioning to him, he said, "You are looking for that religion that does not exist right now on earth, and you can not acquire any of its customs. But what I can tell you now is this: that soon a messenger will come from your land. He will be inspired by Abraham's religion and will nullify all other religions with his customs. Now, you go to him, and when his message becomes manifest, follow him, because the true religion for which you are searching will __.'

"Zayd, having become very happy, immediately headed for Mecca. On the way, those ignorant men—I don't know why—spilled his blood on the ground."

Muhammad, sandals on his feet, was preparing to go to Hirā.

The custom of the Qureish was that whoever was inclined toward virtue, every year in the month of Rajab, to leave Mecca and to spend all of that month on top of that mountain alone, day and night. They believed that he had to be apart from people during that period. He should not see them or hear them. They considered that silence and solitude to be a kind of worship.

In the meantime, at first, the sons of Hashem established that custom. Then other clans did the same. But the Hashemites placed greater effort in it, and in that task, the effort of Muhammad was more than any of them.

Yes, my husband, Abu al-Qāsem, was very attached to sitting in solitude like that. But that year, when he prepared to go to Hirā, I saw him deep in thought because that year, one after the other, surprising happenings had occurred that had caused him to reflect.

Earlier, and all his life, Muhammad had seen visions that, when he was awake, they came true. But when he became forty years of age, and perhaps a little more, his dreams took on a strange quality. All of the things he saw in his dreams were clear and apparent.

What he saw when asleep perhaps can not be called visions because there is no such kind of vision. Abu al-Qāsem's dreams were not like those of others. When he was asleep—just as when awake—he was never unaware of God. (One day, my **mother** had said to me, "My eyes and heart are awake during sleep.") It can be said that they were true dreams. The purity of the enlightenment of his mind and heart was such that he could see all things in their true light.

Once he talked with me about this subject—and during that period he had only told me about his situation—I related those words to my cousin Wāraqa. (Wāraqa was a monotheist and pious man, and he had gathered a great deal of knowledge about religion.) Wāraqa told me, "Cousin, with those stories you told me earlier about that trip of his to Syria, there can be good signs. Perhaps God has designated your husband to be His prophet! For the prophets usually before they are inspired to this task, their hearts are prepared to receive inspiration during sleep. Earlier prophets have received revelations while asleep."

Some time after that, every night, a great and very dignified man would appear to him during sleep. My husband did not know him, and had not seen anyone like him.

After some more time had passed, he said to me one day, "Khadija, that person now appears to me while I am awake."

I asked him, "When and where?"

He said, "It has no particular time or place. In

the city as well as in the desert and on mountain. Sometimes at night and sometimes during the day."

I remember well that from the time he was young, my husband would hear meaningless and distant mumblings which no one else could hear. He sometimes also saw things we did not see. But during these months, those voices had increased. When he was on the road and traveling alone, a murmur would rise up from the bottom of every rock, clod, and thorn bush saying, "Praise to you O' chosen one!"

At that moment, he would look to the right, the left, and behind him, but he would no see anything but rocks, clods, and thorn bushes.

After those occurrences had been repeated numerous times, his eating and sleeping became less and his body started to become ill.

For this reason, that day, as he was preparing to go to retreat like every year at Hirā, and I saw that apprehension in his look, I thought that he had become frightened at seeing that condition of his.

So, I went to his side, kissed him between the eyes, and said, "May my mother and father be sacrifices for you! Why are you pensive like this? You are a healthy and strong man, and all of your ancestors were like that. During all of your life, you lived clean and nothing has come of you but righteousness and virtue. Your eyes have not fallen on impious things and your body has not been polluted by unclean things. You had an attachment to your relatives and you always strove to improve people. You helped the oppressed and were the guardian of those without a caretaker. You were a very worthy helping hand for the needs and trust of other people. For that reason, how can it be that God would allow a demon to overcome you?"

Abu al-Qāsem, in answer to me, smiled and said nothing.

At that time, I prepared a jug of water, a bundle of dry bread, and a container of olive oil for him to take and he left for the mountain of Hirā.

And now Hirā again. The companion of the deep and secretive solitude of Muhammad with those wide views all around, where the strong waves of his thought, without meeting any impediment, spread out in every direction, and spring forward endlessly. Height with the possibility that he see the broad expanse of existence in one place and in one glance. A special kind of seeing, which never occurred for those who remain on the surface of the earth.

From that height, how small, incapable and childlike did people appear! Too, how insignificant were their events, the talk, the struggle, and the quarrels.

How much those people were immersed in heedlessness and daily affairs! How their thoughts had become like a person of lowly habits and had remained far from what they should be.

At that time, the Arab people were attached to the lowliest customs and lived in the worst of conditions. Around them were hard rocks and poisonous food. They spilled one another's blood for the slightest reason and cut their ties with their relatives. Idols were standing among them and they were consumed by sins.

No people were terribly lost and they writhed, amazed and lost, in insurrection and corruption. They were consumed by lust and desire from all sides and self-praise and arrogance had made them mean and distressed.

From long ago, no prophet had arisen. A deep darkness had engaged the world and the people were in a deep sleep.

The thread of all activities had been broken. Fear had taken over their hearts such that o one could find a place of refuge save the sword.

And for this reason, the tree of man's life had turned so yellow that it had no hope of sprouting any leaves or fruit.

Muhammad, on the threshold of his fortieth year of life, was now seeing all of these happenings. But save for sadness and an ambiguous desire for the future he could do nothing. For it had gone beyond that where it could be resolved with the efforts of one or a few persons before him.

Was not there also Zayd, Wāraqa, 'Uthman, and 'Obaydollah? Was Zayd's suffering in this path insignificant? What was the answer of those people for whom his heart burned save abuse, ridicule, pelting with stones, and hitting? And what had he done except, like a fleeting meteor, in that pitch darkness, to open a break for a moment so that in its ray of light, for a moment, they could see the ugliness of their own abominable lives?

Outside Mecca, there were several other persons like them. Muhammad remembered that day in the 'Ukkāz bazaar very well when Qas Sa'edah Ayadi of the Bakr Wā'el clan was riding a red camel and passing among the people and advised them,

"O' people! Gather around me and listen to what I say and learn. Anyone who lived has left this world. And that which can come, will come. It is time that there are in the hearers and lessons on earth."

"Qas truly swore that if you are satisfied with those customs you have. God is displeased with that. There is another religion for God that He likes more than yours."

"O' people! What has happened that you think that people who have come do not return?"

But while he spoke, each of the people was busy with his own trading. Those few persons who listened, save for joking, buffoonery, and ridicule, did not answer Qes.

Truly, how was it that the people really did not think that existence had been arbitrarily created with that much dignity, greatness, complexity, and profundity? Was the meaning of man's life just eating and sleeping, marrying, plundering, assaulting, and things such as that?

Muhammad, looked at the faded sky of sunset for a while. Night gradually arrived and spread its black tent over the earth. The stars appeared one by one here and there in the sky and became more apparent every moment. Wit the coming of night, the silence of the desert and the mountain of Hirā became many times more intense. Greater opportunity for Muhammad so he could pursue his endless thinking in that unsullied solitude and silence.

The night sky was a surprising world for

Muhammad. So large, deep, varied, and full of secrets that it never repeated. A book so rich that every corner—no, every point of it—was a strange and new world.

God forbid that existence, after its surprising creation, would be allowed to wander by itself! This much astonishing order and magnificence is certainly connected with the guidance of a knowing and capable creator.

People can also not be abandoned to themselves. Their deity was never unmindful of them. But how did they come to be afflicted by that condition?

Muhammad was not very preoccupied with his own mind. For from that day he became aware of his own existence, he saw with his heart that he was not alone. Constantly, when work became difficult for him, with guidance from outside and in, paths were opened for him. Whenever in a task I was not appropriate for him, he would use the power of intellect. Thus, when intellect proved incapable, dread and destructiveness would prevent him, or, with a correct vision, the way out of the dilemma would open up for him. Then, if none of these things guided him, a barrier from out side would emerge so that act did not take place. Thus, it did not happen.

Whatever it was, Muhammad, in all situations, found a superior power to help and guide him. A power that for his life he had not found empty from his presence for one moment. But, now, on the verge of intellectual maturity and completeness of thought he saw that his need and thoughts had gone to the very heights of that which was connected to his daily life.

He had realized through the power of intellectual and the guidance of the heart and his deep visions what things were on his correct orientation and which were incorrect. Which were most of the things and the answer those long questions of his about what existence was, constantly, is the way that his wishes were, did not become apparent to him.

Muhammad was illiterate and had not gone to school, and what he wanted was not found among the stories of the Jewish priests of the Christian monks. When he looked intensely, he found many more reasons in the book of nature. In the early morning at the time when it came out of the depth of night, where the sun shone and rose above the horizon; the darkness of evening when it dissolved the lightness of day in itself, the stars, when they were like lights hung on the dark arch of the night sky. The moonlight, desert, and camel even—with their own surprising creation—had very many lessons. For that reason, they were all signs of a very deep and great truth, reality.

But what was that pure reality without diminishment like? The signs with their ineffableness spoke with words for Muhammad. But now after four decades of life and in this mature age of intellect, Muhammad's questions had exceeded the boundary of those signs. His preoccupation had gone beyond himself and had taken on a wider expanse.

What would happen if that pure reality, that deep secret and the key to all the signs and questions were

to speak and after all those years of silence speak again
with his creator?

"Good day cousin!"

"Good day Abu al-Qāsem!"

The voice was that of his cousin, little Ali, and his wife, Khadija. A child and woman who were the kindest persons to Muhammad and the dearest to him. Those two, so as not to arrive unannounced, called out their greeting several steps away from the cave at Hirā.

Happy at their coming, Muhammad left the cave to meet them and called out in answer, "May all your times be good!"

Then, from knowing his right, he caste a deep look into the captivating eyes of his wife and kindly stroked Ali's head with his hand.

Khadija had a large bound handkerchief in her hand and Ali had a jug of water. Although the air was cool and autumnal, large drops of sweat sat on Khadija's wide figure and Ali's brown, wheat-colored face.

Khadija, before she reached the cave, had hesitated for a short while so as to catch her breathe. But her breathing had still not slowed. The paling of her white countenance told clearly the pressure traveling that long distance had on her slight fat body.

Ali, though, joyful and vigorous, without any sign of fatigue, was standing opposite his beloved cousin. It appeared that he was saying to Muhammad with those large bright eyes that a gentle art on its upper line, had given a warm beauty to it, "How happy I am to see you, O' father and cousin!"

Khadija and Ali had traveled the two parasangs from Mecca to the foot of Mount Hirā by camel. For half an hour they had crossed the black and rough rock-strewn areas of the mountain in order to bring water and food to Muhammad.

In the meantime, although he was no more than ten years old, he was a strong and cheerful child. For Khadija, however, descending from Hirā with that steep slope, after living five and a half decades and giving birth to seven children, was difficult, especially since she did not have much experience in this sort of thing. Her slightly fat figure also added to the difficulty of the task.

Continuously, when Muhammad's small amounts of dried bread, olive oil, and water finished, he would return to Mecca and bring back water and food with him. He had told his faithful wife several times not to trouble her self by coming to the mountain. Khadija, however, sometimes refrained from abiding by his wishes.

Abu al-Qāsem took the jug and the bound handkerchief from the hands of his wife and cousin. Then he called them to the inside of the cave. But Khadija said that the air outside was more pleasant.

Abu al-Qāsem went inside the cave, and after placing the food and water in it, came out with his *abā*. He then spread his *abā* out on a rock and asked Khadija and Ali to sit on it. Then he sat down between them facing the Kaʻba.

How much these two were loved by Muhammad! And they loved him very much. However, much they were with one another, silence mixed with the thinking of Muhammad did not allow for much talking. But those telling looks and flowing and lost waves of love between them meant they did not need to say anything.

You do not know how much I miss you Abu al-Qāsem! Thus, how can you expect me to endure a month without seeing you? How bold you are to give the excuse of the difficulty of the road, to deprive me of pleasant moments of seeing you. Did you know that even if there were no need for your food and water, I would still find an excuse to see you and, following the heart, I would fly to you?

My cousin! My father! You are kinder to me than a father. Did you have no idea that I love you more than all my brothers, friends, and even my father? O' that you would never leave me!

Yes, yes! I know all of those things very well. You must also be very aware of my affinity for you. It is for that reason that during these days I refrain from seeing you, because I do not like that, during this period, something else finds its way into my heart except for the remembrance of that absolute reality.

With his hand on Ali's shoulder, Muhammad

asked Khadija about the course of affairs and what was happening in Mecca. Recently, there had been no news. Their godson Zayd had decided to bring food and water for Muhammad with his wife, Baraka, but Khadija had not permitted them, for Khadija wanted to come to Muhammad alone. When Ali had learned of that, like the other times he came to Hirā, he strenuously insisted on accompanying her. Thus, both had come.

Kindly, Muhammad squeezed Ali's shoulder and looked deeply into his face.

Ali's round face opened like a flower from happiness.

After living four years together, the kindness between those two was so deep that they could not stand to be apart one day.

In Mecca, everywhere Muhammad would go, usually Ali was with him. And when they were traveling on the road, Muhammad would say pleasant words to him and treat him affectionately.

My cousin raises me in his own way. He would embrace me much and put me to sleep in his own bed. When he did that, I could smell the pleasing odor of his body. I was always going after him like a baby camel following its mother.

Now, when Muhammad thought about those four years that Ali lived with them, in his heart he thanked the Creator, because if that severe drought and famine had not occurred, that strange affinity between him and this small loveable cousin would not have happened. And too, with that, this possibility had come for Muhammad to somewhat repay his debt to his honorable uncle.

Muhammad assisted his relatives and strangers very much. In that year of drought, he was thinking very hard of how to help Bu Tāleb. Then, one day, I was sitting in the sanctuary when he came to me and said, "Cousin, your brother, Bu Tāleb, has many dependents, and he has no property left. The times are such as you can see. Every person is immersed in his own affairs. Bu Tāleb, however, you know, does not accept aid from anyone because of his high dignity.

"God has given you and me abundance these days, and now no one among the Hashemites is more able than you and me. What do you say that we go to him and each of us take a child from him so as to care for them?"

I said, "That is appropriate."

Thus, I immediately went to Bu Tāleb and in a way so he would not be offended, and I told him of my intention. My brother, after hesitating for a moment, said, "Until this famine subsides...."

I said, "Let it be so."

He said, "Abbās, you know that I can't tolerate being far from 'Aqil. Let him stay with me for now. Of the rest, take whichever one you want."

We said, "We will do what you wish."

Thus, Abu al-Qāsem took Ali and I took Ja'far.

Muhammad, so as to alleviate the silence, looked

toward Ali and jokingly said, "During these days, I was not in Mecca, did you wrestle with any of the children?"

Ali, with a smile mixed with shame, said, "No."

Khadija, laughing, said, "Bu Tāleb was not in Mecca so as to bring an opponent for Ali."

Although what Khadija was somewhat in jest, it was not very inappropriate.

Bu Tāleb, just like other Arabs, enjoyed watching wrestling. Thus, when he was in a good mood, he would gather his sons and his brother's son and arrange to have them wrestle with one another. At the same time, Ali was a big-boned and powerful child. He would throw to the ground whomever he challenged and would defeat him. Bu Tāleb would enjoy seeing that and say, "Ali has come out on top!"

Abu al-Qāsem, after shaking Ali's head affectionately, faced Khadija and asked, "How are our children?"

"Good! But they miss their father."

Then Muhammad asked about Zayd and his wife, Baraka, and Maysara and his wife. Khadija said that all were well and had asked how he was.

"…and your cousin Wāraqa?"

"He is not well."

"Is he ill?"

"No. He is very sad about himself because his eyes no longer see so that he can go to the mountain in retreat and worship. He had still not recovered from his sadness over Zayd 'Amru either."

With the mention of Zayd 'Amru, a heavy pale of sadness settled over Muhammad's large black eyes. He then sighed and said, "Time cures all ills Khadija."

Then his look became ever more distant, so much so that it seemed his spirit was no longer in this world.

Khadija was familiar with her husband's conditions, and she knew that this was one of those moments when he preferred to be alone. So she rose from her place.

Upon seeing her do that, Ali stood up as well. He brought the empty jug and the old cloth out of the cave. After a short farewell, the woman and child set off down the side of the mountain. Meanwhile, Muhammad, though still immersed in his former state, stood facing them. A fresh breeze had begun to blow his long black tresses.

Muhammad, after a short nap, lifted his head off of the sandy ground of the cave of Hirā. The air had a shiver-inducing coolness to it. The night appeared to have reached mid-way.

M turned his head toward the outside. In the sky, the narrow crescent of the moon was scattering its weak light on the mountains of Hirā, Tabir, and the wide southern plain. Mecca, the countryside around it, and the entire world was drowned in a deep sleep. A heavy and strange silence had completely engulfed existence within itself. Not a sound arose from any direction. It was as if that night, the earth and time, had gone to sleep with all living things. The breeze had stopped. If there were a river, it certainly would have stopped moving too.

Earlier, Muhammad had spent most nights awake. But he had never heard nor felt that much silence and calm. He was beset by pain because of the intensity of the absence of sound. It was as if space had found a kind of eternity. Time seemed to have stopped, and existence had been suspended in a moment from deathlessness and **lack of decline**.

The silence and stillness were such that if a plant grew, or a blossom bloomed on a bush, its sound would certainly be heard.

Then, suddenly, in the sky, an intense light appeared of a strange kind and filled all of M's line of vision.

Fearful, he then felt a shudder in his body and soul. A shiver in his body. Spinning in his head. Spinning. Spinning. Until the edge of dizziness.

Pressure. The pressing of the body and spirit. The exiting of something from the body. Bit by bit. Pain. Pain. Pain. Pain even beyond the ability of a strong man like Muhammad. Pain at the last breathe of life. The slow and deadly exodus of the soul from the body.

Then, shivering. The entrance of gentle waves into the body. The cleansing of the spirit in a gentle substance of a kind of light. It seemed like another birth. A new life. The transformation of the nature of the soul. Then, becoming a slight feeling and transparency and translucent. The expansion of the capacity of existence. The fall of the curtains over the eyes, ears, heart, and intellect.

How far existence had been transformed! How alive, beautiful, and profound!

That mass of light suddenly contracted and opened up. Then, from its midst, a very magnificent being appeared. It seemed familiar. It seemed to be that same thing that several; times earlier in dreams and awake had appeared to M. But now it was much more apparent and brighter. It was so large that Muhammad's eyes were filled by it. Its face and figure were like a very handsome man with a cloak[1] of green brocade on its body, wrapped up in a halo of heavenly light.

Muhammad saw it in every corner of the sky where he looked.

---

1. *Jobbeh.* A type of long gown.

Then a voice soft as rain and as pleasant as the sound of streams emerged from it.

"O' Mohammmmad!"

M answered with a quiver in his voice, "Ye....s?"

"Recite!"

"Me? Recite what?"

"The names of your God!"

"H…how should I recite it?"

"Recite in the name of your Lord who created."

M began to recite along with that heavenly being.

"…Created man from a clot of blood.

"Recite! And your Lord is the dearest.

"He is the same one who instructed with the pen.

"And taught man what he did not know.

The recitation had come to an end. The heavenly voice subsided. At that time, again, its speaker appeared in that initial form, and that mass of heavenly light all of a sudden diminished and then disappeared.

A deep feeling of tiredness had overcome Muhammad. He felt himself severely beaten. It was as if his body and all of his bones had been pounded in a mortar. He felt an intense warmth in his body and head. It was as if a furnace had been lighted inside of him. For that reason, his shoulders were shaking wildly from excitement.

Amazed, he wanted to stand up from his place, but no__ remained in his knees. So his feet were folded under his heavy body, and he spread out on the ground. In that position, he placed his forehead on the ground and began to weep.

Bibliography

*Ameneh, Bint osh-Shati*. Trans. Hosayn Azhdari. 3rd ed. Ketabforushi-ye Atrupat.

*Akhbar-e Makkeh. Abu al-Walid Azraqi.* Trans. And ed. Dr. Mahmud Mahdavi Damghani. 1st ed. 1368. Chap va Nashr-e Bonyad.

*Eslamshenasi* (Mashhad). Dr. Ali Shari'ati. Daftar-e Tadvin va Tanzim-e Majmu'eh-ye Asar-e Mo'allem Shahid Doktor Ali Shari'ati.

*E'lam-e Qur'an*. Dr. Mahmud Khaza'eli. 4th ed. 1371. Entesharat-e Amir Kabir.

Al-'asr ol-Jaheli. Showqi Zayf. Trans. Alireza Zakavati Qaraqozlu. 1st ed. 1364. Entesharat-e Amir Kabir.

*Payambar*. Zayn ol-'Abedin Rahnama. 23rd ed. 1363. Ketabforushi-ye Zovvar.

*Tarikh-e Eslam*. Hojjat ol-Eslam Ali Davani. 2nd ed. Daftar-e Entesharat-e Eslami.

*Tarikh-e Payambar-e Eslam*. Dr. Muhammad Ebrahim Ayati va Doktor Abu ol-Qāsem Gorji. 2nd ed. 1361. Entesharat-e Daneshgah-e Tehran.

Tarikh-e Tabari. Muhammad bin Jarir Tabari. Trans. Abu al-Qāsem Payandeh.

Tarikh-e Qur'an. Dr. Mahmud Ramyar. 3rd ed. 1369. Entesharat-e Amir Kabir.

Tarikh-e Makkeh. Amal Amin. Trans. Ahmad Aram.

Tarikhnameh-ye Tabari. Muhammad b. Jarir Tabari. Trans. Attributed to Bal'ami. 2nd ed. 1368. Entesharat-e Nashr-e Now.

Tarikh-e Honar-e Eslami. Kristin Prais (Christine Price). Trans. Mas'ud Rajabnia.

Tarikh-e Ya'qubi. Ahmad Abi Ya'qub. Trans. Dr. Muhammad Ebrahim Ati. 6th ed. 1371. Sherkat-e Enteshrat-e 'Elmi va Farhangi.

Hayat ol-Qolub. Mullah Muhammad Baqer Majlisi. 2nd ed. 1363. Mo'asseseh-ye Matbu'ayi-ye 'Elmi.

*Dar Astanhe-ye Salzad-e Payambar*. Dr. Mahmud Ramyar. 2nd ed. 1365. Daftar-e Nashr-e Farhang-e Eslami.

*Dalayel on-Nabovvat*. Abu Bakr b. Ahmad b. Hosayn Bayhaqi.

*Sirat-e Rasul Allah*. Abu 'Abdullah Muhammad b. Weshaq. Trans. And composition Rafi' od-Din Eshaq Muhammad Hamadani. 2nd ed. 1361. Entesharat-e Khvarazmi.

*Shotor, an keh Kavir ba nam-e u zendeh ast*. Hamid Musavi. Markaz-e Tahqiqat-e Manateq-e Kaviri va Biabani-ye Iran. Daneshgah-e Tehran.

*Sharaf on-Nabi*. Abu Sa'id Khargushi. Trans. Najm od-Din Mahmud Ravandi. Editor and comments: Muhammad Rowshan. 1st ed. 1361. Entesharat-e Babak.

*Farhang-e Mo'in*. Dr. Muhammad Mo'in.

*Qesas-e Qur'an*. Sad rod-Din Balaghi. 11th ed. 1359. Entesharat-e Amir Kabir.

*Qessehha-ye Chahardah Ma'sum*. Mehdi Azar Yazdi.

18th ed. 1369. Ketabha-ye Shokufeh.

*Gozideh-ye tarikh-e Bal'ami*. Abu 'Ali Muhammad b. Muhammad Bal'ami. Editor and commentary: Dr. Reza Anzabinezhad. 4th ed. 1371. Entesharat-e Amir Kabir.

*Mohammad: Payambar-e Azadi*. 'Abd or-Rahman Sharqavi. Trans. Hasan Akbari Marzanak. 1st ed. Entesharat-e Hekmat.

*Mohammad dar shirkhvaragi va khordsali*. Muhammad Showkat Altuni. Trans. Selah od-Din Saljuqi.

*Mohammad (pboh) Khatam-e payambaran*. 2nd ed. 1363. Hosayniyyeh Ershad.

*Makkeh-ey mokarrameh, madineh-ye monavvareh*. Amal Asin. Trans. Ahmad Aram.

*Nahayat ol-mas'ul fi revayat or-rasul*. Sa'id od-Din Muhammad b. Mas'ud Kazaruni. Trans. and ed. 'Abd os-Salam b. 'Ali b. al-Hosayn al-Abarquhi. Ed. Muhammad Ja'far Yahaqi. 1st ed. 1366. Sherkat-e Entesharat-e 'Elmi va Farhangi.

"Men of taste and those familiar with 'research' and 'writing,' together, will realize that height exist in many parts of this collection that appear to exceed the usual ability of 'the pen' or a 'simpler investigation.' This collection, in addition to using all of the author's past experiences, has also opened a new path for which, for sure, praise is deserved."
(Sayyid Muhammad Sadat Akhavi. Chehrehha-ye adabiyyat-e kadkan va nojavanan. No. 12.)


"Sometimes words are not words. They are velvet. The sentences blow in your eyes as soft as a breeze and cleanse the dust from your spirit."
(Hasan Hosayni Sha'er. Majalleh-ye Kayhan-e bachchehha.)


"The writer, with attention to dominance over the elements of the story, has attempted to convey history with the language of a story for his readers. In this area, his writing has been transformed into a readable and attractive work in which there is not just no sign of the dryness of history, but the events of history have been traced in such a manner that its roots in the past have been drawn well."
(Mostafa Delshad Tehrani. *Pezhuheshnameh.*)

That which that Orphan Saw
(The Prophet: From Mission to Emigration
to Ethiopia)

A Novel of the Life of the Prophet
Second Volume

That which that Orphan Saw
(From Mission to Emigration to Ethiopia)

Muhammad Reza Sarshar (Rahgozar)

Rahgozar, Reza, 1332-

That Which That Orphan Saw/ By Muhammad Reza Sarshar (Rahgozar). Mashhad, Behnashr Co., 1380 A.H. (Astan-e Qods-e Razavi Publications. Behnashr Co.; 377.

ISBN 964-333-686-7 (series) 964-333-686-7 (series)

ISBN 964-02-0114-6 (1 volume) 964-333-685-9 (1 volume)

Listing based on FIPA information.

Above the title: novel.

Contents: Vol. 1.      Vol. 2.

(The Prophet: From Mission to the Emigration to Ethiopia).

Muhammad, the Prophet of Islam, 53 years before the Hegira – 11 A.H. – story.

A. Behnashr Co. (Astan Qods Razavi Publications).
B. Title.
C. Title: The Prophet from Birth to Mission.
BP22/9/R86A9              297/93
[297/933]
The National Library of Iran                M 8 1 - 33221

That Which That Orphan Saw (Vol. 2)
(From Mission to the Emigration to Ethiopia)
Muhammad Reza Sarshar (Rahgozar)

2nd ed./1385 A.H.
2200 copies/Raq'i.
Print: The Astan Qods Razavi Institute of
Printing and Publications.
ISBN: (series) 964-333-686-7
(Vol. 2) 964-333-685-9
Copyright protected.
Behshahr (Astan Qods Razavi Publications)
Central Office: Mashhad, S. P. 91375/4969 tel.
8511170, 8511136-7, No. 8515560. Tehran office:
8960620, 8962301

Muhammad leaned on his right hand and lifted his body off of the sandy soil on the floor of the cave. Following those very difficult minutes he had endured, he now more or less felt some strength in his knees. Not very much. Insofar as he could, he stood on his feet and pulled—however strenuous and slowly—his slack and heavy body toward the city and his home.

He stood up. He adjusted his *redā* and *abā* on his shoulders and body and stepped out of Hirā.

The night was the same time as the night before and the sky, the stars, the narrow crescent of the moon were the same, and the mountain of Hirā and the wide southern plain at the foot of it, and Mecca were also the same. But it seemed that behind that apparent tranquility and silence, movement and clamor had begun. It seemed that things were taking place behind the curtain.

The heart of existence, after that earlier standing, beating began again. The tired old world was enlivened and had become young again. On the heels of that stillness and passing death, life began to flow in the veins of the earth. Nature, faced from that deathly stillness of shortly before, was now starting life over again. A deep breathe from the bottom of existence. Such persons with heads lifted up again from a sudden ad incomplete death. A death, and another birth from its heart. Coming out of earlier old and aged skin and the beginning of a new life.

In the sky, it was as if goings and comings had begun. Space seemed full of a sensational hum. Mountain, plain, stone, the thorn of the bush, and the dirt were whispering secretly into the ear of the soul of one another.

"Praise on you O' chosen one of God!"

Muhammad turned his head to this side and that, but he saw nothing around except familiar lifeless nature. There was that same Mount Hirā and its bare black and rough stones. Also, to the south of it, the range of low mountains all around Mecca. Then, the continuation of those mountains which from one direction faced toward Yathrib, with the valleys and simple dry plains bordering them. And from the north were behind those same mountains, until as far as the port of Jidda beside the Red Sea and until the Plain of 'Arafāt and the land of Meni and of Taif.

It was nature end to end, nestled in the bosom of night's darkness. Profound, quiet, and full of secrets, without any speaking being in it.

Muhammad, with beaten body under pressure exceeding endurance, heavy ad slack, by the course of rocky part of the mountain, headed down the road of the mountainside and plains. His strides were slow and hesitating. Every few steps, his weak knees would buckle under the weight of his body. Thus, until those surprising words that he had heard did not sit in his mind, he stopped them the melody of every step.

"Recite in the name of your Lord."

"Who….created."

"Man...."
"From a clot of blood.
"Recite...
"And your Lord
"Is the dearest...."[1]

In this manner, his heart was calmed. But in both his body and mind, he felt as if he had been beaten. His soul and body had been tried and were not prepared for this difficult and secretive connection and realization. Not him, but no one, could endure that strange transformation in his body and mind. The pressure was so much that during those moments he thought that his soul had left his body. Then, his spirit was carried toward a very superior horizon and found greatness and capacity many times more, until that time when he touched that pure spiritual world with all his being and realized the message.

Now, he could sense the residue of that agonizing and difficult condition in his body. Although the air at midnight in the fall had a subtle coolness, Muhammad's condition was feverish. His body was captive to a circle of annoying heat. A narrow stream of sweat was flowing down his bright, even forehead, had passed between his two arched eyebrows and was going toward his large nose. But that was nothing compared to that fear and anxiety that had still not stopped in his heart. That same fear and condensed agitation in the mind. If that sudden loud weeping from its pressure had not subsided, Muhammad's heart would have stopped beating.

---

1. *Koran: al-'Alaq* (The Clot of Blood), 1-3.

Did fate have a new game up its sleeve for him?

A very great bitterness had caused agitation in his mind.

Did he have the capacity to endure this severe test?

He thought about himself and his years of long and painful expectation.

Now that that wait seemed to be coming to an end, did he have the stamina to face that pure and eternal reality that had burned so much in his discovery of desire? Why was he not happy now with all his being and why did he not rejoice? Why had this much uneasiness and fear come to rest in his mind and heart?

He suddenly felt a mysterious transformation in the space around him in the midst of the mountain. Then, on the horizon before him, there where the sky became one with the earth, he saw a surprising light and ether that had covered all of the space from one end to the other.

When he looked closely, he saw that same previous heavenly being amidst that halo of light, whose presence had filled the entire extent of his sight.

Could this be during wakefulness?

He quickly turned his head to the right. Amazing! It was there too! With that same manly appearance. That wonderful beauty and that unearthly magnificence. It was as if it was standing with a thousand wings. Feet wide apart from one another, as if it had planted them on the edge of the sky. This one in the east and that in the west.

In this direction and that...it was there, with that same kind and same form!

A new fear and agitation befell Muhammad's soul.

O' lord…who is he? What does it ant of Muhammad?

Suddenly, that same heavenly and exhilarating voice filled the air and sat in the ear of M's soul.

"O' Muhammad…you are God's prophet, and I am His angel, Gabriel!"

"What?"

"O' Muhammad…you are God's prophet, and I ma His angel, Gabriel!"

"' Lord…what did he hear? Did he hear right?

"O' Muhammad…you are God's prophet, and I am His angel, Gabriel!"

No. This was not a dream! This was clearer and more real than any wakefulness!

Thus, after centuries of silence, the Creator of the world had decided to speak to his servants again? Also, from among all of his innumerable creatures, he had considered him worthy of relating His message to the people!

Ah…this was much more than what his soul had expected or could contain—at least at that moment!

No matter how much Muhammad was continually thinking about the people and their errors and ill-fate, he was however happy about his finding the way and salvation. Could he now rebound after lifting that heavy burden?

That was not an easy task! On the contrary, it was the back-breaking duty of leading all men for as long as men lived on the earth. That was not a threat to the lives of one or two persons. It was taking the reins of all men and guiding them. A task that was impossible except by ignoring himself and sacrificing all in the way of others. Migrating from himself toward God, and from Him toward his Creator. No…this was not an easy task!

Happiness and sadness. Hope and fear. Certainty as well as doubt. What was Muhammad to do with this mix of bitterness and sweetness, this duality of calm escaping the clutch after long years and the new and deep bitterness that had arisen?

The magnificent and heavenly being had gone and had left behind a newly designated prophet, with a sea of various feelings.

The Prophet, with a fever, and with repeated shivers in his shoulders from the excitement, head lowered, and innervated, stepped onto the plain beside Hirā.

Now, his condition was such that he could not endure that undisturbed stillness, silence, and solitude of nature that he looked so much before. He longed for his own home and to be comfortably beside his wife Khadija. It was as if being alone could not endure that much excitement and anxiety all at once. He should have found a sympathetic confidant earlier and conveyed some of that back-breaking load to his shoulders.

O' that this two parasang long road from Hirā to Abtah was a bit shorter! Or that there was one person from his household so he could shorten this long and endless road with him!

That night, I had put Zaynab and Roqiyyeh to bed beside me. Ali was sleeping in another room. I was under the impression that Abu al-Qāsem had stayed in the cave at Hirā. So I had put out the oil lamp and gone to sleep. An hour had not passed, however, when suddenly I started from my sleep for no reason.

I had seen, or not seen, something while asleep I did not know. A vague feeling, however, from the depth of my being, pressed in on my heart telling me my husband, from somewhere far away, was calling me to help him. I was thinking only of him.

At first, I thought that this was a result of the imaginings of the night, the darkness, and sleepiness. But when that agitation continued, I knew Abu al-Qāsem was calling me in his heart wherever he was.

First, I decided to put on my outer garment and go to Hirā, but I saw that it was not appropriate to leave my children alone at that hour of the night and suddenly go out. So I called Zayd, who was a youth, and sent him to look for his godfather. He did not find Abu al-Qāsem, however, and he returned.

When I saw it was like that, my uneasiness increased. For that reason, I decided to go look for him myself when he softly unlocked the door. Just as was Abu al-Qāsem's habit late at night and at inappropriate times.

I knew it was him.

When I opened the door for him, I saw him by the glow of the candle. He was not the same as when he had left. The normal ruddiness in his face was much faded, and his black and penetrating eyes seemed feverish. He had lost so much energy that when he entered the house, he placed his hand on the door and wall and took small, slow steps. In spite of that, the pleasant smell—more pleasant than the smell of all those perfumes that they used—was still with him, so pleasant that I had never smelled an aroma such as that before. Also, his constantly bright face had now become twice as bright.

I went to him fearfully and placed my hand under his arm, and took him by the waist. He put his arms around my shoulders and leaned on me. His body seemed to melt in the fire of fever!

We went like that to the guestroom, which was the first room in the courtyard. Now, no matter how much he leaned on me, he still dragged his feet.

In the room, once he had collapsed on the bed, I sat down beside him and took his hot hands in mine and asked, "Tell me cousin, what happened to you?"

With a voice that seemed to come from the bottom of a well, he explained what had happened.

Upon hearing that, it seemed that the world all at once became noise, such that if shame had not perverted me, and if it had not been the middle of the night, I would have trilled loud and long and filled the city with my rejoicing.

Facing Abu al-Qāsem, I said, "Do you remember, cousin, when earlier Gabriel appeared to you several times and you told me the secret, and that one day I told you that he was not the devil, but an angel?"

My husband, lifeless, nodded his head.

I said, "Abu al-Qāsem, you were always a faithful,

honest, correct man who helped the oppressed and supported right and justice. Your kind heart and admirable attitude, hospitality, your efforts in establishing relations with your relatives is always spoken of by friends and enemies. Thus, how surprising that the Creator of the worlds had selected you to be His prophet!"

This was only right, and there was more than this. From the time he was young, Abu al-Qāsem was never attached to any of these obscene and ugly deeds that were common among all of the Arab youths. In middle age as well, no one had ever seen any error or sin from him. In every moment of his life there was nothing aside from uprightness and fortitude. And it was for that reason that people were so fond of him.

Khadija placed her hand on her husband's shoulder. A furnace fire. But it seemed that earlier disturbance in his look had diminished.

Calm, cousin. Be joyful and firm! Swear to Him in whose hand is Khadija's soul, that this is the reward for all that suffering and abstinence of yours! May being God's prophet be auspicious for you, O' trustworthy one of all the city's people!

Khadija, like a mother, kindly took her husband's hand and had him stand up from the bed.

"Your fever is high Abu al-Qāsem. Come with me to the courtyard so I can pour some water on your head and face so this fever goes down."

The Prophet removed his *'aqal* and took off his *redā* and *abā*. Then he placed all of them on the bed and went with Khadija.

When they reached the end of the twisting courtyard in the darkness, the Prophet sat cross-legged on a square stone.

Khadija lifted the wooden cover from the top of the first urn along the wall and picked up the leathern ladle hanging on the wall. Then she took water from the urn with it and poured it on the head and face of her husband.

After I had poured water in Abu al-Qāsem, and we had returned to the guestroom, he, suffering, lay down on the bed and I sat down beside him. A short time later he said, "Khadija, I feel coldness inside. Throw a blanket over me."

I placed a leather pillow under his head and pulled the *abā* over him. He did not stop shivering, however.

I then brought a blanket and put it on him, but the shaking of his body was so much that the blanket began to shake.

This time, I put a carpet over the blanket until he slowly calmed down. Sometimes, however, a passing wave of shaking would hit his body so fast that the shaking of his body could be seen through the carpet.

After a while had passed, and his breathing had become calm and regular, I knew that he was asleep. So I put on the *redā* and placed the *meqna'eh*[1] over my head and went to the house of my cousin Wāraqa.

---

1. A kind of scarf or veil of cloth worn by women.

Wāraqa's house was a bit father down than ours. I knew from the light in the window of his room that shone in the street that he was awake that night.

I knocked softly on the door. My uncle's daughter—his sister—opened the door. When I entered the house, I saw Sohayb. He came out from my cousin's room. He was leaving. (This Sohayb had been brought from Syria to Mecca a long time ago as a slave, and 'Abdullah Jod'ān had bought him. But because he was a learned man and had many skills, after a short time, he had bought himself back.)

After Sohayb left, I entered the room.

"Good evening cousin!"

"And a good evening to you! Are you not Khadija the Pure?"

"Yes, Wāraqa."

"What has happened for you to leave your own house at this time of night?"

"I had a question and I did not have the patience to wait until morning for its answer."

"Ah! That is good. That's good. Knowing knows neither day nor night. Whatever you learn about it now, knowing it today is better than tomorrow. Tell me now what you to ask."

"Cousin, tell me, do you know who Gabriel is?"

Wāraqa suddenly lifted his bent and bony body off of the ground and half sitting, faced Khadija, stretched out his neck and said, "Huh? Did I hear right? Did you mention the name of Gabriel?"

"Yes, cousin. Tell me who Gabriel is."

Wāraqa prostrated himself. Then, afraid, he lifted his face from the floor and said, "What are you saying Khadija? And why in this city in which God is not worshipped do you mention Gabriel? Now, I swear to Jesus the Messiah that until you tell me whence you learned this name, I will not say a word about him to you!"

"Cousin, I will tell you, but you must promise to conceal this secret until the time of its announcement arrives."

"I will do that cousin. I will do that."

"Tonight, Gabriel appeared to Abu al-Qāsem and spoke to him."

Wāraqa's thin face suddenly opened up and so much blood flowed into it that Khadija could clearly see its instantaneous redness.

"Great God! Great God! These kind of amazing things are signs of his power and wisdom! Tell me now where he appeared to your husband."

"In the cave on Hirā."

Wāraqa's dim eyes started to move quickly in their deep-set sockets.

"Khadija, know that when Gabriel comes down in a land, there will be surprising happenings and news for that land ahead."

Wāraqa, have they written anything about him in those books you have read?"

Wāraqa, with moist eyes, said, "What are you saying Khadija? Gabriel is the great angel of God! He is the messenger and the mediator between creatures and His great prophets. It was he who came down to

Moses and Jesus—praise be on them—and inspired them.”

Electricity jumped from Khadija’s eyes from happiness.

“Cousin, they did not say anything of Muhammad in earlier books?”

Khadija, I myself read in the books of predecessors that God would designate a prophet in this land who is an orphan and He would protect him. He is a poor and humble man, and God would make him in need of nothing. He is amazed and perplexed, and God guides him. He is the last prophet and no prophet will come after him.”

Is there any mention of him apart from these you have said?”

“Yes…Yes, Khadija. The dead speak with him just as they spoke with Jesus. The stones and clods praise him. The trees give witness to his prophethood. Now Khadija, this story you told me, if it is true, know that what Gabriel said to Abu al-Qāsem was the inspiration of the Lord, and he is that same prophet.”

Khadija decided to return to her own house when Wāraqa said, “O’ joy of the women of Q! For three nights I have seen in my sleep that God has sent a messenger to Mecca. Now, among all the people of Mecca, I do not know anyone better than him who is worthy of this position.

Then Khadija bade him farewell and rose from her place.

The day with the spirit of a lion, was breathing life into the slackened skeleton of the city. The darkness gradually dissipated and lightness advanced. Blackness faded and every moment became thinner, and whiteness dominated over it.

Khadija was fast asleep beside her husband on the bed in the guestroom. The Prophet was also in a deep sleep. After that surprising event of the night before and that much excitement and going to sleep late, their sleeping late was not a surprising matter. No matter how much, they were always up by this time.

The Prophet felt a movement hi his soul when the first sparrow sat in the stone floor of the courtyard. At first, he moved heavily under the *abā*, blanket, and carpet. Then he gently raised his eye lids ad the next instant closed his eyes.

No sign of that former fever and shaking remained. However, a soreness in his body and a slight pain in his head was still there.

In the courtyard, the coolness of the last dawn of the fall days that ran from the direction of the desert under the skin of the city caressed the bodies of the sparrow to shiver. Under those thick covers, however, a pleasing warmth had embraced the slack body of the Prophet.

How much his sore body and tired mind begged for sleep! How pleasurable and sweet those moments were!

But those pleasant moments did not last long. The Prophet, tossing between sleep and wakefulness, suddenly heard several sounds resembling the rubbing of metal on metal. Then he heard another sound.

"You with the cover over your head,

"Get up!"[1]

The voice was both strange and familiar. Soft and even, like the gentle murmur of a breeze that goes among the leaves of a palm or the imaginary sound of a stream as it makes its way between small pebble stones in a quiet plain and moves on. But at its root was a fatherly sternness, with a mixture of kindness, softness, and power. Not like a human voice, but clear and transparent like bright and unveiled crystal, cutting and penetrating on the order of a tempered Syrian sword.

Muhammad blinked and stuck his head out from under the covers.

Had he heard correctly? Was this voice coming while he was awake?

In the dark and bright light shining from the windows of the room nothing could be discerned. It was her. Over there, was his faithful wife, Khadija, without covers. Her head was on her left arm, and she was fast sleep. That voice was not from anyone in this house. Not Zayd, not Maysara, and nor any of the others.

Muhammad wanted to pull the covers over his head again and sleep, when he heard that heavenly

---

1. *Koran: al-Modathther* (The Wrapped One), 1-2.

voice, this time somewhat louder, in the ear of his soul while awake.

"You with the covers over your head, get up!"

Ah! How had he forgotten? It was the voice of that same angel from the night before which had appeared to him in the cave at Hirā, and after that, on the horizon of the desert. It was the voice of Gabriel!

Muhammad, like a sinful slave who has failed in the service of his master, and who has heedlessly forgotten him, in a quick motion, raised his head from the leather pillow. He threw the cover aside and sat up. Then he very quickly turned his head all around and like someone started from sleep, brokenly said, "Okay…I am up…I am up! What should I do now?"

"Rise and frighten the people. Mention the greatness of your lord and cleanse your clothes!"

The voice seemed to echo in an empty and barren mountain area and it reverberated several times in the Prophet's mind and repeated in his soul's ear.

O' you with the covers over your head,
Rise and frighten the people,
And mention the greatness of your lord, and cleanse your clothes! O' you with the covers over your head, rise and frighten the people and mention the greatness of your lord, and cleanse your clothes! O'…!

The angel of inspiration had left without leaving any sign of itself except for that pleasant phrase with an admonishing tone that, now, unconsciously, was flowing from the mouth of the Prophet.

"O' you with the covers over your head…."

"Huh… Abu al-Qāsem …? What happened? Are you better now? Do you need anything?"

It was Khadija's tired and sleepy voice. She had awoken from her sleep with the Prophet's raising up in bed and his whispering to himself. She was afraid that the fever was causing her husband to suffer.

Contemplating, the Prophet said, "The time for sleep and my convalescence has ended Khadija!"

When he saw the signs of perplexity in the wide, bright features of Khadija, he explained what had happened to him. Then he went into the courtyard, thinking deeply.

No matter how much Muhammad had been immersed in comfort and well-being from that day he took Khadija as his wife, so much that, if he had wanted, he could have spent the rest of his life enjoying all the usual pleasures of the time. But he never gave in to the heedless life of the body. For that reason, when he thought hard now, he realized that, when confronted with that which this instant had placed on his shoulders, how easy and comfortable and free of trouble that earlier life had been, with all those tasks and efforts and tiring searches for the truth he had done.

Rise O' you, nestled in the bed of security and ease, for your time of sleep and ease has ended until your last breathe of life! Rise and cry out in the world and promise the beginning of a new era!

How good! Rising up for truth was the epitome of Muhammad's desire. He had also always remembered God's high position. However much he mentioned the correct manners of this, it was dear to him…But, what kind of people should he frighten and call to God? With whom should he start? Whom should he call so as to accept them? Would they accept what he said? Would they call him a liar? What tricks did time have in store of which he was ignorant?

"Yes, Abu al-Qāsem. I see you are thinking hard. Now this good news should make you happy!"

The Prophet recounted the disturbance in his mind. Khadija, simple and relieved, like an anxious child, said, "This should not be difficult for you."

Thus, when she saw the sign of query in her husband's eyes, she said, "I am one of the people! First among all of them, offer me your religion. Tell me now what I must do."

The clouds of grief all of the sudden seemed to be pushed to one side in the sky of Muhammad's heart. The dark shadow of sadness diminished in his eyes, and a spark of happiness began to jump in them.

How limpid, empathetic, and companionable this woman was, this wife, this assistant. What an ocean this dear one was.

At the time when Muhammad was indigent and unknown, and Khadija wealthy, well-known, and the object of the attention of all the merchants and young men of the Qureish, she caste all the age-old traditions and customs aside and stepped forward to propose to Muhammad. She then turned over all of her great wealth, without any apprehension or conditions, to him to do with it as he would. To give it to anyone he wanted and for any deed he wanted. That simple woman—say, concubine—submitted entirely to his wants. During these years, like a mother, she gave comfort to his saddened and suffering mind in her sea of mercy. Like a helper, she accompanied him on the difficult road of life. She took half of load of sorrow onto her own shoulders. When difficulties troubled his delicate mind, she sought to console him, she comforted him, and she returned that previous firmness to him.

With Khadija, Muhammad felt less often that he had no one and that he was incapable. Khadija had also brought Muhammad children, the enlighteners of his heart and the giver of warmth to the hearth of his life. Now, too, in this very difficult test, Khadija had become a witness to the correctness of the claim and acceptance of his religion.

"Yes, cousin. Tell me what I must do."

"Ah…yes. First, you must testify to the oneness of God and His high position and superiority."

"And then?"

The Prophet, with the shame that always accompanied him, and he emulated the embarrassment of adolescent maidens, said, "Testify to my prophethood."

Then he told Khadija in what manner to say those things.

Khadija, unhesitatingly, and with great desire, said, "Khadija bears witness that there is no god save the one

Creator, and Muhammad is his slave and messenger."

The Prophet saw Wāraqa while performing the circumambulation. He was also performing the pilgrimage to the Ka'ba. With a shaved bamboo cane in his right hand and placing his other hand on the covered wall of the Ka'ba, he was circling it and muttering under his breathe prayers for his needs to his lord.

When his cane struck the foot of the Messenger of God, he apologized saying, "Ah…forgive me slave of God."

With a gentle smile, the Prophet said, "May God forgive you."

Upon hearing that sweet and familiar voice, the graying pupils of Wāraqa's eyes moved quickly several times in their sockets. In that condition, he said, "Huh! Is it you Abu al-Qāsem?"

With a mixture of sincerity and respect, the Prophet said, "Yes, Wāraqa."

Good…Good. Tell me now nephew, what are you doing and where? What have you seen and heard?"

"Good and charitable things Wāraqa."

Certainly you are coming from the cave at Hirā and you came at this time of evening to circumambulate the Ka'ba. (Because those familiar knew well that Abu al-Qāsem's habit was, when he came back to Mecca from Hirā, to circumambulate the Ka'ba before anything else.)

"Yes."

"Last night your wife related some surprising stories. I would like more, however, to hear all of those adventures from you."

Then, like every seeing person, he turned his head to every side and said, "There should not be anyone except us two persons around here."

"That is how it is."

Wāraqa took the warm and masculine hands of the Prophet of God between his own cold, dry hands and they went together to a corner of the courtyard of the sanctuary, which at that time of evening was empty of any activity.

On the way, before they reached their destination with those steady and slow steps of Wāraqa, he said in jest, "Do you remember, Abu al-Qāsem, that day when you were small and with you nanny, what was her name?"

"Halima."

"Yes, with Halima, you were coming from the desert to Mecca. On the way, she had lost you, and your grandfather quickly had organized all of the people of the city to search for you. He was so afraid."

The Prophet more or less remembered that day. Too, he never forgot that the one who found him beside the road under that large thorn bush was this same Wāraqa. But what a difference between that fresh and fruitful Wāraqa with those honey-colored eyes overflowing with enthusiasm and life, and this suffering, broken old man!

They had come to the side of the porticoes. Wāraqa,

with the help of the P, sat down on a piece of rock that they had placed beside the wall of the portico like a platform. The Prophet sat down beside him and began to speak.

When I again heard the explanation of all those happenings, which I had heard earlier from Kahdijeh, from Abu al-Qāsem's mouth, no doubt remained for me that he was that last prophet and the expected one. Because, first of all, no one had ever heard any incorrect thing from Muhammad. (How could it happen that after forty years, when he lived so virtuously and upright in his actions among us, that he suddenly make such a big lie?)

The second was that all of those signs that had come in the books and stories I had read or heard from predecessors corresponded with his habits and life.

Once the Prophet had finished speaking, Wāraqa took his hand in his and, with a squeeze from excitement, said, "Muhammad, I swear to that lord in whose hand is Wāraqa's soul, that angel that came down to you last night is was that same great protector of God's secret, who earlier had come down to Moses and Jesus. What he said to you was divine inspiration. You are now the last prophet and the best of worldly beings. But you must exercise much firmness, because no man like you has come except that his people have been determined to oppose him. So you, when you reveal your prophecy and invite the people to God, they will call you a liar and cause you to suffer. Then they will run you out of Mecca and will quarrel with you."

Wāraqa sighed from the bottom of his heart and, with watery eyes, said, "If I am with you at that time when your people do that to you, God knows that I will help you every moment."

A large tear from Wāraqa's eye, which was now fixed in a stare far away, dropped on his long white beard and disappeared in it. Then with a voice tha6t seemed to come from a time far off, he added, "That which Gabriel, may his name be exalted, has said to you and will say to you from now on, is that same truth that I pursued to Syria and Jordan and spent my youth and health searching for. Those same things for which Zayd 'Amru crossed all of the Arabian Peninsula and went to Jerusalem and Mesopotamia, and finally gave his life for."

After stopping for a short moment, Wāraqa said, "O' that Zayd was here now to see the right path and the end of his long waiting. However much he was attracted to you, he passed from the world."

"Yes, chosen of God! Earlier, before you became inspired, he bore witness to your prophethood. When news of his murder came, 'Amer, the son of Rabi'a, said to me, 'One day Zayd 'Amru said to me, "Amer, I am anticipating a prophet from among the descendants of Isma'il. I fear, however, that I will not last until his time. Therefore, I have come to believe in him from right now, and I bear witness to his prophethood. Thus, if your life is long, and you see him, convey Zayd's praises to him."

'I asked Zayd, "Won't you tell me his signs?"

'He said, "I will."

'Then he said, "His height is neither short nor tall. He neither has a lot of hair nor little. He has a pleasing complexion that tends toward red. Redness is in his eyes. He also has a fur-like spot with a color tending toward black on his back between his shoulders. His name is Ahmad, and he will be born in this land.

"O' Amer, once he has clearly started his mission, do not be heedless of him, for I have traveled through all the lands looking for the religion of Abraham, and I asked Jews, Christian and fire-worshippers about him. All of them said that this religion will be after this. And they described its messenger more or less like that.'"

Khadija started from her nightly sleep with a sound and the sense of a movement. In the weak glow of the oil lamp that was burning in the mantle she saw her husband. He had risen from the bed and was facing outside to room.

Drowsy, Khadija asked, "Where are you going Abu al-Qāsem? Don't you have anything to do with me?"

The Prophet said, "It is dawn and the time for the morning prayer has come."

Khadija then remembered that last night her husband, when he returned from the mountain, had said that that day Gabriel had appeared to him again at Hirā and had commanded him to pray toward the threshold of God. Then Gabriel himself had begun to make ablutions, and he told the Messenger of God to do that too. Then, with him in front facing Jerusalem[1], he stood and prayed in a special manner, and the Prophet had prayed behind him. Again, Gabriel had said to him to conduct prayers every day five times like that.

Upon recalling that occurrence, KH quickly rose from the bed and went to the courtyard following her husband.

In the courtyard, she brought water from the large earthen jar and began to perform ablutions the way the Prophet had taught her.

---

1. *Bayt ol-moqaddas*: "The Holy House."

Although Khadija, like the other Arab women, had always risen from bed at dawn, she had never risen at this hour. When, on the horizon, a strip of grayish light was becoming apparent and the darkness of night gradually lost its color.

That, in itself, was a new experience for Khadija. Rising at that hour when all of the people were still drowned in sleep and a deep and meaningful silence had enveloped the city. A spiritual and pleasant state had been aroused in her. The world had taken on a different complexion. Life surged like waves in her smallest particles. The sky, stars, mountains, and rocks had now found spirit in her view. Being had taken on a very profound meaning. The sky was not empty. A large spirit, as large as all existence, had been breathed into the world. Countless eyes, at every time of day and night, awake and cognizant, were looking one by one at the actions of human beings, from good to bad. Stones, cods, the dirt, the plains, water, the sky, and that which was in it were not unaware with respect to man. On the contrary, like the mountain which echoed the sounds in itself, every human action, of every kind, resulted in an echo from all existence, no matter how ignorant it was of it.

How much warmth and enthusiasm for life did existence find in this way! And how much wakefulness and intelligence did it want from man!

With guidance from her husband, Khadija poured water on her hand, and with every handful of it, it was as if her heart that was being washed in a divine spring and its encrustations were being reduced. It seemed that the brightness of her eyes was increasing and her mind was being renewed.

The cool breeze of the morning, when it passed over her cheeks, was like a flow from the mercy of God that blew on her thirsty and heat-struck mind.

Who are you Khadija? What did you do that you became worthy of that the Creator of the world and the heavenly angels hold you do dear?

Khadija, upon remembering what her husband had told her last night when returning from Hirā felt an uneasiness in her mind. Following that, tears ran down on her cheeks from the sky of her eyes like a spring downpour, and they mixed with the moisture of her face.

Praise be to you O' Khadija the Pure!

This was the first time that Abu al-Qāsem, upon seeing her, had said to her the phrase, "Be happy."

Not praise from only me, but from the lord, and your superior angel, Gabriel.

Gabriel had brought down this divine message to her husband.

Thus, Khadija's white complexion had taken in a sharp redness because of shame and excitement. Astounded and confused, stuttering, hastily she had said, "Praise be to God, and praise is from Him. And praise to Gabriel the Trustworthy as well!"

The Messenger of God, and, behind him, Khadija, were facing the guesthouse, when suddenly Khadija saw a movement from the second storey of the structure on the threshold of that room where young Ali was sleeping. A shadow, it seemed, in that twilight of the dawn, had come from the room to the door and was standing facing the courtyard.

The outside of the bulky upper body of the specter in that white dishdasha left no doubt in Khadija's mind that it was Ali, the cousin of her husband.

At this time, the P's gaze was drawn to that direction. Ali came down the stairs and, sleepy, asked, "What was it that you were doing cousin?"

"I was performing ablutions."

"For what?"

"To pray to the Creator of the heaven and the earth."

So, the Prophet related the story of the descent of Gabriel and the designation of him. Moreover, he added, "You accept Islam too for God and submit your self to Him….Accept Islam so that you remain virtuous and obey God so that you are saved."

After short hesitation, Ali said, "I must ask my father. For you know, cousin, that I don't do anything without his permission."

So he went down the alley toward his father's house. At this time, the Messenger of God said to him, "Keep this secret hidden from the people, and don't tell anyone about it except my uncle."

Ali said, "I will do that."

But when he reached the door of the house, he stopped. With his head down, he thought for a while. Then he returned and said, "I will do what you said cousin. Now offer Islam to me."

Reflective, the Prophet said, "What happened Ali that you changed your mind?"

Ali said, "I thought to myself that my Creator, when he decided to create me, He did not consult with my father. So it is not necessary that I consult with anyone about accepting His religion and worshipping Him."

The Messenger of God became very happy and in his heart congratulated him. Then he said, "First, you must bear witness to the one Creator that there is no god save Him. In all of existence, He is unique and without equal. He had no offspring, and He is pure and infallible."

Ali did that.

The Prophet then said, "Now, you must testify that Muhammad is the slave of God and His messenger."

Ali did that.

Happy, the Messenger of God opened his arms and took Ali in a tight embrace and then said, "Know, Ali, that God can do what He wants. It is God who gives life and causes death; takes up and brings down. He makes one independent and reliant."

Ali said, "That is how it is."

The Prophet placed his hand on his shoulder and said, "I swear to the God of the Ka'ba, Ali that you have been directed toward truth and you have reached divine growth and success."

Then he began to perform the ablutions. Thereafter,

he taught Khadija and Ali the rituals. Also, at that moment, he said, "Ali, prayer connects the thinking of man with the God of heaven and earth. It prevents him from indecency and impurity."

After that, all three went to a room on the third floor of the building. There, the Messenger of God stood in front and Ali and Khadija stood behind him, and they began the two prostration prayer of the morning.

Of the people, the third person to go toward my husband Abu al-Qāsem was Zayd, his freed slave.

Hakim Hezām, on a trip to Syria, had brought Zayd with him along with a group of other slaves. Hakim's occupation was slave trading.

Zayd was an adolescent at that time, almost fifteen years of age. The signs of virtue ad intelligence were clearly visible in his olive-colored eyes and brown, open face.

That day when my aunt, Khadija, came to my house to see Zayd, she asked about his life. I told her that he was from the Kalb tribe, who apparently live around the Dumah al-Jandal. The Kalbis interacted and traded with the Jews and Christians, but a group of hiwaymen had attacked them. (I learned this story after buying Zayd.) Among the prisoners they got was this Zayd. Thus, they put him up for sale in the bazaar of Dumah al-Jandal. I bought him for four hundred dirhams, but on that day, when I saw my aunt ask about him, I gave him to her as a gift on her marriage to Amin.

My aunt happily accepted. After a while had passed, however, I knew that her husband had become fond of Zayd, and my aunt gave that young slave to him. Amin then freed him and accepted him as a child of the family. Thus, he was named Zayd Muhammad.

At the beginning, being away from my tribe and family was very difficult. So much so that, after the capture and enslavement, I wept openly and in private, day and night, and I was very dejected. Until I was taken to the house of my mistress Khadija. I saw so much good from her and her husband that all of that sadness seemed to vanish. For the kindness and repose I saw in that house, I had never seen before in my own tribe and family.

When our son Zayd was taken prisoner, his mother, Tha'laba, and I became crazy because of the excess of grief. It was such that I could any do any work. Thus, I sold whatever camels and goats I had, mounted a fast came, and went off to look for him. But when I reached the slave bazaar at Dumah al-Jandal, all of the merchants had left and there was not sign of them. Until, following many long years, I learned that a merchant from Mecca had bought him.

So, again, I got a few provisions and set off for Mecca this time. I slept neither night nor day, and I did not rest. I traveled constantly, so much that both I and my camel were close to dying. I traveled, mourned, and wept profusely until I reached Mecca.

Without any hesitation, I started to search for him. They directed me to Abu al-Qāsem's house. When I went there and saw Zayd, I did not recognize him at first. Zayd was now a strapping young man, well fed, living well, and raised well. It seemed he was not from a nomadic tribe, but one of the noble and great ones of the Arabs.

When Abu al-Qāsem learned that I was Zayd's father, he was very kind to me. When I was returning, I said to him, "Young man, take the price of this boy now and give him back to me."

He said, "I will not say the price. I freed him so he can do whatever he wants, either go back with you to his own people ad tribe, or, like before, stay here and be our son."

How surprising that my son would choose to stay with them.

At first, I tried very hard to take him back with me. He did not agree, however. When I saw that, I acquiesced to that, and I knew that his good fortune was right there. I then returned, happy, and I took his mother to Mecca to see him. From then on, whenever we missed Zayd, we went to Mecca to see him. Until J heard that his godfather Baraka had given him a wife. After that, they told me that Abu al-Qāsem had brought a new religion and that Zayd had accepted his religion.

From Yemen, I had trading to do with Abd al-Muttaleb's son Abbās in Mecca. Aside from giving money on interest, he sometimes also did business, mostly in perfumes.

Earlier, Abbās himself would come to Yemen to purchase perfume, but that year he had sent me a message that I bring him various kinds of perfume from Yemen.

When I reached Mecca, I did not find Abbās in

his house. I went to the sanctuary and found him there. In the sanctuary, however, before I found him, I saw a middle-aged man with a masculine body, with collyrium on his large eyes and full eyebrows had made more attractive.

The man first looked at the sky and the sun. Then he went to the Zamzam well. He went politely and removed his *abā* from his shoulders and spread in on the ground and stood mannerly on it. At that moment, a youth with big bones and brown skin, who resembled the Syrians, and a woman with a full figure, stood behind him in that same manner.

I was busy watching them and their surprising movements when Abbās came up to me. He hugged and greeted me. Then, since he knew that I was engrossed in the activity of those four persons, he said, "'Afif Kandi, do you know who that young man is?"

I said, "I do not know him."

He said, "He is Muhammad, son of 'Abdullah, my nephew."

Then he said, "And that boy? Do you recognize him?"

I said, "I do not know him."

He said, "It is another nephew of mine, Ali, the son of Bu Tāleb."

I said, "Does the leader of the Qureish know that his so has accepted this religion?"

He said, "Yes. I heard that one day he came in unexpectedly on them when they were praying like that. Then he asked Ali about what was happening. Ali said that that was the supplication in the custom of Islam, and that he believed in the one high God and His messenger, Muhammad, and that he had confirmed what he had brought. After hesitating a while, Bu Tāleb had said, 'Doubtless, he does not ask anything of you but goodness and correctness. So be with him.'"

This was a very surprising thing, that the leader of the tribe and city, who was not of the people of Mecca, it was not proper to deliberate more than that about that. Thus, I asked, "That handsome young man, who is he?"

Abbās said, "He is Zayd, Muhammad's godson, and that woman in Khadija, the wife of Muhammad."

I said, "Khadija, the daughter of Khowaylad, the famous merchant of Mecca?"

He said, "Yes, 'Afif. For some time, my nephew has been saying that the Creator of the heaven and the earth has designated him to establish this religion and that he is the messenger of God. But right now, no one in all the world believes in this religion outside of these three individuals."

That day, on seeing their humility, manners, and sincerity before their creator, the thought suddenly occurred to me that, "O' that I was the fourth person among them."

It was dusk, and in the sanctuary men were sitting in groups and talking. I was sitting in my own clan's circle. One man of my people said, "Have you never heard the story of that nomad with the idol of Sa'd, son of 'Abasa?"

For a time, I had been ill, and I had not come out of the house. For that reason, I did not know anything about that happening. He said, "The story is like this 'Abasa. A man from the desert took several of his camels and had decided to offer them as gifts to Sa'd, the idol of his tribe, and he set off for the place of that idol. When he drew near it, I don't know what happened that the camels stampeded and fled in all directions. He went after the, but the camels were scattered in the desert and he did not find any of them. After he had tired of chasing them, angry, he picked a stone from off of the ground and threw it at Sa'd and it hit its head, and he said, "Nothing good comes to you from the Creator of the world."

Then, he went after his camels again, and at that time sang,

"We came to Sa'd so he could gather us and make us one.

"But he scattered us and made us far from one another.

"Thus, we will no longer be followers of Sa'd.

"And is Sa'd other than a piece of stone,

"That has ended up in a corner of the earth,

"And does not have any good or bad?"

After reciting that story, the man smiled and remained silent. An old man among them grimaced and said, "From that day, the young son of Abd al-Muttaleb began to talk from heaven and negated all of our gods, the belief of some of the young Arabs in the idols has weakened. So it is likely that this kind of thing will occur."

At that time, Amru 'Abasa unconsciously recalled the story of Amr ol-Qays that had happened years before.

A group had killed Amr ol-Qays' father. He wanted to leave the tribe to take revenge. Members of the tribe advised him that before he tainted his hands with someone's blood, he should go to the tribe's idol and seek its view on that subject.

That is what he did, and on the way, he went to the temple of Dhu al-Khalsa. (The god of that temple was a piece of white stone.) So he caste lots with special wooden arrows, three times. Each of the three times the arrows of prevention came up.

Amr ol-Qays, angry, broke all of the arrows, beat the head and face of the idol with them, and said, "O' damned one! If your own father had killed you, would you have prevented me from taking revenge against him?"

Thus, those last words of his became a proverb and people recited it.

Suddenly, Amr had a tumult in his heart. It was as if all of the sudden he lost all of his repose and calmness.

Your life is more than half gone 'Amru! How long will you remain of two minds and in doubt? Rise 'Amru! Rise and hurry toward Muhammad's house! Is he not the most honest man and the most trustworthy of all the Qureish? Rise and listen to what he says. Perhaps there is reality therein, and it will please you!

Without a word, 'Amru pried himself from his spot and headed down the road. The men of the people were so busy with their talking that no one paid any attention to that condition of his in order to ask him about his intention.

Immersed in his own thoughts, 'Amru was going toward Abtah. When he placed the story of that nomad beside that of Amr ol-Qays, and, with what he knew about the idols in those years, he weighed them, and he realized that those weaknesses in some people's belief were not entirely inappropriate. When he thought a lot, he saw that, however much he searched to join with the people in all the traditions of worship, in the depths of his heart he never liked those stone gods, and he did not have sincere belief in them. Just as it happened that someone with his own hands came or made something with stone, clay, dates, or such like, and men worship it and petition it!

'Amru had heard words earlier from Zayd 'Amru

more or less along those lines, and those same words had added to his weakening belief in the idols. Zayd's work was only the destruction of the people's old structure of belief. He did not have any new custom to put in the place of those ruins. 'Amru, however, once he had destroyed, then built. He rejected and in its place he built new roads. Thus, hearing what he said was necessary.

Once I had entered Abu al-Qāsem's house, before he could take me to the room, I took both of his hands and said, "Amin, tell me in detail what your affair is!"

He smiled, and with that, like lightening that appears in the sky, for several moments his pearly white teeth appeared between his two lips and disappeared. Then, joyful, he took me to the guestroom of his house and showed me to a couch.

I asked, "Amin, what are you doing?"

He said, "I am one of the slaves of the Creator of the worlds, and His messenger to the other servants."

I asked, "What had God designated you to do?"

He said, "That He be praised without any partners, bloodletting be eliminated, and kinsmen be treated kindly."

I said, "Who is with you in this matter?"

He said, "A freeman, a freed slave, and a woman. (He meant Ali, the son of Bu Tāleb, Zayd, his godson, and Khadija, his wife.)

I said, "Now open you arms so I can conclude an agreement of friendship and faithfulness with you."

His arms opened. I made a contract with him in

Islam, and I considered myself the fourth Muslim.

Bu Zar. Just like all days, had left his small herd of goats and camels someplace was preparing to pray to his Creator in his own special manner.

No thing could be found for his camels and goats to eat on that barren and rock-strewn ground except for a few *moghilān* thorn bushes. Also, at that hot time of day, and with the shining of the sun on that valley gripped between the low mountains, there was no shade so he could find shelter from the deadly burning heat. In that corner of the valley where the sides of the mountains were so smooth and wall-like that it was as if a hand had cut them intentionally. Without any crevice or over hang so he could save himself in their safety from the lethal spears of the sun. But in that distant crevice in the middle of the White Mountain the herd had found a cave-like opening for itself and side by side had crouched on the ground and were resting.

Bu Zar was unconcerned with the heat and burning of the sun. No matter how much in these three years that he had washed his hands of idol worshipping, sometimes it would happen that, when he was immersed in worshipping his god, he would forget himself such that he would be unable to endure the intensity of the heat and, exhausted, he would splay on the ground until his brother, Anays, would come searching for him and find him like that and save him from death.

Bu Zar, like other days, relinquished the reins of himself to the hands of his heart and turned in the direction his heart told him and then stood in prayer.

One day, hand in hand with Bu Zar, I was going. In that situation with my fingers intertwined with his, I asked, "Tell me so I know, did you not pray during the time of the Days of Ignorance?"

He said, "Yes, 'Obaydollah."

I said, "To whom, Jonāda?"

He said, "To the Creator of the people of the world."

I said, "You prayed facing which direction?"

He said, "In which ever direction God caused me to face, son of Sāmet."

I said, "How did you find the way among heedless people who were all idol-worshippers?"

He said, "It is a long story."

So we sat in the shade of the wall and he began like this:

"You know, 'Obaydollah, that my tribe was very poor. All of their possessions were small herds of camels and goats. In a good year, with much rain, our lives more or less passed. But if the year was dry, all of those animals would die or, fearing death ourselves, we would kill them. At that time, the custom of the tribe was to gather wood from the *sal'* tree and a tree that bears quickly whose name was *'ashr* and to tie these to the tail of a cow and they took that cow up a mountain and threw it in a fire to burn. When the fire began to blaze, the cow, fearful and bellowing, would begin to flee. Then the people would consider that flaming running cow similar to lightening and those cries of the cow to resemble thunder. They believed that after that rain would pour down from the sky.

"One day, when I saw the burning of the cow in that manner, I felt very sorry for it. Thus, I thought 'What is this? What relation does rain have with it?'

"And that is what happened. That cow burned, fell down the mountain, and no rain came down."

"At that time, a crier called out among the people that every person who had a sacrifice, we will leave the next day for the temple of the tribe's idol, Manāt, to worship. Because it was several days to Yanbu'."

"I had not participated in the actions of my people for some time, and I had thought a lot about their customs. And for that reason, my belief in those idols, traditions, and forms of worship diminished greatly. However, I had not become so confident in that as to refrain from cooperating with them in those deeds."

Bu Zar, it seemed, was trying to remember something. He hesitated for a moment, and then added, "Yes, 'Obaydollah! The next day, with my brother, we each mounted a female camel and set out after the people traveling toward the location of the idol Manāt in Nakhla[1]."

"We arrived there after traveling several days, and every person offered his own sacrifice as a gift to the great idol. Also, Anays, on our behalf, placed a jug of

---

1. *Nakhla* means "a date palm tree" in Arabic.

camel's milk at the foot of Manāt.

"Once the supplication for rain and pilgrimage to the idol ended, and we began our return, I turned to face backwards and saw a dog that had turned over our jug and had begun drinking the milk.

"Anays, angry, wanted to go to the dog and run it off. I don't know what happened, however, that I prevented him from doing that and said to him, 'What need does our capable god have for the support of a weak servant? Have patience now until we see what happens.'

"The dog, however, was not satisfied with drinking the milk of the people's god. Once it had finished that, such as the habit of dogs is, it raised one of its legs up and urinated on the foot of Manat. Then, once relieved, it went about its business without any worry.

"Upon seeing that, I said to nays, 'How can that be our god when a lowly dog did such a thing to it?'

"Anays fell into thought. But I, from then on, put aside my small doubts remaining in my heart. I completely stopped worshipping the idols and began searching for the true Creator.

"After I had had that thinking for a time, I found signs in existence that guided me to Him. I realized that a world this large, complicated, and profound could not be created by the hands of man. Creation must have a creator that is greater than all existence and more powerful than all the individual creatures. It exists, although we can not see it. No matter how much we try, our thinking can not comprehend its origin and all of the aspects of its existence, for it is limitless and our understanding is quite restricted. God is so great that our small intellect can never encompass Him.

"Thus, I strove hard to purify my heart and being, and I hesitated in speech and action until my heart, bit by bit, gained enlightenment and a surprising happiness enveloped my being, whereupon the veils fell away from my heart and eyes one by one. I knew I had to use both my intellect and heart together and know them anew.

"When the people saw that, they called me an infidel and turned their backs on me. Big and small, young and old, they ridiculed me and began to reprimand me, except for my brother and mother. But I continued on my own path despite them.

"I was in that condition three years until one day at dusk, and with the tribe, I was sitting at the door of the tent very saddened. At that moment, I saw a man riding a camel who was heading to Aswa. I called out to him to come down from the camel and to rest s while in that tent.

"Once he had drunk a goblet of milk, rested a little, I asked him about what he had seen and heard n the road. He said he was returning from Mecca. He also said that in Mecca things were happening. A man there had emerged who maintained that revelations were coming to him from heaven. He had brought a new religion, and he had placed a single god in place of all the gods.

"I wanted to hear more about that man, but that traveler did not know any more about him.

"Once he had gone, I called Anays and told him the story. The next day, I saw him off to Mecca to go to that man, hear what he said and learn it well, and, upon returning, tell me point by point.

Bu Zar, with all of that patience, had become very impatient these few days! He had become so impatient and ill-tempered, like children tired of long waiting, that he could not even tolerate the talk of his mother, whom he loved very much. It was as if the extent of his patience and endurance for waiting was only to that day.

Astounded at that condition, Bu Zar sometimes thought to himself if that traveler had not come that day and brought that surprising news for him, would that intolerance and impatience have plagued him?

Ashamed of his own amazement and dizziness, he opened his arms and went toward his young brother.

"Not tired Anays?"

"Thank you brother."

I am grateful to you for protecting the honor of you brother like this and for doing as he wished.

He kindly kissed the dusty head and face of Anays and took him to the protection of the shade of the mountain that had now appeared for a while.

"Aren't you thirsty Anays?"

"No, brother, on the road I first went to the tribe. Mother gave me a container of milk. Then, since I knew you had come from the tribe with a herd, I came here."

Bu Zar placed his hand on the broad shoulder of his brother gently and staring into his clear eyes, said, "I am grateful Anays. I am very grateful! Now quickly tell me what you saw and heard."

Anays sat on a rock ad removed his kaffiyyeh from his head. Then, with the stained, old sleeve of his dishdasha, he wiped the sweat from his forehead and said, "I tried to do what you requested without the people knowing my intention.

"First, in the sanctuary, I spent time in circles of people of every clan, which were all over at sundown. Most of the talk was about that man. His name, just as the traveler had told you, is Muhammad, the son of Abdullah, the son of Abd al-Muttaleb. His father had passed away before he opened his eyes to this world. Then his mother, Amaneh, the daughter of Wahb, from the clan of the Bani Zohreh, raised him.

"In short, his mother also passed away when he was small, and his grandfather, and then his uncle, Bu Tāleb, raised him."

"Bu Tāleb, the leader of the Qureish and Mecca?"

"Yes, brother. Then he took KH, the daughter of Khowaylad, in marriage. Before he claimed prophethood, he was known among his own people for virtuosity, truthfulness, trustworthiness, and patience. So much so that they gave him the title of Amin. In this matter, both his friends and his enemies are of like mind. For no one in these forty years has ever seen anything bad or indecent in his actions or talk. It is for that reason that his people, no matter how much they consider him an infidel for his religion and do not believe his claims to prophecy, just as before, they give him things in confidence, and no one knows anyone more correct or faithful than him."

"Did you see him yourself Anays?"

"I saw him, brother, several times. At dusk and sometimes in the dawn when he came to visit the Ka'ba. He would be thinking and preoccupied, and he was immersed in deep and log silence. When he was walking, he took long strides and with each step he seemed to hesitate for a moment. He wore simple, but clean, clothes of white Egyptian cotton or striped Yemeni cloth. On top of those, he wore a thin *abā*. Otherwise, he had an Iraqi turban on his head and sandals of leather on his feet.

"When he was coming, before he would appear, one could detect his pleasant smell, which was mostly of musk. It was as if a halo of perfume constantly enveloped him."

"He was a little taller than average, but he was not tall. His head had a masculine greatness. His shoulders were broad. He had strong arms, long hands, and long fingers. The bones of his hands and feet were big, and his stomach was even with his chest.

"His face was so bright that it was as if the sun shone on it. It was so beautiful that I have never seen a man as handsome as him until this day. The color of his skin was not pale white, but neither was it brownish. It was whitish mixed with red.

"He had a broad forehead and connected eyebrows. There was a surprising penetration and effect in his wide, almond-colored eyes, such that they grabbed the on-looker and did not let him go. His cheeks were even, and his beard was black and full. But he kept his thick mustache short. He had a long nose, and his mouth was proportional to the other members of his face. His laugh was never more than a smile. He also had teeth that were white, bright, and apart from one another.

"One day, a group of men engaged him in a discussion, and the opportunity arose for me to hear him talk.

"When he spoke, he did not look at the face or eyes of the listeners, but he looked at the sky through the corner of his eye. The essence of his voice was high, and its tenor was more beautiful than that of all people. He spoke very audibly, clearly, and fluently. What he said was related to one another. When others poke, he did not interrupt their talk, and he was patient with their loquacity, except for when they began to talk nonsense."

Bu Zar, no matter how much unquenchable enthusiasm he had to hear whatever related to that newly emerged prophet, he was more desirous to know his teachings. Was that the same noble of the Qureish who must bring an end to his long and painful waiting?

"And what he said? Tell me about that Anays."

"I did not have the opportunity to hear much of his speech because those who were engaged in talking with him and hearing his answers tried to reject his words more than discovering a truth. But I heard during that and also from other people that never had any abuse been heard from him and no one had ever been seen to quarrel or argue with him. He always invited people to do good and he refrained from ugly or bad things. He now also believes that the Creator of the world is one, without a partner, and unseen. He was before all the people and creatures and He will always be after them, forever. He is the Creator of all existence. He was not born, and He did not give birth to anyone. There is no one like Him or equal to Him. He does not need His creatures. To speak with Him and request of Him needs no intermediary, for He is situated in all pure hearts.

"He forbade people from burying their daughters alive and he instructed the children to respect their father and mother and to do good to them. He also called the slave-owners to be moderate and lenient with their slaves, for the slaves, in his view, are human beings like their owners. There is no difference between white and black, rich and poor, master and slave, except in terms of righteousness, correctness, and virtuous behavior."

What did Bu Zar want other than these things? All that inner effort and energy, had it guided him to something other than this? Other than this alleviating medicine, what could cure the old pain of the mental illness of the Arabs?

The period of rest and repose and shrinking away and only being concerned with one's own affairs had passed. Bu Zar had to discontinue the worn-out loneliness and turn to the direction of this pure and boiling spring. The time for removing the dust of years of turbidity from the heart and being has come.

Bu Zar, not knowing his head from his foot, began to go.

"Where to brother?"

"To Mecca, Anays."

"But why not wait until tomorrow? Provisions for the road…?"

"Nothing, Anays. I can't bear to linger even an hour. If I don't take off right now, I will lose my repose."

Bu Zar said that and headed for his camel on the other side of the valley.

O' lord, look upon me!

Bu Zar was not one of those people who were bound to the stomachs and repose. Before he was Bu Zar, he was an Arab nomad and the Arab of the desert had an old affinity for thirst and hunger. Beyond that, in the desert, those two were twins with one another. There, there was mostly hunger, thirst, and poverty. The nature of the desert was indigent and insatiable. And sometimes if it became satiable, it did not last long—one or two months from the end of winter and a month at the beginning of spring. Or, if a tribe plundered and quarreled, it would sometimes acquire more spoils. Nothing else. There was taking care oneself and restraining one's self in eating. For that reason, there was never that little bit of daily food. Sometimes there was also becoming lost in the desert, for days, and finishing the provisions, such that the scream of the stomach and intestines from the pain of being empty rose to heaven. Then the pain became such that there was no recourse left but to deceive them. Tying a stone over the dry stomach, dry and stuck together, on the waist....

Bu Zar was also a patient child of the desert. In addition to that, during those three or four years removed from the tribe, he had so trained and built his body that the food of a small child filled him up.

But after three days of traveling and the finishing of all the meager provisions for the journey, now at the third dusk of hunger, tying a stone to the stomach accomplished nothing, and those few coins spent at the caravanserai had bee spent on his camel.

There were those things. More than that however, the unrequited source of not having seen that newly emerged prophet bothered Bu Zar. What had happened that in these three days after Bu Zar had entered Mecca and had spent all the hours of nights and days in the sanctuary that he had not come to the sanctuary even once? Had not Anays said that he usually came every day to visit the Ka'ba? Wasn't this another examination by the Creator to test again with the touchstone of experience Bu Zar's firmness on the path of his belief?

The difficulty of the task was that he had to keep his own desire hidden from the pagans so that no one knew his intention. If not, finding a man named Muhammad was not that difficult.

Bu Zar's brown and sunburned face, with that tough skin like dried leather, and that tall lean stature, and those worn-out clothes, he was wearing. It was clear from afar to any on-looker that he was a poor man from the desert. That was also a huge impediment for him to search while he was in the city, especially in the quarter of Abtah, which was the location of the wealthy and noble of Mecca.

So what was Bu Zar to do? How long could he endure this painful wandering?

O' Lord, look upon me!

Bu Zar headed toward the Zamzam well so that by drinking its water he could calm his stomach pains for a while.

It was sundown, and all around the sanctuary groups of men of the ten tribes of the Qureish were gathered and talking. Amidst the talk, above all Bu Zar could hear one name clearly, Muhammad.

Their talk seemed to be questioning: what did Muhammad maintain? What was his purpose with those words? Did he not know what insurrection and revolt those kinds of words could cause?

Bu Zar had himself heard many of those words and that caviling from the old men and leaders of the people in the tribe, which created no desire to hear them again from the mouths of those men drowning in well-being and self-praise. What was strange was that the rest of the matter and the essence of the words of both groups were of one kind. However much they depended on increasing their own knowledge and common sense, they explained those same meanings in glossier folds and a more complicated manner.

Bu Zar pulled a pail of water from the well of Zamzam. As he was pouring water into his dry water-skin, he suddenly realized all the voices and commotion had suddenly subsided. The pail in his hand, he turned his head around. Several hands had turned to the Bani Hashem gate.

Bu Zar turned his head to that side. An aged man with a special dignity and repose was coming toward the Ka'ba.

Bu Zar at first thought that that man was that same newly arisen prophet. So he wanted to quickly leave the pail and water-skin and go over there. But when he looked more closely, he knew that he had been mistaken. Although that man clearly had the signs of greatness in his face and glance, and the way the men behaved towards him showed his high position relative to them, it was very different from what Anays had described to him. First of all, the hair on the head and face of this man was completely white. Secondly, he appeared to be fatter than Muhammad.

The old dignified man was wearing simple white clothes, saying that he was not a wealthy man. But so much high naturalness and self-sufficiency emanated from his gaze that any on-looker respected him unconsciously in his heart.

Bu Zar quickly poured all the water in the pail into the water-skin and tied the mouth of the water-skin with a long leather cord. Then he threw the water-skin over his shoulder, and so as not to attract any looks to himself, went forward so as to see what that man was doing. Perhaps he could help him to attain his goal.

Yes, he had not been mistaken. The whispers and low talk of the men with each other made it clear to Bu Zar that that good-looking and attractive old man was Bu Tāleb, the uncle of Muhammad.

Upon realizing that point, a great joy raced into Bu Zar's heart. He had finally found someone who knew Muhammad and the enemies of Muhammad were apprehensive of him. Thus, his hope was that this man would take Bu Zar's tired and needy hands and guide him to Muhammad.

By the time Bu Tāleb's circumambulation and his talks with a few of the men had ended, dusk had passed and might was casting its shadow over the city.

Once the servants of the Ka'ba had begun lighting the torches and oil lamps, Bu Tāleb began to leave the sanctuary.

It was a good opportunity for Bu Zar to bring an end to that bitter and long three day wait.

"O' sir!"

Bu Tāleb had just stepped out of the Bani Hashem gate when he heard that voice. He then turned toward the voice.

In that twilight, he saw a tall, middle-aged man in ragged clothes, with a small water-skin o his shoulder. The bones of his chest were sticking out of the rent in the collar of his purple dishdasha due to his extreme thinness.

Bu Tāleb at first thought that he was a Bedouin who was stranded and wanted to ask for help. But once he looked at him, upon seeing that bright face ad those lively and penetrating eyes that seemed to emit a strange kind of fire in his depths, he clearly realized that his task must be something else.

"Yes, sir. Were you talking to me?"

"Yes, sir. I wanted you to assist me and show me to your nephew, Muhammad."

No matter how much the voice of this Bedouin appeared tired and worn-out, from its depth, the signs of steely determination and uprightness were clear.

Bu Tāleb, beset with doubt, said, "Muhammad? What is your business with him at this time of night?"

Bu Zar, helplessly and imploringly, said, "I am not an enemy, sir. My name is Jonādeh Jothdab. I am from the Ghaffār tribe. For a long time I have been searching for the truth. Until I heard that in Mecca a man had appeared and he more or less says those things which I am looking for. I gave up my livelihood and headed for this city in total confusion to see him and hear what he has to say. Thus, if I find him to be true, I will pledge myself to him and follow his way."

There was a truth and enthusiasm in the words and voice of that strange man that caused Bu Tāleb's heart to shiver in his chest. Also for that reason, without another question, he said, "Let it be so!" Now follow a ways behind me so it appears you don't know me at all. On the way, though, when I stop, you go on and pass me until you reach the house of my nephew, and I will point it out to you."

Bu Zar, with tears of joy in his eyes, said, "I am grateful to you, sir. I will do as you say."

So he took off following a few steps behind.

Bu Zar, pleased with that night he had spent with the Prophet, was going to the sanctuary. It was as if he had died and come to life again. That he was sick, and after many long years, all of the sudden, taking in a life-giving breathe into his frame, he had found his health again, entirely. A lost person alone and without support who had now found his way and had placed a very large mountain behind him. Or like a thirsty person who after days of thirst reaches the spring of life and has become satisfied.

He discovered in himself a deep feeling of deathlessness. As if, relative to death, he had become invulnerable. As if in all the world no one and no thing could harm him.

From that moment his thin dry hands were situated between those of the Messenger of God, it was as if a clear flow of water, like a wave, rushed into his body and would not go out. Then his heart became strongly warm, such that whoever saw his face earlier and saw it now would realize in a moment that this Bu Zar could not be that earlier Bu Zar. In those eyes, there was now so much light of life, happiness, and certainty, that it seemed that if he looked at a stone he would influence it and cause it to break up.

How pleased it was, passing through the lax and vain wadi of bewilderment and arriving at the firm, safe house of certainty.

Bu Zar remembered the earlier long periods of wandering. How much he had thought in his long periods of solitude! Sometimes his brain and heart had been so pressured by the intensity of effect and amazement that he wanted to beat his head against a rock repeatedly until his brain became distracted! Then he would scream from the bottom of his heart such that even the camels—with those large hearts of theirs—would be startled at seeing him in that state.

During those periods, however much he had turned away from the idols and all of the superstitions of the people, it was still as if something secret continuously pained him. It was as if he had a dear lost object that he could not find. Calm and repose would not return to him. Now, though, what else did he want that he had not already acquired?

The heart and mind of Bu Zar again went to that which he had experienced last night.

Bravo, man of god!

"May praise and the mercy of God be on you too. Relate where you are from and what you do."

"My name is Jondab and my nickname is Bu Zar, of the tribe of Ghaffār, in the land of Yanbu'. Four days journey from Mecca and three days to Yathrib. We are a poor people who live in a dry and barren land. Nothing controls us but a few habits and mean and worthless customs. The people of our tribe are mostly quick to understand and clever. But they are very naïve, and they have raw and uncultivated minds. For that reason, their sharp emotions dominate their intellects. They become overjoyed at once verse of poetry and with another become entirely angry and vengeful. In short, they are ignorant people subject to thoughts full of baseless wisdom."

"Though they apparently worship idols, religion and tradition has no firm foundation among them. They have nothing to do with the other world, hell, or heaven. They only look to the idols when they have a material want, to help them and free them from something hindering them."

"Among my people, oppressing others and attacking people is common. There is nothing indecent about it. More than that, they take pride in their oppressions and they recite poetry in praise of them. For a while, though, I have separated my self from theirs, guided by intellect and confirmation of the heart, and I have given up worshipping the idols. Then I heard a man in Mecca has emerged who travels that same path for which I have long searched. I went to him until they showed me to you. Now man of God, offer your religion to me so I know hoe it is.:

Pleased, the Prophet took him to his home. Then, he warmly welcomed him and, until part of the night had passed, he answered his endless questions. The he had said, "Jonādeh, Islam is bearing witness that God is more than the one Creator, and Muhammad is His messenger. Then institute prayer."

Without any hesitation, Bu Zar repeated those two oaths. Then he had taught him the method of ablutions and prayer.

Once he had executed the first prayer with the leadership of the Prophet, the Messenger of God had said, "Bu Zar, know that prayer is the pillar of Islam."

At dawn, at the time when he was infatuated with the greatness and attractiveness of the Prophet, and he had decided to leaver his house, the Messenger of God had said to him to keep his Islam hidden from the Meccans so he would not be bothered by them. Bu Zar, however, had said with any hesitation, "How can I keep this great inner movement hidden? I swear to that God who has motivated you to truth that I will yell my belief and aim at the top of every mountain and neighborhood, and I will not conceal my faith attachment to you from any powerful person!"

Then he had asked what his duty was. The Prophet had said to go to his own people and call them to Islam. Once the time of the summoning became clear, and Islam had gained a foothold, he was to return to Mecca.


"O' chosen of God, give me an order now to light my path.

"Bu Zar, always say the truth, no matter how detrimental you."

"What else?"

"Do not fear the abuse of the people, when on your God's path."

"And what else?"

"Have sympathy for the oppressed and be their companion."

"Go on, Messenger of God."

"Know, Bu Zar, that no one will reach the position of abstention until he calculates for himself that the partner gets t from his partner. So know that whence he eats and whence he drinks and whence he wears clothes. Is it permitted or is it forbidden?"

"He who gives no importance to how he acquires his property, God will not consider important whence He throws him into the fire."

"And too, my mother and father?"

"When they ask you something you don't know, say 'I don't know,' so you are freed from its bad result."

Bu Zar, overcome with amazement, reached the sanctuary. He felt himself so capable that he could stand before all the people of the world.

"I bear witness that there is no god save the single Creator, and Muhammad is His messenger."

A voice reached the ears of several of the persons who had come to visit their idols inn the morning and some others who were talking ort passing through the middle of the sanctuary. But it seemed by what he heard they were certain. After a short delay, they went about their business. One or two of the idol persons, however, turned their heads toward the voice.

Was that voice from this tall stranger wearing rags?

When Bu Zar saw that, he mounted the stone of sacrifice between the idols of Asāf and Naʿela. Then, facing them, who were busy circling around their own tribe's idol and rubbing it, he shouted, "People, Jonāda

Jondab of the Ghaffār tribe now testifies before you that there is no god but the single Creator and Muhammad is His messenger."

Bu Zar's loud voice, which did not correspond with his thin body, drew all the men and those few old women towards him

What is that stupid Bedouin saying?

"People, I am Bu Zar, of the Ghaffar tribe...."

"What are you saying little man?"

"O' you benighted ad lost people!"

"Beat him, because he said something insulting to our gods!"

"This mouthy infidel has to be killed to serve as a lesson to others!"

But Bu Zar's clear voice was louder than all the other voices.

"I testify that there is no god but the single Creator and I testify that Muhammad is His messenger."

Amidst that angry commotion that was intensifying every moment, a wooden shoe whistled and suddenly struck his head, and his kaffiyyeh, faded by the sun, fell to one side. Then a fist fell on his nose, and blood dripped on his clothes. And then unceasing fists, kicks, and blows rained down on his wrinkled head and body.

Bu Zar, half conscious, saw himself being pulled to one side every minute, and he heard constant shouts of abuse that were raining down right and left.

At first, there was pain, and deadly, like that of

severe blows. Numbness then came, and the pain gradually subsided.

At this moment, a shout was heard by the aggressors.

"Shame on you! What is this you are doing killing this man like this? Did you not hear him say he is of the Ghaffar tribe? Don't your trading caravans going to Syria pass by his tribe?"

Upon hearing the words of Abbās 'Abd al-Muttaleb, the angry people all at once stopped beating Bu Zar. Now, signs of fear more or less could be seen in the faces of some of them who were engaged in business. For they well knew t hat if he died by their hands, that would be the end of safety and security for the caravans of the Qureish.

Thus, two of them, giving advice, picked the half-dead Bedouin up off the ground and slowly carried him to the Zamzam well. They poured water on his head and face there and washed the blood from his body and face. Then, they poured a gulp of water down his throat until bit by bit he regained strength and came to.

Once the people had gone about their business, Bu Zar with a bitter smile n his lips, stood from his place and, hobbling and biting his lip from pain, moved toward the Ka'ba.

One day I was going down a street—and at this time nearly twenty-three years of my life had passed—when I saw my father. He said, "Where are you going Ja'far?"

I said, "My uncle, Abbās, has sent me to retrieve some money in the quarter of Abtah."

He said, "I am also going to see your cousin and brother. "

It had been a while that I had not seen them because Ali was with our cousin, Abu al-Qāsem, and I lived in the house of our uncle, Abbās. Thus, days sometimes passed and no opportunity arose to see one another. For that reason, when I saw that, I decided first to go see them with father and then go about my uncle's business.

For some time I had known that our cousin had adopted a new religion, and I was very curious to know more about that event. For that reason, one day when I saw Ali, I asked about that religion. He explained it to me. He also said that he had converted to that religion. Then laughing, he added, "One day I had gone to the valley of Bu Tāleb with our cousin to pray. Suddenly, father appeared there and saw us in that situation. Until that day, he did not know anything about that religion.

"He waited until our prayers had finished. I was very afraid in that situation because I had not told father anything about my accepting Islam.

"Deep in thought, father turned to face Abu al-Qāsem and said, 'Nephew, tell me what religion this is that you have created and what worship this is you are doing.'

"Our cousin said, 'Uncle, know that this is the religion of truth and the religion of the angels, the prophets, and our great ancestor Abraham, the Friend of God.[1] The high Lord has inspired me and sent me as a prophet to the people to call them to Islam. Now, the worthiest person to hear my wisdom and to accept my claim and to help me in this affair is you uncle.'

"Then he related to him the commands and teachings of this religion in details.

"After a long hesitation, father said, 'Let me think about this.'

"Then he added, 'Have peace of mind, though, that as long as Bu Tāleb lives and breathes, he will not fail to support you and will not let anyone harm you.'

"Then, again, he turned to me and said, 'Have you also accepted this religion Ali?'

"Fearful, I said, 'Yes, father.'

"He said, 'What kind of worship was it you were doing?'

"I said, 'It was a prayer, father, that we do for the single Creator. In this religion, doing it is incumbent on the people.'

"Father said, 'My son, no one has ever heard a lie from your cousin until now, so keep this religion, accompany your cousin, and don't be far from his

---

1. Abraham is referred to as *Khalil Allāh* [friend of God] in the Koran.

service, for he does not say anything to you but good.'

"That day, when I heard those words from my brother, I had a strong urge to go to our cousin and learn more about the new religion. But some time passed and I did not have the opportunity. Until the day that event took place."

Upon seeing those two, the Messenger of God met them joyfully and greeted them. Then Ali spread out a blanket of goat's hair in the shade and on it placed two cushions beside the wall. The Prophet showed those two to the blanket and told Baraka to bring a cool sherbet for them. At that time he said to Bu Tāleb, "While you rest and gain some repose, we will pray."

Bu Tāleb said, "So do it nephew."

The Messenger of God stood on another blanket and Ali stood behind him on the right and they began to pray.

Bu Tāleb stared at them both for a while. Then he said to Ja'far, "Get up Ja'far! Get up and be the other wing of your cousin!"

Ja'far, amazed and also happy, rose from his place and went barefoot toward those two. He then stood on the left side of the Prophet and, without knowing the manner of that worship, began to follow them.

Bu Tāleb was happily immersed in watching that scene for a while. Then he felt an agitation in his heart and slowly his lips began to move,

"In the difficulties of the time,

"Ali and Ja'far are my crutch,

"And Muhammad too,

"He is like one of my sons,
"I swear to the gods of the Ka'ba,
"That I will not let him be injured,
"Or my sons leave him alone.
"O' Ali and Ja'far!
"Always assist your cousin,
"Who, of all your uncles,
"Only his father has the same father and mother as
your father."

"Yes, 'Abd al-Ka'ba, where to?[1] I see that you are in a big hurry!"

That is what 'Uthman 'Affān thought. From the time Bu Bakr returned from the trip to Syria and had heard that talk about Amin, he had become strongly desirous of seeing him. But he did not want anyone to learn about that.

"Yes, 'Uthman, I am going to see a friend."

'Uthman came closer, said hello, and heard the answer. Then he added, "It is a long time that I have not seen you Bu Bakr. They said you were on a trip to Syria."

"Yes, I was with a trading caravan in Syria."

"You certainly brought a lot of beautiful Syrian cloth back with you."

For many years Bu Bakr's main business was in cloth and clothes. So what kind of question was this that his friend 'Uthman was asking? Especially since 'Uthman was himself a well-respected cloth seller in Mecca? Bu Bakr, with his own special insight, realized that this had to be an excuse for something else. He did not say anything, however, until his friend spoke up.

'Uthman started walking shoulder to shoulder with Bu Bakr.

"Okay, 'Abd al-Ka'ba, what is the news from Syria?

---

1. *'Abd al-Ka'ba* means "Slave (or servant) of the Ka'ba."

Before, when you returned from a trading trip, you related what you heard and saw for your friends."

What 'Uthman said was correct. Most of the Meccans interacted with Bu Bakr and did business with him. Some also came to see him about interpreting dreams or hearing him talk. Also, at times, when differences arose about knowing the ancestors or lineages among them, they would turn to him, because in Mecca he was one of those men who knew the lineages of the Arabs well, and that was considered an important skill. Bu Bakr also enjoyed interacting with the people. Since he spoke well and had a good appearance, people desired to discuss with him. Among them, however, some like 'Uthman had closer friendships and relations with him because their occupations were more or less the same, and also because 'Uthman only had tow or three years difference in age with Bu Bakr.

Bu Bakr was slightly less than fifty then.

"Where are you yourself going 'Uthman?"

"I was going to the bazaar and my shop. I am not in a hurry, however. I learned last night you had returned from the trip. I went to see you this morning, but you were not at home. I intended to see you and also to see what cloth and clothes you have brought!"

"That is good. That is good. Now that night in coming on, I will stay in my shop some other day until you come."

"That will be fine."

The two friends passed leisurely through the

sloping alleys of Mecca and were going toward the quarter of Abtah. Bu Bakr asked about their friends and what each one was doing. 'Uthman asked again about what Bu Bakr had seen and heard on his trip.

"'Odā, the son of Hātam, recently ceased worshipping the gods and turned to the Christian religion."

"Are you serious Abd al-Ka'ba?"

"Yes. That story is all over the Hejaz."

"What a surprising story! It's as if a ruckus has erupted among the Arabs! One by one, they are turning their backs on their fathers' customs."

Bu Bakr knew towards whom the allusion in 'Uthman's words was aimed. Like Bu Bakr, 'Uthman was also easy-going and eloquent. For that reason, he always spoke guardedly so no one was hurt. There was a difference between Bu Bakr and 'Uthman, however. When he saw fit, he openly said what was in his heart and believed, however gently. Especially when he saw that his listener was a man like 'Uthman who never insisted much on any talk and did not take on a grudge.

"It has been a long time that in Syria, Yemen, Iran, and other lands no one worships idols. In Yathrib and around it there are many people who practice Jewish customs."

Accepting, 'Uthman nodded his head. Thus, it was clear that his mind was busy with something else.

"And Hātam's son" What happened to him to quit his fathers' religion?"

"Good evening!"

There was a bent old man standing beside the wall and greeting all of the passersby in the hope of receiving a small coin.

"And a good evening to you!"

Bu Bakr placed a copper coin in his palm and they started to move on.

"It is a long story 'Uthman. In short, one day 'Oda decided to sacrifice a camel and was heading toward the place of worship of his tribe's idol, Falas. (I had seen this temple and idol during a trip. The idol of Falas resembled a human, a black man. It was amidst a mountain.)

The tribe of Tayy has a strong belief in that idol, so much that they take many sacrifices and presents and make vows to it. Falas' position relative to them is such that once criminal has taken refuge with it, he is safe, and no one has the right to bother him."

"Yes, that day when 'Oda reached the temple, a camel belonging to a man—his name was Malek, the son of Kolthum Shamji—escaped from the herd and came toward Falas' temple. Thus, Malek mounted his horse and went after it. He found the camel with Sayfi, the caretaker of the temple. He wanted to take back his camel, but Sayfi said, 'The camel belongs to your god Falas.'

"Malek did not accept that and asked for his camel again.

"Sayfi answered him saying, 'Malek, with you break the agreement with Falas?'

"Angry, Malek drew his sword from his scabbard and attacked him. Terrified, Sayfi turned the camel over to him. So, facing Falas, he sang for a moment,

"'O' god of ours,

"'Today, Malek, the son of Kolthum, attacked you with a bare sword and broke the agreement of service to you and my honor.

"'Even though earlier I was dearly liked by my people.'

"Then he cursed Malek a lot.

"Upon seeing that event, 'Oda, amazed, said to those around, 'Look and see what Falas will do to him!'

"After some time had passed and nothing happened to Malek, Hatam's son's belief in the gods weakened, and he stopped worshipping the idols and turned to the Christian religion."

O hearing that story, 'Uthman thought for a while and did not say anything. Then, with his head down, he moved his head in contemplation and said, "What can I say And al-Ka'ba? It seems the way of the world has changed. 'Oda is the greatest man of his people and he is famous among all of the Arabs.

Thus, it is likely that this will have repercussions."

Bu Zar said, "Yes! That is what I was thinking too!"

Thus, tired from that long conversation and determined that he not inform 'Uthman of his intention, he smiled and said, "Tomorrow in the morning I will be looking for you."

Then he said farewell and at the bend of a street disappeared from 'Uthman's eyesight.

When he neared Muhammad's house, he quickly looked in every direction. The street was empty of people.

Agilely, Bu Bakr hit the iron knocker against the door. The voice if a youth said, "Who are you?"

It was the voice of Zayd.

"I am not a stranger."

"Come inside."

Bu Bakr entered the house. He passed through the wide foyer behind the door and reached the large courtyard of the house.

Zayd came to greet him.

"Is Abu al-Qāsem here?"

"Yes, he is."

Zayd took Bu Bakr to the guestroom.

After several minutes, Bu Bakr heard steps. Abu al-Qāsem then entered the room.

Bu Bakr rose from his place and greeted him. Abu al-Qāsem answered him and welcomed him.

They then sat down beside one another on the couch and Zayd brought them a container of thick raisins from Taif.

The Prophet wanted to ask about Bu Bakr, his children, and his business in Syria, but when he looked at his white boney face, he saw haste and anxiety in his eyes that was inconsistent with that experienced nature and the resoluteness that was always in it. For that reason, so speaking would be easier for him, and so as not to have him wait more on him, he said softly, "Be calm Bu Bakr. Do you have something for me to do?"

"Yes, Abu al-Qāsem. I came to you so you could tell me about that religion you brought."

The Messenger of God spoke in detail about what had happened to him—about Gabriel coming down from heaven and those words he said to him—and how Islam came and its instructions. Meanwhile, Bu Bakr sometimes asked questions and the Prophet answered them.

Once the Messenger of God had finished, Bu Bakr took his right hand in his two hands and said, "You were right Amin, that no one has heard anything but the truth from you. Now I too testify that there is no god save the single Creator and I testify that you are His messenger."

"Yes, Khāled, I have heard talk about you."

A bit confused, Khāled said, "What talk father?"

Sa'id twisted the short stick in his hand, fixed his sparkling eyes on his young child, and angrily said, "What talk? Don't you know about them?"

That is how his interaction with the Prophet had not remained hidden from the idolaters, and they had relayed that news to his father.

Khāled had no fear for himself, because there was no doubt anyone now for him that that religion Muhammad had brought was true. However, he also knew how much animosity his father had for Islam. That which had made him anxious was that before the time had come, this event had been revealed.

When Sa'id saw his son's silence, he added, "Is it correct what they are saying about you? Have you become an unbeliever in your father's religion and converted to the religion of the young man of 'Abd al-Muttaleb?"

Again, Khāled did not say anything, for he knew that any word from him would make the spark of his father's anger even hotter, and then it was not clear what would happen, especially with that thick stick that was in Sa'id's hand. The house being empty of his mother and sister left no doubt for Khāled what ideas his father had in mind.

Sa'id let his thick, heavy body down on the wooden

platform beside the wall and said, "Okay, if you relate to me what happened, I will forgive your sin. Now, sit down beside me and relate to me in detail what this man says and what happened that you were attracted to him."

He wanted to use a moderate tone of voice so as to make his son certain about what was saying. But Khāled knew his father's character well, and that this promise was only empty. Thus, the affair had gone far beyond hiding something to be efficacious. So he thought to himself that since it had come this far, it was better that the benefit from this opportunity and that story he had to relate. It should affect his father's heart and free him from the error of his ways.

"Will you allow me father to finish what I have to say and then do with me what you will?"

"I promise."

"Yes, father, I have converted to Islam for a while.

"I knew about that. Tell me now what happened for you to do that without my permission."

"Earlier, before Amin brought this new religion, I had a very surprising dream."

"A dream? What dream? Why didn't you tell me about it?"

"One night I dreamed that darkness had enveloped Mecca end to end, such that the mountains and plains around it could not be seen. Suddenly, a light with the brightness of one lamp began to come from the well of Zamzam, and the higher it went, the bigger and brighter it became. Then once it had gone to the sky, first I saw the Ka'ba in its rays. Until that brightness became so great that no mountain or plain remained except for what I saw. That light went still higher in the sky and then, on another side, it began to descend.. Until there in its rays the date groves of Yathrib appeared before me. So bright that the unripe dates could be clearly seen on the branches of the palms. At this time, from amidst that shining, I heard a voice that said, "The Creator of the worlds is pure! The Creator of the world is pure! The word of God had been completed. Ahriman[1] the evil one has been enchained, and good fortune has looked upon these people. The Prophet for teaching those who have not learned has come, and that which was written by the pen of fate became apparent."

"Good! Good!"

"When I related this dream to Wāraqa Nowfel, he thought about it for a while. Then he said, 'This is a surprising dream! I think that this is a sign of a coming event among the children of 'Abd al-Muttaleb, because that light you mentioned issued from Zamzam.'"

"And when 'Abd al-Muttaleb's young man claimed to speak with heaven, you thought that was the interpretation of your dream! Then you hurried toward him and submitted to what he said! Is it not so?"

"No father."

"So how was it? What happened for it to come to this where you go astray like this?"

"Forgive me father. My intention is not to be impudent toward you. But since you said it, I must tell it."

---

1. In Zoroastrian theology, the deity Ahriman is associated with darkness and evil, while Ahura Mazda is associated with light and goodness.

"Relate it! Don't be afraid! You probably had other dreams like that. No?"

"Yes, father. A month ago I had another surprising dream."

"Okay. Okay."

"I saw in a dream that there was an expanse of five before me. The fire sent up tongues of flame to the sky ad made all of that which was around it ashes. Suddenly, you came, and you have determined to throw me into the flames. All of the sudden, I saw Amin, who appeared before us and placed his hand on my collar and saved me from that calamity."

Sa'id sarcastically said, "Most certainly, you ate something heavy that night."

Then his voice took on a friendly tone and he said, "Son, you never thought so crudely before. What person have you seen who, following the dream, quit the old religion of his fathers and became an unbeliever?"

With his head lowered, Khāled said, "These dreams caused me to think very deeply. But I was not satisfied with them."

"Ah!"

"I asked about his teachings and talk from those persons who had been attached to Amin, and I found all of them to be in accordance with intellect."

"Intellect? Which intellect? Your own weak and inexpressive intellect?"

Khāled did not say anything.

"Okay, tell your father some about those eloquent teachings and words so he does not remain deprived.

What world did you see? Perhaps it will have an effect on my hard heart too and after a lifetime, I will recognize anew the path out of the well!"

Without any concern for his father's sarcasm and allusions, Khāled said, "The command is only from the one Creator, that deity whose ability has no limit. He was neither born nor begotten. He has always been and He will always be. He has no equal. He is greater than anything we can imagine. For that reason, He can not be restricted by a place like the Ka'ba and larger than that. At every moment, He is everywhere. And for that reason, speaking with Him and wanting something from Him needs no intermediary like the gods."

"The Creator of the worlds has no form. There is no body. He is one. In that respect, it is proper that He be worshipped."

"In other words, our gods are all invalid! Woe to you my son! You have chosen to follow someone who has become an unbeliever in the religion of your fathers!"

"Yes! I am a follower of that which he has said!"

"This instruction that Muhammad has brought does nothing but cause separation between wife, husband, father, and children, and brothers. His teachings have caused such in the hearts of base people that they are opposed to noble people. The slave is equal to his master, and this kind of nonsense will not lead to anything except misfortune for the people and agitation in their affairs."

"He does not speak for himself father."

"These words smell like infidelity and insurrection,

and I will not allow these words to be spoken in my house. Now this night I will give you the opportunity to return from this path. If you do not, I will do with you what the uncle of 'Uthman 'Affān did with him."

Was this father's animosity toward the new religion really that profound that he would put shackles and chains on his hands and feet and torture him?

"I thought about this a lot father. Muhammad's words are in agreement with the intellect and the heart."

Angry, Khāled said, "You have done a stupid thing! Your actions have now reached the point where you oppose me!"

"Amin wants nothing but good for the people."

Sa'id's face turned blue from anger. Then, suddenly, like wild rue falling on a fire,[1] he jumped from his spot and attacked his child.

"Now you are giving me advice, you misled infidel?"

Then there were blows from the stick that rained down on Khāled's head and face.

Sa'id was foaming at the mouth and beating. It was as if he had become crazy. Was this short and small-framed youth not the same Khāled who was his joy and whom until yesterday he had loved so much? He beat without any concern, with profound vengeance. It seemed he wanted to kill him. He was beating hard, beating and shouting abuses.

Before Khāled could move, he was pinned under

---

1. In many eastern societies, including that of Iran, wild rue or *esfand* is sprinkled over a fire or coals and its smoke is believed to have certain beneficial qualities, including that of driving away the evil eye. When it touches the heat, the seeds oftentimes jump into the air.

the heavy blows of his father. It was only possible for him to protect his head and face from the injuries of the stick with his two hands. Subsequently, several blows hit his head and face, and after that, blood covered all of his young face. Then his eyes went blank and he fell to the ground. For a while, he did not hear or feel anything.

Sa'id, seeing his son like that, became frightened and stopped beating him.

Then he threw the stick to one side and lowered his weary body onto the couch.

After a while, Khāled slowly came to, lifted his beaten and injured body up off of the ground, gathered what reservoir of strength he had in his legs and limped toward the street.

In that condition, from behind, he heard the voice of his father saying, "There is no place anymore for you in my house!"

Khāled said in his heart, "The day has arrived for the servants of the Creator, not for people like you father."

Thus, he walked down the street and went toward the house of the Messenger of God.

A long time passed and no revelation came to Abu al-Qāsem. At first, he did not think much about that, because he well knew what time a revelation had to come to him. But when some more time passed like that, he became saddened and began to contemplate.

In order to rid him of that sadness, I said to him, "Abu al-Qāsem. Perhaps this halt to the revelations is because those earlier sufferings and sacrifices that sometimes occurred for that state will intensify! Or your desire for that will increase and you will be better prepared to receive the revelation!

A while later, my husband waited patiently in the hopes that perhaps some wisdom from the Creator would come, and he revealed no impatience. It was clear, however, that that time was very difficult for him, so difficult that it seemed it was the most unpleasant period of his life.

I, who was like a son to the Messenger of God in his house and with him, saw that he, like a candle, burned without a sound, melted, and his body continuously shrunk. That former enthusiasm and happiness that had appeared in him after the coming down of the first revelation had completely left his being. That brilliance of desire, life, and hope had left his eyes and in its stead a heavy shadow of vexing sadness had settled until Khadija, I, and Ali feared that this grief would kill the Messenger of God.

It was Abu al-Qāsem's habit at night, when all of the people were asleep and Mecca had become drowned in silence and calm, to go atop the roof of the house or to a corner of the courtyard, sit alone, and busy himself with prayer and supplication with the Creator. This situation, however, from the view of Umm Jamil, the wife of Abu Lahab, whose house was one or two houses down from ours, had not remained hidden, because she was one of those women who was always interfering in the affairs of others in order to learn more about other's lives. Then one day, my husband fell ill and his sickness became so serious that he could not stay awake several nights.

The next day, when he went to the sanctuary, on the way, Umm Jamil stopped him and said to him, "Heh, Muhammad, it seems your devil has abandoned you and has left you to yourself!"

Upon hearing that, a certain sadness came down over the Prophet's face. I wanted to say something in response to her, but Abu al-Qāsem signaled me to be silent with his hand, and he himself did not say anything.

In Mecca, this news circulated. The idolaters again were gladdened. When the Messenger of God passed by some place, they quietly said to one another, "Muhammad's god has abandoned him, and he does not send anyone else to him."

The Prophet, depressed, was facing toward Hirā and was deep in thought.

What had happened that that he could not find that earlier brightness in his mind ad thought? Why had that first enthusiasm and activity in his being turned to silence? Why had this bitter and depressing emptiness rested in his soul and stayed the night?

Had the lord forsaken him and left him alone? But for what reason? Had he committed some sin or error which he did not know about?

Earlier, one day, when his gloom had been much because of this situation, he headed for the mountain and plain and on the height of Mount Tabir he moaned and lamented. After he had passed some time in that way, Gabriel suddenly appeared to him and said, "Muhammad, you are really the Messenger of the Creator of the world." But no other revelation came. He was left again, in a dead and silent world empty of every kind of enthusiasm and hope.

In this black period, he burned in a fire of enthusiasm and vacillated between fear and hope. Day to day, he added to the hours of thinking and supplication to his lord.

With the recalling of that which had happened to him during this period laden with sadness, the Prophet's heart became pressured by bitterness, grief, and pain, and his mouth became poisonous, so much so that, unconsciously, his voice rose to the sky in a moan.

His anticipation lasted a long time and his longing had reached its end. On the other hand, the insurrection and sarcasm of the enemies angered his heart very much.

More that that, no tolerance for patience remained now for the Prophet. So much so that, death seemed very sweet to him opposed to that great disillusionment and heavy loneliness. O' that he had left the world and not been left to himself, abandoned! Or that they at least had told him what the reason for this abandonment was!

The Prophet sat on a rock on the slope of Mount Tabir, and, restless, leaned his body against a rock ad began to weep bitterly. The dam of self-restraint burst and a flood of tears, with loud and uncontrolled sobbing, flowed down his face.

Suddenly, however, before his weeping could go on, he felt a movement in his being. Then, he discovered a calmness inside his body. His body became heavy, and then all of those conditions that had appeared in him earlier when inspiration came to him.

The end of the long days of waiting....The manipulation of the special messenger of God, Gabriel.

"In the name of God, the Merciful, the Compassionate."

"Swear to the beginning of the day,

"And swear to the night, when it becomes calm and withdrawn,

"That your Lord has not forsaken you and is not angry with you. Certainly the other world is better than this world for you. Also, be quick so your God forgives you and you become glad.

"Did He not find you an orphan and protect you?

"Did He not find you lost and wandering and show

you the way?
    "Did He not find you poor and make you rich?
    "Thus, do not you bother the orphan,
    "And do not run the oppressed from you.
    "And always speak the blessings of your Lord."[1]

---

1. *Koran, al-Dohā* (The Glorious Morning Light), 1-11.

Finally, dawn broke, and the long evening of Sohayb connected to the day. Sohayb, tired from the sleeplessness and anxious thoughts of the night, decided to get up to go to Muhammad and hear his words from his own mouth again. Thus, he quickly got out of bed and went to the courtyard of the house. There, he washed his face and head with water from a small jug. Then he stepped into the street and set out for Safā.

In these three years that Muhammad's voice could be heard in Mecca, and talk of his was everywhere and in every gathering, Sohayb had more or less heard all of those remarks. Among them was that Muhammad believed that the Creator of the world was other than one of these stone gods that the people worship. He was everywhere. For that reason, He could neither be seen nor felt.

Sohayb found these words t correspond with reason, because from the beginning he was not very attached t the idols and idol-worshiping with that he remembered from the customs of the Zoroastrians and the days of his childhood in Obbola and Mosul and also what he had seen of the religion of the Byzantines during the time of his youth and slavery in Rum, the customs of worshipping idols were very surprising in his view and appeared feeble. But at that time, when he was Abdullah Jod'ān's slave, the opportunity did not arise for him to penetrate those matters. When Abdullah freed him, he became so engrossed in business, work, and increasing his wealth that he was completely heedless of those thoughts. Now, however, on the threshold of his fiftieth year of life and immersed in well-being, he found himself tired of life, such that after all that life and effort, his spirit hungered for death.

Truly, what had happened that he, with all that knowledge and experience with life and the world, of which most of the Meccans were jealous, had become so immersed in heedlessness and daily activities? It was there years that a man named Muhammad with that high position among the Qureish had caused an uproar in the city and spoke of a new caution, and Sohayb had not gone to him once, and had not become attracted to his talk? In those years, nearly forty persons—most of them were less in terms of knowledge, experience, and age that Sohayb—turned to him and had verified the corrections of his head in the crib of sleeping, eating, and low and petty thoughts. Until that time that—several days before— that affairs came up for Muhammad's followers.

It was late afternoon and I had returned to Mecca from Taif with several of my companions. When we drew close to Mecca, suddenly, from one of the many ravines that surrounded the city, a clamor of voices arose.

We turned the heads of the camels in that direction and quickly headed for that ravine. There, we saw several Meccans who had attacked a group of Muhammad's followers, and blood was flowing from the hand of one of the idol-worshippers.

We quickly dismounted from our camels and went among them ad separated them from one another. When we asked about the incident, Muhammad's followers told us, "It was time for our worship and we had come to this ravine for our prayer, when suddenly this group—we did not know from which direction— appeared. They considered our religion to be base and wanted to prevent us from carrying out our prayers. So, trouble started and we attacked one another."

The other groups said the same thing. They said that amidst the quarrel, Sa'd Waqqās picked up the jaw bone of a camel from off the ground and with it broke the head of one of them.

This Sa'd was one of the bravest and most noble men of Mecca. But he was rough and impatient man. Too, he was, through Ameneh, the mother of Muhammad, a relative of his. Thus, when this event took place, the followers of Muhammad became fearful and sought refuge in the house of Zayd Arqam, who was situated on the slope of the small mountain of Safā. Thus, they carried out their prayers there and worshipped their lord.


Safā had emerged after the large and small buildings and could be seen. Despite the fact that the alley was empty of passersby in those first hours of the day, Sohayb stood still for a while and looked behind him.

Surprisingly, though, in that grayish weather, he saw an apparition which, on seeing him, stopped coming and backed against a wall.

Sohayb's heart began to last faster. Was that man tall? Was he one of the informants of the Qureish? Perhaps he was going around the house of Zayd Arqam in order to inform him of the comings and goings of people to it!

Sohayb wanted to go back or take a detour and go from a different direction. But he thought to himself that no matter what, this news would not stay covered. Because he was too well-known for that man, if he was an informant, not to recognize him. So he gathered up his nerve and quickly went toward that specter.

"Hey, who re you?"

"Is it you Sohayb?"

"Yes. And who are you? And what are you doing following me?"

"I...I am 'Ammār. 'Ammār Yāser. I was not following you Sohayb."

"Then why did you hide?"

"I came this way on some business that...."

'Ammār, after a moment, seemed to overcome his vacillation and added, "I didn't want anyone to know about my destination."

Happy at this honesty, he said, "Perhaps we are both going to one destination."

Then, without allowing any opportunity to think, he said to 'Ammār, "Are you going to Safā as well?"

"Yes."

"To the house of Zayd Arqam?"

"Yes, Sohayb."

"So there is no need for anymore delay. Let's go before someone else shows up."

Then they both set off.

Along the way, Sohayb asked, "What happened, 'Ammār, that you want to see Amin?"

A sweet smile lit up 'Ammār's tan-colored face. Then, as if a happy thought had passed through his mind, his sheepish eyes stand at an indistinct point. In the distance and he said, "You know Sohayb that I am five years older than Abu al-Qāsem. The first time I met him was when we both were youths. At that time I saw so many noble acts by him that I became enamored of him. Then, in youth, when Amin was the caravan leader of the Qureish on the trip to Syria, I was with him. At that time, I was still the slave of Abu Hodhayba, and he had not faced me. On that trip, I saw so many surprising things from him that I was sure that this Amin was very different from all the other people, both Arabs and others. I always watched his way of life until I knew that I had not erred. For I noticed that among the Qureish and in all of Mecca, no one could match his ability. Then, one day, I heard that Wāraqa Nowfel had said to someone, "So-and-so, know that the sky is pregnant with a secret."

Then, after some time had passed, and the matter of Amin speaking from heaven came up, I heard again that Wāraqa had said, "…and the child will be the bearer of that secret."

"Therefore, Sohayb, I had less fear earlier, now,

after these three years, with what I have heard from the teachings of Muhammad, I am now certain that he is telling the truth with his claim. I have come now to join with him and save myself from the fire of hell."

Sohayb, deep in thought for a while, walked in step with 'Ammār and didn't say anything. When he first learned of 'Ammār's decision, he thought that 'Ammār for that reason had been attracted to Muhammad because Amin considered all people, from the freedmen to the slaves, equal. In Amin's words, men, like the teeth of a comb, are the same before God. In the presence of the lord, the powerful and weak, the high and the low, the master and servant, there is no difference between them. If there was superiority, it was inn abstinence, actions, and speech.

At the start, Sohayb believed that 'Ammār Yāser, although he had not been a slave for a while, nonetheless, since his mother, Somayyeh, just as before, was a slave of the family of Bani Makhzum, his turning to Amin could thus be for that reason. Upon hearing that from 'Ammār, however, he knew that his attraction to this new tradition had more profundity than these events, and it was far from any personal motive or greed.

They had arrived at Zayd Arqam's house. The sun was now descending behind the mountain of children on the east side of Mecca.

Sohayb stopped first to look around. 'Ammār hurried toward the large door of the house and the banging of the iron knocker rang our.

"Who are you?"

"An acquaintance...I am 'Ammār Yāser, together with Sohayb."

"Sohayb the Roman?"[1]

"Yes, Sohayb the son of Sinān."

"What is your business?"

Impatient, 'Ammār said, "To hear Amin talk and ….."

His words had still not finished when the door cracked open and that same voice said, "Come inside."


We saw there a group of people, including Ali, Ja'far, Bu Tāleb, Zayd, 'Amru 'Abasa, Bu Bakr Abi Qohafa, 'Uthman 'Affān, Zobayr 'Awwām, Khāled Sa'id, 'Abd or-Rahmān, 'Awf, Sa'd Waqqās, Talha 'Obaydollah, Khabhad Arat, Sa'id Zayd, Arqam Arqam, and 'Abdullah Mas'ud. All of them were men of good name, and they were sitting in a circle around the jewel, Amin.

Amin, on seeing us, stood up with a happy face.

Once we had sat in the circle too, he told Abdullah Mas'ud to continue reciting his Koran.

That is what Abdullah did, and we two listened. He read very well. What he read, like a goblet of cool water that is poured down a parched throat in a dry desert, flowed in my thirsty mind. How sweet and delicious it was, that life-giving water! Why had I deprived myself of it until that day?

Upon hearing each verse, it was as if an invisible chain was unloosened from the foot of my soul. Then my spirit became light and slowly rose upwards. At

---

1. "Roman" is a translation "Rum," indicating that he was originally from one of the regions of the Byzantine Empire.

that moment, my view of the world all of the sudden transformed. It seemed as if that burnt rocky ground suddenly began to turn green all over. The green gardens of Taif and Syria, it seemed, suddenly embraced it on every side. Melodious and small birds faced towards it from every place and sat on every branch and their heavenly songs filled every space. New leaves and blossoms of every color grew on every brittle and narrow branch of every tree, and emitted the most pleasant fragrances in the world into the air. In the meantime, I saw myself like a dear one who is lost and then found again after a long time. I wept profusely. Not from sadness or grief, but from the abundance of enthusiasm. What witchcraft was hidden in those words and in that kind of recitation! It was not clear to me. I suddenly came to myself, however, and saw that for Sohayb, like me, tears were streaming down the width of his round face, and tears were dripping from his black and white hairs of his face onto his expensive *redā*. Then I saw him take Amin's right hand between his hands and from the bottom of his heart testifying to the oneness of the Creator of the world and the prophethood of Muhammad. After him, I did that.

Until night that day, I was with 'Ammār in the house of Arqam. The Messenger of God spoke to us about Islam and his friends taught us how to pray. Abdullah Mas'ud taught us several chapters of the Koran.

In the middle of the day, after performing the

noonday prayer and eating a simple meal, a few persons rested in a room of that large house.

I was fast asleep when suddenly I was awakened by some commotion. The sound came from a room on the other side of the courtyard. Several of the men, happy, were saying, "God is great!"

At first, I thought that it might also be one of the customs of Islam, but when I went over there, I knew that new verses had come to the Messenger of God. After three years, God had now told his envoy to make the claim public and call all of the people to Islam.

"Make apparent that for which you were sent, and turn your face away from the idolaters.

"We will protect you from those who ridicule,

"Those who believe in other gods along with the one Creator, thus be quick so they know.

"And we know well that you are vexed by their words.

"So remember to praise your Creator and be one of those who prostrates.

"And worship your lord until the moment of you death arrives."[1]


Ali caste his final glance on the large guestroom of his uncle's house which he himself had remodeled. From large Arabian carpets with thick geometrical designs of camels, deserts, and palm trees and in sharp and singular colors of black, yellow and green, and wide margins in red, clean, were spread out on the floor of the room. The five double doors of wood of the room

---

1. *Koran: al-Hijr* (The Rocky Path), 94-9.

were open, and the gentle evening breeze was playing with the curtains, which were pulled to one side. All around the room, small cushions of sheep skin filled with wool and in a beautiful arrangement were leaned against the wall. Opposite every two cushions was a clay cup of Taif raisins or roasted wheat. That the wife of his uncle, Hāres, himself had given to Ali. On both the left and the right side of the room, two torches were ready in their places on the wall. And on the upper shelf beside them two fruits were situated.

The atmosphere was darkening and bit by bit the time for the coming of the guests neared. In the heart of the adolescent Ali, moment to moment, the feeling of happiness and fear were replacing one another. Happiness from the great amount of work, all of whose execution the Prophet had entrusted to him and which Ali had now carried out, and the fear of finishing the work.

It was one or two earlier when the Prophet had summoned him and said, "Ali, God has commanded me to warn the relatives close to me and to call them to Islam. With the history I have with them, that affair was difficult for me because I thought that if I do that, they will find a good manner and method for that task, I remained quiet for a while until today when Gabriel again came to me and said, 'Deliver that which you have been commanded and turn your back on the idolaters.'"

Thus he recited the verses that had come to him on that subject.

"Frighten your close relatives.

"And with each one of the believers who follows you bring down the wing of humility.

"Thus, if they are recalcitrant to you, say, 'I am disgusted with that you are doing.

"And trust in God, the Victorious and Compassionate.

"He who sees you, when you rise.

"And sees your prayers with the other prayers.

"Surely He is the Hearing, the Knowing.

Then he ordered, "Ali, roast the thigh of a sheep and prepare a goblet of yoghurt drink.[1] Then, invite all of the relatives for supper, so I can speak with them."

Ali said, "I will do that cousin, but whither should I invite them?"

The Prophet, after some hesitation, said, "Some of them may avoid coming to my house. And your father's house is not large enough to accommodate all of them. But I think for the others that the house of our older uncle Hāres will suffice because no one had any problem with him so as to avoid going to his house."

Ali said, "Okay cousin."

Then, he wanted to ask about the reason for the small amount of food he had asked for, but shame prevented him from asking. Also, since he knew the Prophet did not do anything without a reason, he certainly had a purpose in doing that.

With the sound of talk that arose from the direction of the doors of the house, Ali came out of the guestroom. It was his strong uncle, Hamza. Moore

---

1. Text: *dugh*: a drink comprised of mixture of yoghurt, water, and salt.

or less the same age as his uncle, Abu al-Qāsem, with that medium height and thick body and long locks and thick neck that had made him noticeable among the men of the tribe and Mecca.

Those two, at the foot of the mud stairs of the guestroom, met each other face to face. Ali wished his uncle a good evening, and Hamza, with a friendly pat on the shoulder, answered him.

Had this strong man of pure heart and few words, whose thoughts and actions were only of exercise, hunting, and wrestling, accept the claim of the Messenger of God?

It was unlikely, because although he did not have most of the view of the other men of the Qureish, nonetheless, in thought and belief, he was not much different from them. Except that with all his amazing dignity and great strength, and besides that rough manner, he had a transparent, bright and spotless heart. Also, he liked his nephew Muhammad, who was also his milk brother, because, besides being his nephew and brother, Muhammad was also his playmate in childhood and adolescence. Hamza, like Muhammad, had lost his father in childhood, and with the death of ‘Abd al-Muttaleb both had suffered not having a father. And also asking that period it had made a strong connection between them.

When Ali stopped into the courtyard, he saw the Prophet, who had just arrived. He was wearing clothes entirely white with an *abā* the color of a yellow camel, and a green turban was wrapped around his head. He seemed in a bit of a hurry, as if he feared he was late.

Before Ali had the opportunity to welcome him, the Prophet said hello and asked how things were going. Ali said that all those things he had said had been done. The Prophet gently squeezed Ali's right shoulder in thanks. Then he went to the guestroom.

Ali stood beside the large door of the house. The other invitees arrived one by one to a few at a time and entered the house. Ali wished them a pleasant evening and directed them toward the guestroom.

The first of them was his father, Bu Tāleb. Upon seeing his slightly sunken shoulders and broken figure, Ali's heart contracted.

Then there was his oldest uncle, the head of their family, Hāres, who was not al home and had come. He was now close to eighty years old, an old and stooped man who had nothing to do with anyone and preferred that no one have anything to do with him. He was withdrawn into himself and went straight ahead. It seemed he was passing the last months of his life. Thus, it was quite unlikely that he would put aside his rooted old belief now and accept the worship of the single lord.

Then there was Zobayr, who came, with his usual freshness, good thoughts, and joking nature. Although he did not have a very firm belief in the idols, there was not much hope he would be attracted to Islam, because he was the kind of man who was not attracted to any kind of belief, did not bother with those kinds of things. He was infatuated with desire, wine, and love-sickness, and a man of action, easy-going, and without any patience or thought of tomorrow.

His other uncles, 'Abbās also came, with those same expensive and fancy clothes and that gait mixed with his pride. There was no hope of him coming to Islam either, because 'Abbās was the keeper of the Ka'ba's covering, and his position and greatness was dependent in the existence of the idols. Too, a large part of his tremendous wealth had come from taking interest. Now, this custom the Prophet had brought had considered idol-worship and the taking of interest to be incorrect.

The evening had become dark and the men of the family had more or less all come. Ali thought he would go to the guestroom when, in that twilight, a shape appeared at the turn of the dirt alley. It was heavy-set and fat. Ali knew from that loose coming and dragging of the feet on the ground and the sound of the irregular beating of his cane in the ground of the alley an wheezing of his breath that it had to be his uncle Bu Tāleb, the great merchant of Mecca whose marriage with the wealthy sister of Bu Sufiān had doubled his power. Straightforward in manner without any concealment or complication, but as the instrument of his selfish, vengeful, and egotistical wife, very quick to anger and foul-mouthed, always frowning and with sparks of anger coming from his eyes. So red in the face that it seemed a furnace burned there. Thus, they called him Bu Lahab.[1] What he did not have was thought and thinking. Religion, tradition, and the idols were so dear to him that a large part of his business depended on them.

---

1. i.e. "father" or "possessor of the flame."

On seeing him, and before he could be hurt by that bitter and biting tongue, Ali slipped inside the house and went to where the guests were.

In the guestroom, two torches burned on the two walls on both sides of the room, and all the men of the family—save Bu Lahab—had gathered, two by two to in groups, talking and listening, with laughing and joking. Their commotion and noise filled the room. The Prophet, however, as was the custom for the host, was sitting beside the door.

On seeing Ali, he quietly said, "Now bring the food."

Ali quickly went to that corner of the courtyard where two large stone ovens stood. The foods had been prepared some time earlier, but so as not to get cold, Ali placed them on the ovens and in the ovens a fire had kept the, warm.

At this time, Zayd came and with Ali's request began to carry the containers.

Ali picked up a round large tray from among the vessels. He poured the pot of cooked bulgur wheat onto a tray with a copper ladle. He pulled the roasted sheep's thigh of the skewer and placed in on the wheat and took the tray of food to the room.

By the time he reached the guestroom, Zayd had spread out the large white cotton cloth on the floor of the room and had set the clay glazed azure and brown plates at the four corners of his cloth. The Prophet took the tray from him and placed it in the middle of the cloth.

The guests, surprised at seeing that tray of food, at

first looked at each other and then at Abu al-Qāsem, because it was quite clear that that much food was only enough for two or three of them, because there were those among them who could eat a whole roasted goat at one sitting.

When the Prophet saw that, he went up, mentioned the name of God, and gave each one of them a plate of bulgur wheat. But a lot of couscous was till left on the tray. The he pulled apart the thigh of the sheep and gave each one of them a large piece of the roasted meat and still not of the thigh was on the tray.

Upon seeing that, all—save the Prophet and Ali— unbelieving, began to eat. Only BL, as always, began to mock.

"I swear to the gods that this friend of yours had done sorcery!"

The Prophet sighed deeply so as to suppress his anger at this inappropriate accusation of his uncle. He looked at the front and back of his right hand and said nothing.

Hāres, who was sitting at the head of the assembly, asked for water. With a sign of the Messenger of God, Ali went out of the room and brought a goblet of yoghurt-water that had been made ahead of time from the other side of the ovens. The goblet went from hand to hand until it rested in the tired and shaking hands of Hāres. Hāres drank from it until satisfied, but, surprisingly, the goblet of *dugh*[1] did not seem to have become less!

On seeing that, the others also took the goblet from

---

1. A drink consisting of yoghurt mixed with water.

one another one by one and drank. Again, however, a lot of *dugh* was left in the container. Although there were persons among them who could drink all of the *dugh* in the goblet in one sitting.

At this time, the Prophet began top speak and looking at Bu Lahab he said, "You saw how this little amount of food and drink of yours filled all of you even though witchcraft does not satisfy you."

The men, some in their hearts and some with their heads, confirmed the correctness of his words. Bu Lahab refrained from answering.

Ali and Zayd came in again and with alacrity picked up the plates and cloth.

Now it was time for the Prophet to make his main point. Again, however, that former fear came into his heart. There were men from the highest and most noble Arab families, such that a poet had said of them, "When God wants to bring a state into existence, He creates such persons for that. These are the seeds of God, not the seeds of men." Thus, the acceptance or rejection of his invitation by them could have great meaning for other Arab clans. If they rejected him, his work with the other tribes would be very hard, because those tribes looked to the Quriesh and the sons of Hāshem and what they did so they could do the same.

So as not to allow that fear to advance, the Prophet stood up and with an attractive voice started to speak.

"First, I give thanks to the great Creator, who is worthy of praise. I seek aide from Him and confirm that there is not lord but Him. He is one and has no partner.

"My relatives, know that I want good for you, and I have only good thoughts about you.

"I swear to God that I am His prophet who has been chosen for you and all mankind. I swear that you will die the same way you sleep, and you will awoken the same way you got up from sleep, and you will be held accountable.

"For sure, heaven exists, hell exists, and they are eternal.

"Children of Abd al-Muttaleb, Gabriel came down from God and told to me to invite my close relatives to their lord and make them fear disobedience toward Him.

"I swear to God that I do not know of a chivalrous man among the Arabs who has brought something better for his people than what I have brought for you."

Bu Tāleb interrupted the Prophet and sarcastically said, "We very much desire and are impatient to receive that same gift nephew!"

Without answering him, the Prophet added, "I have brought good fortune into this world and the next for you. I will say two phrases that are easy to say, but hard to do. By saying these two phrases, you will be saved from hell and enter heaven."

Bu Lahab, with that same tone, said, "Won't you tell us those two magical phrases nephew?"

Without showing his discomfort, the Prophet said, "Confirm that there is no creator save the one Creator and I am his messenger."

Then, before Bu Lahab could say another snide remark, he added, "Now, which one of you will help me in this affair so he can be my brother's successor, and representative among you after me?"

He stopped speaking after saying those phrases and looked at his relatives. There was virtue and truth in what he said that affected the hardest of hearts, but among them only the voice of Bu Lahab arose, and the rest, as if struck by lightening, were glued to their places.

"You consider yourself the chosen of God and you seek assistance from us?"

Had the Prophet himself earlier not thought that they are not persons to accept the customs of God? Nevertheless, he had begun his difficult work, so he had to carry on to the end.

Not even one person from among them answered the Prophet's invitation. When I saw that, I, who was younger and smaller than any of them, stepped forward and said, "Messenger of God, if some of them speak, I will come to you and help you."

Bu Lahab sarcastically said, "That's enough from you little boy! Go ahead with your work with him!"

The Prophet placed his hand on my shoulder and said, "Sit down."

Then he repeated his invitation again, and again no one responded.

I stood up again and said, "I am ready to support you, Messenger of God!"

He said, "Sit down."

Then, for a third time, he repeated his invitation. Again, no one responded, even with a simple word. So I, for a third time, stood up and repeated my previous words.

The Prophet this time placed his hand on my neck and said, "This is my brother, successor, and representative among you. Listen to what he says and accept it."

The relatives laughed, and Bu Lahab said to my father, "Did you hear brother? Your nephew has ordered you to listen to your son and to follow him! Congratulations for your son's leadership!"

Depressed, the Prophet did not move and said nothing.

Then a commotion erupted and one after another they stood up, until, with that, Bu Tāleb, sympathetic, said to the Prophet, "You have delivered the message of your lord my son, and we have heard it. Now let us look at it."

Bu Lahab, however, on hearing that, raised his voice. "Sons of 'Abd al-Muttaleb, be quick before this relative of you with his affair gives you a lot of trouble. Listen to my advice and get away from him before others. Distance yourself from him, for on that day, both in this affair will be your loss, because if you help him, you will be killed. And if you let him go, you will become lowly to do what they want with him."

In response to him, Bu Tāleb began to speak with his quivering voice so that all could hear, and he said, "O' shame of the family, I swear to the god of the

Ka'ba that we are prepared to help him, and we will help him to the end."

Then he said to the Prophet, "Nephew, whenever you decide to call persons to your god, let us know so we can take up arms and accompany you."

They then left the room one by one and headed for their own houses.

After all of them had left, the Prophet headed for Abtah with Ali's hand in his. They had still not gone far down the street when he heard a voice.

"Nephew, wait a minute!"

The Prophet and Ali turned around. It was their middle-aged uncle 'Obaydollah Hāres.

"Get up! Get up! Get up!"

The dawn had just broken, the sun was just coming up over the eastern horizon, and the people were slowly becoming busy with a new day, when suddenly, this admonishing cry arose. Then, in that innervating silence of dawn, the voice traveled through that rocky valley and hit the mountains in every direction and echoed several times.

"Get up….Get up….Get up…."

Have hiwaymen attacked the city? It was not unlikely, because their custom was that when they wanted to conduct a large raid, they would attack people at this time of day.

Yes! Most certainly it is raiders! Because this phrase in this loud of a voice at this time of the morning could have no other meaning.

"Get up! You sleepy head immersed in heedlessness for the enemy is very near!"

This was not an easy phrase to put aside and give it no value. So the people, curious, fearful, or some curious and terrified, most, pale in the face, dropped what ever they were doing and turned their heads in every direction looking for the direction of the voice.

The cry came from Safā, a high place on the mountain of Bu Qobays looking out over Mecca and the Ka'ba. That same place where the idol Mojāver or-

Rih[1] was. A loud and clear voice with a high quality, which with each wave was accompanied by a measure of purity, correctness, and fatherly kindness.

But whose voice was it? What person had gone atop that height, feeling sorry for the people, thinking to warn them of the great and close danger at this time of the morning and with such deep fear, wake the up and warned them?

Now, however, there was not time to linger. Time was short. And…perhaps it was too late.

"O' families of Ghāleb, get up! "O' families of Lo'ay, get up! O' families of Morreh, get up! O' families of Kelāb, get up! Get up all of you Qureish!"

Aha! The voice was that of son of Abdullah! The most honest and virtuous man in the city. He who was the most famous and trustworthy person in Mecca.

"It is Amin! Hurry!"

Those who were awake quickly woke those who were asleep. Those sitting stood up. Those standing started to walk. Those walking began to run. Of all fo the Q—the Bani Mohāreb, Bani Hāres, Bani Taym Adram, Bani 'Adi, Bani Sahm, Bani Jomah, Bani Taym Morrah, Bani Makhzum, and the Bani Hāshem— each one heard this voice and quickly took action.

From one end to the other, the city all of the sudden became full of activity. The people, like ants on whose den water had suddenly been poured, poured out of the open mouths of the rooms and houses. The stream of people—men, women, large, small, young and old—flowed into the streets until those streams

---

1. "Near the wind."

came together at the bazaar between the sanctuary and Safā. Thereafter, there was a river of people that headed toward Safā and the place where Amin was standing, hurrying, roaring, and loud.

An old man, with a cane and breathing heavily was passing with difficulty over the steep hillside, all of the rocks, of Bu Qobays. A young man, his grandson, was caring for and helping him so that he was not hurt by the people. A young, dark woman who had a child in her arms hanging on her flaccid breast, unaware of the gaze of passersby, was going along quickly with them. In that same situation, with the other hand, she was pulling along her own small and ill-clad daughter. Some, the man, woman, and children of a family, as a group, were all together. Also, slaves, masters, the lowly and the noble, were all mixed together. It was as if all ay once all of those feelings of superiority and divisions had disappeared.

In Safā was Amin, standing atop the highest point on a rock. Around him were several of his followers, Abdullah Mas'ud, Zayd Arqam, Sohayb, Sinān, Sa'id Zaid, Sa'd Waqqās, the young Ali Tāleb, and Zayd Hāreseh.

It seemed there was no raid, because this pleasant expression on the face of Amin and his followers showed no sign of it. So what had happened that the grandson of 'Abd al-Muttaleb had called them there? What was his reason for that surprising action?

The people had no doubt at all that Amin of the people was not a liar or that he was not doing some senseless thing. What was that great matter, however, that had caused him to do that?

The Meccans had gathered just as the Prophet had expected them to do. So those who were nearer—and most of them were women, children, youths, and poor people—sat down on the flat rock of Safā. Those who were father back, however—and most of them were the elderly, great, wealthy, and famous among the people—sat down on pieces of stone or leaned against rocks or remained standing. All eyes were staring at the Prophet. Some were obviously curious and waiting anxiously, and a group, with completely burning curiosity in their souls, with a touch of pride in their looks, trying to cover up their inner inclinations. But now there was nothing but a little in them of those fears and anxieties. In the looks of Muhammad's followers, however, an unearthly apprehension was pulsing.

Once Amin Hoshām and Bu Lahab arrived, a voice from among those gathered said, "Now you and all the clans of Qureish are here! Say what has happened Muhammad!"

The voice so familiar that the speaker was well-known to the listeners. It was Bu Sufiān, the most famous of the merchants of Mecca, the wealthiest of them, very much desirous of leadership of the Qureish. He was leaning his short frame against a high stone slab, and with his hand on his waist, he was standing at the edge of the people.

The Prophet, who seemed to be waiting for that question, and with a voice that easily reached all of those assembled, began to speak.

"People, what was I like until now among you?"

What was this that Amin was asking? Had the people seen or heard anyone better than him?

A woman whom Muhammad did not recognize said, "You were the most honest, the most virtuous, and the most beneficent of the people."

Then, from all sides, voices arose to confirm what she had said,

"Now, if I inform you that behind this mountain a large army is preparing to attack you, would you believe me?"

"We would believe you, son of Abdullah."

"Yes, we have never heard anything incorrect from you."

"We have seen wrongs from ourselves, but not from Abu al-Qāsem."

"You and I are like what happened to that watchman who at dawn saw an enemy army far away that was attacking. So, thinking that the enemy would arrive before him, he went to his own tribe and there yelled out, 'People, get up and save yourselves from danger and death.'"

Perplexity became visible in the faces, but that bewilderment did not last long.

"Now people, I am warning you of a danger larger than that. O' family of Ghāleb. O' family of Lo'ayy. O' family of Mazzeh. O' family of Kelab. O' all of the Qureish, I am warning you of a very severe and difficult punishment. Your enemy is the incorrect beliefs and customs of yours. Arise in yourself and save your own soul from those."

"What are you saying Muhammad? Why are you speaking so obliquely?"

"People, know that the caravan guide never lies to them. I swear to God that if all the people turn away from righteousness, I will not speak dishonestly to you. And if all of them decide to lead you into incorrectness and annihilation, I will not do that."

After a short hesitation, the Prophet added, "People, it is true that I was sent by your lord and I am His messenger to you and all men. That same lord who possesses heaven and earth. There is no creator save Him."

"God had chosen me to prevent you from disobeying Him and to call you to the right path. Thus, I warn you a painful punishment and invite you to salvation and virtue.

"People, worship the single and incomparable Creator, and give up these idols that neither benefit you nor harm you, nor create, nor give sustenance, nor bring to life, nor cause death.

"I do not want any payment or recompense from you except that you say, 'There is no god save the single Creator.' Then follow me so you are rescued from the fire of hell and divine punishment."

"I swear to the gods that you have bought tremendous lowliness to us nephew! May you and this religion you have brought be damned and all of those things you have asked us to do! Death to you. What was this gibberish to hear which you dragged the people at this time of day like this?"

It was the voice of Bu Lahab, who, having seen Bu

Tāleb far off, interrupted the speech of his nephew. Bu Lahab shouted toward the people, "It appears that this man has lost hi senses. So go home and do not give him any thought."

After him could be heard the voices of 'Ās Wā'el and 'Amru Heshām.

"What is this you are saying, you who cut off the young peoples' talk?"

"You are pouring water in a sieve Muhammad."

Then Bu Sufiān and Shayba Rabi'a and some others of the leaders of the Qureish spoke out against what the Messenger of God had said. Then the commotion became so much that no one could hear what the Prophet said.

First, Bu Lahab, and after him the other leaders of the people and then a group of people turned away from the Prophet and began to go back.

The Messenger of God, sad, was descending from that rock when suddenly a piece of rock, roaring, streaked across the sky and landed on his shining forehead. Zayd saw that Bu Lahab had thrown that stone.

Before the Prophet could regain his composure, another rock hit his arm. And after that one, other stones rained down on his head and body.

At this time, Abdullah Mas'ud and the other Moslems who were scattered around the Prophet, quickly ran forward and, like a circle, placed their heads and bodies to shield him until they could get out of the place.

"That day when Bu Lahab, 'Amru, and others threw stones did not let us clearly understand what Amin was saying.

Omayya rubbed the back of his hand on the front of that idol with the colored clothes beside which he was sitting and said in answer to Walid Moghayera, "His claim was that heaven is speaking to him and that he has been assigned to bring a new religion. A group has also in secret joined him and they pray to the superior God."

'Amru Heshām adjusted himself on the reed mat on which he sat and angrily said, "I hope that if some have joined his religion, I will beat their heads like those of snakes. And too, if I see Muhammad come inside the sanctuary and prostrate to any besides Hobal, I will hit his head so hard with a rock that his followers will take heed."

"All of you know of the ill-feeling I have for Muhammad and it is not less than the enmity any of you have for him. But 'Amru, you yourself know that it is three years that he is preaching like this. Until now when he did it openly. We are afraid that what he is doing will divide the people and bring about problems. The solution to his actions, however, is not what you think it is."

Annoyed, 'Amru said, "So what is the solution Omayya? Should what has come to us from him until today not be a lesson for us? All of you saw how in the beginning when he began to preach, we laughed at him derisively and totally ignored what he said. Until a few persons joined him and began to follow his religion. Also, yesterday, you saw how he became so bold as to speak to all of the people and to warn them of the fires of hell. Now, you, who are one of the leaders of your family, are speaking like that. Do you not think that if things keep going like this, tomorrow we will lose control of all affairs and something will happen that should not?

"My opinion is that as long as Min has this incomparable position among the Qureish, his work can not be prevented like this. You know very well that equality can not be attained for his position among the people. Until today, except for this preaching he has started to do, you have not seen any improper action from him. He is that same person who at the time of placing the black stone everyone accepted his judgment and that great conflict came to a resolution with him and his correct thinking. Our children like him, and the indigent, orphans, widows, and slaves support him with their hearts and souls."

Walid Moghayera interrupted him and said, "We are well aware of what you have said and more than that. But tell us now what your opinion is on this subject and what you are thinking about it."

"I think that this religion of which Muhammad thinks he is its prophet will not find many followers among the Qureish."

'Amru Heshām, in his own particular tone, which

was tinged with pride and sarcasm, said, "When did you start thinking like that Omayya?"

"From the time this religion appeared very difficult."

Omayya, when he saw the signs of confusion in the faces of 'Amru and Walid, added, "Amin is not doing anything but following the tradition of 'Abd al-Muttaleb. The style of some of these families is to think differently about the world, the traditions of religion and worship and to follow a different path. On this path, you seek your own peace of mind and they prefer difficulties for themselves. First of all, Amin prays five times a day. Another is he does not charge interest, and in all affairs he treats slaves leniently, as if they are equal to him. He does not drink wine, does not gamble, and he does not consider those pastimes we have as appropriate for him. Or during the hajj, we Qureish and the people of Mecca do not go outside the precincts of the sanctuary and to which the other tribes go. But Amin does all of those things, at a time when others do not have the ability to accept that much hardship in religion. And earlier, was not there Zayd 'Amru and Warāqa Nawfel and Abdullah Jahsh and 'Uthmān Howayreth who said these sorts of things? And Muhammad is one like them! I understand that for several days a number of youths and a few of the poor people are following him. Soon, however, they will turn away from him and return to the religion of their fathers. Also, think about this, that your quarrel with him may become the cause for the Hāshem family's suffering and division may appear within the tribe."

'Amru wanted to say something in answer to Omayya when suddenly a voice arose from the direction of the Ka'ba.

"Know, people, that there is no lord save the single Creator, and I am his messenger to you."

That phrase was repeated three times.

The voice was that of Amin, bright, clear, without fault, carrying. He was standing on top of the rock of Ismail facing those circumambulating the Ka'ba and with his hands opened towards them and in a loud cry he was saying those words. Then all the persons who were circling the Ka'ba and the people who were visiting the idols at dusk or passing the evening with friends in the sanctuary, began to go towards him. Some, like 'Amru Heshām, angry, and another group out of surprise and curiosity.

Once they had gathered around Muhammad, his voice rang out again.

"People, follow me so you have an Arab leader and people who are not Arab submit to you and become c commanders in heaven too."

A surprised old man asked, "Who is this man?"

'Amru Heshām said, "He is deluded a man who has become prisoner to his own alluring visions."

Omayya said, "He is the son of Abdullah who has recently become mad and who clothes his nonsensical thoughts in the attire of rhythm and rhyme."

'Amru Heshām suddenly split the crowd of people and went forward, screamed in Muhammad's face, "What kind of insurrection is this you have started and what tricks are you pulling? Do you think that one god is better than three hundred or more? What use to us is that god that can not be seen or touched and can not be seen by anyone but you?"

The Prophet, softly, yet firmly, said, "Amru, if you have suffered harm, a problem has come up, or your wealth is in danger from whom do you seek assistance?"

'Amru did not answer that clever response from the Prophet. But a youth from amidst those assembled stretched his hands out to heaven and said, "From the most high God, Abu al-Qāsem!"

And that is the way it was, because most of them, even though they worshipped the idols, they believed that those were their mediums with the Great Creator. For that reason, the Prophet had asked that question of 'Amru, and 'Amru had refused to answer.

The Prophet said, "So, since the God of the heavens answers your cries and helps you, why do you create partners for Him?"

The matter was becoming knotty and difficult. At this point, the thick deep voice of Walid Moghayera rang out, "Muhammad, since I am the senior man in Mecca and 'Omayr Thaqafi is the senior man of the people of Taif, and, with all that wealth and possessions, the angels did not come down to us and did not make us prophets, but they came down to you, the orphan of Bu Tāleb, who did not give you much in the way of possessions? Is that possible?"

That is the way it was. Walid was one of the famous wise men of Mecca, such that some called him the wise man of the Arabs. He was an old man whom the people asked to judge in their matters.

Earlier, however, before the Prophet opened his mouth to answer Walid, voices of insult, sarcasm, and rejection arose from every side.

"If you are honest in your invitation, why do you not walk on water son of Abdullah?"

"Are you not that same orphan who was raised at the table of your grandfather and uncle and who was raised above others by the wealth of your wife? What has happened now that you speak from heaven?"

"Did God not have anyone else like you to choose as His prophet?"

"...."

The Prophet wanted to answer their questions, but the uproar had become so much that even if he yelled, his voce would not go beyond himself. On the other hand, their antagonistic questions and criticisms were very familiar to him. They were more or less the same words that earlier peoples had said to their prophets, and God, in some way, had given them an answer. It seemed the ignorant and blind of heart of every people, in every age, were more or less the same, and those among them who looked for excuses were the same. Thus, if they were given answers a thousand times, they would never be satisfied because they did not have ears for hearing or intelligence for evaluating or thinking, or hearts for learning a lesson. In addition to those things, it was very clear that their questions were not from ambiguity or to search for a realization of the answer and to lessen their ignorance. On the contrary, all of it was seeking excuses and intended to reject and deny. In any case, whatever it was, it was not a search for the truth or inclination toward knowing so that the Prophet could answer it. True, these were of that group of people who did not know and did not want to know. They were not sleepers who could be awakened, but blind-hearted people who had put themselves to sleep. What person could awaken sleepers such as them?

The Prophet, so as to rein in his anger, looked at the back of his hand for a while. It seemed then that he was not seeing any of those benighted people. A path opened up for him amidst them and he went to the Ka'ba to circumambulate it. So he listened to the waves of confusion and their sarcastic talk, which were their farewell to him.

"Okay, Walid. What was the outcome of your business with the son of Abdullah? The way I see it, you went away light and came back heavy. Do not tell me you were bewitched by his talk too!"

The month of the hajj was near and with the coming of all the people from the Arab Peninsula to Mecca it was not unlikely that Amin would go among them and invite them to his religion. So with all those surprising new things and new method in explanation and other incomparable special ties of witchcraft that are in the words of his Koran and had no precedent in the language of the Arabs. How many of a group of the people became infuriated and were attracted to him. For that reason, so that they could think of a solution for this action of his as soon as possible, that day in the late afternoon they had gathered in the large house of Walid Moghayera, because he was their superior in intelligence, cleverness, perspicacity, and experience. They wanted Walid to go to Amin and listen closely to what he says in order to determine what they could relate those words to that had amazed them and had surprised them very much.

That is what Walid did. It was very clear, however, that he did not come back the way he had left.

Walid adjusted his heavy body on his own special cushion and said, "The affairs of 'Abd al-Muttaleb's son is as we thought."

Sarcastically 'Amru Heshām said, "What's the story uncle?"

Walid leaned his thick body against the cushion filled with camel hair, his deep-set eyes stared at an invisible point far off, and said, "I went to him and said, 'Muhammad, Recite your poem for me."

He said firmly, "Walid, what I say to the people is not a poem. It is the word of God, Who had also sent former prophets." Then he said some more very amazing things like that to me.

"'Amru, of all the intelligent men of the Arabs, in elegance, measured words, management, and correct views, you are well-known to them. What is this you are telling me now?"

It was not Walid's habit when speaking to answer the raw and undigested question of ignorant men. He was one of the handful of eloquent speakers in the Hejaz. Many of the Arab poets recited verses for him, and every poem he approved of was considered selected. What had happened now whereby someone like 'Amru spoke to him like this about this subject? And for that reason, with obvious annoyance in his face from that hasty judgment of his nephew, thoughtfully, he lowered his head, and said nothing. When Shayba Rabi'a saw that, he asked, "Can you relate to us some parts of what he told you?"

In a low voice, Walid said, "I can."

Then he began to recite.

"Hā, mim."[1]

"A book that had come from that forgiving

---

1. These are two letter of the Arabic alphabet. Letters precede several of the chapters in the Koran.

and compassionate One. An Arabic Koran for the knowing. It is both good news and cautioning. Most of them, however, have turned away from it and do not hear its words."

They said, "Our hearts are closed to that you call us, and we are hard of hearing, and there is a curtain between you and us. Thus, you go about your business and we will go about our business.

"Say, 'I am a human being like you. I have received inspiration that your god us a simple god. So turn to Him and ask forgiveness from Him. And woe be the idolaters!

"Those who do not give *zakāt*[1] and have no faith in the other world.

"For those who have faith and do commendable acts those is endless reward.

"Say: 'Will you disbelieve in He who made the world in two days and for whom you raise up partners? He is the Lord of the worlds!

"He created mountains on the earth, and he gave it abundant blessings, and He created all the creatures in one day out of four days. All alike for all those who want.

"Then, He started on the sky, and it was full of smoke. Then He said to the sky and the earth, 'Come, whether you want to or not.'

They said, 'Obeying, we have come.'

"Then He caused the seven heavens to appear in two days, and He inspired the work of each heaven by it.

---

1. The alms that Moslems give to the poor and needy. It is one of the five pillars of Islam.

"And He embellished the heaven of Farvardin with lights, and We were pleased by it. This was the work of Him, the Victorious, the Knowing.

"Thus, if they turned their faces away, say, 'We warn you of that same lightening that struck 'Ād and Thamud.

"Truly, these words had no equal or precedence in the Arabic language. It poured forth from the power of explanation and demonstration. A kind of spiritual epic and poetic feeling and special steadfastness were mixed together, special spiritual music reverberated from one end to the other of it and brought unadulterated happiness to the heart. Thus, it had a surprising effect on satisfying the listeners."

Omayya Khalaf said thoughtfully, "Yes, Muhammad's sharp weapon is his speech. They say that he calls each part of these words a verse, and has given a striking name to each one: 'The Opening,' 'The People,' 'The Daybreak,' 'Purity of Faith,' 'Succor,' 'The Disbelievers,' 'Small Kindnesses,' 'The Qureish,' 'The Elephant,' 'The Traducer,' 'The Declining Day,' 'Rivalry in Worldly Increase,' 'The Calamity,' 'The Coursers,' 'The Earthquake,' 'The Clot,'…and names such as those. His followers write these verses on lamb's skin or deer, a polished rocks, or wide and thick stems of date palms so they endure. Many of them have memorized them, and recite them every day and in every place with a loud voice and pleasing cadence, such that when other people hear them, they are very effected and listen to them."

Walid said, "That is how it is. I heard that in every

meeting one or two persons with good voices recite the chapters or parts of one chapter, and some who have more knowledge than others speak about them."

"Yes, uncle. It seems that of those of them with the best voices, one of them is Abdullah Mas'ud, that man with the small body, who yesterday desired to let others hear his beautiful voice. But what happened to him."

"That strife they said yesterday happened in the sanctuary was because of his reciting the Koran, Bu Hakam!"

"Yes, uncle. The religion of the son of Abdullah had so emboldened that lowly man with family or claim that yesterday he came to the sanctuary, stood of the place of Abraham, and in a loud voice began reading the Koran. We beat him so badly though that he will not have such nonsensical urges after a month when he gets out of bed."

"That is an amazing story! So the followers of the son of Abdullah have gone so high that one of them, a weakling like Abdullah Mas'ud, reads the Koran in the sanctuary in a loud voice!"

"Yes, Omayya! I heard that after that Muhammad told his followers that he had been ordered by his god that the Moslems should reveal their religion. One day his followers come together and said, 'These Qureish had not heard the Koran until today.' He then said, 'Who among you is ready to sell himself to God and enter the sanctuary and read a chapter of the Koran in a loud voice?' Abdullah Mas'ud said, 'I.' You know that of Muhammad's friends, he is lower than many of them and has fewer relatives. For that reason, Muhammad said, 'So he has to stand up to that task who has a clan so that when the idolaters want to make it hard for him, to stop them.' Do you know, though, what Abdullah Mas'ud answered? Huh? 'My God will protect me!' Thus, at that time, when a lot of people had gathered in the sanctuary, he entered there and began to recite. I was in the sanctuary at that time. It was dark. When his voice rose up, the people gathered around him. I asked him, 'Son of a concubine, what is this you are reciting?' He said, 'It is something from God.' Then all of us jumped on him and beat him. But that lowly and brainless man kept on reciting. We beat him and he recited. We beat him hard and he recited until that chapter finished and he fainted."

"But Bu Hāshem, I do not think this is the solution to Muhammad's followers."

"Why do you think that Omayya?"

"Because I heard it from one of my slaves after that incident."

"Huh? Son of Khalaf, what did you hear?"

"Last night, I heard that slave whisper to his wife and say, 'When Abdullah Mas'ud, bloodied and beaten, returned to his friends, on seeing him Abu al-Qāsem was hurt. Then he said to him, 'I was afraid this would happen to you.' But Abdullah said, 'This I easy for me, Messenger of God. I swear to God that His enemies have never in my view appeared so despicable as today. If you want, I will go again tomorrow and recite another chapter.' Until they said to him, 'That is enough! You said to them what they disliked.'"

On hearing that story, a pale of hopelessness fell over the eyes burning from the anxiety of 'Amru Heshām's life, and he did not say any more. Thus, a heavy silence caste its shadow over the assembly.

It is true that the situation was not as simple as they first thought. Also, the effect of the influence of Amin's words on these forty persons who had been attracted to him had become much more. As far as those like 'Amru Heshām, who was considered a famous merchant in Mecca and one of the leaders of his people, no matter how much his effort was obvious in ridiculing Amin, in secret, his view towards him was different.

One night, 'Amru Heshām had come out of his house to hear the Koran in secret from the people and to understand the secret of its effect on the hearts of the people, because he had heard that they Prophet prayed in the middle of the night, in that room of his house. That borders the street, and in his prayers he reads the Koran in a loud voice.

It so happened that on that night, Bu Sufiān Harb and Akhnas Sharif had come from their house with the same intention and were going toward the Prophet's house. Thus, each was standing in a dark corner behind the wall, in a way they could not see one another. By the time the Prophet's prayer had ended, those three were heading to their own homes. At that time, they saw one another and started to reproach one another by saying, "It was not proper for us to hear the Koran from Muhammad because if the people see what we are doing, they will think that this is a proper religion and many will chose to follow Muhammad."

Surprisingly, however, when night came again, that same desire came over them and they went behind the wall of Muhammad's house and started to listen to the Koran from him. Until that time when they saw one another and had said those words of reproach. Then they had said to one another, "Muhammad will soon captivate our hearts, and if we listen to his Koran again, we will probably become believers of his message." So they made an agreement with each other not to listen to Muhammad's Koran.

On the way, after they had left, Akhnas, unknown to Amru, said to Bu Sufiān, "Bu Hanzala, what is your view of this Koran of Muhammad?" Sufiān Harb said, "I swear to the three daughters of god, Lāt, Manāt, and 'Uzzā, that I found it to be very pleasing. Even though I understood part of it and did not know what its purpose was and did not understand another part and did not know what its point was." Then, Akhnas asked the same question of 'Amru Heshām. 'Amru, however, answered that, "I did not hear anything that was useful."

So, when he saw disbelief I those two, he had said, "Do you want to tell me what the truth of the situation is that Muhammad is pursuing?" His two companions said, "Tell us Bu Hakam." 'Amru said, "Know that this clan with our clan, Bani Makhzum, is constantly in rivalry in honor and greatness in order to get ahead. But every place where they achieved, we were even with them, such that they never surpassed us or became equal. If they gave food to the indigent, we gave it too. If they gave something to the people, we did too. When they gave refuge to the weak, we did that too. If they supported the weak, we did too. When they could not do anything else, they provoked this Muhammad to begin claiming to be a prophet and to he brought another religion. He says that heaven is speaking to him so that we can not equal them in that affair and their superiority over us will be obvious. I tell you now that, swearing to all the gods, I will never have faith in Muhammad's religion even if my head is separated from my body."

At that time, Akhnas and Sufiān realized that all of his words were because of envy.

Now, since they had been so astounded by the terms and secrets of this talk, how were they to protect the others from its magical effects?

However much they feared and were ashamed to relate it, even though they wanted, when they heard those melodious chapters with that profound substance inside, all of their self-restraint and steadfastness was shattered. A spiritual joy rushed into their souls. An agitation appeared in the depths of their beings, far-off but very familiar—however dumb—memories moved their depressed minds. It seemed inside them a return to a familiar thing lost—something lost from a time without beginning that for a long time they had forgotten—had occurred. Then a sweet and superior sadness filled their hearts. Their hearts softened, and the attraction to righteousness, goodness, kindness, and recompensing the virtuousness that they had lost awoke in that. It was as if they realized anew how dry, rough, bitter, dark, and empty their lives were of every correct calm and pleasure, and how much better their lives could be, but were not. How much higher their position in the world could be than what they were.

Those verses seemed to be inner whips on the sleeping skeleton of their conscious that stirred them from their heedlessness and familiarized them with a painful waking. It wanted a special knowing and awareness from them. It drew them to question and try themselves. Like a lancet, it went in the old and dirty abscesses of their being, so that after that, it could bring hope of well-being and prosperity for them.

But it was not clear for them why there was this fearful and surprising effect. From the sweetness and special melody of that speech, or its large roots that they recognized the signs of it in the foundation of their being and complete existence? This Muhammad, who had not learned to write or read and earlier had never recited poetry, *saj'*[1], spoken or such like, suddenly found this ability where with this speech he could do these kinds of surprising things! To the extent that, on this subject, one day a knowledgeable person in speech had said, "It is replete beyond these words—like the branches of a tree—full of fruit and under it—like the roots of an old tree."

This strange excitement that it had stirred in their hearts, and from that their spirit had become warm,

---

1. The style of rhymed prose.

was it only the incomparable melody and special rhythm hidden in it? From what category did this intoxicating joy that rushed into the soul bit by bit on hearing those even and rhythmical words and existence expanded with that and the heart opened up? What magical speech was this that resembled poetry, but was not poetry, and which sometimes seemed like *saj'*, but was not *saj*?

These, and many of these questions, were the same ones that on that day had carried away those persons and sent them to the old and wise speech master of the tribe—Walid—so he could familiarize them with the pure and impure. Now, though, Walid in whom they had placed hope, after a short talk with Muhammad, had himself been attracted to the magic circle of his speech so much that he avoided doing to the end what they wanted from him.

But what could Walid do? What could he say to that waiting group he saw staring at his mouth? Should he tell them the truth of what he had experienced? Should he say that when Muhammad reached the last verse, in a moment, a fast shaking wave had hit his spine and made all of the hairs of his body stand on end?

"Well, uncle, will you not say something? Are you not going to say something? Have you become enamored of Muhammad's religion and left us ashamed and disappointed?"

"No, 'Amru. I am still of your religion. But I heard some difficult speech from him that causes bodies to shiver."

Is what he says poetry as some say?"

"You know very well that there is not one among you as familiar with poetry as I. I am familiar with all the kinds of odes, *rajaz*,[1] and poetry attributed to the spirits even. Therefore, I swear to the gods that what he says does not resemble any of those styles. It is very sweet. It is as if it is covered with a magical halo all around. The rising and falling of his speech is abundant. It seeks superiority over every thing and no speech excels it. That speech beats everything."

"A sermon[2] is not verse?"

"A sermon is not either, because a sermon's speech is connected and this speech appears scattered and some of it resembles other parts. Also, the way I said, there is a sweetness in it that can not be described."

"So perhaps it is like the speech of the Jewish priests."

"I have also heard the Jewish priests speak a lot. What he says is not like the humming of the Jewish priests or their magical whisperings. No doubt that these words I heard today from Muhammad can not be the kind of talk of human beings and the jinn."

"What are you saying? That we spread the word that he has been taken over by spirits and is crazy?"

"That must not be said either, because there are none of those signs that possessed and crazy persons have, such as doubts, depression, and the nervousness of that condition. And for that reason, if we say that, we see no benefit except for the people accusing us of lying and abandoning us."

---

1. A genre of Arabic poetry.
2. *Khotba.*

"Now uncle, you tell us what are we to tell the other people—Arabs and non-Arabs—so the religion of our ancestors does not go under and they are attracted to him?"

Walid placed his hand under his chin. He squeezed his narrow and long white beard in his fist and began to think deeply for a while with his head down.

Then he raised his head and facing those assembled said, "In any case, whatever they say about him will be wrong. But it seems of the things you said, it is better that you say, 'This sorcery that that is learned with difficulty and Muhammad learned it from someone else.' Or hearing that, divisions will develop between persons, father, brother, spouse, and their relatives."

The he encouraged them to watch their young people.

The talk had become drawn out and gone on until late at night. Walid said to the guests to sweeten their mouths with the bowls of halva, dates, and raisins. But that talk had left such a bitter taste in their mouths that they did not feel like eating any confectionaries, especially 'Amru, who had no medicine for the pain in his head except old wine. Thus, they rose one by one and went to their own homes.

Outside, the sky was clear and full of stars, and the new crescent moon little by little rose into the sky behind the conical peak of Hirā.

It was late afternoon, and some time was left until the sun would descend into the eastern well. In that situation, and before those people invited arrived, Ali, Ja'far, 'Aqil,, Tāleb, and their sisters, Hind and Rayhāna, were busy cleaning and preparing the guest house and small courtyard. In the kitchen, then another, Fatima, was preparing sherbet and dates and cooking halva in the round copper utensils.

But Bu Tāleb was sitting on the mud steps of the roof immersed in his own far-away and long thoughts. Also, because after seventy-eight years of life and he had spent more than four decades of that in poverty and hardship, now he no longer had that ability to help his children and wife in these kinds of things.

How selfish and ignorant they are, these people! They want me to turn over my own nephew to them so they can shed his blood and after that I will bring their youth to me and raise him.

"O' Bu Tāleb, you know well that at this hour, among all the Qureish, there is no youth more beautiful, better or stronger that 'Omāra, the son of Moghayera. Also, among the people, no one has the fame of his father. Now you have not submitted to our request, except this request of ours: a man for a man! We will give you 'Omāra to be yours in place of Muhammad and as his blood price. And you turn Muhammad over to us so we can spill his blood, because we do not have any more patience in the face of what you nephew is ding to our religion."

"People! What a bad thought is this you have! How can I take your child and raise him and give my own child to you so you can kill him? What person has done that for me to do it too?"

"Bu Tāleb! No matter how much the people seek your happiness and follow you, there is no way you can not want their happiness. Until today, if it was not obvious for me, I would know now that they are just and you are not."

"You are lying Mot'am. The people have given no justice to me, and you, who are one of their leaders, are not saying this with good intentions. They have gathered to denigrate me and to incite the Qureish against me. I think that you have come out with them to oppose me and my nephew and that those words are nothing but excuses. Now, if this is correct, go back and do what you want. I will, as far as I am capable, oppose you. If I could not, you know my intention. If I have not made it clear until here, I will now say, know people that whoever is an enemy of Muhammad, I am their enemy. And whoever is an enemy of Muhammad's religion, I am the enemy of his religion."

Yesterday, after Bu Tāleb had said his final words, the leaders of the people had stood up and left his house. Today, however, Bu Tāleb dreamed that last night all of them had gathered in Walid Moghayera's house and agreed from then on to pursue open antagonism with Muhammad and to oppose him. So Bu Tāleb summoned the men of Bani Hāshem to his house to inform them of that development and to express his own view about it.

Bu Tāleb, with all those years he had lived among these people and that familiarity he had with their habits and thinking, it was quite clear that from then on very difficult days lay ahead for his nephew. That Muhammad had brought up of beliefs and about the gods and idols was not an easy matter for the people to put aside. Others had nothing to say to him as long as he did his worship in private because they had felling of fear from him. So, when they came face to face with one another, they said laughingly and jokingly, "The young child of 'Abd al-Muttaleb is speaking from heaven!" But from the time he called all the people to his religion and denigrated their religion and gods, and spoke about the burning of their forefathers—who had died unbelievers—in the fires of hell, the situation changed. First, they began by ridiculing and bothering him. When that did not work, they complained to Bu Tāleb.

"Bu Tāleb! Although we try to please you in whatever we d, we are determined not do something to cloud your memory, you do not consider us at all and do not try to please us."

"What has happened son of Harb?"

"Sometime ago I came to you with this same 'Othba, Shayba, Rabi'a, 'Ās Wā'el, Aswad Muttaleb,

Tobaya, Monabba, Hajjāj, and Walid Moghayera, who are with us now, and we told you, "This nephew of yours has given up the religion of the fathers and ancestors and has revealed another religion. He is responsible for the good and bad of this deal. But why does he accuses our gods of inadmissible and consider us and our fathers lost and unbelievers and lead the people astray? So we wanted you to give advice so he quits that. You said to us gently and sought to console us and sent us off. But he started doing the same thing again, but he did even more. Now, Bu Tāleb, we have come to you to tell you for the last two, you are a great, noble man and our chief among us, and the head of the people. Tell us, what are we to do? If your nephew's intention in this action is to seek mastery and superiority among the people, he should be told to desist from these words so we ourselves give him what he seeks. If he wants wealth, we will put it in his hands so he can do with it what he likes. But if he is not pleased with those things, we will have no choice but to resort to the language of our swords until he or we remain in Mecca."

On hearing those words, Bu Tāleb's mind became very preoccupied. In the meantime, what could he do? Muhammad was not a child, and he did not speak those words from an urge or as a game so he can stop him doing it with old wisdom. On the other hand, the experience of long years of life and familiarity with the thinking of the people convinced him not to ignore this warning of theirs. For that reason, think of a solution. So he summoned Muhammad and told him the story.

It is difficult for me to battle with the people my child. I think that it would be proper for you to moderate your acts with them in this matter and go slowly.

Suddenly, blood raced into Muhammad's rosy complexion, and the blue vein between his eye brows popped out. But in order to suppress his anger toward his uncle, he looked at his palm and the back of his hand for a while. Then, in a voice shaking a little from the suppression of anger, he had said, "Uncle, God did not send me to provide the world and be attached to it. He inspired me to deliver His message and lead towards Him. I swear to that God in whose hand is Muhammad's soul that if the Qureish place the small in my right hand and the moon in my left, and say to me, "Stop doing this," I will not desist. I will try my hardest to attain my intention and make Islam manifest until the time my death arrives."

So, tears had begun running from his eyes, he was tired on his feet, and he was walking along.

Bu Tāleb's heart had become tight in his eyes, he was tired on his feet, and he was walking along.

Bu Tāleb's heart had become tight in his chest with seeing the sorrow of the only memorial of his brother. It appeared that Muhammad thought from those words of his that perhaps his uncle had decided to stop supporting him and to give him and the people up to each other. Thus, regretting what he had said, he had quickly taken it back, had hung his head, and had said, "My son, I know that you are giving advice to the people and that you speak the truth. So be happy that I will be here to be your joy. Now, carry out God's command, do what you want, and repeat, and do not think of anyone, for as long as your uncle is not buried, no one will have the power to tell you anything."

Bu Tāleb stood up and carried his hefty body toward the guestroom. The sun had now hidden its face from the city, and the coolness of the autumn weather was becoming cold. Little by little it was affecting the bones in his old body, and sharp pains were streaking through his knees and hips.

On seeing his father move toward the guestroom, Ali ran up and brought the blankets of skin for him from another room of the house. He then spread the blanket filled with camel wool against the wall.

Bu Tāleb sat on the skin and thanked the son. By the time Hind placed the burning oil lamp on the mantle, three guests had arrived. The oldest of 'Abd al-Muttaleb's sons, Hāres, tall and slender, with a bent back, and who had a cane. Hamza, with that thick stature of a wrestler and a manly and confident face. The other was Bu Lahab, of medium height, fat, and slack, with blond hair on his head and face, and eyes slightly crossed, weak, careless, and easy-going, but with the pride and confidence of prosperous merchants in his look and speech.

Although Bu Tāleb was not very pleased by the actions and habits of Bu Lahab, he nevertheless at times saw things from him that sparked a glimmer of hope in his heart. Those caused him to always decide not to run him from him and try to reform him. Thus, he stood up for him too and, smiling, greeted him.

Forsooth, what a surprising mixture this brother was! He had many faults, though he was not without virtues either. Sometimes, in that respect, he was very helpful. In the same way, he could be very bad, even though the blood of a great and virtuous man like 'Abd al-Muttaleb was flowing in his veins and he had been raised by him. From that time on, however, when he had taken a daughter of the Umayyad family as his wife, his virtues had gradually lessened and his bad qualities had become ascendant. Following the unveiling of their nephew's preaching, he and his wife had become two of his reproachers, until he had spoken out harshly against him like that when Muhammad summoned the relatives to Hāres' house. Another time was that day at Safā, he was one of the first persons to reject the invitation of his nephew and torment him like that. But yesterday when he heard that the people had said bad things about him because of Bu Tāleb's support of Muhammad, angered, he had said, "Stop bothering this old man, for he has completely gone over to his nephew's side, such that Muhammad will not be killed as long as Bu Tāleb is not killed. And Bu Tāleb will not be killed until all of the Bani Hāshem are killed. And Bani Hāshem will not be killed until all of the people of Mecca are killed. People, you know full well that I have no quarrel with Muhammad. But I swear to the gods that if you do not stop harassing this old man, I will be compelled to side with him."

The men of the family came one by one and each, depending on his age and position, sat down in his own place. All knew about that assembly last that the clans of the Qureish had organized agreement to fight Muhammad and whoever supported him. Therefore, there is not much need to repeat what had gone on between them. So, after all had assembled, Bu Tāleb, after reciting a poem in which he praised Bu Lahab, he said to the men of the family, "Abu al-Qāsem, good or bad, in agreement with you or not, is from your family and clan, and his greatness and honor is the greatness and honor of each one of you. The same way the insulting of him and the denigration of him is the same as insulting of all of the people and the denigration of each one of the individuals of your family."

"The children of Hāshem have lived proudly until this day, and this high position that you have among the Qureish is the first of the sacrifices of your fathers. Now you must protect this greatness and leave it in place for those in the future. So try not to don the attire of baseness."

"People, Abu al-Qāsem has not spoiled his own family's clothes with shame for you to be ashamed of it. I understand that what he has brought does not correspond with what some of you believe. Do not forget that earlier he always assisted your poor and helped your needy, and was the pride and glory of the family. Also remember that position that he had in childhood with your father and grandfather, 'Abd al-Muttaleb, and his request about Muhammad with his last breathe of life."

"Brothers and nephews, you must support Abu al-Qāsem! Help him. And if the Qureish raise the banner of war against him, you fight them too so the enemies become hopeless at the division among themselves and withdraw their covetousness of you!"

When Bu Tāleb's words ceased, Ali, Ja'far, 'Aqil, and Tāleb brought several large bowls of sherbet and some goblets and trays of halva and dates into the room and offered them to the men of the family. Some of the men proceeded to eat and drink and another group talked about that subject. Several persons—such as Hāres, Hamza, Bu Lahab, and 'Abbas—were withdrawn and deep in thought. If anyone had anything to say, they kept it to themselves, with that reminder Bu Tāleb had made about 'Abd al-Muttaleb's request concerning Muhammad and that pride Abu al-Qāsem had bestowed on the family and they did not say anything.

In truth, how had they forgotten how many surprising things they had seen in childhood and adolescence from that orphan beloved by all the family. From those strange visions that Āmina had seen when pregnant to that happening at the time of Muhammad's birth. Those stories Halima Sa'diya had told from the period of his infancy and the words of Bohayra the monk of Syria. That title of "Amin" that the people had given him because of his exceptional uprightness and faithfulness.

Were all those signs not enough for them to know that Abu al-Qāsem was not one of those persons who lies and makes baseless claims?

"We heard and follow."

"Yes! We will do what you say Bu Tāleb."

"No matter how much we've been hurt by Abu al-Qāsem's words, we will take the side of the family in this matter and will stand with you until death."

"I will also make a contract with you in this matter brother."

"Count me and my sons in too Bu Tāleb."

"Did you hear, Umm Jamil, what new song Muhammad has played for us?"

"No! Tell me so I know what the story is."

"Abd al-'Uzzā, with suppressed anger, said, like those whose *qabā*[1] has been burned,

""May Bu Lahab's hands be cut off, and death to him!"

"His wealth and what he has earned has not benefited him.

"Soon he will fall into a blazing fire.,

"And his wife will carry the firewood for that fire.

"Until a rope of date palm fibers is around his neck.

"Woe to Muhammad! He is lampooning us! We will do something to him until he repents!

"Calm! Calm woman!"

"What calm? He has not left us any honor with that poetry of his. If those words are spread about, first his followers, and then our enemies, and finally the slaves and small children will speak of him everywhere. And like the Seven Hanging Poems[2] they will go from heart to heart to other generations."

"Certainly, earlier, before we could do something, it has become like that, because his followers, who understand this to be the heavenly word and the speech of God, and write it down and memorize it,

---

1. A kind of long gown open in front.
2. Al-*Mo'allaqāt*: Famous poems by pre-Islamic poets that were hung from the door of the Ka'ba.

and all the time and everywhere recite it, thinking it has spiritual benefit. Others too learn it and mutter it to themselves, infatuated by the cadence and beauty of its words. I think the last persons who learned of it were you and I!"

The husband and wife began to think deeply. After all those quarrels they had had with Abu al-Qāsem, and the extent of those torments they had caused him, they did not think that one day a blow so deadly from him would descend on their life and being.

Umm Jamil, like the other people, knew the place of speech among the Arabs. Especially since she was herself a poetess and she was very familiar with the tenor, value, and endurance of it. In the view of her and her people, speech was not a simple compilation of several new and soulless words or idle talk that only come with reading or hearing and then was relegated to the basket of forgetfulness and was rewarded from memories as if it had never been. But every expression, whenever it was in a new position, or created an image in a mind, ad was being spoken, was a living existence with spirit, flowing, capable, endurable, and effective. Especially when it was clad in poetry, *saj'*, and things like those. Woe be the day when this speech was uttered about for our men of the people— like the Qureish—and was considered heavenly and had guardians as enthusiastic and believing as the followers of Muhammad!

Yes! Muhammad, with that surprising patience of his, face to face with their tortuous torments; it seemed at first had put them into a deep sleep of heedlessness, and then at exactly the place where those two considered themselves well protected by him. He had answered them by saying that worse than that could not happen.

'Abd al-Uzzā was not a tolerant, moderate, or patient man. His hot-headedness, quickness to anger, and sharp tongue were the talk of all the people of Mecca. Every person—even before they knew him—on seeing those eyes emitting evil, eyebrows always knitted, protruding red cheeks, quickly realized from which class of people he was. And it was because of that that he had acquired the title of Bu Lahab.[1] Now, however, he was so astounded by this deadly blow of Muhammad that he did not see in him the ability to give an answer.

Bu Lahab, now, broken and collapsed in on himself, was lounging on a carpet with his waist propped up on a cushion and thinking about his past actions with his nephew.

For sure, Muhammad had not done anything bad to Bu Lahab or his wife. He and Khadija were the best neighbors for them. In almost two decades of being neighbors no one had seen anything to annoy them from that husband, wife, their children, or even their slaves. It was because of that that Bu Lahab, with all that wealth and fame in the city and among the other Arab tribes, when he decided to chose spouses for his sons 'Othba and 'Othyaba, he could not find anyone better than Roqiyyeh and Umm Kolthum, the daughters of his nephew. And his wife, being from the

---

1.

family of Bani Omayya, and having precedence among her relatives, was very happy with those marriages. But what had they done to these peaceful and gentle relatives and neighbors? First, they had convinced their sons, without having done anything wrong, to break off their marriages and send those two to their father's house. (Roqiyyeh, after her marriage to 'Otba and Umm Kolthum when she had just become engaged to 'Otahyba.) and Bu Lahab had also sworn that until Muhammad did not renounce those words, he would also prevent others from marrying his daughters. That action had so disturbed Muhammad and Khadija that Abu al-Qāsem, broken-hearted, raised his hands to the sky and cursed them.

O' God, have one of Your fierce animals attack 'Otbā!

(That was the first time the people heard Abu al-Qāsem curse someone.) There were sarcastic and stupid remarks that those two said about Abu al-Qāsem, and there were nonsensical things they spread behind his back.

In addition to those, everywhere Muhammad decided to speak to the people and reveal his religion to them, Bu Lahab was the first enemy to stand against him and made it very difficult for him. The last of those acts was a month earlier in the bazaar of the tribe of Hodayl, Zi Majār, All the people of the Arabian Peninsula. After spending twenty days at the 'Ukkāz bazaar which was one parasang away, so as to the plain of 'Arafat to spend the remaining nine days of the month of Zi Qa'da there is trading, talking, the conclusion of contracts, and then go to Mecca. Abu al-Qāsem, seeking to benefit from that opportunity, went to that bazaar. But Bu Lahab, Walid Moghayera, Nazr Hāres, and some others of their friends, aware of his decision, followed him so as to block the path every time he misled the people.

On that day, Abu al-Qāsem was wearing a red *redā* that was very pleasing in that instance. Every place he saw a group of people standing around, he went to them and invited them to the one God.

I and those for whom I have been designated are like that man who went to his own people and said, "I saw an enemy army with my own eyes, and I warn you of them without concealing a thing. Think about saving yourself from them." A group accepted what he said and left during the night. With that opportunity they had, they rescued their lives and property. But another group considered what he said to be a lie and did not move until the enemy army arrives and kills all of them. This is a story that resembles that which I brought and they follow. Those people who resist and consider the truth I brought to be a lie."

Therefore, Bu Lahab, who was wearing a new *redā* of cloth from Aden, was following him and threw a stone at his foot so hard that blood lowed from his shin and he said, "People, I am 'Abd al-'Uzzā, the son of 'Abd al-Muttaleb, and this is my nephew. Know that he is a big liar. Do not listen to him and do not accept what he says lest he deceive you and turn you away from your fathers' religion."

Walid Moghayera supported him.

People, I who am also one of the leaders of the Bani Makhzum pull you aside lest you hear his words. Know that sorcery is in this man's speech that attracts and possesses. It has words that, when people hear them, divisions appear among them and dispersal occurs. Beware that you do not gather about him and listen to him!

Those who knew Muhammad's background had doubts.

Yes, it must be like that, because if he were right, first his family and tribe would turn to him.

"We will do what you said."

Bu Lahab knew very well how much his standing against the religion for which his nephew claimed to be the prophet bothered Muhammad and thrilled his enemies. Because that point itself was a very important pretext for them, that "If Muhammad's claim is true, why does his family and uncle not even support and follow him in this matter?" In that case, in the tradition of the people and tribe of the Arabs, the structure and foundation of the matter must be like that.

If other were not aware too, Bu Lahab himself was well aware that belief in the gods was not very deep or well-grounded so as to continuously submit to this matter without security. Also, the religion that his nephew claimed, if it had followers among the Arabs, would become cause for mastering the family of Hāshem over all of them so much that Bu Lahab would benefit from that mastery too.

I want to say something, once I say it, the Arabs will bow their heads in obedience to you and the others will become indebted to you.

"That is good! Since it is like that, I will say ten words! Now, tell me, what are those words nephew?"

"That you say, 'There is no god save the single Creator.'"

"How surprising! You want to make all of the gods one?"

It made little difference to Bu Lahab whether there was one god or more because he had no interest in there affairs from the beginning. He possessed a lot of wealth, of many gardens and very large fields in Taif where his slaves were busy protecting and cultivating them. All these had come from the paying of interest and trade during the three forbidden months[1] when the people of the Arabian Peninsula came on pilgrimage to their idols. Now, then Muhammad had a claim, like this if three-hundred and sixty gods were gathered intone and all the idols of the tribes disappeared, who would go to Mecca then to do business with Bu Lahab and other merchants like him and add to his tremendous wealth? No. This was not something Bu

1.

Lahab could accept.

Umm Jamil more or less had the same fear of quarreling with Muhammad because she was herself a wealthy woman and her wealth was more than most of the Qureish men. Her brother, Bu Sufiān, was one of the interest-takers in Mecca and one of the great merchants of the Qureish. More than that, if Muhammad's religion took hold in Mecca, the leadership of the Qureish would go to Muhammad and the Bani Hāshem. That was not what Umm Jamil and her family wanted and because of that Umm Jamil was throwing more fuel on the fire that was burning between her husband and Muhammad.

Earlier, Umm Jamil had made fun of Muhammad. She had belittled Muhammad in those poems. Thus, in women's gatherings, he recited those derisive poems and they clapped at their rhythm and danced, or their men, children, and slaves read them in the alleys and bazaars and laughed derisively. But Muhammad did not take those poems personally and he did not become angry hearing them.

Throwing stones at Abu al-Qāsem's house—one of her obstacles on his claim's path—had not achieved anything. Profligate youths whom Umm Jamil had encouraged to do that at night had thrown a lot of stones at his house several times. They had broken several windows, his storage room, and had frightened the people of the house. In spite of that, Muhammad, as was his habit, had been patient and had asked his wife and children to be patient too.

Again, Umm Jamil herself once or twice had

thrown a polluted womb of a goat into their food on the oven in a corner of the courtyard from off the roof.

O' children of 'Abd Manāf! What kind of neighborliness is this?

Although she never actually said it, it was however clear that she meant the neighbors on either side—them and 'Aqaba Abi Mo'ayt.

At night as well, Bu Lahab and Umm Jamil would put thorns or animal dung on the road and in front of their house. Sometimes Muhammad would step on them without seeing them and be either hurt or dirtied. Sometimes too Umm Jamil would pursued her female slaves to pour dirt and ashes in his head or when she herself saw Abu al-Qāsem in the lane, she would point and say mockingly, "People, look at this good-for-nothing orphan who harbors visions of mastery over the Quriesh in his head!"

Umm Jamil, when she thought hard, realized that she and her husband had done like that very many times with Abu al-Qāsem and had bothered him a lot, but he had always been patient. For that reason, they had never thought that Muhammad, who was that gentle and forgiving, would one day attack them like that and tear their base out by its roots.

Umm Jamil, burning with the fire of revenge, could not sit down more than that. She therefore stood up and put on her clothes to go out.

"Where to Umm Jamil?"

"I am uneasy. Before night comes, I am going to

the sanctuary to find out the reaction to this affair among the people."

Bu Lahab, fearful of the hot temper and abusive language of his wife, said, "Okay, do it. But control yourself and do not do anything stupid. This affair of Muhammad must be answered at its own time and place."

Then he laughed evilly and said, "Yes! The kind of response that will break his back, like he broke our backs!"

Umm Jamil, having barely heard the last words of her husband, came out of the room and house and headed toward the sanctuary in that cool air of late afternoon. She had pulled the thin white gold embroidered scarf over her mouth and nose so as not to be recognized. For she thought that with those rhythmical and melodious words Muhammad had spoken about her and her husband, all eyes would now be looking for them and so as to rain down their poisoned arrow-like look and sarcasm upon them.

She, with all that pride and sense of superiority she had, she felt herself now mean, humble, and fallen. She saw that she did not have the strength like before to stick her chest out, to raise her head, to let the two strands of thick locks of hair wave in the wind on either side of her head, to stare into the distance with pride with her attractive black eyes, and to walk proudly. In her inner sanctum that earlier had never tasted defeat or humility, something had collapsed. In her heart, it seemed the cavity of her mouth was open, a vacuum, hollow, a feeling of emptiness….

The sanctuary, like every late afternoon, was filled with people. Some were performing pilgrimage to the idols of their people or tribe and worshipping with them. A group was circling the Ka'ba and saying the special prayers for circumambulation. Others, a few at a time, were coming and going or gathered together talking. Umm Jamil, hidden from the others, went to the Ka'ba. On the way, she was listening carefully in order to gear the people's words to one another. Perhaps they would be about her and her husband. But every person was preoccupied with his own affairs. Also, these kinds of talks took place mostly in circles of men who sat together. Women were not allowed in them.

Umm Jamil was circling the Ka'ba and among the people when suddenly she saw Bu Bakr, who was sitting on the stone of Ismail. Thinking that Muhammad might also be beside him, blood suddenly rushed into her brain and she could not think of anything else. So, in an instant, she saw she had picked up a stone from off of the ground and, raising it high, was going toward the stone of Ismail and Bu Bakr.

Bu Bakr was busy talking with the Prophet when suddenly, guided by an inner sense, he lifted his head and saw a pair of unruly eyes among the people who were circumambulating the Ka'ba. The fire of uncontrollable anger leapt from the eyes and they were staring at them. It was a woman whose mouth and nose were covered by a silken white shawl. But, from the gentle twisting of her left eye, the heavily made-up face, and that lewd walk that resembled dancing when angry, he knew without any doubt that she must be Bu Lahab's wife. Therefore, when he saw the stone in her hand, he said with an obvious shiver in his voice, "Messenger of god, your uncle's wife is coming. It is better you get up and leave, because she is a woman, and I am afraid for you."

The Prophet, with his usual calm, said, "It is the will of God. She will not see me."

Then he began reciting several verses from the Koran. By the time he recited, "When you recite the Koran, We will place a curtain between you and those who do not believe in the next world."

The recitation of that verse had just finished when Umm Jamil, yelling and screaming, sprang in their direction. In that threatening situation, she bounced the stone in her hand and screamed, "Where is he who says improper things about our fathers and who our idols have made angry?"

A few heads turned toward her and Bu Bakr's heart began beating faster.

"He was right here, daughter of Harb Omayya."

Umm Jamil stood over him with the stone in her hand and in a loud voice said, "I swear to the gods that if I had found him, I would have beat this stone against his head and killed him. Son of Abi Qahāfa, your companion's affair has gone so far that he is ridiculing me and my husband. Does he not know that I am a poet too and that I can ridicule him as well?"

Bu Bakr, fearful, said, "No, daughter of Harb. I swear to the God of the Ka'ba that he has not ridiculed you. My companion is not a poet and does not know what poetry is."

"No. He said that my husband and I will go to hell and that a string of palm fiber will be tied to my neck."

Bu Bakr, unable to answer, said, "Why do you not ask him yourself Umm Jamil?"

"If I had seen him, I would not have asked you where he is!"

When she saw several people staring in amazement at her, Umm Jamil dropped the stone and as she was turning away from Bu Bakr and the Prophet she said, "Unless I do not see him!"

Then, with sagging shoulders, she headed out of the sanctuary. But a few steps away, she suddenly tripped over her dress and fell to the ground.

Even angrier, she got up and said hatefully, "Death to the slanderer!"

The Prophet said to Bu Bakr, "Did you see how God deflected the abuse of the Quriesh from me? They mention every kind of despicable thing with ugliness and damn it. Even though God has named me 'praiseworthy'."[1]

---

1. In Arabic, the name "Muhammad" means "He who is praised."

When the Prophet went in to the sanctuary, he saw groups of Qureish men who were gathered in circles all around several idols. After he went further, he saw a group of them who were raising an idol in its place. The idol resembled a young woman, with a narrow and extended body, from white stone.

Further away, he saw several persons busy around the image of a man carved from a rough blue stone. One was hanging a large ostrich egg with strips of string around the neck of that idol. A young thin man was fastening earrings of colorful stones on his two ears.

The Prophet wanted to pass by them and go to their usual place between the black stone and the Yemeni column and pray the afternoon prayer. But when he saw those men fall on the ground after decorating that idol and prostrate towards it, he did not feel like leaving them in that situation. So he went beside them and said in a friendly manner, "With this you are doing, you are opposing your fathers, Abraham and Ismail—peace be upon them."

The men, amazed, raised their heads from the ground. The Prophet recognized 'Ās Wā'el Sahm and Hāres Qays 'Adi Sahmi among them. Those two were among those five persosn who, more than the others, were standing in front of him and who, openly and clandestinely, tormented him.

'Ās, so as to conceal his anger, softly said, "Why do you say that son of Abdullah?"

"Because they did not worship idols, but they praised the Creator."

'Ās, having no answer, hesitatingly said, "Muhammad, we worship those idols out of love for the superior God."

Hāres Qays added to what he said, "So they can be our mediators with the superior God and bring us nearer to Him."

Then a breeze of inspiration suddenly blew on the Prophet's mind and heart and he recited to them:

"Say, 'If you love God, follow me so He will love you too and forgive your sins, for He is the Forgiving, the Merciful.'

"Say, 'Obey your God and His messenger. So if they turn their faces away, they know that He does not like the unbelievers.'"

It was as if a lock had been placed in the mouths of all of those men. They cold not give any answer. They only looked at the Prophet, who went on his way to a point in the sanctuary in order to pray.

There where the Prophet prayed was outside the circle of people who were circumambulating the Ka'ba. That place, although it was beside the Holy House, nonetheless, facing the Ka'ba, it was between the Yemeni column and the Black Stone.

The Prophet took the *abā* from his shoulders and spread it on the sand covering the sanctuary. He stood on it and began to pray.

At this time, anew, it seemed the lock had been unlocked from the tongues of those men.

"Did you see how he denigrated our religion and fathers and considered our intellects nothing?"

"With the abusive things he says about our gods, if we do not stop him, they will become angrier with us and blessings will leave our lives."

Suddenly, a flasj of ill-naturedness jumped from the eyes of 'Ās. Then, as if he had a secret to say to his friends, he called the other men to him with his two hands and in a way his voice did not go beyond them, he said, "When I came, in the quarter of Harura I saw that they were sacrificing a camel. What do you say if we bring the dirty paunch of that camel and when Muhammad prostrates himself, throw it on his back so that he does not do his prayers in the sanctuary anymore?"

All made clear their happiness with that by laughing loudly. 'Ās then called one of his slaves, who was a thin youth with brown skin and was rubbing a cloth over the head and face of the tribe's idol, and sent him to bring the paunch.

'Ās had not thought completely inopportunely. Earlier, when the Prophet had gone to the sanctuary, normally his godson Zayd Hāres and the young Ali were with him. When he stopped to pray so that he not be bothered by the unbelievers and idolaters, those two would stood on either side of him and guard him. During those hours, more or less, from the Bani Hāshem, there were men and women in the sanctuary as well. Now, however, the sanctuary was empty of all of them. Too, the Prophet, when he began praying, became so engrossed in his worship that he was totally unaware of what went on around him. So, for 'Ās, Hāres, and their friends, the best opportunity had come to humiliate him and to do something to him so that after that he would not be impudent toward their religion.

The young slave arrived with the large paunch filled with the filth of the camel.

'They had just butchered it when I arrived."

It was as he said. When steam rose up from the paunch and what was in it, and the unpleasant smell that dispersed in the air. It clearly showed that the paunch had been taken from the stomach of the camel only moments before.

Before the opportunity was lost, 'Ās said to his slave, "Hide behind an idol near Muhammad and when he prostrates, put this paunch upside down between his shoulders so his head and body are polluted by it."

On hearing that order, the slave thought for a minute, he lost strength in his knees, because even though he did not know Muhammad or have any attachment to him, neither was he his enemy. On the contrary, when he thought hard, he saw that his owner and the other wealthy Qureish were so frightened of the words of this good man, that like the other slaves, he felt lightness and happiness in his heart. Therefore, how could he refuse the order of his master?

'Ās, when he saw the hesitation of his slave, looked at him. That evil look caste so much fear into the heart of the young slave that he went to Muhammad without saying anything.

The Prophet had just placed his forehead on the ground when he suddenly felt something heavy, wet, and warm between his shoulders, and a strong unpleasant smell assaulted his nose. He heard the sound of quick steps going away.

When he lifted his head from prostration, that thing fell on the ground and a smelly slim ran over his back and dirtied his clothes. He then heard voices roaring with laughter, mockery, and buffoonery.

The Prophet finished his prayer and turned his head toward whence the voices came. It was 'Ās, Wā'el, Hāres Qays, and those other persons with whom he had spoken a bit earlier.

The Prophet's gaze was so intense that their laughs vanished from their lips.

The Messenger of God, dejected, rose from the ground. Timid, he shook the dung from his back, picked up the *abā* from the ground, and quickly—in a way that had not been seen from him—went out of the sanctuary.

His annoyance and anger had become extreme. He saw that his abundant patience before the harassment and verbal abuse of the people, rather than softening their hearts toward him and preparing them for accepting his claim, had made them more rude day by day, until now, when they had done that to him in the protected sanctuary of the Ka'ba!

In the beginning, they were satisfied to speak with him and debate, or ridicule him, either openly or in private. Then, when the support of Bu Tāleb and the family of Hāshem increased, and they saw that it was not possible to kill him, they instigated the ignorant and stupid of the people to verbally torment him. Sometimes they called him a liar. At times they accused him of being a poet. One day they said he was a magician. Another day they called him mad. The Prophet heard all those things, but he did not take it to heart, except that he ordered his friends to confront them verbally when need be.

Thus, things became more difficult than this, until when he left the house, whichever of the people he passed—small and large, freedman and slave—when they saw him, they made a face and sometimes also cursed him and said improper things to him, or they placed children along his path and they threw stones at him, so much that the hits of the stones caused injury and blood would run from his head, face, and body.

In that situation, however much their actions caused him great pain on his body and in his heart, he nonetheless exercised patience and concealed his pain and sorrow in his heart. Until that time when he was returning to his house and Khadija, like a kind mother, would put balm on his injuries and clean his clothes, wipe the dust from his head and face, and with a sweet voice console him saying,


Abu al-Qāsem, do not bother yourself over the ignorance and vengefulness of those people because every person who attained the position you did would be envious of him and what he said they would call a lie and would quarrel with him and torment him. But be happy that soon the lord will help his religion and humble your enemies and bring the people under your command.

Now, however, things had gone beyond where patience and silence would solve that.

Suddenly, the Prophet found himself before the humble house of his uncle. He quickly banged the knocker.

"Who is it?"

The voice was that of his uncle's kind wife, Fatima Asad.

The Prophet said his name. He heard the voices of Fatima and Bu Tāleb together from inside calling him joyfully to come inside.

The Prophet mentioned the name of the lord and entered the courtyard by the short door of the house.

Bu Tāleb was sitting on a straw mat and leaning against a small cushion in the portico of the living room. The Prophet greeted him and his wife, and they warmly replied to him. But Bu Tāleb realized from the tone of his words and the knitted brow of his nephew that he was not his usual self. So when he saw that, he did not have his *abā* on his shoulders, that impression of his intensified.

"What has happened nephew? You do not appear to be well."

"Uncle, I came to ask what my position is with you."

Bu Tāleb, surprised at the tone of his speech and words, asked, "Why do you ask that nephew?"

The Prophet repeated that same question, but this time in a different way. "Do I not have any position with you uncle?"

There was a slight trembling in his clear responding voice that caused the heart to shivering Bu Tāleb's kind heart.

"Speak more openly my son! What has happened to you?"

The Prophet, choked up, turned his face and showed the dirtied back of his clothes to his uncle.

Bu Tāleb started and did not seem to believe what he saw. After blinking several times, he angrily asked, "Who?"

It was as if an angry wind had descended into his throat and did not allow him to speak any more than that.

"'Ās Wā'el, Hāres Qays Sahmi, and several of their relatives."

"Tāleb! Where is Tāleb?"

Tāleb quickly came down from the roof of the house. On seeing the Prophet, he greeted him and answered.

"Yes, father. Did you want me?"

Bu Tāleb, who was now busy putting on his *redā* and fastening the turban around his head, said, "Right now go and find your uncle Hamza and take him to the sanctuary with you."

His tone was so penetrating and angry that Tāleb did not consider it proper at that moment to ask what had happened or the reason for that.

"I will do it father."

He then quickly went into the street. Following him, Bu Tāleb, who had now fastened his sword about his waist and pulled his *abā* over his shoulders, headed for the street. The Prophet followed after him without saying anything.

Bu Tāleb walked so fast and passed through the rocky and sloping streets along the route that the Prophet had problems staying up with him. He was so preoccupied that on the way he did not hear, or ignored, the greetings of several men and women.

Uncle and nephew, in a deep silence and without speaking a word, were in the sanctuary in a few minutes.

'Ās, Hāres, and their companions had not yet left the sanctuary. Bu Tāleb, casting sharp glances this way and that, found them and, like a falcon descending on its prey, he hurried toward them.

On seeing his state, the faces of all of them paled, and the hands and feet of the slave who had done that began to shake so much that it seemed he was in the throws of death.

'Ās and Hāres decided to stand up to honor the headman of the tribe and to overcome the fear of being belittled that had afflicted their hearts. Suddenly, however, Bu Tāleb, with a quick movement that was surprising for a man of that age, slung one side of his *abā* aside and loudly pulled his sword from its scabbard and held his hand and sword high above the heads of that group and like thunder shouted, "No one move from his place!"

At that same time, Tāleb, with Hamza, arrived. The terror of that assembly doubled when they saw the large figure of Hamza. 'Ās, with no strength in his hands or feet, wanted to say something when Bu Tāleb yelled, "Quiet 'Ās! I swear to the God of the Ka'ba that whoever opens his mouth, I will sever his neck with this sword."

Then, facing Tāleb, he said, "Bring that paunch here with all the dung inside it."

Tāleb's look was inquisitive, because his father, because of his great anger, had forgotten to make clear where the paunch had fallen. On realizing that situation, the Prophet indicated with is hand to that part of the sanctuary where the paunch still lay.

Tāleb nimbly ran over there, picked up the paunch from off of the ground, and returned to them.

Hamza, saying nothing, looked intently upon that scene, just realizing what had happened to make his brother so angry. Thus, little by little, flames of anger jumped from his penetrating eyes. At this time, Bu Tāleb seemed to have just noticed his brother and said, "Now, Hamza, do to those impudent and stupid persons what they did to your nephew. Take this paunch with its filth and rub it on the beards and heads of these one by one."

Hamezeh looked at Bu Tāleb questioningly. He did not at first think that this order of his was serious. But seeing the unforgiving and firm look of the old man convinced him to step forward and do what he had said.

For the Prophet, no matter how full his heart was with pain from that group, nonetheless, he could not stand to watch them be humiliated that much. For that reason, he turned his face away so as to accept that much humiliation of them a little easier. From what he could hear, one of them said with a shaking in his voice, "Nephew, what you have already done to us is enough!"

Hamza, tired, but happy, was returning from hunting on his agile Arabian horse. After days and days of work, these two days of riding after game in the mountains around the city had renewed his soul, and he was prepared to pursue his won profession again for many days.

He spent most of his time trading goods just like most of the men of the Qureish. But there was a big difference with them. Hamza had not spent all his time and life working and accumulating wealth. First of all, he had not made the worship of property and gathering of capital his profession like most of them. He gave just enough value to property for what he needed in his daily life. When his income reached that level, he was gladdened, and he spent the remainder of his time on exercising, wrestling, and hunting, to which he was very attached. The other was that this attachment and inclination to those things kept him from falling into the whirlpool of many of the wasteful and ugly things of the time. Even though in terms of his looks, form, strength, and family he was one of the eminent men of the city, he was satisfied with two wives, and he had three children from them. His son, Ya'li, had been raised in such a way that, like himself, he was attached to exercise and hunting, and most of the time, like his father, he was hunting and accompanied him.

The horse Samand, happy from the two days it had run in the springtime environment around the city, now had cocked its head to the right and easy and unhurriedly was passing through the wide streets at the end of the city.

After a hard midday rain, Mecca now had very fine air. The moist smell and rainy earth pulsed in the space and brought about a sweet sleepy looseness in the tired bodies of the rider and mount. But the those acquainted with the habit of its rider knew that the time to relax had still not come. First, they had to go to the sanctuary so Hamza, in his consistent manner, could go around the Ka'ba seven times. At that time, the men of the people, who had gathered to spend time in the afternoon and evening in the sanctuary, called him to their circle so he could relate in detail what had happened during his most recent hunt. They informed Hamza of what had happened in the city, until he pitched his black tent at night above the city and the people, individually or in groups, headed for their homes.

"Heh Bu Ya'li!"

The voice was that of an old woman. Hamza pulled on his reins and stopped the horse and turned toward the voice.

"Wait a minute hero of the world!"

Yes, the voice was that of a short, small old woman. The woman was wearing old clothes faded by the sun, and, weeping, was coming toward him from the door of a house on the small hill of Safā.

On seeing that, Hamza thought that that woman

was wronged and poor and had come to him for justice, because such persons sometimes approached him and he more or less approved of their wants.

"Woman, who are you? What has happened to you?"

The woman came near. One or two steps away from the horse she stopped, and with a lump in her throat, said, "I am one of Abdullah Jod'an's female slaves, whose house is in this passageway. Young man, noting has happened to me. My weeping is for your nephew, Amin."

On hearing that, Hamza quickly took his foot out of the stirrup and came down from the horse. He did that so fast that his foot struck the deer that was tied to the back of the horse and the carcass hung to one side.

Hamza unconsciously dropped the reins and took hold of the old bony shoulders of the woman with both hands and asked "Abu al-Qāsem? What has happened to him?"

"What can I say Hamza about what Bu Hakam did to him today? O' that you were here to see what Amin endured at his hands!"

"What did he do? Where?"

He said whatever ugly words and curses he knew to Amin and his religion. And he was not satisfied with that. He beat him over the head with a stone until blood flowed from it."

"…and my nephew…? What did he do in return?"

"Nothing! It was clear that he had suffered much, but he did not answer his curses nor to his beating with the stone. I only saw that he put a kerchief over the wound, and when 'Amru dispersed the people from around him, he went to the house of Arqam."

"How did that happen woman?"

Now her voice was accompanied by a visible shaking from anger increasing every moment.

"Nothing! At the beginning of this event, I was busy sweeping in front of the house of my master, and I saw what happened from the start. Fist, Abu al-Qāsem was standing and a group of people—of men, women, and children—were around him and he spoke to them of his religion, until suddenly 'Amru Heshām and several other men of the Bani Makhzum arrived. 'Amru wanted the people around Amin to disperse, but when he saw the people continued to stand there, he began to belittle Amin's religion, and he cursed bitterly Amin and his religion. So much that the color of your nephew's face first turned red and then became dark on hearing those words. But he bit his lip and did not answer 'Amru's curses. Until...."

"Where is this 'Amru now?"

"He went to the sanctuary with his friends."

Hamza did not wait any longer to hear the rest of the old woman's words. Suddenly, his enormous body jumped like wild rue on a fire and in the blink of an eye he jumped on his horse, which was now in a corner of the street where it had found some grass and was busy eating it. He spurred the animal on the steep slope of the street.

How impudent 'Amru Heshām—that stupid and vengeful man—had become! While Hamza—a brave man whom all Meccans respected and feared his grandiosity and dignity—was Abu al-Qāsem's uncle, how had someone like 'Amru dared to do something like that to him in front of others? Did the people not say how he was a great hunter of lions? And with him around, they had done such a thing to his nephew?

In addition to the fact that Abu al-Qāsem was the nephew of Hamza, his mother was the daughter of the uncle of Haleh—the mother of Hamza. In addition to that, he was like a brother to Hamza, because when they were infants, the female slave of Bu Lahab, Thowayba, had nursed Hamza for a while and then Muhammad. For that reason, those two were brothers through milk. Thus, although Hamza was two years older, in childhood those two played together and were friends. And Hamza, like Muhammad, had lost his father in childhood and had been swallowed by the shadow of the other sons of 'Abd al-Muttaleb. Hamza well remembered that when his father, AM, passed away, it was as if Muhammad, like him, became an orphan. Those, and Muhammad's good nature, from childhood had built a stronger tie between them than one between an uncle and his nephew. 'Amru, however!

It was clear to Hamza that 'Amru's animosity toward Muhammad was not entirely because of the gods and customs of the fathers, because before his nephew brought this new religion, 'Amru harbored rancor towards him and was very envious of him.

It was first on that trading trip to Syria when Muhammad was the leader of the caravan for

Khadija, and the merchants of Bani Hāshem had selected him to be the leader of the caravan. Thus, when Khadija, with all that wealth and those suitors, after she rejected all of her suitors, including ʿAmru, and suddenly wanted Muhammad, that animosity and envy ʿAmru had became deeper until he was always in wait of Muhammad so that with any excuse ad at every opportunity, he could pour the poison of his animosity into his mouth. But his fear of the men of Bani Hāshem, especially Bu Tāleb and Hamza, was that he would go far ahead in that endeavor and they would stop him. Now that Muhammad had brought a new religion, however, and most of the Bani Hāshem did not follow him in that it seemed the anger had awakened in ʿAmru's heart that perhaps their support of Muhammad had lessened and the time had come to attack this old rival again and sweeten his bitter mouth, heedless that as long as Hamza was on the earth he would not allow that.

Beyond those things, the denouncing of Muhammad was also the denouncing of all of this family, the Bani Hāshem. Among the Arabs, insulting was not just a few words that were spoken in anger and like a wind in the air was left and a little later disappeared until no sign remained of it and it was forgotten. Every word had a spirit, personality, and life. Good or bad, ugly or beautiful, down or up. When it was born with either a mouth or a pen, it was embodied in the minds, and it took on the appearance of reality. Thus, it followed its long life—a life sometimes longer than the life of the speaker. It opened its way among the minds and in the course of years and proceeded. In the mirror of thoughts and by the way of other mouths and pens it became more and more. It bore and caused to be borne. Sometimes it took on new faces. It built or destroyed. It killed or bestowed life. It humbled or raised up.

In the sanctuary, on the porch of the Bani Hāshem, we were sitting around 'Amru and listening to what he had done to Muhammad an hour before and at times laughed loudly, when we suddenly noticed that the commotion in the sanctuary had subsided a bit. Then we saw 'Amru stop speaking and his gaze remained toward the Bani Hāshem gate. Then the redness of his cheeks very clearly drained away and gradually its color became yellow like the color of straw.

Surprised and fearful, I followed his stare and knew why Amru's disposition had become transformed. The lion hunter of Mecca, the hearing of whose name caused the backs of their necks to shiver, was coming toward us with a look that no one had ever seen on him before.

He was afoot, but it was clear he was coming straight from hunting, and he had tied his horse outside the sanctuary. He was wearing his outer garment of lion's skin and a hat of the same was on his head. A wide belt of leather the color of saffron, had made what he wore straight, and he had high boots of leather that same color on his feet. Hanging on his waist was a sword with a silver scabbard, and under that belt a Syrian dagger was in its scabbard. Behind his left shoulder was a quiver with several arrows, such that when you looked at him from the front, the feathered ends of the arrows were visible above his shoulders. Then here was his long bow that he was carrying on his back.

Hamza was the eye and light, not just of the Bani Hāshem, but of all the Qureish. With that medium height that approached tall and that bulky figure—wide chest, thick arms whose ripples were clearly visible through his clothes—full shoulders and bulging neck—resembled the most splendid of forms from which some tribes made their god of war. Or this thought overtook the mind, that those builders had made their own forms from him.

He approached in such a way that the ground of the sanctuary shook under his steps. He paid no attention to any of the persons along the way, as if he saw nothing save the point on which his eyes were set.

On seeing that form frowning and dark from anger, all of the on-lookers were certain that something serious was about to happen.

When Hamza reached the porch, he went straight to 'Amru, and before we were aware or had the opportunity to get up, he suddenly took the bow from his shoulder and raised it and quickly brought it down on 'Amru's head. Then we saw the strongman of our family—'Amru —that his form crumpled in pain and blood flowed over his face from the large cut that had appeared on his forehead. Then Hamza, angry, said to 'Amru, "You thought Muhammad was defenseless, so you abused him and you beat him with a stone!"

At this time, the men of the tribe, who had slowly come to their senses, stirred from places and were going to attack Hamza in support of 'Amru. Surprisingly, though, 'Amru, with all that pride, restrained himself from doing that and did not respond to that blow of Hamza. On the contrary, with a low voice he said, "It was my mistake. I said very impudent things to his nephew."

Once everyone had calmed down, an old man said in a shaky voice, "Hamza, the way you are supporting him, perhaps you have given up the religion of the ancestors too and have accepted the customs of your nephew?"

This was the same fear that 'Amru had had.

May our serious quarrel with Muhammad not be the cause for Hamza to accept his religion out of honor for his relative!

For in that condition, Muhammad's supporters found a great support like Hamza, and the task became very difficult for their enemies. It was also for that reason that 'Amru had taken the shame of that blow from Hamza on himself and had not said a thing.

"It is like that, what person can keep me from it? Now the rightness of what Muhammad says is clear to all the people!"

Hamza, after saying that, raised his voice,

"Know that if I had not chosen his religion before today, now I choose it, and what he says, I say also."

Thus, with a loud voice that echoed throughout the sanctuary, he added, "I testify that there is not lord but the Creator and Muhammad is His messenger."

'Ammār, when he saw the narrow ray of light that shone inside from the crack in the sheep fold, he lifted his head from the ground.

Pain rushed from one end of his body to the other. It seemed his body had been placed in a stone pestle and had been beaten hard.

His wounds were now beginning to throb. With every beat of his pulse, a murderous pain rose up in his being. Then, in the moment between each beat of his pulse, the pain subsided slightly until, with the beat of the next pulse, it manifested itself even more intensely.

'Ammār thought that he could stand pain and hardship much more than his father, seventy years of whose life had now passed, and his mother, who was a sickly old woman of almost sixty years of age, even though he was no longer young.

A rooster crowed from far way. On hearing its voice, Yāser rolled over and moaned.

After the passing of many hours in that stinking prison of Bu Jahl, awake and with severe pain, sleep had just come to him briefly when that sound woke him. What a sweet dream it was though! He was in his childhood and his younger brother, who had disappeared during the trip and had not come home to Yemen again, in a large garden, like the large green gardens of San'a, but more beautiful than them, were following one another. And as they were coming, their happy yelling filled the space of the garden.

Seeing that dream had filled Yāser's head with saltiness.

What was the interpretation of this surprising and sweet dream? What was about to happen that he had seen this kind of dream, during this difficult period when, with his wife and two sons, he was constantly under the torments and tortures of the Bani Makhzum clan every day and his thought every night was whether the next day he had the patience to endure this torture?

That is right, what had happened to their brother? Why had there not been any other sign of him?

Yāser remembered that day when he was young and with his two brothers Mālek and Hāres, and they had decided to go to Mecca to find their brother.

At that time, Mecca had more rule and order than today. The great man of the city was 'Abd al-Muttaleb, and all of the people obeyed him. Also, the blessings in the city were a lot. Yāser, who was from a poor family of the Modhaj clan of the 'Anas tribe, on seeing that daily ampleness and abundance of work, business, and order in the city, he had decided from then on to give up his homeland and to take up residence in that city. Because, although Mecca seemed no more than a depressing land of rocks next to Yemen with all that water, greenness, trees, and natural beauty, from that time when the Ethiopians ruled over their land, especially from the time of Abraha had become the king of Yemen, its commercial activity and the abundance and happiness of the people had left it.

No one had the urge to work. Friendship, kindness, and righteousness had declined among the people, and vengefulness, pessimism, hard heartedness, and unrighteousness had taken their place. For that reason, the young people, who had enthusiasm in their heads and more passion for life in their hearts, headed off for other lands and never came back. Yāser's brother had emigrated with that same passion. Then Yāser, on seeing Mecca, had followed his brother and stayed in this city. Then, since in the Hejaz no one could live alone without a people or tribe, he concluded an agreement with the Bu Hodayfa, one of the merchants of the Bani Makhzum, who was a reputable man, and he had come under his protection. At that time, he was a young man of twenty years of age.

He was with Bu Hodayfa for a while until his thinking and behavior was approved by his confederate, and Bu Hodayfa gave him a concubine of his by the name of Somayya as a wife.

Yāser let out a deep sigh of relief and thought about his fate. Had he spent fifty years of his life in this burning land of rocks until now someone like Bu Jahl had put him, his wife, and his two children in chains like animals and to do with him as he liked?

"Son, 'Ammār, are you awake?"

"Yes father."

"My eyes can not see well. Look and see whether the time of the morning prayer has come."

"It has father. The dawn has been shining for a while."

Yāser turned toward his wife who was father away

and who had put her two thin hands under her pillow.

"Are you awake Somayya?"

The old woman had not been able to sleep until now because of the fever. But so as not to cause her husband and sons to worry more, she had said nothing about it. With a voice from which the intensity of the sickness could be heard, she said, "Yes, Bu 'Ammār[1], I am awake."

"And you Abdullah?"

"Yes father. I am awake too."

"This unbeliever does not give us any water to do ablutions. So get up and do *tayyamun*[2] and pray the morning prayer."

One by one, they did *tayyamun* against the wall of the stable. Then Yāser stood in front and his sons stood behind him on either side. Somayya, however, sat behind them because she had not the strength to stand.

"God is the greatest…."

When the prayer was finished, Somayya stretched out right here where she was sitting. On seeing that, 'Ammār went to his mother and placed her head on his knee.

"Do you have a fever mother?"

"Do not worry my son."

How much patience this woman had! If it had not been for that deep faith and the consolation of the Prophet, they might not have had that much patience and self-control. In the meantime, 'Ammār, his brother, and his father had not experienced the torment that

---

1. i.e. "father of 'Ammār."

2. Ablutions done without water.

Somayya had because only Somayya had endured it. From the time the leaders of each people had begun to torture the Moslems of its own clan, the first persons of this family to be tortured had been Somayya.

Those days, 'Ammār, his brother, and his father saw how Bu Jahl, every day and several times, came to the house of his uncle Bu Hodayfa and beat the body of this old and weak woman with a whip until blood flowed from the marks of the whip. Sometimes Somayya fainted from the intensity of the pain. But they could do nothing because Somayya was Bu Hodayfa's concubine, and Bu Hodayfa, under pressure from the tribe, had let them do what they wanted to her. Perhaps she would quit following Muhammad.

During that period, one day 'Ammār, his heart bleeding from that happening, went to the Prophet to see if he could do something about his mother's situation.

Messenger of God, they are tormenting my mother very harshly and she is in a very bad condition.

The Prophet had said, "Be patient 'Ammār."

Thereafter, he had raised his hands to heaven and had said, "O' God. Let no one from Yāser's family be punished with the fires of hell!"

Then, 'Ammār became very ashamed that he had complained to the Messenger of God because he knew that this was not just his mother who had been imprisoned, tortured, and tormented by the idolaters and unbelievers. All the slaves who accepted

Islam were beset by this onerous wrath. Had not the Messenger of God himself continually been exposed to torment and abuse? And if 'Ammār only had the grief of his mother, the Prophet had the sorrow for all the Moslems.

Now, though, could that weak old woman stand up to that painful torture?

With the shining of the first ray of sunlight of the dawn inside from the slits in one pair of the sheep fold, activity began in the house. After a while, one of the concubines opened the cell and brought a small loaf of barley bread and a jug of water for each one of them.

That was their food until evening. Therefore they should not have forgone it. For that reason, however hard it was, the father and sons ate their own bread, but Somayya could not eat more than one or two bites.

The last bite had still not gone down their throats when one of Bu Jahl's tall slaves came and summoned them. It became clear that they would take them to Bahtā that day, in the southern portion of Mecca, and, like several days ago, torture them.

They set out with Yāser and Abdullah in front and Anwar following them with the weight of his mother on him and with his hand around her.

In the street, on seeing Bu Jahl, whose nose was flared and waiting for them, Anwar said, "My mother is sick and has a fever 'Amru. Do not bother her today so she can get a little better."

Bu Jahl, appearing to have heard some good news, let out a loud laugh and said, "Why do you not want

Muhammad's one and omnipotent god to heal her?"

Anar, fearing that Bu Jahl would say something ugly about God and His messenger, did not say anything else.

So Bu Jahl advanced with a long whip in his hand and those four persons followed him. Two hefty and black Ethiopian slaves of Bu Jahl—one tall and the other short—whose upper bodies were bare and were wearing red skirts to below the knees, followed them with tools for torture in their hands.

On the way, there was nothing but angry looks empty of kindness and poisonous words, abuses, and mockery of the unbelievers and idolaters. Sometimes they also passed children who were playing and there were stones that were thrown at them by them. So that the stones not strike their faces, they had to raise their hands.

Among the on-lookers there were sometimes Moslems who, saddened and weary, watched them and with their looks reflected all their empathy.

Finally, they reached the place of torture in the rocky plain.

The summer sun had still not reached the middle of the sky, but the ground of that barren plain was cooked by the heat. On recalling that pervious torture that they had experienced in that harsh place, an ominous fear assaulted the hearts of each one of those four persons unconsciously, and their pulses sped up. Then, as if a poison had been distributed in their veins, life went out of their hands and feet, and suddenly their knees began to shake.

Bu Jahl, as if he sensed their inner states by their paleness, said with a laugh from pleasure, "What? What do you say?"

Trying to conceal his helplessness, Yāser said, "We seek refuge in God from the evil of every malevolent oppressor."

On hearing those words. Bu Jahl let out an intoxicated laugh and said, "Which god? The one who has helped you these few days?"

He said to his slaves, "Tie their hands and feet to these stakes because today is another day."

Tow dexterous slaves ran forward.

The tying did not take but a few minutes. Then Bu Jahl went forward, whip in hand.

"Today, before your torture begins, I will give you an opportunity to stop this stubbornness and with that, you can buy your life and freedom. Come out of this error Muhammad has led you into and come to the religion of your ancestors. Condemn his and his god before all the people and like before go back to your life and work."

The answer was silence. Yāser, in that position of his with his back to the wooden stake stuck in the ground and with his hands and feet tied to the stake with rough rope, he said, "Death is better for us than that kind of life you promise us."

Somayya, who, because of how tight her hands were pulled back, her thin chest was jutting out under her worn-out flowery cloak, nodded her head along with her husband.

Bu Jahl looked at Anwar and Abdullah. These two

also had no answer save a meaningful silence.

On seeing that, Bu Jahl suddenly broke and caved in inside. Even though they were his prisoners, these few days it was he every time who had kneeled to those four persons. Thus, with blind rage and out of distress, he rushed at them and began to beat them about the head and body with the whip. He beat them and showered them with indecent curses. It was clear from the way he hit that this time it was more than to cause them to give up their religion. The intention was to empty his bag filled with anger and revenge inside him.

"I will kill you! I will beat you so much that your soul leaves your body! Today I will finish my business with you."

Somayya fainted with the first blow and her delicate head hung on her chest. Yāser was no better than her, but he tried not to give in. It was harder for Abdullah and Anwar. They endured because the greater strength of their bodies meant they did not faint. Thus, they were the targets of most of the blows. They wept and put their screams of pain by calling the name of god and asking His help in their heart.

"O' God, come to our aid!"

'Ammār, after those ruthless blows one after the other and that inner pressure and burning, suddenly felt pressure on his heart. Then, breathing heavily, he placed the whip to the side and went to that shade that was in one corner and sat on the straw mat that his slaves had just spread out for him.

Sweat was rolling down his head and face, and his

color was turning from red to yellow now.

As he had earlier ordered, tow slaves were busy lighting a fire in a stone furnace in a far corner.

'Amru looked straight ahead,, breathing heavily. Like previous days, several of the youths of the city had gathered to see the torture of Yāser's family, and their number increased every moment. All, whispering, looked on the lowliness of those four persons, half alive and crumpled up. It was as if they did not dare go closer or speak louder for fear of 'Amru's anger. Suddenly, from among them, a man who had just arrived went to the middle of the area and went toward the wooden stakes without paying any attention to 'Amru.

'Amru, on seeing him and what he was doing, half stood where he was. It was Muhammad!

Without looking at Bu Jahl, the Prophet—as if it was not him—with a saddened face, caste a glance at those four persons. Then he gently stroked the heads and faces of 'Ammār, Yāser, and Abdullah and empathetically said, "Be patient, family of Yāser, for your reward is heaven."

He raised his two hands toward heaven and said, " O' God, make them steadfast and give them a good reward!"

On seeing the Prophet, Somayya seemed to find new life and raised her head—enough to see all the on-lookers—and said, "I bear witness that you are the Messenger of God and that that good news which you bring is true."

The Prophet prayed for her and left.

After he left, 'Amru, who, like someone bewitched, had remained motionless where he sat, suddenly jumped from his place.

"Lay them down on the ground!"

The slaves went to them and one by one untied the ropes from their hands. They laid them down on the rocky ground baking from the burning heat of the summer sun, and tied them hands and feet to four stakes I the ground in four directions.

"Fire!"

The short slave went to the flaming furnace and with long tongs that were lying beside it picked up a large coal from the fire of the furnace and came forward.

With a sign of his hand, Amru pointed to Somayya.

"Put it on her foot."

Some of the youths and adolescents who now filled all of the area, fearful, turned their heads away.

Suddenly, the loud and long scream of Somayya broke the heavy silence of the plain.

Following that, the sound of a louder and more drawn out scream from her rose up and the smell of burnt meat filled the air. Then the sound of painful sobbing from the incapability of 'Ammār and Abdullah arose.

Somayya fainted, but a dark smoke still rose into the air from the sole of her foot.

As tears, like a flood, rolled down his aged and wrinkled face and became lost in his thick white beard, Yāser, without a sound, prayed for his suffering wife.

'Amru, who had now come beside his prisoners,

wanted water.

The short slave, from a jug that was under the shade, poured water into a clay goblet beside it and gave it to his master. 'Ammār took the goblet and sprinkled that and water on the head and chest of Somayya all at once. A sort wave of shivering rushed through the head and shoulders of the old woman. Filled with pain, she the raised her eyelids.

Bu Jahl gave her an ugly curse and said, "I am not going to let you go today until you speak well of our gods and speak ill of Muhammad, or you will be killed."

Somayya trained her lifeless and feverish eyes on the thing, evil-filled eyes of Bu Jahl filled with revenge, and suddenly with a voice so loud no one had heard from her during those days, screamed, "Death to you and your gods Bu Jahl!"

A commotion arose among the on-lookers. Bu Jahl again lost control of himself. He suddenly raised his right foot and with all his strength brought it down on the empty stomach of the old woman. Then, in the blink of an eye, he took the dagger from the scabbard on his belt, knelt beside Somayya and raised his hand with the dagger and several times, one after another, he plunged the dagger into her stomach.

On seeing that scene, several of the small children watching, screeching, began to flee.

'Ammār and Abdullah, amazed, were staring at their mother Somayya when, after a quick shiver, with out movement, she fell to one side and her eyes, fixed, kept staring at a point.

Tears flowing, Yāser said, "We are all from God and we return to Him. May heaven be pleasant for you brave woman."

Bu Jahl, with snicker, cleaned the bloody dagger with the sleeve of Somayya's cloak. He placed it in the scabbard and went toward Yāser.

"Now it is your turn you old jackal! You saw that 'Amru is not a joking man. Either say what I wanted from you, or expect a more ominous fate than what your unfortunate wife had!"

An animal electricity now shone in his black penetrating eyes.

"'Amru, you are needlessly tormenting yourself and us! You think we fear death in the way of God? With that deed, you bought eternal damnation and gave the honor of martyrdom to that virtuous woman. It is a source of pride for me that my wife became the first martyr of Islam. For you it is a great shame that you became the first killer of a Moslem. O' that...."

"Take this you errant and lowly fellow!"

Bu Jahl, like an angry wolf, flew at Yāser and began to pummel the side and stomach of the old man with a rain of deadly kicks. But the suffering body of Yāser did not need that much beating, because with the fifth kick, the breath twisted inside his breast and did not return. The old man crumpled up as much as his feet and hands tied to the four stakes allowed. He let out a long groan. His feet turned blue, and his mouth remained half open.

"Hard-hearted! Hard-hearted! Death to you! Death to you! Death to you!"

It was the long cry of Abdullah that rang through the plain one after another and repeatedly.

Bu Jahl, tired from that relentless struggle, said to the tall slave, "Whip him until he dies or he says what we want him to say."

He added to the other slave, "And you! Strip this other one and put chain mail on him!"

The slaves did what he ordered. Then it was the whistle of the whip that continuously split the air and descended on the bare body of Abdullah, and with every blow the cries of pain of the young son of Yāser pained the hearts of the on-lookers.

The sun had risen into the sky and was approaching midday when bit by bit the deadly and wearing torture of 'Ammār began. The chain mail got hotter and hotter every moment and its rings, like melted strips, burned Anwar's skin and flesh, and went into his body bruised by torture.

'Ammār tried not to show his weakness in front of Bu Jahl, the idolaters, and the unbelievers who had gathered to observe their torture, although he knew very well that looking and not yelling before that severe torture was beyond the endurance and ability of any human being. In the meantime, however, what he did show was that he could endure the painful martyrdom of his oppressed father, and the deathly torment of his brother and himself, and not allow the grief and deadly pain to buckle his knees and give in to the wants of the enemies of God. So, he allowed the tears to drip like a flood onto his weak and burnt cheeks. Some times he did not refrain from allowing his weeping to turn into sobbing so that the enemies could hear. Because if he did not allow himself to do that, it was for fear that from the tremendous pressure on his mind and body—both—would tear them apart. Among the tears, weeping, and intermittent screams, he constantly remembered the name of God in his heart, mind, and on his tongue, and sought help in being firm. 'Ammār, in that condition, where he had closed his long attractive and pleasant eyes so the blazing sun would not take away the sight of his eyes, sometimes he realized—with opportunities between bitter thoughts and the pain of the body and mind—he hear voices of those around that it seemed the intensifying heat of the sun had scattered the on-lookers and sent them to the cool shades of their homes. Too, his brother had fainted under the soul-melting blows of the whip and the heat of the sun because no sound came from him now.

'Ammār opened his eyes and turned his head toward him apprehensively.

Surprisingly, though, after blinking several times, he could see his brother's face there under the blinding light of the sun, he could not discern find any sign of life in him. Blood had covered all his young and muscular chest and arms, and his face had fallen on its side on the burning dirt and stones. A thin stream of congealed blood was falling in the dirt from the cover of his narrow lips, and his eyelids, with those large beautiful eyelashes, had remained half open.

'Ammār did not see any more than that, and suddenly lost consciousness.

That condition of his, from the view of the short slave, who had now for sometime taken the whip from the hand of the first and was beating the body of Abdullah unmercifully, did not go unnoticed. The slave, with all his affinity for the heat and sun, was now himself really feeling dizzy and tired from the intensity of the shining of the sun on his head and half-naked body. Facing 'Amru, who had a goblet of wine in his hand and was leaning against a cushion, he said, "Master, I think the bodies of both of them have lost life."

'Amru, calm and weak from the heat, seemed to have heard about the death of a sheep, put the goblet of wine to one side, picked up the colorful fan woven of palm leaves from the ground and came towards the slave fanning himself.

First he looked at 'Ammār.

"I do not think this one is dead."

Not all of the individuals if this family had to die like this, because if it happened like that, with a doubt, 'Amru would have lost in that wager and the correct victors would be them and Muhammad. But if one of them remained and became disgusted with Muhammad and his God, the end result would be different. Meanwhile, Somayya and Yāser, though healthy and active, in any case, they were all ad on the verge of old age. Abdullah and 'Ammār, however, were young and strong. Especially 'Ammār, with that tall broad-shouldered stature, intelligence, skill, correctness, internal and external beauty and flexibility, were strongly attracted to Amru's uncle, Bu

Hodhayfa.

"Water!"

The tall slave, who was waiting in a corner of the shade with both hands over his chest, brought a cup of cool water from the jug.

'Amru took the cup from him and poured the water from it all at once on the head and face of 'Ammār. 'Ammār let out a short moan and without opening his eyes, moved his head a little. 'Amru let out a short laughed and said, "Good for you! It is still too soon for you to die! I still have a lot to do with you."

Then he turned to Abdullah. He picked up his face from the ground with his foot and knew on seeing those half-open eyes and that dried stream of blood at the corner of his mouth, that he was finished. "Too bad!"

Now, only 'Ammār was left. He must not die before he had done what was wanted.

Be very careful hat this one does not die. Torture him, but not so he gives up the ghost. He must also bear the oppression of his father, mother, and brother. We have to get out of this one's throat what those did not say."

The short slave went to the shade, knowing his job, and returned with a cool cup of water. He sat on the ground, took 'Ammār's head in his lap, and poured the water into his mouth one gulp at a time.

The coolness of the water—more or less—returned to 'Ammār's body the strength it had lost. Then, again, he felt the pain of the body and the burning of the rings of melted iron of the chain on his body, and his repeated cries hurt Amru's ears.

"You see that there is no one to help! This murderous heat seems to have caused your lord to go to the cool shade and room! The most fruitful persons to you seem to be now me and these two slaves. Your father, mother, and brother have been killed and are totally oblivious to you. Learn from them and save your soul from this pain and suffering. We do not want you to do anything but say a few words!"

But before he finished speaking, 'Ammār had fainted again.

"O' Messenger of God, 'Ammār also turned away from Islam and returned to the religion of idolatry."

"Yes Messenger of God, I heard that too."

"'Ammār? After experiencing all that torture and the martyrdom of his mother, father, and brother?"

"Yes, Sohayb."

"That 'Ammār whom I know would not do that until his soul had left his body."

"That is how it happened Sohayb."

"How did it happen that 'Ammār's mother, father, and brother, who became believers with him, did not renounce Islam until the verge of death and he with that much belief does like that?"

"Sohayb, perhaps they would not do otherwise whoever it was with that torture the leaders of the Bani Makhzum did to 'Ammār."

"Yes, I also heard that Bu Jahl changed his manner of torturing 'Ammār after the martyrdom of Somayya, Yāser, and Abdullah. If he had not, certainly 'Ammār would have become a martyr without giving them what they wanted."

Saddened, the Prophet was sitting in a corner of the large guestroom of Arqam and said nothing. He was listening to his friends' talk, but his heart was with 'Ammār.

What did 'Ammār, now alone with that hurting body and that memorable and agitated mind in his poor hovel, do? How could he endure that sudden difficult loneliness?

With a signal from the Prophet, his followers entrusted and the mother, father, and brother of 'Ammār to the ground with much dignity. It was because of that that one or two of the friends, such as Bilāl and Mos'ab 'Omayr, whose Islam was still not known to the idolaters, nursed 'Ammār. But in 'Ammār's situation, he had more need for empathy and sympathy. Anyway, with those informers the enemy had, it was not prudent for the Prophet himself to go see him.

"Messenger of God, how do you see this affair?"

"Which affair Sohayb?"

"I can not believe these words because the 'Ammār I know has a being filled with belief in God, and Islam is mixed with his flesh and blood."

Hearing that, the followers of Muhammad remembered what they had heard earlier from his mouth about 'Ammār:

"'Ammār is that same skin between my eyes and nose."

And that is how it was, because 'Ammār was very close to the Prophet and there was never a day he did not see the Messenger of God. So how did it happen that such a person did that?

Doubtless, it was the same thing the Prophet had said.

That fear and grief that had caste a shadow over the assembly at the beginning seemed to suddenly go away and again the hearts became bitter. Thus, with the Prophet's signal, Abdullah Mas'ud began to recite several verses from the Koran in a pleasant voice. Verses about the correctness of the promises of God for the believers, and heaven which was their reward in the other world. There they would have neither fear nor grief. He said. And he promised the unbelievers and idolaters a painful punishment.

Hearing these verses was a cool breeze that blew in their burning insides and bestowed a surprising calm on their agitated minds. So, in their hearts such longing to see the lord and be forced from that life full of suffering was awakened, that they became envious of those first three martyrs. Each one of them wished in their hearts to have been in the place of those three persons.

Abdullah Mas'ud's recitation of the Koran had still not finished when someone knocked on the door. One long knock. A wait. Then two knocks, one after the other, but shorter than the first knock.

It was one of their own, because they had knocked on the door just as they had agreed. Therefore, Zayd Arqam went up on the wooden stool that was under the window of the room, stuck his head out of the small window, and after a moment brought his head inside and said, "It is Bilāl and Khabāb Arat, and someone whose face is not very visible."

Khāled Sa'id quickly got up and went to the courtyard to open the door for them.

This Khāled, from that day his father ran him out of the house, went to the Prophet and lived in his house. Thus, like a son who serves his father, he was away with him ad he liked to perform work for the Messenger of God himself.

We were in the room when the three entered. Then we were surprised to see that that man whose face was covered was 'Ammār. His head face, and body were so scarred that I only recognized him after a few moments.

His face was very swollen and all around his eyes was blue. His forehead and head were broken and balm had been put on them and bandaged. It was clear that he did not have the strength to come there himself. Therefore, after some of the night had passed, Bialal and Khabāb had brought him.

'Ammār threw himself at the hands and feet of the Prophet and wept bitterly.

The Messenger of God raised him from the ground ad offered his condolences on the martyrdom of his mother, father, and brother. Following the Prophet's example, one by one, each of us offered his condolences.

After 'Ammār calmed down a bit, weeping, he asked forgiveness from the Prophet.

The Prophet said, "What has happened 'Ammār?"

'Ammār said, weeping and despondent, "Messenger of God, that happened which should not have happened. The idolaters did not free me, and they tortured me so much that I dared offend you and spoke favorably of their idols."

The Prophet wiped the tears from 'Ammār's large eyes with his hand and asked, "At that time when you said those words, what was your heart like 'Ammār?"

'Ammār, a lump in his throat, and with a voice shaking from fever, said, "The belief in my heart was firm and my certainty had not decreased even a little bit."

The Prophet, kind, said, "So, from what you said, you have nothing to fear."

Then he added, "If they tortured you again and you saw yourself in difficulty, repeat what you said today."

We saw here that a state like the occasional desert of inspiration touched the Prophet. (You know that of all those states, one was the inspiration that fell on his heart. Then verses would begin to flow from his mouth.) Then he recited,

"Anyone who, after faith, becomes a nonbeliever in his God, not he who was forced to do that, when his heart was calm with his faith; but someone who opens his heart to non-belief, garners God's anger and a great punishment awaits him."

"This, was because they like the life of this world more than the life of the other world; and God does not guide the unbelievers."

"They are persons on whose hearts, ears, and eyes God has placed a seal and they are ignorant.

"Thus, they will necessarily in that world also be of those who experience loss."[1]

---

1. *An-Nahl* (The Ant): 106-9.

The hot summer sun had just risen in the sky when Omaya Khalaf went to see Bilāl.

Bilāl knew that—a new period of his torture—much harsher than before—had begun, because the torture by his owner Abdullah Jod'an did not produce any result from him and he did not give up being Muhammad's follower. This same Omaya, whose hard-heartedness was on all the people's tongues, was sent by the tribe to learn about Bilāl's torture.

Before he could think about what he was expecting, unconsciously Bilāl's heart began to beat faster. But there was no escape except to either give in to what Omaya and the other chiefs of the Bani Jomah wanted, or to firmly endure all those tortures.

Omaya took the end of rough woolen rope around Bilāl's neck in her hand and headed for the street. Bilāl necessarily followed after her. They headed toward the dry and hot plain on the edge of Bathā.

Bilāl thought to himself in that condition, "Like an animal was following his own oppressive owner."

It was not other than that either. It was true that the worth of a slave for someone like Omaya was sometimes less than that of an animal.

On remembering the bitter end and the sad fate of the fellow believers, a sudden anger overtook Bilāl. Thus, unconsciously, he ground his firm, wide white teeth so hard together that the sound could be heard in the hot street empty of any passersby. True, why must a group of a few people like Omaya Khalaf, Abdullah Jod'an, Bu Jahl, Bu Sufiān, and such like, who had all the blessings, comforts, ad freedoms, and opposed to them a large group such as Bilāl, his brother, sister, and mother, spend all their life in slavery, suffering, and torment?

What custom was this that the first group was allowed to take his father and mother from their homeland of Ethiopia four and a half decades ago and with force bring them to another land and take all their worldly possessions from them and do whatever they wanted with them?

When Bilāl thought hard about all of his life of twenty-five or six years, he did not see one hour of freedom and repose for himself because he had been born a slave. Since his father, Rabāh, and mother, Hamāma, were slaves of the clan of the Bani Jomah when he opened his eyes to the world. The custom was that the children of slaves were considered slaves of the owner of his father and mother.

Before he met the Prophet and heard what he said about slaves, Bilāl did not feel bad about his fate. No matter how much, earlier, depending on his nature, from the way he saw himself and other slaves, he became very depressed. But with that tradition that was common among the Arabs, and those words the masters constantly uttered into the ears of their slaves, gradually they arrived at the belief that the axis of his creation was situated around here. Some were created to be superior and to be masters. Another group to be slaves of the first group. Especially because those slaves were black and not Arabs. Until he became acquainted with the Prophet and know it was not like how they said. All human being are from one essence, and their mothers and fathers are the same. If God made them different classed and tribes, it was so they would know one another. White is neither superior to black nor Arab to non-Arab. All human beings—of every color, ethnicity, class, and family—are equal to one another like the ribs in the chest. If there is superiority, it is in abstinence, virtue, and honesty. Thus, God, from the mouth of His prophet, ordered the slave-owners to treat their slaves like their own relatives and families, not to give them tasks beyond their capability, be kind to them, give them the same things to eat as them, clothe them as themselves, and many teachings like that that, if the slave-owners did them, slavery would not remain as it is.

When Bilāl heard those teachings, the world and life took on a different shape and color in his view because contrary to the idols, in the view of this god whom the Prophet had made known, he, who was a black Ethiopian slave, was no different than his owner, Abdullah Jod'an, except that he had more ability,, with favorable actions and speech to reach position much higher than his master before their lord. Thus, when he mentioned those teachings to his master, as if waiting after a long time of thirst, she had arrived at a bubbling spring of cool and delicious water. Tears had appeared in her large black eyes and without any discussion she had accepted that religion.

Bilāl drew a hand around his neck. The line of wounds from the rope had become fresh on his neck and blood was coming from them in several places. Several days earlier, before Bilāl and his mother were given to Omaya Khalaf, his owner had put that rope on his neck. At that time he had given the end of it to the children city, so they could lead him through the streets and neighborhoods like an animal and throw rocks at him.

That is how it was when I was the guardian of the small idol temple especially for Abdullah Jod'an. (There was one of these shrines in the house of each of the wealthy and great men of the Qureish. They kept the idol particular to the family there and they performed their prayers to it every morning.) Abdullah Jod'an had twelve slaves. He liked me the most. Therefore, he entrusted me with the keeping of the special shrine.

One day, according to earlier tradition, he, his children, and his dependants came to that shrine to perform the ritual. Earlier, I had performed those rituals with them. That day, I had accepted Islam for a while, but Abdullah did not know that.

When they prostrated before the idol, I prostrated as well. But I prostrated to the one Lord, as was the manner of the Moslems.

What I did was not unnoticed by the sharp eyes of Abdullah. So he stopped his own worship and angrily said to me, "Are you prostrating to the god of Muhammad?"

I had no choice but to reveal my secret, and I said,

"Yes, I prostrate to that Lord Who is superior to all existence."

He became very upset and slapped in the mouth with his hand, so hard that my mouth filled up with blood. Then he tied me up in a room day and night and gave me nothing to eat or drink.

He opened the door the next day and wanted me to renounce the Prophet and to return to the religion of the tribe. I did not accept. He brought a rough rope, tied it around my neck, took me to the street, and gave the end of the rope to the children so they could lead me through the streets and neighborhoods and curse the Prophet and his religion.

Thus, that day, those children pulled me so much this way and that, and the people threw stones at me, that blood ran from my neck and various places in my body.

That day, Abdullah had become annoyed at what Bilāl's mother and sister, 'Agra, and his brother, Khāled, were doing, because he knew Bilāl's mother had also accepted the new religion. So, when Bilāl was returned to the house, bruised, pale, and shaking from hunger and thirst, Abdullah had whipped his mother, who was tied to a column, in front of him. Hamāma had wept and moaned, but she did not say what Abdullah wanted her to.

Once Hamāma had lost consciousness, Abdullah said to Bilāl, "Do you not feel sorry for your mother? Why do you not come out of Muhammad's magic circle?"

Bilāl, feeling as if he was about to faint, had spoken of the love and infatuation of the just Lord. Then facing his mother, he had recited,

""How sweet is suffering of the friend.

"And how beautiful and awe-inspiring is your firmness and standing up for him!"

Then, facing Omaya, he had yelled,

"You are torturing her, but her body is now so empty of anything other than God that she does not feel the pain of your torture.

"On the contrary, the more torture there is, the happier her soul and mind, which are filled with God's compassion, become." She does not feel the pain, but she tastes the punishment and pressure of the truth and worshipping the one God.

"Should I feel sorry for her because such a God has made her the object of His love?"

Hoping to understand a point amidst his words, Abdullah had listened to what he said until the end. Then, angry, he had started beating him until he fell down out of breath.

"Lay down!"

"What?"

"I said lay down on the ground you errant and unfortunate man!"

They had reached that part of the desert on the outskirts of the quarter of Bathā where black rock walls rose up on three sides.

The high rocks and the ground bordering them like clack mirrors, smooth and shining, glistened before the melting sun. The air at that time of day was so hot that no person could bear to touch the mountain or put a bare foot on the rocky soil. It was as if inside the earth there was a large furnace of fire burning, melting, and flaming.

Omaya, wearied by the burning heat of the air, beat the whip against Bilāl's body and yelled, "I said lay down you impudent and damned man!"

When she saw Bilāl's hesitation, she put her foot on the back of his and with both hands pushed against his chest.

Before he realized it, the bare back of Bilāl had fallen on the sharp and burning pebbles upon the ground and his two hands and feet were tied in four directions to four large stakes in the ground. The he clearly realized that in a moment, al over his back, as if he were on burning nails. His skin was blistering and swelling. He saw that Omaya, breathing heavily and sweating profusely, was rolling a large stone over the ground towards him.

So as not to let fear the opportunity to slip into his heart, Bilāl lowered his eyelids when the stone suddenly rested on his chest. Such a sound arose from the bones in his chest that he thought his ribs had caved in. The breath in his chest stopped coming and got so tight that he thought it would not come out. But neither his ribs were broken nor after that did he suffocate. It was as if, once again, his young strength, bulk, the strength of his bones, and his healthy body had come to his aid so as to prevent this tragic event from happening. Or perhaps Omaya, aware of the extent of his endurance, had placed a stone to take him close to death nut not to kill him. Wearying, slow, and severe pain and suffering that remove ability and brought one to one's knees, and make one humble, but did not kill.

Bilāl tried to move the rock off of his chest to one side by moving his body. Omaya, though, had kept his arms and legs so straight and the weight of the rock had taken so much strength out of him, that nothing happened except that his pain increased and the pressure on the left side of his chest cavity became so much that not much was left until his ribs on that side broke. In any case, struggling was useless, because Omaya, clever, was standing over him and she was staring at him with her bulging and round fish-like eyes so nothing went wrong.

"It is useless to struggle Bilāl! Forget about thinking that you can save yourself from this suffering, because except for increasing your own pain and causing me more trouble, you will not achieve anything. If you want salvation, do what I want from you. Say, "I believe in Lāt and Uzzā."

With his large black eyes building out from pain and pressing from his sockets, Bilāl said in a broken voice, "He is one! He is one!"

It was as if his strength and breath went with saying each word and did not return for several moments until he had regained some strength again and said the next word.

Omaya, with her knee on the ground, sank her fingers into the curly and thick black hair of Bilāl and said, "Say, 'I believe in Lāt and Uzzā!' I swear to the gods that you will stay like this until you die or you will renounce the god of Muhammad and worship Lāt and Uzzā."

Bilāl, with a voice that seemed to come from the bottom of a deep well, and broken, said, "I am disgusted with…Lāt and Uzzā."

When Omaya heard that, impatient from the heat and angry at her defeat, quickly took the rock off his chest, such that pain ran through Bilāl's entire body and his scream rose up to heaven. Then she sat on his chest and placed her large hands around his bruised throat and began to squeeze like a madman.

At first, Bilāl tried to move his body so as to free his throat from her hands. With those bound hands feet, however, and with that heavy body of Omaya like a mountain, he could not do anything. So he vigorously with his last built of strength, however, much he could, to draw air into his throat and chest. But the sound of gurgling came out of his throat, he suddenly felt his mind was beginning to turn dark. Then his whole body went limp and stopped moving.

"What are you doing Omaya?"

Tired and weak, Omaya raised her head. It was 'Amru 'Ās, one of the intelligent and clever young men of the Qureish.

"You will kill him like that Omaya!"

Breathing heavily and sweating, Omaya got up from off of Bilāl's chest. Her head had begun to hurt because of the unmerciful burning of the sun, and her eyes were two bowls of blood from the heat and anger. She was so fatigued that she seemed to have been tortured by her slave and had been brought to her knees.

In that situation, Bilāl moved and gradually regained consciousness. But he had lost so much strength that not much life was visible in his eyes. For that reason, when she saw him like that, Omaya, like an executioner, stood over him and said, "Say it. If you do not, I will kill you!"

As if his voice would not come out of his throat any more, Bilāl this time pointed to the sky with his finger and his lips moved in that same previous manner, saying "He is one! He is one!"

"Good after noon Omaya."

"And good afternoon to you Abdullah."

"I am grateful Omaya. I can see that you are still busy with this young man of mine in this murderous heat where everyone has sought out a corner and is resting."

"What can I say Abdullah? I am fed up with this ugly black and he does not cooperate."

"What about his mother Omaya?"

"She is even worse. That old woman, though, is nothing more than a decrepit and sick old woman whose life will not last more than a few more years perhaps. I also noticed that the more I torture that old white-haired woman, the more her son's insistence in what he said and his belief increases. God forbid that that woman, if she dies by our hands, this young man will never give up his following Muhammad and his firmness in his path will become several times more."

Abdullah Jod'an pulled the edge of the shade to one side and looked at Bilāl again. Bilāl's tall figure, with that narrow waist, was laying on his back on the burning and rocky ground, and his feet and hands were tied to four stakes driven into the ground in four directions and with rough ropes. At various places on his very brown and bare body whose color was tending towards blackness, there were signs of small and large wounds, new and old, healed fistula of the whip and other torture marks could be clearly seen. As on previous days, was a large black stone on his chest, which a little and curly hair covered. His large Ethiopian face which had little hair growing on it was grimaced from the unbearable pain and his tongue out of his mouth because of the intense heat and thirst and he panted. In spite of that, he showed very few signs of defeat or giving up.

"Will you not give him water Omaya?"

"Not during the day. But I give him water every dusk until the next morning so he does not die."

"Omaya, try not to let him die. He is a very valuable slave. Of all the slave I have, none of them has his health, industriousness, virtue, or skill. Do not look at how thin he is. In strength, he equals two or three strong men. He is so fit that there is not an ounce of fat on him. All of it is veins and fat and muscle. He has very thick and heavy bones. Rather than his body being of flesh, skin, and bone, it is of iron, silver, and catgut."

"Yes! If I did not know, during this week I have been tortured, I knew. Without him, whoever it might be, with this much torture, they would not be able to stand more than two or three days. Either they would have surrendered or died. But he stands up and suffers and does not show any sign of weakness."

"All of those are right Omaya, but his mind must not be overlooked. You are aware that before he became Muhammad's follower, Bilāl was very dear to me, and I favored him over all of my slaves. He was born in my house, and he has spent all his life in that house. For that reason, I know him very well. From childhood and adolescence he had that big and beautiful spirit and upright heart and will. From the time he was small, when he considered a task correct, and had set his mind on executing it, no one could dissuade him from doing it. For that reason, I fear that he will die in your hands and not relinquish his belief."

"Yes, Abdullah! If I did not believe in your talk earlier, I have reached it in those few days. Not just me, but Bu Hakam, with that much viciousness and dexterity inn torturing the followers of Muhammad, could not achieve anything with this slave of yours."

"Yes! He came here yesterday. Then, so her could humiliate me in front of some of the men of our clan, he boastfully said, 'Yes, son of Khalaf. I learned you are still at where you started after several days!'

"He thought that I had demonstrated more weakness than him in this task.

"I was angered by what he said, but because I was familiar with the details of the matter, so as to show to others how difficult it was, I said, 'Both the thief and the goat are present.' Now, this is the ball and this the field. If you can hit it better, be my guest!'"[1]

After what I said, Bu Hakam had no choice but to roll up his sleeves and enter the arena. I and all those men stood and watched to see what he did. The result was the same, though. Midday arrived and Bu Hakam fell down breathing hard and had not achieved anything.

"No!"

---

1. This is a reference to the game of polo, which did not exist in the Arabian Peninsula in the 6th or 7th *centuries A.D.*

"Yes Abdullah. He did what ever he had up his sleeves and special ways to torment and torture the slaves and none of them worked. Until he took hold of Bilāl's feet and pulled his naked and bruised body over the stones and rocks so much that thorns went through his skin and flesh and still that stubborn black kept saying 'He is one! He is one!' He wept and amidst the weeping he laughed and said, 'He is one! He is one!'"

"So that is the way it is Omaya. To tell you the truth, in my seven decades of life, I have never seen a group like the followers of 'Abd al-Muttaleb's grandson to be so steadfast in their belief."

"The surprising thing is that now they very openly and loudly speak badly about Lāt and Uzzā, may their names be exalted.

"Let me say one thing to comfort you Omaya. The fear of danger and death is meaningless to them. Muhammad's magic has so overtaken their minds and bodies that they are prepared to be torn to pieces and they will still not give up their faith. It is as if they consider our bitterest torture to be the sweetest gift in the way of their god. They believe that the more they offer in His way, the nearer they will become to Him."

"Yes. That is how it is."

Omaya, from the orange-colored clay flagon beside, poured some wine in a clay goblet that same color and extended the goblet toward Abdullah Jod'an. Then, with a mix of anger and sarcasm, she said, "Probably, though, they do not show it, in their hearts they are grateful that we are making it easier for them to get near their god."

"I do not want to drink any. I drank a lot before coming to you."

Omaya raised the goblet to his lips and drank all the wine at once. He then placed the goblet on the ground and wiped her lip and drooping mustache and started to think.

Abdullah also stopped talking . His old eyes were now staring at an invisible point straight ahead.

This last word of Omaya, with that tent of mockery and joking, was completely correct. Although it was not hard to believe that Abdullah, if he had heard that talk earlier from Bilāl, he would never have been able to believe it.

Abdullah was not feeling all that well that day, and he had stayed in his own home. He suddenly saw Bilāl, breathing hard and sweating, throw himself in to the house and close the door behind him.

Abdullah had still not revived from that action of his when he heard the sound of a ruckus and yelling in the street. They repeatedly knocked on the door.


"Abdullah, have you given up the religion of your fathers too?"

"I? What stupid things are these you are saying?"

"Then why are you hiding your deviant slave I your house?"

"My deviant slave? Of whom are you speaking?"

"Of that impudent young slave of yours! That black Ethiopian."

"The son of Rabāh the Ethiopia."

"Oh! You are talking about Bilāl."

"Yes. That is the one."

"Why are you saying these things about him? Has Bilāl done something you did not like?"

"What is worse than this Abdullah, than that today what he did to our idols in the sanctuary?"

"Bilāl?"

"Yes, Bilāl."

"Now, if you are true to your word, and you are not cooperating with your slave, hand him over to us so we can punish him for what he did."

"Calm! Calm! These embellishments that you claimed do not go with me. So that you do not have the least amount of doubt about this matter, I will now make a contract with you that if someone found a sign that I have turned my back on the customs of the ancestors, I will sacrifice one hundred camels at the foot of Lāt and Uzzā. Also, if it becomes clear to me that my slave did what you say to the idols of the tribe, I will do to him what you want."

:That is good."

"Let it be so."

"Calm! Calm! Now, with any uproar, one of you come forward and explain to me what Bilāl did."

"I will do it Abdullah."

"Come closer and tell me what you want to say."

"Abdullah, what I am going to say, I saw with my own two eyes and heard."

"I agree. Say it."

"In the sanctuary, we were sitting by the rock of Ismail and talking with one another. I was sitting in such a way that I could see the other wall of the Ka'ba from the corner of my eye. Then suddenly I saw someone come to that row of idols that were on that side and look around, searching. I became suspicious of his behavior. Then, in a way as if I did not see him, I kept my face toward my companions and watched him from the corner of my eye until I saw him suddenly spit on the idols and say to them, 'What losers are those unfortunate ones who worship you!"

"And he said that several times."

"I ran towards him yelling and when the other men learned what was happening, they accompanied me. But he fled, and we did not catch him."

"How surprising! Bilāl! O' Bilāl!"

"Yes, master."

"Is it true what they are saying about you? Did you do that to our idols in the Ka'ba?"

"Yes, master."

"Woe on you! So your actions have come to this?"

Abdullah, appearing to run the troubling thoughts out of his mind, ran his thick hairy hand over his forehead and eyes and said to Omaya, "I could not do anything. I whipped him. I kept him hungry and thirsty. I tied him up in the skin of smelly beef and kept him in it so long that he was suffocating and turning blue from the lack of air. I tortured his mother in front of him…. But he stuck to maintaining his belief and what he said. And you did what you could to him. Also—the way you say—'Amru Heshām, who is an expert in this, used whatever he had in his bag. Now, like this, and under this sun, which doubtless is causing his brain to boil, he has fallen on the ground and he still sticks to his word. How does this end? Are you not afraid that his surprising persistence in this path may be that he will cause the slaves, people, and downtrodden to go towards him and his religion?"

"It is as you say Abdullah. Let me tell you the truth: I do not know what to do in this matter. Before you came, I was torturing him, and I thought that today, if he did not do what I wanted, I would kill him. Until I saw Waraqa coming with his cane."

"Waraqa Nawfel?"

"Yes."

"You are right, Omaya. Has not Waraqa gone toward the customs of Muhammad?"

"I do not think so. I do not believe that they say he has chosen the young religion of Christianity because the Christians do not believe in the Ka'ba or have affinity for it. Now that he has not stopped circumambulating the Ka'ba during all these years."

"I also think that Waraqa, more than being a Christian, is a Hanif, because he, like the Hanifs, did not worship the idols, nor drink wine, and he did not eat the meat of the animals that were sacrificed to the idols. I think that because he knows Hebrew and he translated the *Injil*[1] into Arabic, people thought he was a Christian. If not, he has never spoken openly about his religion with others. But now I think that he, like Bu Tāleb, in his heart has gone toward the customs of Muhammad and he does not speak about his own belief."

---

1. The *Injil* as it is used in the Koran is usually identified with the four Gospels in the New Testament.

"Why Abdullah?"

"I do not really know the reason for that. Perhaps old age and weakness have compelled him to do that because his habit was like from youth when he would not quarrel with anyone over his own belief. If he was a monotheist, he only wanted that for himself. It was his inner and sincere belief. He did not claim to guide or lead the other people. He did not attack the idols of the fatherly beliefs of the tribe. He did not reject the multiple gods in speech. He did not lead his own people astray. All of those words he said to the people were stories about the times of their masters and prophets that he seemed to have learned from the *Injil*. So the people heard those stories and tales and they enjoyed them and they held Waraqa in high regard. His teachings of monotheism never rested from his repetition, was asking the people to be kind, lenient, and moderate with one another and distancing themselves from conflict and viciousness and vengefulness. For that reason, perhaps he now fears that if he reveals his own belief in Muhammad's religion, he will be harassed by us. Or it can also be that the belief that by concealing his own belief, he can better help Muhammad's religion."

"The reason for that can be both of those which you said."

"It is not improbable. But until he makes clear his own belief in Muhammad or he has done something inappropriate toward our gods and our fathers, it is not proper for us to do anything to him."

"In that case, neither should we be negligent of

him."

"Why Omaya?"

"I was going to say this when the discussion went in a different direction."

"Say it now what you saw."

"Yes! I was saying that yesterday shortly after noon, I was taking this black slave of yours when Waraqa came along with his cane. At the time, the rock was on Bilāl's chest, and he kept saying to himself, 'He is one! He is one!' Sometimes he would say "O' God, help me! O' God help me!'

Waraqa wept, went near him, and said, "Yes, He is one Bilāl."

Contemptuously I said to him, "Huh? What happened old man that at this time of day when dogs and locusts do not stir from their place for fear of the heat, you, with your decrepitude and blindness, are going into the mountains and desert?"

He said, "Are you not ashamed Omaya that you are doing that to the slaves of God? What need of yours does all this torturing you do to this young man satisfy?"

I said, "His life is in my hands and I will do with him what I want."

He said, "What kind of injustice is this that you are doing to him?"

I said, "The first ones to do him injust9ce are those who allowed him to go astray and who misled him."

He said, "I swear to God that id he does like this, they will build a building over his grave and I will weep for him so much every day and I will rub myself on it seeking blessings from it until it becomes a place of pilgrimage for the people."

I became very angry at this talk of his and I also became afraid. But so as not to show my anger, I said, "Do not be saddened Waraqa, for if he was going to die, he would have died in these few days."

He turned toward Bilāl again and said, "Be patient Bilāl, for He will answer your cry for help."

"Amazing!"

"Yes, Abdullah. That is the way it is."

Abdullah Jod'an, as he struggled to get up and go, said, "I placed his life in your hands, so you can do what you think is proper. But Omaya, end his affair soon so this story does not become larger than this."

Omaya nodded her head.

After AJ had left, Omaya pulled the jug to him ad poured its water over his head and face so it might remove the irritating heat of those ill-omened thoughts from his head. Then he laid down a while on the small couch inside the shade and began to think.

His eyelids were getting heavy. O' that we were in his house now and sleeping in his cool room.

"Heh! Son of Khalaf! Omaya!"

Omaya started from her place and sat on the couch.

"What?"

"No, son of Qohāqa."

Omaya looked there where Bilāl was tied down on the burning ground to four stakes. Bilāl was stretched out on the ground with that same rock on his chest. It appeared that he had passed out from the excessive pressure and heat.

Omaya stared at Bu Bakr with his eyes sad from his fatigue and heat.

"What do you want with me?"

"I heard that Abdullah Jod'an entrusted this slave to you."

"So what?"

"I would like to buy him. Are you willing to sell?"

"He is a bad-natured slave and sick right now. How can such a slave be useful to you?"

"You state the price of your goods."

"I will not sell him until I know why you want to buy him."

"You know why Omaya."

Bu Bahr turned his face away from Omaya and started to go back the way he had come.

"I had decided to do you a service and before you lose what he is worth, to buy him back from you."

Omaya's heart began to beat faster. O' that she had accepted his offer. That could have ended this whole affair, which had gone on too long.

Bu Bakr turned around half way away,

"Another suggestion Omaya!"

"Huh!"

"I have a white slave who is even stronger than this one. You take that white one with a black heart from me and give me this black one with a white heart."

This was an even trade that brought no shame with it for the Bani Jomah and others would not gossip about it.

I accept."

"Good."

Bu Bakr picked up the stone from Bilāl's chest and untied the ropes from his hands and feet. Bilāl did not have the strength to stand up. Bu Bakr helped him to rise from his place.

Omaya turned her face away from them so her gaze would not fall on Bilāl. Even though Bilāl was now so the prisoner of a fever that he saw things in a foggy and dark halo.

Those tow prepared to leave when Omaya sarcastically said, "You have become the loser 'Abd al-Ka'ba. I would have been happy with half this price."

Bu Bakr said, "It is not the way you think Omaya! It was you who suffered loss, because if you wanted several times this price, I would have paid it to you."

So he took Bilāl's hand in his and left there.

That evening, according to the former tradition, we had gathered in the house of Arqam. Our gathering every day there had several reasons. Among them was that we did not have the ability to gather in the sanctuary like the idolaters every evening. Another was that in these assemblies, one of us would recite the Koran. Thereafter, we would talk about those verses that were recited, and if we had a question, we asked the Prophet. Aside from those, we learned about each other's life, and if someone had the ability to help another, he did.

We all gathered that day, and still sometime was left until the Prophet arrived. When I saw all of the friends, I saw no sign of Khabāb Arat. This Khabāb was a good-natured and simple youth without any deception. He was the slave of a woman of the Bani Zohreh clan. Her name was Umm Anmār. Khabāb was a blacksmith. He was especially skilled at repairing swords. So Umm Anmār had started him up a shop, and every evening, whatever Khabāb had made from that work, she would take it from him.

Before he was inspired, the Messenger of God knew him and had a friendship with him and had empathy for him. After that, when the invitation began, Khabāb was one of the first persons—they say he was the sixth man—who chose to follow him.

That occurrence remained secret for several years,

until the idolaters learned of his becoming a Moslem and told Umm Anmār about the matter. From then on, his torturing began. First, Umm Anmār every day ordered another of her slaves to tie his hands and feet. Then, she heat a piece of iron in the furnace and placed it on Khabāb's head, and told him to stop following the Prophet. That woman did that to him so much that little by little all of the hair on the front of Khabāb's head fell out, and his head constantly had a severe pain.

Khabāb took his complaint to the Messenger of God. The Prophet prayed that God would give him an opening. After a short time had passed, such a pain appeared in Umm Anmār's head that she howled like a dog. She then tried the medicines that various persons suggested, but her pain did not subside. Until someone said to her, "The only cure for your pain is to heat some iron and place it on your head."

Amazingly, from then on, when pain afflicted her head, she went to Khabāb so he could heat some iron and place it on her head until the pain eased a little.

Umm Anmār, from then on, left Khabāb to himself. But her family followed up with torturing him.

Of that torture, one was that they would have him wear a chain mail on his bare body and have him stand in front of the fire of the furnace until the armor melted and the rings of it went into his skin and flesh. But he did not scream from the pain and he did not give in to their demands.

This was one of those days when the torturing and tormenting of Khabāb had become more intense.

Therefore, when I did not see him among the others. I became afraid for him. Until Bilāl began to speak about what had happened to Khabāb that day.

"Today, I had gone to the plain on the edge of Batha. The men of the Bani Zohreh were torturing Khabāb and a large group of the youths and children of the city had gathered to watch. Once all of their torture of Khabāb was ineffective, out of great anger, it seemed that one of them went crazy, because suddenly without any discussion, he picked up Khabāb's half-alive body from off of the ground and threw it on the red-hot fire of the furnace that was burning father away. He pressed his feet on his chest so much that Khabāb, after letting out several blood-curdling screams, fainted. When the smell of burning flesh and fat filled the air, several of the on-lookers ran forward and freed Khabāb from the grasp of that man. Then, we saw that the fire of the furnace had been put out by Khabāb's body."

Weeping, Bilāl ended what he was saying. It was clear that remembering that ominous scene had hurt his heart very much. What could he say? What had they accomplished? When the Messenger and Prophet of God was himself under constant harassment from his enemies and did not do anything but have patience, what could they who had chosen to be his followers do?

The idolaters began to ridicule, castigate, and denigrate us. When they got nowhere with that, they began to torment and torture.

At first, only the Prophet was the aim of their harassment. All the women of Mecca broke off their relations with Khadija, and she became very lonely. They would say to her, "You took a crazy person as a husband."

When the Prophet was in his house, his neighbors on both sides—'Ās Wā'el, Bu Lahab, and his wife—took away the repose of him, his wife, and their children. When they prepared to leave the house, they would pour those things on his path or say those ugly things to him.

They persuaded the crazy people, ignorant children, and sometimes even some of the slaves, men and women, to block his way wherever they saw him or follow him and say, "Crazy person, liar, sorcerer…! Crazy person, liar, sorcerer!" in order to destroy his greatness and dignity and to humiliate him in front of the people.

When those did not produce results either, the identification and harassment of his followers began

The most extreme of them was Bu Jahl. When he learned that someone had converted to Islam, he quickly went to his clan. If that person was a slave or refugee, he convinced his clan to torture him to death or quit following the Prophet. If he was a free man, he would go to him himself and castigate him very badly and say, "You left the religion of your ancestors, who were better than you? Know that from now on we will consider you ignorant and stupid. We will consider your view and belief ugly, and we will trample your honor and pride."

If he was a merchant, he would frighten him. "We will ruin your business and destroy your property."

I had made several swords for 'Ās Wā'el Sahmi. A while passed after that occurrence, and since he knew that I had accepted Islam, he did not pay for them. One day I went to him to collect that debt. Just like earlier days, he said, "I do not have any money today to give you."

I said, "'Ās, I am not going through the door of your house today to collect my debt."

He said, "Khabāb, what happened that today you are insisting like this on getting your money?"

I said, "Because I know why you will not pay your debt."

He said, "Yes. It is the reason that you imagine! Khabāb, you have become an unbeliever in our religion, and I consider the taking of the property of an unbeliever like you to be permissible for me. Know that I will not pay any debt to you until the day you stop following Muhammad's religion and become an unbeliever for him."

I said, "And you know that I will never be an unbeliever for him, until the time you die and are raised up on the Day of Judgment, and there I will collect my debt from you."

'Ās sarcastically said, "Do that, Khabāb! Give me until that day and exercise patience until I enter the heaven you talk about and collect some of that gold, silver, and jewels then and pay my debt to you!"

They did the same, even worse than that, to the slaves and weak Moslems. They beat some so much and kept them so hungry and thirsty that they no longer had the strength to stand up. So they said what they wanted. Especially, following the martyrdom of Somayya, Yāser, and Abdullah, when the Prophet had given them permission, when their life was in danger, to say blasphemous things and save themselves.

Some of the Moslem slaves had come close to dying under torture, until there was not choice but to buy them from them. The last of them was Bilāl, and that was at the time when the Prophet and his friends no longer had any money.

"Bu Bakr, if we had something, we would have bought Bilāl from the unbelievers."

"What are you saying Messenger of God? Do you want me to go to your uncle, 'Abbās, and ask him for help in this matter?"

"Do that Bu Bakr."

But how long could this method be pursued?

When Howza accepted Islam, a fervor had over taken the Moslems, because with his attachment to them, Islam acquired so much power that if one hundred persons had all at once converted to Islam, the followers of the Messenger of God would not have become so powerful. Upon his becoming a Moslem, the enemies necessarily began thinking of killing the Prophet. (Even though their unity against him and his followers increased.) Therefore, the number of Moslems as opposed to their enemies was not enough for them to have the power to oppose then face to face.

But patience to what degree? What kind of life was this that they had?


"My God, earlier when we were idolaters, we had a very high position among our people, and no one dared say one untoward word to us. How is it that now that we have turned to Islam, we have to endure all those humiliating and bitter things and not respond?"

"It is as you say 'Abd or-Rahmān. But now we have instructions to forgive."


"Messenger of God, we the slaves and the weak are experiencing a lot of oppression and torment at the hands of the idolaters. Do you not want the Lord to help us?"

"You are being hasty Khabāb. There were persons among the followers of earlier prophets who experienced more torment than you, and they did not demonstrate impatience. They scratched one of them with iron combs so much that all of his flesh and fat fell off. They put a saw to another's head and split it in two. But even wit that, they did not renounce their religion."

"Be patient my friends! I swear to your Lord and God, at His own time, will assert His religion and He will bring this affair to a close. Until a rider can go from San'a to Hadramawt and fear nothing but God."

But where was that assistance from the all-powerful Lord? At what time would it occur?

"Hāres Zama'a, Qays Faka, Bu Qays Walid Moghayera, Ali Omaya Khalaf, and 'Ās Monebba, after those tortures they experienced from their own families, renounced Islam and became idolaters again! Has not the time for that aid arrived?"

"There are persons whose soul the angels praise, when they allowed themselves to be oppressed. They ask them, 'What were you doing?' They say, 'On the earth, we had become humble people.' The angels say, 'Was not God's earth expansive enough for you to migrate?' Their place is in hell, and their end is bad."[1]

The men were saddened and had drawn their heads into their shells of bitter and saddening thoughts that, except for a few individuals, they did not notice the Prophet's coming. So, when those few individuals answered his greeting, the others came to and greeted the Prophet. But sadness rested so heavily on their hearts that the entrance of the Prophet and his smiles that always created joy could not untie the knot from their knitted faces.

The Prophet asked each of them how he was and they answered him. Outside, the sun had left the sky for some time. The remaining redness from that had so diminished from the horizon, and had become faint ad gradually was mixing with the growing darkness of the evening. Two of the first stars of the night were

---

1. *Al-Nesā* (The women), 97.

sparkling.

Bilāl, on seeing the look of the Prophet at the side of the courtyard, knew that the time for the dusk call to prayer had arrived. So he rose from his place and after a glance at the sky, began to say the call to prayer with his pleasant and carrying voice.

When the edifying heavenly expressions resounded in the air with that pure and pleasant voice, all of those former anxieties seemed to become ever more insignificant. Until all of the sudden nothing of them was left. Remembering the compassionate one Lord replaced thoughts of bitter helplessness, and allowed no room for any other thought. The tumultuous waves of the hearts calmed down, and the agitation of the minds quieted. Calm. A great calmness, like the expanse of a sea, on a calm and moonlit night, soft, calm, and smooth.

"Hurry to prayer!"

Those who needed to do ablutions hurried toward the courtyard.

"…Hurry to the best deeds."

All of them straightened their rows behind the Prophet.

"…Rise for prayer."

They stood up.

"The high, one Lord is the greatest."

Then there was the sweet and familiar voice of the Prophet which, upon hearing it, the soul was renewed. The boiling spring of phrases one after the other of prayer, that flowed from his tongue I the space of the room and could be heard by the ears of each one of them and washed their hearts in it and bestowed brightness and carried them with it to the much higher horizons.

"Praise be to You and the mercy of God and His blessings."

Silence for a time. Every person occupied with his own personal praises. Then the praises of the group. After that, the Prophet stood up facing the men praying. First, he mentioned the name of god. Then, as if aware of what had passed in the hearts of his friends, he spoke about their difficult tasks effected by the torments of the idolaters and unbelievers and he gave good news to the patient ones about the divine reward and nearness of assistance and relief from their Lord. Then he turned the talk to migration in the way of God and his religion and added, "God's earth is wide and it is allowed for those believing in one god, when they see their faith is in danger, to migrate."

The he recited,

"That person who migrates in the way of God will find many successes and openings. Whoever leaves of his own house to migrate toward his God and Prophet and dies on that road, God is responsible for his reward. And God is forgiving and compassionate."[1]

---

1. *Al-Nesā* (The women), 100.

It was dusk and the Prophet, just like on other days, was going to Arqam's house. His head lowered, he murmured that verse that had come down to him the day before and he was deep in thought.

"That person who migrates in the way of God will find much success and many openings. And every person who leaves his own house to migrate towards God and His prophet...."

The Lord had opened a crack for the salvation of the Moslems following a long time of suffering. Now was the time for them to think themselves what persons and how they were to migrate toward which land? This was a difficult trial for which every person may not be capable. Detaching the heart from friend, country, home, possessions, relatives, work, business, and accepting the suffering and danger of the long journey and living in a faraway and alien land was not an easy task. On the contrary, it needed deep belief and firm determination.

No matter how his followers had stood beside him in these five very difficult years, they were not all the same. Thus, before all else, these difficulties of this path had to be revealed.

Although he himself had not gone without benefit from the torments of the Qureish, the Prophet, nonetheless the Prophet knew the extent of their impudence toward him, because the fear that God had put in the hearts of the idolaters of him and the support of his uncle Bu Tāleb, does not offer them much opportunity in this task. His unprotected friends, however, were in difficult straights and suffering, without the Messenger of God having the ability to support them.

It was surprising that the torture and torment had encompassed all the Moslems—from slaves and weak persons to the great and noble.

On nearing the house of Arqam, the Prophet slowed his steps. At the turn in the street, he turned his head and looked behind him. In that light and darkness of dusk, there was no one in the street except an old man clad in rags who was slowly limping toward the bottom of the hill of Safā.

Before he raised his hand to knock on the door, Zayd Arqam opened the door in front of him.

The men were sitting in wait for him in orderly rows in the large room of the house and the room beside it that had no opening to it.

Once the dusk prayer and the supplications after it were ended, all the assembled in the larger room, and the Messenger of God began to speak. First he praised and thanked the Lord. Then he spoke about the verses that had come down concerning migration.

Migration was a commendable tradition that before them had existed among the peoples, nations, and worshippers of God. Whenever the life of a people became difficult in the land of their own fathers, and they could no longer bear them, this was the best method for saving their religion and themselves from danger and injury. At the beginning, the task was very difficult and its future was indefinite. Nevertheless, it eventually had a good conclusion.

The people of Moses found freedom, self-respect, and greatness after that great migration from Egypt, and they acquired the world. When the friends of the love left their families and city to protect their faith, they came under the protection of the omnipotent Lord, until their graves became the place of pilgrimage for other peoples. Aside from those, did not Mecca itself come into being with the migration of Hājer and Ismail to it? Was not the rule of the Qureish over these beating hearts and the trading intersection of the Arabian Peninsula and all the Arabs other than the first of their migration to this place?

From the beginning of creation, man has always been migrating in search of a better living. So why should they do that, or when did they allow fear into their hearts?

The words of the Messenger of God caste excitement in their hearts and the men began to think. Now, when the Moslems had neither the power nor the permission to fight their enemies, it was better that they grasped onto this.

"Messenger of god, what you say is that we should migrate like those earlier people have?"

"This is not God's order for everyone, and no one is compelled to do it. Every person needs to weigh his own condition until he realizes whether it is best for him to stay or go. So let him do it."

"What will you do Messenger of God?"

"My situation, day, and duty is not the same as yours. For that reason, I will stay in Mecca as long as God's order for my migration has not come."

"But where should we go to be safe from the pursuit and revenge of the unbelievers and idolaters?"

"God's earth is expansive, and every part of it is different. Select a place where you are more able and worship God."

When these words came out of the Prophet's mouth, and sigh of regret arose from all the breasts because aside from the other difficulties, the desire had remained in each of their hearts that the world come when they could freely worship their Lord the proper way without any fear or restraint, and practice the customs of His religion.

"You will know Prophet that many of us are poor people in our own land and we have a difficult life. How are we to live in an alien land?"

Before the Prophet could answer him, Abdullah Mas'ud answered him with the word of God.

"Every person who migrates in the way of God, he will find many successes and openings in the earth."

Then he added, "The poverty of many of us is not from inability or lack of qualifications. It issues from the incorrectness of the laws and the thinking that dominates society. In other words, those whose profit and dominance depends on this situation have imposed it on us. Though in a society with another way of thinking and other laws our fate would be very different."

As always, Abdullah Mas'ud's words were correct.

Thus, nothing else was said about this matter. Now all the questions concerned which land they were to go to so that things be the way that the Messenger of God said.

The closest city to Mecca was Taif, but it was not possible to go there because the people there were like the Meccans, unbelievers and idolaters. Also, the large temple to the idol Uzzā was in that city, and God had spoken badly of that idol in the Koran. For that reason, they, like the Meccans, were antagonistic toward the Prophet and his followers. The second was that the nearness of the road to Taif was reason that the leaders of the Qureish were always pursuing migrants and molesting them.

'Uthman Maz'un said, "It is not possible to go to Yemen or Persia either, because the rulers of Yemen takes orders from Chosroes, and Chosroes Parviz is a very arbitrary king. He is very disgusted and fearful of every new custom. Besides that, Persia and Rome, both, are very far from Mecca."

'Obaydollah Johsh said, "Although Yathrib is better than Taif, it is closer to Persia and Rome, but that does not work for this either, because the large quarrel between us 'Ās and Khazraj has made life for the people of the city difficult."

'Āmer Rabi'a said, "Besides that, there is no protection for us in Yathrib. Wherever we go, without support, we will not be safe from the pursuit and harassment of the Qureish."

In the beginning, when the way to migration had been opened with the permission of God, everyone had found that to be quite easy. Then a great wave of happiness ran through the harts of the oppressed. Now, though, they realized that the task was not as easy as they thought. So silence over came the assembly and the men fell into reflection.

At this time the Prophet began to speak.

"If you go to Ethiopia, it will be profitable for you. Ethiopia is a good land. A just and able ruler governs there and no one is oppressed in his country. Stay in that land until God opens a way. Then, if you want, you can come back to me."

It was as the Prophet had said. Ethiopia was far away from the influence of Persia, Rome, and the Qureish. Although its people were Christians, they did not have some of the inhumane ideas, perversions, or self-praise. More than that, the country of the Negus was on the other side of the Red Sea, and the Quriesh did not know how to sail a ship or fight on the sea. Thus, in that land, the Moslems were safe in every respect.

The merchants of Mecca were constantly in contact with Ethiopia. They took various kinds of goods there and brought goods from there. In Mecca many of the slaves were Ethiopian. For that reason, the Meccans were very familiar with that land and its people. The road to there from Mecca by sea was close to three days. Thus, it was closer than Syria or Yemen. Its ruler, the Negus, was a knowledgeable and open-minded man who followed the Christian religion. But his belief was not blind or superstitious. He was a man always searching for truth, and he had not closed his ears to hearing other words. For that reason, he was not hard on the followers of other religions. They lived free in his country. Why would he not do that with the Moslems?

At the intersection of those two roads where one went to the right toward the port of Jidda and the other turned slightly toward the north until on the edge of the Red Sea it connected with the port of Sho'ayba, the beautiful youth of the Bani 'Abd od-Dār alit from his camel.

He was hungry. So he took out from the saddlebag a package of food that Khadija had prepared for him to take along. It had several pieces of barley bread, a copper bowl of date halva, a contained of olive oil, and several pieces if dried and salted meat. The wife of the Prophet had given all of the emigrants those same foods that she had prepared for her daughter, Roqiyyeh, and her husband, 'At the intersection of those two roads where one went to the right toward the port of Jidda and the other turned slightly toward the north until on the edge of the Red Sea it connected with the port of Sho'ayba, the beautiful youth of the Bani 'Abd od-Dār alit from his camel.

He was hungry. So he took out from the saddlebag a package of food that Khadija had prepared for him to take along. It had several pieces of barley bread, a copper bowl of date halva, a contained of olive oil, and several pieces if dried and salted meat. The wife of the Prophet had given all of the emigrants those same foods that she had prepared for her daughter, Roqiyyeh, and her husband, 'Uthmān 'Affān. Also, the

Messenger of God had come to see each one of them off and had prayed for them.

Mos'ab picked up the piece of sun-dried bread, closed the bundle of food, and began to eat.

The night was slowly approaching midnight. A short while before a soft breeze had begun to blow from the east and brought the smell of the fetidness and dampness of the sea with it.

The moonlight of the beginning of the tenth of Rajab shone and the sandy road glistened like a silver line in its light.

Mos'ab 'Omayr, as a precaution, took his trusty camel behind a sand dune and had it kneel while he stood beside it. He was looking toward Mecca with his attractive black eyes so as to direct each one of his companions toward the port of Sho'ayb as they arrived.

When the news of the emigration of some of the Moslems reached Mos'ab, he had immediately decided to accompany them. So that is what he did. He was aware, though, that when his mother and father learned of that, they would immediately send someone after him in order to bring him back to Mecca. For that reason, he was very anxious that his traveling companions arrive quickly and distance themselves from the people.

His emigration was not because of fear of torture or the torment of the clan or a feeling of weakness before them. On the contrary, Mos'ab was in pursuit of a broad horizon so that in it he could freely worship the new and dignified God free from every barrier, fence, or hindrance of his mother, father, and relatives. So that he could speak with others about his new discoveries and realizations about it and invite others to it.

Earlier, his life was very empty and directionless. Now it had much feeling of enthusiasm, elation, and joy. In appearance, Mos'ab lacked nothing in terms of what others knew as good fortune and happiness. All of the great men of the city praised him. The youths were envious of him. The young girls of the city were enamored of him and desired him.

He was from a very large family. His third grandfather, 'Abd od-Dār Qosā, was the holder of the key of the city, the carrier of the flag of the Qureish, the water carrier and host of the pilgrims to the Ka'ba, and the head of the assembly House. Thus, his children, one of them being Mos'ab, had access to that large assembly from childhood, while, except for others like him, others remained bereft of it until they reached the age of forty.

His father, 'Omayr Hāshem, was one of the wealthy men of Mecca. He liked Mos'ab very much and fulfilled all of his wants. His mother, Khanās Mālek, with all that toughness with her children, her behavior toward Mos'ab was quite soft and gentle. Khanās considered Mos'ab to be the apple of her eye and her peace of mind. She was very pleased with him. She was prouder to have him than the others. She loved him like her own dear soul.

When that youthful child, with that stature and medium build, soft and delicate skin, happy and pleasant face and open forehead walked gracefully before her, it seemed they gave all the joys of the world to that wealthy and middle-aged woman. Thus, she did not shirk in any effort to making the child comfortable and happy. She attired Mos'ab in the most beautiful and expensive clothes. She bought the rarest perfumes for him. And she gave him the most delicious foods and drinks to eat.

As far as Mos'ab could remember, he had not wanted anything except what was made available to him or that was prepared for him a short while after that. He had a happy disposition, good habits, a calm disposition, and gentle morals. He had nothing to do with roughness. His outlook on the world and people was very bright and accompanied by good-will. He was honest, and he liked truthfulness. But when he reached the beginning of youth, he began to make himself look pretty and attractive, as was customary at the time. He spent all his days with his peers in play, passing time, thoughtless things, and having a good time. He was very happy with that kind of living free of every restriction. He wore new clothes and shoes every day whose prices were sometimes a hundred times the prices of the clothes of the poor people. He was always beautifying his thick attractive hair. He would put so much oil on his hair, and amber on it, that the sun and moon were reflected in it. He sprinkled so much perfume on himself that, when he passed through the streets, his fragrant smell lingered in the air.

The charming youth of Mecca came and went, and

attracted hearts to him. In the city, all the talk was about him. He was praised, and he fostered kindness, happiness, and desire in the hearts. He was gladdened and he dispersed enthusiasm, happiness, and frenzy about him. But the time suddenly arrived when, like someone has eaten one food a lot and constantly—no mater how delicious and desirable—he gradually became disgusted with all that happiness and joy. Tired of all that every-day repetition, he fell into thinking.

And then?

He avoided his friends, and for several days, alone, he would go to the plain around the city. An opportunity to think about those things in which he had earlier been immersed up to his neck.

He now realized that with all those encounters how much his life was hollow, empty, and sterile. Without any aim. Very low, closed, and narrow. Without correctness or diversity.

How much attending to his body had made him heedless of his mind. At that time, day by day, his skeleton became obese from too much satiety. His spirit kept becoming thinner and more afflicted from the intensity of hunger and thirst, until it came very close to death.

He realized that those joys were no more than bubbles on the surface of his stagnant life. In his continued heedlessness, his mind was depressed from the abundance of grief.

It was not futile that with all that success, he did not feel good-fortune in the bottom of his heart. It seemed he had lost something that he could not find. His life did not take on meaning or depth. But what that lost object was, he could not understand.

He thought, "Is life merely all this eating, sleeping, seeking gratification, playing, biding time, prinking one's self, and praise from others? And then the period of middle-age, selecting a spouse, an occupation, work, children, and then…?"

No! That kind of life could not be accepted by his heart. He could not see in himself the ability to accept long years of this kind of monotonous and wearisome life, like his fathers. That life was so cheap that it was as if by the price of discovering the spirit, it continuously added to the growth of the belly, their mean wants did not go beyond the narrow framework of their house and room.

Fresh glances inside himself brought newer questions in their wake.

"Truly, whence did we come? Whither will we go after death? What is the work of this activity?"

No idol could give an answer to these questions. Those spiritless forms were built by the hands of people and they could not protect themselves without their care and nursing. Neither did the old men of the people have clear answers to those questions. So who must fill those deep fissures between what was and what his spirit and heart sought and could not find?

In the late afternoon, saddened, he headed for the sanctuary and sat in a corner. His eyes were glued to the traffic, the circumambulations, the prostrations, and the supplications of the people to the Ka'ba ad their idols. But he did not understand anything from them. He was not deep in thought either. He had a special condition. It was as if his mind and senses had all stopped functioning.

Farther away, several persons were sitting in a circle on the ground. They were talking about the orphan of Abdullah who was deceiving a larger group of the people day by day and leading them away from the traditions of their fathers.

The story of Abdullah's Muhammad and his claims to be speaking with heaven was not a new thing. In Mecca, for several years what he said had been talked about. Surprisingly, though, was that until that day, Mos'ab had not thought about it. He was so pleased with his life and busy with his own affairs that his mind was not occupied by those kinds of things. He thought that those words and quarrels were between the leaders and elders of the people and Muhammad Amin.

Mos'ab did not think about the idols either. He had nothing to do with them either. He had neither any need to make requests of them, nor was there any injury from them so as to plead with them to rid him of it. The idols were things like those other things around him that from the beginning—when he opened his eyes to the world—he had seen them. Thus, he thought that it had to be like that. Now, though, the affair was of a different sort. For that reason, when he heard the name of Muhammad in their talk, all of the sudden a spark shot through his mind.

He was not like the slaves and lower people so as to be deceived by the words of another, even if it was Muhammad Amin. So, it was better that he heard what he said. Whatever it was, it could not hurt him.

He knew from the talk of those men that the followers of Muhammad gathered every evening in the house of Arqam and he went to them. So he decided to go to that house.

He hesitated for a while. Once the evening star appeared, he started down the road of the hill of Safā. Muhammad's friends, surprised, but warm and kind, accepted Mos'ab among them. He sat beside them and began to listen to Muhammad's words....

The braying of a camel brought Mos'ab out of that state. He stroked the soft moist snout of the animal with his hand to calm it. Then he extended his neck and gazed toward the other side of the sand dune. A fox, frightened, ran from one side of the road to the other side of it and disappeared in some *moghaylan* thorn bushes. Then, silence again caste its shadow over the plain. There was still no sign of his traveling companions.

Mos'ab sat n the ground and with his back against the camel wrapped his hands around his knees and looked at the few stars in the sky.

How quickly time had passed! From then on, Mos'ab went every night to that house and quenched the thirst of his spirit with the clear stream of the speech of God and His messenger and washed his burning soul in its calming and pleasant coolness. He had found what he had lost.

From the idolaters, 'Uthmān Talha would clandestinely in the evening go around the house of Arqam in order to learn who those persons were connected to Muhammad. He was the first to learn of Mos'ab's ventures to that house.

Then he told Bu Sufiān that, "The adornment of the Qureish, Mos'ab 'Omayr, goes to the house of Arqam Arqam in the evenings and the orphan of Abdullah breathes his sorcery on him there."

That situation destroyed the Qureish very much because earlier when talk of those who gathered around Muhammad came up, they said disparagingly, "They are nothing more than a group of lowly and ignorant people."

Now, though, with this development, what were they to do?

Finally, they thought they would go to Mos'ab's father, Abu Zarāra, and tell him about what was happening.

Mos'ab's father could not believe it at first. Once he became certain, first he tried to dissuade his son from that affair with gentleness ad moderation.

It was useless.

Then the mother and father deprived him of money, clothes, drink, and other enjoyments.

That was very severe punishment, but cutting off the heart from the new religion was more difficult than that.

So they imprisoned their beloved child in the basement of the house and chained and shackled his hands and feet so he could not go to Muhammad and his friends. Yet, no matter how harsh that was, it was ineffective, and it increased Mos'ab's thirst for Islam. Until they decreased his food and water and did not give him any thing but a little water and a loaf of barley bread each day.

The coddled young man became sick and weak. Still, though, he did not relinquish his new religion. He continuously prayed in front of their angry eyes and he recited what he had learned of chapters and verses of the Koran in a loud voice. Until the situation changed, and his mother and father could no longer stand it.

At that time, his mother placed her hands over her ears and screamed from the bottom of her heart and insulted him. Then his father came toward shim with a whip in his hands and beat him with it so much over the head and body that Mos'ab, bloody and battered, lost consciousness.

In the end, like a bird freed from the cage, he hurried to the Prophet again, until the time of the emigration to Ehtiopia came. He fled his father's house and joined the emigrants.

Aside from Mos'ab, ten men and four woman wanted to emigrate. Someone from every clan of the Qureish, so that the idolaters could not threaten them. It also showed that the people of Islam were from all of the Qureish, not one or a few of its clans. In that way, whoever was determined to kill this group would make all of the tribes their enemy.

Mos‘ab let out a sigh of happiness. He stood up on the back of the camel and faced toward the road to Mecca. There was nothing on the road. With that, in that former days silence, it seemed like a defect had occurred. It was as if a mute and faraway tumult was in the air. The moon had now risen into the sky, the sign that the night had reached its middle.

Mos‘ab sat down on his camel. Sleep had made his eyelids heavy. Then, distancing it from himself, he stood up. Then he sat on his feet and stood up again. Several times. He had to endure until his friends arrived.

The Prophet's habit was that when he sent three persons somewhere, he made one of them the leader.

On that journey, he had made ‘Uthmān Maz’un the leader of that group. ‘Uthmān was a good man from the friends of the Messenger of God, and he had firm trust in him He prayed a lot and he liked God and his Prophet, and he was the fourteenth Moslem.

‘Uthmān had told his traveling companions to leave Mecca one at a time and separately so that no one would discover their secret. He had told them to take the road to Jidda. But he had told Mos‘ab secretly to go ahead and stay at that crossroads. When the companions arrived, and tell them to go toward the port of Sho‘ayba. That instruction was so that if someone from that group was taken by the enemy, they would not know their destination and divulge it, and if they followed them, they would not find them soon because the Meccans all went to Ethiopia by the road to Jidda.

On the road, Mos'ab saw several camels that were coming. When the light of the moon shone on them, he saw a woman and a man on the first camel.

He hid until they came nearer. Then he realized from their voices that those two were Roqiyya and 'Uthmān 'Affān, the daughter and son-in-law of the Prophet. Then he recognized the others one by one. On the second camel were Abu Hodayfa and his wife Sahla, The third camel had Abu Salma 'Abd al-Asad and his wife, Umm Salma in its back. Then there was Zobayr 'Awwām, Abdullah Mas'ud, Abd ar-Rahmān 'Awf, 'Āmer Rabi'a and his wife, Layla, Khāteb 'Amru, Abu Sabra Abi Rohm, and Sohayl Bayzā, who were all sitting two by two on a camel and coming at a gallop.

Mos'ab, in a way so as not to frighten them, slowly came out from behind the dune and greeted them. Then he directed them toward the port of Sho'ayba.

'Uthmān 'Affān asked, "Why Sho'ayba?"

Mos'ab said, "'Uthmān Maz'un wanted that."

Abdullah Mas'ud said, "Where is my brother 'Uthmān now?"

"'Uthmān went to Sho'ayba earlier to find a ship."

Abu Salma said, "It is not unlikely that the idolaters are following us right now. Therefore, it is not prudent to linger."

Mos'ab said, "So be it."

He quietly took the shackles from his camel's feet, sat on the animal, and started galloping after the caravan.

In this way, at dawn, they were in the port of Sho'ayba. Then Mos'ab had to take the borrowed camels of the travelers to the quarter of the fishermen and give them to an old fisherman. Then, as 'Uthmān Maz'un had said, he would take those camels back to Mecca and return them to their owner, who was a nomad. Now, though, the fear of all of them was what were they supposed to do if there was no ship at the port of Sho'ayba? Sooner or later, the Qureish would learn about their secret migration and would send groups in pursuit of them. Then they would find them and detain them and certainly increase the torment and torture of them. But that is much more bitter and detrimental for the Moslems, because in that way the Qureish would take the last hope of salvation from them. Then, if other people were inclined to go toward Islam, on seeing that bitter end of the emigrants, they would wash their hands of making it known, because the other tribes would stand aside in that dispute between the Moslems and the idolaters of the Qureish and would wait to see which one was victorious. For that reason, as long as this quarrel was like this, or the Moslems, if they were defeated in it, they would not turn to the new religion, but if the idolaters and unbelievers got hold of the emigrants, they would benefit greatly from it because with that they would add to their own position and dignity before others. Thus, this emigration had to be completed at any cost.

Aware of all these events, the emigrants kept on galloping and in that same condition they remembered their lord and sought assistance from Him.

"O' seeing and able God!

"You who are kinder to your servants then their mothers!

"O' You who are closer to us than the vein in our neck!

"You gave us permission to do this task,

"And You earlier ordered in Your heavenly look!

"He who helps my religion and takes a step in my way,

"I will help him.

"And I will make his steps firm.

"Now that time for performing that promise had arrived.

"So hear these lonely and tired servants of Yours."

The swell of the sea now became clearer. Then came the sound of the small waves of water that softly lapped against the rocks the rocks and reached to the ears of the emigrants.

Gradually the blackness of the port became visible.

"We have arrived."

"Thank God!"

"So far there is no one following us."

"Do not become fearful. It is the promise of the true God."

Amidst the darkness that was becoming less every moment of the early morning, the crowd of the port slowly took shape and the lines of the roofs and walls of the buildings became clearer every moment. Then the buildings, streets, and neighborhoods became distinguishable from one another.

At the edge of the Red Sea, there was a long line of houses and huts from the north to the south. The buildings were low, of stone, and small, and no sound came from anywhere. The villages of the port was totally immersed in the sleep of the night. There was only the soft sound of the waves that, with their ancient and splendid melody could be heard once every few moments.

Mos'ab 'Omayr went ahead.

"Our meeting with 'Uthmān Maz'un is at the jetty."

All of them followed him silently. They must not disturb the sleep and repose of the small port.

Finding the jetty was not difficult. The tall masts of two ships could be seen from afar. Therefore, the small caravan moved in that direction like a thin line.

The sea was calm and its smooth and even surface shone on the clear moonlight like a large and polished mirror. Two small ships were resting on it at a distance from the shore and moved gently like cradles. A strand of long rope was connecting the bow of one to the back of the other one. The front ship had unfurled and hoisted it sails. On the deck of the two ships several men were moving about. At various places on the shore small fishing boats were resting easily on the sand or lying on their side. In the direction of the ships, a tall, heavy-set man was praying and was absorbed in worship and praying to his lord. His white dishdasha shone in the half alive darkness of the shore and the hems of his kafiyya moved gently in the gentle northerly breeze.

All went toward time, happy.

'Uthamn Maz'un said to us that one of those two ships had been sitting in the mud for several days. Thus, these days the crew were busy clearing beneath it.

The others had also come to their aid. That night, when the moon rose above the horizon, the tide had come in and the water was rising.

The ship was freed from the mud at dawn and floated on the water/

The destination of both ships was Ethiopia. 'Uthmān Maz'un had spoken with its captain about taking us with them. We prayed the morning prayer when the cock crows and we took upon our few belongings and went to the ships with three boats. So seven persons sat in one ship and weight in the other, each paying half a dinar as a fee. Before the ships lifted anchor and set off, all our eyes were on the shore and we were fearful, except for 'Uthmān Maz'un and Abdullah Mas'ud, who were calm, and as always their lips moved in remembrance.

Once the sun had risen, the two ships began to move into the heart of the sea. Not more than a few minutes had passed, however, when the crew pointed toward the port, and our captain said, "It appears that several horsemen have arrived and are waving their hands toward us."

Slowly, I said t 'Uthmān Maz'un, "They seem to have followed us."

'Uthmān said, "Rest easy Mos'ab, for they can not reach us."

The captain shaded his eyes with his hand and stared at the shore for a while. Then he said to the crew, "There must be trouble. There is no room on our ship for more travelers."

I saw those sent by the Qureish as they got off their horses and sat in tow boats. But by the time the boats began to move under oar power, our ships were miles from the shore.

So we all knelt on the deck and prayed the prayer of gratitude.

"Now 'Uthmān, tell me in detail. What happened that after four months without any questioning of the Messenger of God and without his permission, you came back to Mecca from Ehtiopia?"

It was nighttimes. The Moslems were setting all around the large room of Arqam's house and their eyes were fixed with amazement on 'Uthmān Maz'un, Mos'ab 'Omayr, Zobayr 'Awwām, and 'Abd or-Rahmān 'Awf.

'Uthmān, his head lowered, said, "I accept that it was my fault. I was deceived. The friends, with what I said to them, were misled and they returned."

Ja'far Bu Tāleb said, "Your position in Islam and near the prophet is not concealed from anyone 'Uthmān. But what happened that things came to this?"

'Uthmān Maz'un, saddened, said, "When we reached Ethiopia, we went straight to be city of Ka'bar, where the Negus himself was. Since our number was small there, none of the officials of the Negus asked the reason for our going to that land. It is not unlikely that they thought that we were merchants or that we had gone to that land for work.

"We stayed in a caravanserai until we gradually found houses for ourselves. But after three months being there in the month of Ramazān a trading caravan came from Mecca to Ka'bar. I spoke with a slave from the caravan incognito and asked about news from Mecca. He said that the animosity between the Qureish, Muhammad, and his friends had ended.

"I was amazed. What had happened for all that vengeance, oppression, and torment to end so quickly? So I asked him to relate to me in detail on that subject what he knew had happened. He said, 'One day this happened in the sanctuary. Muhammad and his fries were sitting beside the Ka'ba. Hamza was also with them. Then Muhammad's condition became transformed. His friends said that that was the sign of the descent of the word of God to him.'

"'The Qureish, who had heard about that earlier, but had never seen it , curious, gathered around him and his friends until they became a large crowd. I was one of them.'

"'After it passed like that for a while, Muhammad caste his *abā* to one side. His color was pale like the moonlight, and his body was completely soaked in sweat. Then he recited:

-In the name of God, the Compassionate, the Merciful.

-Swear to that star that disappeared,

-For your friend has not gone astray nor has he swerved,

-And he does not speak nonsense.

-This speech is nothing but what is revealed to him.'[1]

'Until he recited:

-Thus, did you see Lāt and Uzzā?

-And Manāt, that other idol of the three?[2]

---

1. Koran, *An-Najm* (The Star), 1-4.

2. Koran, *An-Najm*, 19-20.

"'When Muhammad's speech came to here, all of those people who were gathered in the sanctuary around him suddenly became very happy, and they recited with him—may the intercession of those beautiful and high-flying birds be accepted by God.[1]

"'They did not say anything else then. Until Muhammad's talk reached when he said, 'Were you surprised by those words, and you laughed and did not weep? You were heedless. Prostrate yourself to God and worship Him.'"

"At that time he stopped speaking and placed his head on the ground. Then all of the people—his friends and the Qureish—prostrated themselves and placed their foreheads on the ground. I did that too. At the last moment I saw that Walid Moghayera, the elder of the Bani Makhzum, with that self-importance he had, picked up a fistful of dirt for the ground and rubbed it on his forehead. After that, the people dispersed.

"From that day, the Qureish said, 'Muhammad, after that animosity he had toward our idols, finally believes in them by the command of his God, and he spoke of them respectfully."

'Uthmān Maz'un sighed and added, "It was clear to me that the word of the Messenger of God was the truth. What he never says is lawful. For that reason, we thought tat God, the Great and High, had drawn the hearts of the idolaters towards Islam! So I went to

---

1. This was an incantation that the idolaters recited when circumambulating the Ka'ba when honoring those three idols. Comparing the idols to sea gulls was because they fly very high in the sky. They compared the idols to them because of their high value and position.

the friends and told the about that event and what I thought about it. They were happy. All of us decided to return to Mecca.

"When we reached the outskirts of Mecca, we learned from a shepherd that it was not as that slave had told us and that the animosity of the idolaters toward Islam persisted. Necessarily, every person entered Mecca under the protection of someone. Except for Abdullah Mas'ud, who entered the city unprotected. After two days, he suddenly returned to Ethiopia.

After saying that, 'Uthmān Maz'un put his head down and his lips began to move in saying a prayer.

Ja'far said, "What happened was not like you related. You were not at fault in this matter because that day the events occurred one after the other and together in such a way that even many of those persons who were in the sanctuary were very perplexed or in error, and those persons who were not there, because the idolaters had dispersed in the city, thought that the Messenger of God had respected Lāt, Manāt, and Uzzā and had prostrated to them. So the idolaters, when they saw that, believed in him and joined him."

Mos'ab 'Omayr asked, "But what really happened? What happened for things to become like that?"

Ja'far said, "That day, the chapter 'The Star'[1] came down to the prophet. When he began to recite it for us, some of the idolaters also stood up and listened. Some, though, as always, said nonsensical things and trilled their voices and caused a commotion to

---

1. i.e. an-*Najm*, the 53rd chapter of the Koran.

whistled and clapped. They made meaningless sounds so no one could hear the Messenger of God until the Prophet reached the verse where God mentions Lāt, Manāt, and Uzzā. At that time, all of the idolaters—seeming to think that the Prophet had believed in them and had shown respect to their idols—became very happy. As a group they began to say their own prayer for circumambulation for those three idols: 'May the intercession with God of those beautiful and highflying birds be accepted.'"

Bilāl, who had been silent until then, began to speak and said, "Whereas, if they had listened correctly to the verse before and father that verse where Lāt, Manāt, and Uzzā are mentioned, they would have become angry because it is relate din those verses,

'Do you have a son and it a daughter?

'Thus is a division contrary to justice.'

'These are nothing but what you and your fathers have given to them, and God has not sent any cause for them. They only follow your own thinking and desires. Now they have guided them from God.'[1]

The Messenger of God recited and they were busy murmuring or embroiled in their own baseless thoughts. Until he reached the verse of prostration. Then the Prophet prostrated himself. We prostrated with him. Then we saw that the idolaters too—perhaps with that same earlier understanding of theirs—prostrated themselves with us."

'Uthmān Maz'un and Mos'ab 'Omayr and Zobayr 'Awwām let out a sigh of relief. Their grimaced faces

---

1.

relaxed and grins appeared on their lips. But the young Mos'ab began to laugh very loudly, so much that, even though he tried hard to restrain himself, his even shoulders began to shake from the intensity of the laughter.

Then the others asked about their condition and time on that trip, and they told them about their time in Mecca. What the emigrants had heard about the decrease in the harassment of the idolaters and unbelievers of the Moslems was not completely misleading. But it had a cause separate from what some thought.

"When you emigrated to Ethiopia, their torment and torture of us decreased somewhat. It seemed their leaders had gathered in the Assembly House and though among themselves that aside from those torments and tortures not having any effect, they had had the opposite effect. Because, with the emigration of a group of the Moslems from Mecca, that religion would spread to other lands and thus add to its luster. Also, some of them said that in that way, the emigrants might join forces with the Negus so that he comes to Mecca with his army and, like Abraha, aim to pummel them. For that reason, until they could think of another solution, the refrained from bothering us for a while. Until the month of Ramazān when some of their leaders spoke with the Prophet about reconciliation. But when they realized that he would not quit his proselytizing, they again began harassing us, until Shawwal[1] arrived and you returned and things

---

1. The tenth month of the Arabic lunar year.

became even worse that what they had been before.

Those who had returned from Ethiopia had seen the sins of the intensification of that harassment. By the time they reached the gates of Mecca, they realized that the unbelievers and idolaters were looking to punish them. For that reason, first, they had to put themselves under the protection of a prominent man of the Qureish and then enter the city.

Arqam Arqam said, "From the day you returned, the intensity of the harassment from the Qureish has increased. It seems they thought that this journey was fruitless and that you regretted it. Thus, we have no choice but to stay in Mecca and submit to their torments and tortures."

A shadow of grief again settled over the faces of ‘Uthmān Maz‘un and Mos‘ab ‘Omayr and Zobayr ‘Awwām, for they knew that this time they would also be at fault. Their smallest fault was that hey had insisted on returning without knowing the opinion of the Messenger of God.

A while passed in silence. Then ‘Uthmān Maz‘un said, "Things will not stay like this. If God helps, we will make up for it."

Zobayr ‘Awwām said, "How?"

"If God and his Messenger permit, we will return. The idolaters will see that God's hand is higher than theirs."

In the name of the One, the Forgiving, the Compassionate.

"O' traveler
"Deliver my message to the people of that city
"Know that they are very desirous to deliver the verses of God and His religion to the people.
"Especially to the monotheists and His servants, who are being tormented and tortured beside His house.
"Say to them,
"We found God's earth large.
"And we were saved from humiliation and suffering.
"So, do not submit to shame in life and death in the poverty of the body
"So you do not deserve reprobation in that world!"

Zayd, my brother, what you read is the last poem by Abdullah Haws Qays. He recited it last night among the friends in the caravanserai.

Umm Salma heard that I intended to write a letter. She told me to write, "When we reached Ethiopia, we came under the protection of the Negus, who is a good support for us. Now we are free to protect our own religion, and we worship God without any hindrance. We are not bothers nor do we hear any harsh or biting words."

Zobayr 'Awwām also said to inform his aunt Khadija and his nephew, the Messenger of God, of his good health.

In short!

You had said that when we reached Ethiopia, whatever the situation was and whatever happened, to inform you in detail about what we see and what happens to us. Now, thirteen days after leaving Mecca I now have that opportunity to do that.

First of all, let me tell you about the scroll on which this letter is being written, because there is nothing like it in Mecca. The people of Egypt make these scrolls, and its name is 'papyrus'. Papyrus is a plant that grows in swamps, especially along the Nile River. The Egyptians make these sift, desirable, and bright scrolls from those plants. This ink I am using to write is also made by the people of Egypt. I am sending one of these scrolls for you so you can show the other friends.

But let me tell you about our trip. I was traveling with Bu Tāleb's Ja'far, 'Uthmān Maz'un, and several other friends. The trip from Mecca to the port of Jidda by camel took less than three days. A Bedouin had said, 'The length of this road is ten to twelve parasangs.' This time we left Mecca with ease, and openly, and set out because no one followed us with the intention of blocking our path or to make us return. In Jidda, though, we stayed two days until the other traveling companions arrived one by one.

All of us together were seventy-one persons. With

Abdullah Mas'ud, who had returned to Ethiopia before us, we were seventy-two. In this group, fifteen persons were those first emigrants to Ethiopia who were deceived and returned to Mecca and emigrated again. We are fifteen women and forty-nine men of the Qureish and eight men who are not of the Qureish. There are also several children with us.

This time, however, the leadership of the group was with Ja'far, who had come with his wife, Asma 'Omays. Although Ja'far was young, and they say that his age was not more than twenty-one, he was however quite capable and worthy of his task.

This time we found two ships that were not carrying cargo, only passengers. So half boarded one ship and half boarded the other. All of the women, however, boarded one ship with their husbands.

We were at sea for three days and half of another. On the way, we passed several islands. One of those islands is named 'Aqal. They said that on that island there is a spring whose name is 'Aqal. The natives drink from it and say that it has a beneficial effect on the mind and intellect. They also say that near the shore there is another island by the name of Saqtara. On that island a plant grows from which they obtain Saqtari Aloes. They say that that medicine is only found on that island.

Our captain was a man from Egypt, and the crew was also either from Egypt or Ethiopia. He was a man of middle age and experienced because he had spent his life on the sea. So, before we reached the other shore, he told us very interesting stories about the sea and its amazing things. First, that sea is a branch of the Indian Ocean, sticking out into the land, narrow and long. On one side of that sea is Arabia and on the other the land of Zang, which they call the Barharian Peninsula.

The Ethiopian shore s opposite Yemen and ha many towns and cities. Among them are Zila', Dahlak, and Nāse'. We dropped anchor at Zila' and went ashore.

In Ethiopia we traveled for four days by camel until we reached Ka'bar. There, we stayed at the same caravanserai we did the other time. On the second day, Ja'far went to the Negus' palace and gave the Prophet's letter to him. In that letter, after praising God, the Messenger of God wrote about us for the Negus and had made a request.


In the name of God, the Beneficent, the Merciful.

From Muhammad the Messenger of God, to the Negus Asham, the king of Ethiopia.

You have good relations with us. I praise the Creator before you, Who has no partner an Who is the upright commander of all deficiencies, t. He has no deficiency or corruption. He is the savior of the people from terror and anxiety and the guardian of the daily needs and life of his servants. I bear witness that Jesus, the son of Mary, is the Holy Spirit and His word, who placed him inside the virgin Mary, and Mary became pregnant with him. God created Jesus by healing His spirit into Mary in the same way. He gave life to Adam by His own hand and by breathing spirit into his skeleton.

I summon you to the unequalled God, to the continual of obedience to Him, and to following me and my divine book, for I have truly been sent by God.

Truly, I have delivered the command of God and offer my good wishes and wisdom. So accept my advice.

And praise and security from God's retribution on him who follows guidance.

Ja'far related to us, "I found the Negus to be a far-thinking, good-natured, and knowledgeable man. His countenance is, like men of God, glowing and pleasant. After his minister of court read the Prophet's letter, the Negus, sitting on his throne, thought for a while. Then he took the letter and stared at it for a while. He then asked me several questions about the Prophet, Islam, and my companions. It was clear from his question that earlier he had heard about their religion. Finally, he said, 'It is not permissible for me to prevent the servants of God from entering His land. In Ethiopia, the followers of all the religions are free to worship their own god, and one of those is you. Put your baggage down and begin your new life in this land.'"

But Ethiopia is a surprising land. It has hot weather, and except for the Nile, which is a very large river and full of water, there is not much water flowing through it. For that reason, in those places that are far from the Nile, there are few villages or people, and its rainfall is little.

In their figures, the Ethiopians are like Bilāl.

They have black skin, wide and short noses, wide and protruding lips, and stocky bodies. Their height is medium and their hair is short and curly. The language of the Ethiopians differs from ours. But their merchants, courtiers, slave-traders and some others more or less know Arabic. The Negus and most of his courtiers are very familiar with our language.

Its crops are wheat, barley, rye, and coffee. Of fruit, it also has a lot of grape and pomegranates. There is also a fruit there by the name of banana. There is no fruit like it in Mecca. It has bunches like grapes. On every bunch there are almost twelve fruit, slim and long like cucumbers.

Of the special animals in this land, there are elephants and giraffes. Our people saw elephants in that army Abraha brought to Mecca, but they have not seen giraffes. The giraffe is that same animal that some call a camel-cow-leopard, because its head is like a camel's, its hooves, horns, and teeth like a cow's, and its skin like that of a leopard. Its legs are also like those of a camel. But its tail resembles the tail of a deer. It has a long neck, and its front feet are longer than its back ones. Some of the Ethiopians believe that the giraffe only exists in this land. They also say that this animal is a mixture of a camel, hyena, and a mountain cow.

One of the occupations of this land is hunting elephants. On the methods they use in that which they learned from the Zangians is that they chase the herd of elephants toward special trees. Those trees are so many that when the elephants eat their leaves, they lose consciousness. Then they go to the animals and tie them with chains and shackles. Some also kill them for their ivory.

I will now finish until the next letter. All of the friends are healthy, and we have not experienced anything but rest and kindness until today. Tell the Prophet and friends to have peace of mind regarding us. I only regret being far from the friends, especially the Messenger of God. I myself am not forgetful of the Prophet for one moment.

> He whose face is like a Chinese mirror
> In which I saw my own image.
> He remembers me with the coming of the sun,
> And I recall him when the sun sets.

This Ethiopian merchant who has delivered the letter is a good man. Arab merchants are constantly going and coming in this land. We hear the news from Mecca from them. Therefore, if there is any message, tell it to those merchants or in a letter.

In the name of God, the Beneficent, the Merciful
From Zayd 'Amru to Mos'ab 'Omayr


Those whose separation was anticipated, migrated.
At the time of departure, a crow with burned feathers and wings passed by.
Its covetous beak resembled a pair of scissors that severed us from one another.
O' crow!
Those whose distance you cried out,
They were all awake and anxious for the long night of preparation.


Greetings to you and your companions!
Joy to you who opened a new chapter in the history of God's religion with your great migration. At the time of saying farewell I heard 'Uthmān 'Affān tell the Prophet, "We emigrated the first time, and now we are emigrating again, but you were not with us either time."
The Prophet said, "You are migrating toward God and me. Both this migration toward God and toward me belong to you."
In this land, the friends are always remembering you, and after every prayer, they pray for you. Your letter arrived just as you sent it. This is a good manner which the idolaters will not find out until too late,

because Bu Tāleb, although he is the chief of the Qureish, because he has not expressed Islam before them until today, they do not suspect him.

I read to the friends all the things you wrote or related it to them. They thanked God and rejoiced. Even though the news from Mecca more or less reaches there, some of the events are hidden, so that they may not be as clear as they actually are, or they many not see it in their interest to make them clear. For that reason, whenever there is an opportunity, I will write about those events for you.

The first is that the second migration of our friends to Ethiopia was very effective. It frightened the idol worshippers and caused them to think.

When you returned to Mecca from your first migration, they, thinking that that journey was ineffective, and did not have any benefit for the friends of Muhammad, they became even more impudent in harassing us. For that same reason, at the time when you left on the second migration, no one blocked your road or followed you in order to bring you back to Mecca. Now things have changed though, because merchants have brought news from Ethiopia that in that land the emigrants and their children are comfortable and at ease. They are serving the God of Muhammad with all their hearts. Also, when that *qasida*[1] that Abdullah Haws recited in Ethiopia arrived here, in the city a tumult erupted, to the extent that our children say it during their games and they excite sparks of anger from the idolaters even more.

---

1. A type of poem in Arabic.

This news has stirred hope in the hearts of the friends though. Those other people who were inclined towards Islam have less fear in explaining what is in their hearts, because they believe that God's earth is expansive. If they suffer, in Mecca they can migrate and save themselves from the torment of the enemies.

In that respect, that news delivered a severe blow to the pride of the Qureish and their seeing themselves as superior. From the regret that they now realize that the work of the religion of God is beyond their decision and desire, so they can do whatever they want.

What has reached us about this relates that the leaders of the idolaters gathered in the Assembly House to discuss this matter. They decided to send emissaries along with many gifts to the court of the Negus to speak badly of you so that Ashama Abharāz will drive you out and close that crack of hope for the Moslems. Then they could say all about that, "We will not take our hands off of the followers of Muhammad no matter where they go, just as we did with the emigrants!", so that the other lovers of this religion know what will come to them in the end.

Thus, a few days ago, they sent 'Amru 'Ās and Abdullah Abi Rabi'a to that land to do that. That same day, your letter arrived, those two passed before the eyes of the Prophet and the friends with heavy loads of gifts on the backs of camels and heading for Jidda.

They said that those gifts were leather from Taif, Arabian ambergris, Indian incense, Persian perfume, striped Yemeni cottons, Chinese silk, and two beautiful and fast Arabian horses. It appears they are taking with them expensive gifts for all of the ministers and courtiers of the Negus.

When he learned about that, your father, Bu Tāleb, said a poem and seems to have sent it to the Negus. That poem is now on all of our tongues and everyone has entrusted it to memory. Yesterday, when it was recited in the house of Zayd Arqam, I wrote it down, and I am writing it here for you.

Oh that I knew what Ja'far was doing in that far-off land
And what Amru As and the enemies wanted to do.
I do not know whether Ja'far and his companions have the Negus' support,
Or whether the king no longer looks on them with favor.
O' king of Ethiopia, you are devoid of every undesirable thing.
You re a great and elevated man.
Thus, you will not look harshly upon he who turns to you.
Know that by giving shelter to these defenseless monotheists,
The Creator of the world will make you more powerful than before
And will provide all the beneficial means for you.
You are the giving being that is the gift of all.
And those who are near and far from you, both benefit from that.

Another occurrence you may be surprised to hear about—just as whoever heard has been surprised—is that 'Omar Khattāb has accepted Islam. That can not be other than a miracle of the Koran.

You also know that 'Omar was one of those who harassed the Moslems and was very harsh with them, such that the word Islam and the name of the Prophet could not be spoken in front of him or else he would insult and be very upset. You may not know, however, that in the beginning, he was one of those persons who tortured the Moslem slaves until they renounced their religion. He helped his uncle, BJ, in that.

He beat Zenniza the Rumi and Labiba, the concubine of the Bani Makhzum clan, so hard with a whip that they were badly bloodied. Then he said, "They have to die or give up Muhammad's religion!"

But those two young women did not wash their hands of Islam. Bu Bakr then bought and freed them.

But the case of 'Omar accepting Islam....

When he became a Moslem, he related to us that, "I was very angry that day about why the Qureish were getting along with the orphan of the Bani Hāshem like that so that he could darken their day like a dark night! I thought to myself, 'From that day Muhammad made those claims, divisions emerged among the people and it removed comfort and tranquility from the city. So, if it was removed, all of those disturbances and animosities would be removed. Now, though, because the leaders of the people are refraining from doing that, it is better that I do it and cause that uprising to calm down.'"

In that way, 'Omar, following his hot temper and nature, pulled his sword from its scabbard and with that tremendous and rough voice, raising an uproar, went looking for the Messenger of God in every street and neighborhood so he could kill him.

On the way, whoever saw 'Omar, with that two-meter height, thick body, and dark face, which dark anger had turned into a grimace, terrified, got out of his way. They had then told him that Muhammad was in a house beside the Safā bazaars, and that forty persons—one of them being the powerful man Hamza—were protecting him. In that case, he headed for the house of Arqam.

At that time, Na'im Abdullah had seen him. (This Na'im was 'Omar's friend and from the same clan. Sometime before, however, he had accepted Islam, but, out of fear, he did not reveal it.)

Na'im related to us that, "When I realized what he intended to do, in order to keep the Prophet out of danger, I said, 'What a wrong idea this is that you are doing son of Khattāb! Do not deceive yourself like this 'Omar. If you kill Muhammad, the children of Hāshem and 'Abd al-Muttaleb will not let you live on this earth. If you intend to correct things, first correct the members of your own house. Then set your sights on Muhammad!'

"'Omar stood up and, astounded, asked, 'The members of my house?'

"I said, 'Yes, 'Omar. Know that your sister and her husband have both taken Muhammad's religion.'

(Although they were cousins, Sa'id Zayd and 'Omar Khattāb had taken each other's sisters as wives.)

"When he heard that. 'Omar's anger became even more intense. So, from that locale, he set out for the house of his sister to kill her and her husband.

At that same time, Khabāb Arat was with Fatima Khattāb and Sa'id Zayd. (Because he secretly went from the Prophet to them to teach them the Koran.) When 'Omar knocked on the door, and they understood who it was, Khabāb fled and hid in a room on the other side of the courtyard. Fatima also hid that skin on which a chapter of the Koran was written under the rug.

'Omar, however, heard their voices reading the Koran from behind the door. Fatima Khattāb related what happened next like this:

When my brother entered the house, he angrily asked, "What was that singing I heard?"

I said, "You did not hear anything, and we did not sing anything."

'Omar became angry and grabbed my husband by the collar to kill him. When I saw that, I rose and grabbed onto him in order to stop him. 'Omar, though, threw me to the side. I hit the wall and, my head was cut, blood ran down my cheek.

When that happened, we caste our secrecy aside and said, "Yes, 'Omar, we follow Muhammad, and we have accepted his religion. Even if you tear us to pieces now, we will not renounce Islam."

'Omar said, "When I saw their steadfastness and that blood that was running down my sister's face and which had colored her clothes, my heart suddenly softened. I then took my hands off of them ad said to my sister, "Give that writing to me now that you were reading so I can see what it is for myself."

Fatima said, "That is the word of God, and we are afraid to give it to you."

'Omar said, "Read something from those words so I can listen."

His sister took the writing and read:

"Tāhā

"We did not send the Koran to you for you to suffer.

"It is only a warning for he who fears.

"It has come down from someone who has created the heavens and the earth.

"Forgiving God is ensconced on His throne.

"What is in the heavens and the earth and in between them, and that which is under the ground, all of it belongs to Him.

"And if you say something aloud, he is aware of the hidden and more hidden secret."[1]

Sa'id Zayd said, "I watched my cousin closely, and I saw that with each verse that Fatima read, the drawn lines on his face gradually opened up and the dark anger in his face lightened. Then, little by little the color left his face.

---

1. Koran, Tāhā, 1-7.

He leaned back against the wall and began to think.

Once Fatima had stopped reading, 'Omar sat down on the carpet on the ground and began to weep. Then he said, "What nice words these are, and what a great speaker it is."

We also began to cry on seeing his condition.

Meanwhile, 'Omar asked, "Where is Muhammad now?"

Fatima said, "What do you want with him?"

'Omar said, "To go to God and His religion. I have learned late that these idols do not do anything for us."

At that time, Khabāb came out of his hiding place. Then he and I, along with 'Omar, went to Arqam Arqam's house so the Messenger of god could offer Islam to 'Omar, and he accepted.

That event made us very pleased, but it made the idolaters very vexed. As a result, when Bu Jahl learned of it, he became very depressed, and he ran 'Omar off with the worst kinds of words. Because, aside from being the former enemy of his nephew with the Moslems, he was also the ambassador of the Qureish, and that news reached every where.

In short, with what had happened until today, it can be said that after all these years of pressure and suffering, it seems the page of time has been turned back and that a new era has begun for us. Among the other signs of that was the transformation of the condition of the pharaoh of Mecca, Bu Sufiān.

Prior to these happening, every time the Prophet

and his claim were mentioned in front of Bu Sufiān, he would straighten his neck, his jowl would rest on his chest, and with a smirk mixed with mockery he would say, "He is one of those like Waraqa and Omaya, who accepted the Christian religion on reading the *Torah* and *Injil*. They talked about it everywhere and invited the people to it! Sooner or later the fire of the claim of the son of Abdullah will also go out, and he will join up with the caravan of those who have been forgotten."

But from the time of his daughter, Ramla, and her husband, 'Obaydollah Jahsh, emigrated to Ethiopia, and then this news came from you, it seems his back broke.

Now, just as before, as a group, we go with the Prophet to circumambulate the Ka'ba, and we sometimes also pray in the sanctuary.

Send me some more letter like that one.

Farewell.

In the name of God, the Beneficent, and Merciful

From Mos'ab 'Omayr to Zayd 'Amru

Your letter arrived, and I related what you wrote in it to the friends. During these days, however, events have taken place, both bitter and sweet.

First is that, before your letter, 'Amru As and Abdullah Rabi'a entered Ka'bar. Then, a day had not gone by when a messenger came from the Negus and said, "Tomorrow, two hours before noon, send your leaders to the court."

I asked the reason. He said, "Two emissaries have come to the court from the heads of Mecca and have said bad things about you so that the king returns you to Mecca. But the Negus has said, "These people have chosen me from all the kings and they sought refuge with me. Therefore, until I hear what they say about you, I can not expel them from my land."

We knew what the story was! We all became sad and fearful, and the world closed in on us. We said, "The affair has come to a head, and this pleasant period will not endure. The deceivers of the Qureish have also deceived the Negus."

We lost our repose and calm that day. No one could sleep that night for fear. In the meantime, the children and women were more restless and weary. Therefore, we sat down to think of a solution.

At first a while passed in talking about which

person would speak the next day and what he would do.

Abdullah Mas'ud, as always, consoled us with the word of God.

"They plot and God plots as well. Truly, God is the best of plotters."[1]

Thus, we were all agreed that we would say what God and His prophet had said and not utter anything but the truth. At that time Ja'far said, "No one say anything before the Negus. I will be the speaker tomorrow."

It was agreed, because Ja'far, besides being our leader, was also a brave man and a capable speaker.

Of the others, it was decided that 'Uthmān Maz'un, 'Uthmān 'Affān, 'Uthmān 'Uthmān, Abdullah Mas'ud, 'Obaydollah Jahsh, Zobayr 'Awwām, Abdullah Hāres, Sa'd Waqqās, 'Abd or-Rahman 'Awf, and I would be with Ja'far.

Then we dispersed. But I saw friends who spread carpets here and there in the courtyard of the caravanserai and were praying until dawn.

We slept a little after the morning prayer. After we arose, we performed the ablution as Ja'far had requested and donned our best attire, rubbed ambergris on our heads and musk on our bodies, and went to the Negus' court.

The people had assembled in the palace in a large hall. The hall had a high ceiling with columns of white

---

1. Koran, *Āl-e 'Omrān*, 54.

stone. Its floor was covered in red and white marble. Large metal chandeliers from Syria hung from the ceiling. There were large wooden windows all around the hall opened to the four directions. Behind them were colored glass—yellow, green, red, and blue, from which the light of the sun shone from behind them into the interior and bestowed it with a beautiful appearance. The floor of the hall was a little higher at the end. There, a silver throne of ivory stood. The Negus was seated on the throne. He was an old man, of medium height and heavy body. The darkness of his skin was less that that of his courtiers. He had a wide face and two large wrinkles on both sides of his jaw. He had an even nose and intelligent eyes. The hairs on his head and face were short, curly, and wavy, and a lot of white strands were growing among them. He was wearing a white cloak which had become straight with a belt around his body. Over that fine cloak was a *redā*, which was also white. But the two flaps on that *redā* were decorated with colored string, rubies, and emeralds. His shoes were of thin leather and open on top. Diamond-like jewels glittered on their surface.

The Negus was sitting dignified and grave on his throne, and he had a cane with a round head and silver covering in his hand. Behind the throne a young woman was standing and fanning him with a large fan of peacock feathers.

On wither side of the throne there were platforms of ebony. On one side the bishops were sitting with white cloaks and caps. The senior of them was the nearest person to the Negus and he had a gold cross in his hand. Then the priests, with the special black and straight *redā* and hats were sitting. A *Torah* and *Injil* were opened in each one's hand. Behind them were the nuns. Their hats and clothes were of one cloth and dark, and their wrists were tied with a cord. On the left side of the Negus were his confidants and ministers—they were also knowledgeable in religion—and his military commanders. Then, on both sides of the hall were platforms. On them were sitting the courtiers with the same kind of special clothes. 'Amru As and Abdullah Rabi'a were among them in the left side.

Once we entered the hall, all heads turned toward us. We all greeted the Negus with one voice. But we did not fall on the ground as was the custom in the courts of kings.

A commotion arose among those assembled, and the chamberlain of the king said to us angrily, "Fall on the ground and kiss it!"

He said it I Arabic with a particular cadence, the same way the Negus spoke after him. It made us very happy that we could speak to the king without a translator.

Ja'far said in answer to the chamberlain, "Forgive us, for we do not prostrate our selves before anyone save the Creator."

At this time, I saw that 'Amru As looked at his companion, Abdullah Rabi'a, and smiled in victory. The chamberlain then showed us to the right side of the hall and to a platform in front of those two.

Silence fell over the hall for a moment, until the Negus opened his mouth and said, "Why do you not prostrate?"

His voice was calm, and no anger or rancor could be sensed in it. Ja'far stood up facing him and said, "Long live the king. Because our prophet has told us not to worship any but the Creator of the world, and we only prostrate to Him."

The Negus was silent for a few moments. The he pointed toward the emissaries of the Qureish and told us what they had said and why they had come. Then 'Amru As stood and said, "King of kings, this is a group of corrupt people who have fled their own people, and come to this land to corrupt your people as well."

Ja'far said, "May the king be healthy. Ask them whether we are their slaves."

The Negus looked at 'Amru As and Abdullah Rabi'a. Glib-tongued, 'Amru As said, "No! But we are great and noble freemen!"

Ja'far said, "Have we killed someone and blood is on our hands?"

'Amru As said, "No."

Ja'far said, "Did we steal property from anyone?"

'Amru As said, "No."

Ja'far said, "So what do you want that you have followed us to this far-off land? Was it other than that in your city you harassed us so much that we had to leave our friends, relatives, homes, businesses, and work and go to a foreign land?"

'Amru As said, "O' king! Their sin is that they fostered division among their own people and removed calm from our city."

The Negus said, "How?"

'Amru As said, "For some time a man has risen up in Mecca and has made a false claim, and has brought a new religion. He said surprising things that correspond neither with our religion nor with yours. No one has veer heard anything like them before. That man humiliates our religion and gods and invites other to follow him. Some of the slaves, women, youths, and poor people have been led astray and have become his followers."

Looking toward us, the Negus said, "What religion is this that you have erected?"

Ja'far said, " O' king! We were ignorant people who worshipped idols of stone and wood that we ourselves had built. We ate corpses and the property of the dead father. We did not refrain from doing any indecent thing. Our habit was to oppress the weak, torment our neighbor, and cause others to suffer. No law was exercised except the will of the powerful and warriors. Until the Lord of the world designated a man from among us to send. He is from the noblest of the Arab families, and all the people know him as being virtuous, truthful, and just. He is that same prophet of whom Jesus—peace be upon him—gave the good news about his coming, and his name is Ahmad or Muhammad.

"The Messenger of God prevented us from worshipping the idols, drinking wine, gambling, fornication, oppressing slaves and the weak, stealing, the unrighteous spilling of blood, and taking interest, and he called us to pray, give alms, be good to relatives and the lowly, and to honor girls and women. He recited the word of God for us and decreased the darkness in our hearts and souls with its brightness. With this religion slaves realized that they are human beings like their masters and God had created them free. White is neither superior to black, nor is Arab to non-Arab. If there is any superiority, it comes from abstinence. The women know that they are created equal to men , and like them they have rights and choices. The weak found that to be a powerful support for them. The intelligent of the people gravitated toward this religion for the reason that its customs and commands are compatible with intelligence ad they saw much good-fortune and the repose of men. Thus, they gathered to it one by one or in groups. They submitted to it. We were of all those. But the people began to oppose us and began to oppress and harass us and caused us constant suffering. The Messenger of God, when he saw that, told us that there is a God-fearing and just ruler in this land who will give us refuge. So we—women and men, old and young, and children set out on a long and difficult road. We passed through burning deserts and turbulent seas and aught refuge with you. Now, since the idolaters know that here is pleasant for us, they have sent these emissaries so you can turn us over to them and they can take us back to Mecca and caste us into suffering and calamity again."

The Negus said, "Jesus the messiah also came to teach these same words."

Then he added, "Yu do not remember anything

from the book that your Prophet brought for you?"

Ja'far said, "I do."

The Negus said, "Recite it."

Ja'far began to recite the chapter of "Maryam" with that pleasant and sad voice of his until he reached this verse:

"Remember Mary in this book when she fled from her family to a place in the east.

"She pulled a curtain between herself and them, and We sent out spirit to her, and it appeared to her in the form of a human being.

"Mary said, 'I seek refuge from you with God the forgiving so that you be chaste.'

"It said, 'I have been sent by you Lord to bestow on you a virtuous son.'

"She said, 'How can I have a child when no man has touched me and I have done nothing bad?'

"It said, 'Your Lord has said thus: <This is easy for Me, and We will make that son a sign and gift for the people.> This is a task that They have ordered.'

"Thus, she became pregnant, and it took her with it to a far-away place.

"The pangs of birth took her to a date palm tree. She said, 'O' that I had died before this and had been forgotten.'

"The infant called out from under her. 'Do not grieve. Your Lord has caused a stream to flow under your feet.'

"Shake the date palm so that fresh dates fall for you to gather.'"[1]

---

1. Koran, *Maryam*, 16-25.

I was immersed in the word of God and the tone and cadence of Ja'far. When I emerged from that state of selflessness, I saw that the Negus, bishops, priests, and nuns were weeping. The y wept so much that the *Torah* and *Injil* in front of the Negus became mist from his tears.

Thus, the Negus opened his mouth and said, "This speech and what Jesus the Messiah brought are both the rays from a single light."

The senior bishop said, "This speech has the color of eternity. Its qualities ate pieces of diamonds, clear and flawless."

The chief minister of the Negus—whom they said was also knowledgeable in the Christian religion—said, "Its interior is very beautiful and its exterior profound. There is a special melodiousness and surprising __ in it that brings joy to the heart and makes the soul happy."

'Amru As grimaced and said, "But they are saying very impudent things about Jesus."

Looking toward Ja'far, the Negus said, "What do you say about Jesus the Messiah?"

Ja'far at first hesitated and seemed to have doubts in answering. Then he said, "O' king. We say the same things about Jesus—peace be upon him—that God and His messenger say."

The Negus said, "And what is that?"

Ja'far said, "He is the servant of God and His messenger. Jesus is the soul of God and the word of God whom he sent to Maryam, the maiden without a husband, and was placed in her so his so his incomparable power, without a father, would come into existence from Maryam."

The Negus drew a line with his cane in front of his foot and said, "The difference between you and us on this matter is as thin as this line."

Some of the bishops, priests, and nuns breathed deeply and rustled. The Negus looked toward them and said, "No matter how much you clamor!"

Then, facing us, he said, "Now go and be at ease for you are under my protection, and no one will touch you."

He told his chief minister, "As long as this group works and does business, give them whatever clothes and food they need."

We thanked him and went to our friends, happy. The next day we heard that the Negus had returned all those gifts the emissaries from the Qureish had brought and had told them, "If you pour all the gold and silver in the world before me, I will not give this group to you."

I think that after this event the leaders of idolatry will stop bothering us. But with what happened that day in the court, there is the fear that the courtiers of the Negus, some of whom are those learned men in the Christian religion, will become our enemies and began to harass is. Because they consider Jesus—peace be upon him—to be the son of God, and believe in the trinity of the Father, the Son, and the Holy Ghost. However, many there were some among them who contemplated what Ja'far had recited from the Koran and did not say anything until the end.

The other news is that yesterday Ja'far's wife gave birth to a son. We were all happy at that and considered it a good omen. I saw him, and he is a beautiful and healthy boy. They named him Abdullah.

Until the next letter. Peace.

In the name of God, the beneficent, the Merciful
From Zayd Hāresa to Mos'ab 'Omayr

Greetings to you and the other friends with you! Your letter arrived and was the reason for the happiness of your co-religionists and the anger and grief of the idolaters. Earlier, 'Amru As and Abdullah Rabi'a brought all the gifts back and the people more or less learned about their defeat. But the way you wrote, the events were much higher than what we had thought.

In Mecca, the talk is that before you went to the Negus' court, 'Amru As went to the countries, bishop, and priests and had given them all of them from those gifts so that would take his side with the king. They had said, "The return of these refugees from Ethiopia will not decrease anything from the king until he decides to do it. So be strong, and we will say to the Negus what is beneficial in this matter."

So, they had spoken with the Negus about turning you over to the emissaries of the Qureish. The Negus summoned 'Amru 'Ās and questioned him. Then he said, "The way you said, your people have to be happy about the flight of this group because with their flight, the animosity toward them will diminish. So why do you insist on taking them back now?"

'Amru 'Ās had said, "Until this group is punished, the root of this insurrection will not be extirpated."

The Negus had said, "The source of this insurrection there is you. Why did you leave it and pursue this group?"

The courtiers had stood up in support of 'Amru 'Ās. It seems that the Negus had realized in secret what had happened because of their insistence in this matter.

Thus, angry, he had said, "The words of those emigrants must be heard too." Then he judged between them.

At court, once those words had come up, the Negus had said to his confidants to give back all those gifts that they had taken from them.

Not a work had passed since the return of those emissaries thought when a group of bishops and priests came to Mecca. They were looking for the Prophet, and they met him in the sanctuary. On that day, I was not with the Messenger of God. But Zayd Arqam, who was there, told me about what happened. "They were twenty persons, all of them old. First they went to the leaders of the idolaters and asked about the Prophet, from childhood until that day.

The senior of them, who was also older than the others, spoke first and said, "This group you see are all from the leaders and learned men of the Christians. We came here to this land from spiritual domain of Ethiopia so as to inquire about your religion."

We knew that this followed these talks that Ja'far had said in the court of the Negus.

The Prophet said, "That is good! Ask, and you will be answered."

At this time, many of the idolaters ad their leaders had gathered around us and were watching.

Each one of those prominent Christian questioned the prophet about his father and mother. They asked about his childhood, what he had experienced and seen, or what he had heard. Then they asked about the condition of the Messenger of God when at the time of the coming down of inspiration. They also posed questions about former religions and communities. They also asked what his god had said about their tradition.

The prophet answered all of their questions. They wanted him to recite something from the Koran. The Messenger of God recited several verses from the chapter "**Manda**" with that heavenly voice of his.

"In the name of God, the Beneficent, the Merciful.

"The day that God gathers the prophets together and asks, 'What did they answer to your invitation,' they say, 'We do not know anything, for you are the Knower of the unseen.'

"God said to Jesus of Maryam, 'Remember the blessing that I granted to you and your mother. That time I had the Holy Spirit assist you so you could say it both in the cradle and when grown up. I taught you the book, wisdom, the *Torah*, and the *Injil*. That time when, by My command, you made something resembling a bird from clay and breathed life into it, and, by My command, it became a bird. And you healed a person blind from birth and a leper, and you brought the dead out of the grave by my command.

And when you went to the tribe of Israel with these clear proofs, and prevented them from harming you. And from among them those were unbelievers said that 'This is nothing but obvious sorcery.'

And I gave inspiration to the Apostles, 'Have faith in Me and my Prophet.'

"They said, 'We believe. Witness that we submit.'

"And the Apostles asked. 'O' Jesus of Mary, can your Lord send down food to us from heaven?'

"He said, 'We want to eat of that food so our hearts are comforted, and we know that you told us correctly and we can bear witness to it.'

"Jesus of Mary said, 'O' God. O' our Lord, send down food from heaven for us so it can be a gift ad a sign from You for us and those who come after us. And give us daily bread, for you are the best giver of daily bread.'

"God said, 'I will send down that food for you, but whomever of you who becomes an unbeliever after that, I will punish him in a way I have never punished any person in the world.'

"And then God said to Jesus of Mary, 'Did you tell the people, <Take me and my mother as a god apart from God?> He said, <O' pure God, I do not deserve to say something of which I am unworthy! If I said something like that, You yourself know, for You know that which goes on within me and I am ignorant of what is in Your essence, because You are the most knowledgeable about the unseen.>

"Other than what you have commanded, I did not say, 'God, worship my lord and your lord.' As long as I was with them, I was the guardian of their faith. And when You ran me out, You became their protector. And You are omniscient.'

"If You punish them, they are Your servants. And when You forgive, You are the most Powerful, the Wise."[1]

As the prophet recited, tears flowed from their eyes and made their cheeks and beards wet. Then the Messenger of God invited them to Islam. They all bore witness to his prophethood and accepted Islam. The senior one of them said, "How can we not have a faith when all of those signs that have come in the *Injil* and other books of our about *Farqelit* are obvious in your dear being?"

When that group left the sanctuary, a group of the leaders of the Qureish approached, angry, and Bu Jahl said to them, "We have not seen anyone more ignorant than you!"

The senior man of that group asked, "Why do you say that sir?"

Bu Jahl said, "What did you do?"

The leader of the group from Ethiopia said, "What have we done so upset you so much?"

Bu Jahl said, "Did you not come from your people to investigate this man? So what happened that, before this man, you turned away from the religion of your fathers and designated his claim as correct?"

The leader of those emissaries said, "We know

---

1. Koran, *al-Mā'eda* (The table spread), 109-118.

what we were sent for, and we are also acquainted with your tradition. You are very attracted to the faith of your ancestors. Now that we are following our own lost ones, and we do not want anything but prosperity for our people."

The idolaters were quite vexed by that account, and it made them very fearful. So it is not unlikely that they will employ new deceits and plots again. But the prophet and we are clever as well, and the hand of God is over their hand.

Farewell.

In the name of God, the Beneficent, the Merciful.

From Mos'ab 'Omayr to Zayd Hāresa!

Peace on the Prophet of God and on his faithful friends! The letter that you sent arrived on time. The reason its answer was late was because we were not in Ka'bar for a while. When we returned, those merchants who were to take my letter had left.

But the reason for being away....

From that day Ja'far said those words about Jesus—peace be upon him—and some of those confidants of the Negus were disturbed, the situation in Ka'bar changed, because the people of Ethiopia knew that what the Negus believed concerning their prophet was different from theirs. So when that group of bishops and priests returned from Mecca and had become Moslems, some of the courtiers and other bishops and priests said that, "This was because of the Negus action. He is inclined toward Islam, and he has turned away from the king rose up and those countries joined him and encouraged the people to result.

When the Negus saw that, he secretly sent someone to us at night and said, "I have prepared two ships with captains for you on the bank of the Nile. Gather up your things and go there at night. Then get on those ships and wait. Then, if I am victorious over my enemies, come back. If they prevailed over me, however, take the ships and go wherever you want."

On hearing that news, we became very distraught. So, frightened, we did that, and we went to the other side of the Nile and waited. In the meantime, we did not sleep at night nor were we calm during the day. We prayed constantly and called on God to make the Negus victorious over his enemies.

After three days had passed, we decided to get news from him. Among us, Zobayr 'Awwām was a good swimmer and an agile young man, so we sent him to do that. Zobayr filled a large skin with air, laid down on it, and went to the other side of the river. When he returned, he was still on the water when we rushed to meet him on the deck of the ship. Zobayr then cried out from afar, "Joy to you, for the Negus has been victorious over his enemies, and God has put the rebels in their place."

An uproar occurred on the ship, and he related what he had seen or heard.

"The rebels had encircled the Negus' palace in order to remove the Negus from his throne and kill him. The Negus was opposing them with his friends. But he did not begin to fight. First, he went atop the roof of the palace and spoke to them. He said, "O' people of Ethiopia, was I not your king?"

All in one voice, the people said, "You were."

He said, "Did I not act justly with you?"

They said, "Yes."

He said, "Then why have you rebelled against me?"

They said, "You have turned away from our religion, and you have another belief about Jesus the Messiah."

Some had also yelled, "You have gone toward Islam and being a Moslem."

He asked, "What do you believe about Jesus the Messiah?"

They said, "Our belief is that Jesus is the son of God. You, however, said that he is the servant of God."

The Negus grimaced and yelled out, "What person heard that I said such a thing?"

No one from among the people had heard such a thing.

At that time, the Negus placed his left hand on his right arm and said, "I also say that about Jesus the Messiah."

When they heard those words, most of the people dispersed from around the palace, happy and praising him. But some of the bishops and priests and a group of the people continued to stand there, and the leader of the rebellion said, "This talk is nothing but a deception! You have to explicitly say what your belief is concerning Jesus the messiah."

Then one of the priests among them said, "When he said that, his hand was on the amulet tied to his hem. Ii must be seen what prayer is written on it."

Another had added, "Most certainly that same blasphemous belief of his about Jesus is written in that amulet."

A discussion had arisen among those who had remained. Some had said that the matter was not as that priest had said. Another group, however, were I accordance with that priest. So, again, a number of them had dispersed. At this time the Negus had told his friends to either disperse those remaining, apprehend them, or kill them.

Fighting erupted between the two groups. Most of the rebels were killed and some were apprehended and tied up. The fighting had just ended when Zobayr 'Awwām arrived.

Yes, Mos'ab! That rebellion ended like that, "The Negus was victorious over his enemies."

So, when we returned to our caravanserai, your letter for me had arrived, and that event occurred so I could answer it. Now we are doing better than we were before. The Negus, either secretly or openly, strive as much as possible for one comfort and success. So far that now he has ordered that fine house be built for us in a nice area. He has also sent a messenger to Ja'far to say that, "Let me know if you need anything."

Some of the companions, each according to his own situation, has found an occupation and is engaged in it. Most of them are busy trading in the bazaar.

For that reason, I think that most of the friends believe that they will stay in this land until an opening from God occurs in Mecca for the Moslems. Nonetheless, most of us still long for our friends and Mecca. And being far from the Prophet has made all of us impatient.

Farewell.

Bibliography

*Āsār ol-bilād va ākhbār al-'ebād*. Zakaria bin Muhammad bin Mahmud Qazvini. trans. Jahangir Mirza Qajar. ed. Mir Hashem Mohaddes. 1373.

*E'lām-e Qor'ān*. Dr. Mahmud Khazā'eli. 1371.

*Al-'asr al-Jāheli*. Showqi Zayf. trans. Alireza Zakavati Qaragozlu. 1364.

*Enqelāb-e takāmoli-ye Islām*. Jalal od-Din Farsi. n.d.

*Bā Payghambar*. Dr. Bint al-Shati. trans. Dr. Sayyid Muhammad Radmanesh. 1377.

*Payghambar*. Zayn al-Abedin Rahnama. 1363.

*Pirāmun-e sireh-ye nabavi*. Dr. Taha Hosayn. trans. Badr od-Din Ketabi. 1362.

*Payghambar va yārān*. Muhammad Ali 'Alami.

*Tārikh-e Islām*. Hojjat ol-Islam Ali Davani. n.d.

*Tārikh-e payghambar-e Islām*. Dr. Muhammad Ebrahim Ayati and Dr. Abu al-Qasem Gorji. 1361.

*Tārikh-e Tabari*. Muhammad bin Jarir Tabari. trans. Abu al-Qasem Payandeh. 1375.

*Tārikh-e Arab*. Filip Hitti. trans. Abu al-Qasem Payandeh.

*Tārikh-e Kāmel*. 'Ezz od-Din ibn Asir. trans. Dr. Muhammad Hosayn Rowhani. 1374.

*Tārikhnāmeh-ye Tabari*. Bal'ami. ed. Muhammad Rowshan. 1368.

*Tārikh-e Ya'qubi*. Ahmad bin Abi Ya'qub. trans. Dr. Muhammad Ebrahim Ayati. 1371.

*Tohfah al-ahbāb*. Shaykh 'Abbas Qomi.

*Tutiā-ye didegān*. Shaykh 'Abbas Qomi.

*Hayāt al-Qolub*. Mulla Muhammad Baqer Majlesi. 1363.

*Dāstanhā-ye mā*. Hojjat al-Islam Ali Davani. 1371.

*Darshā'i az tārikh-e tahlili-ye Islām*. Hojjat al-Islam Sayyid Hashem Rasuli Mahallati. 1368.

*Dar maslakh-e 'eshq*. Ali Musavi Garmarudi. 1358.

*Dalāyel al-Nabovvat*. Abu Bakr bin Ahmad bin Hosayn Bayhaqi.

*Zendegāni-ye Muhammad (PBOH)*. Hojjat al-Islam Muhammad Muhammadi Ashtehardi. 1373.

*Zendegāni-ye por eftekhār-e Bilāl Habashi*. Hojjat ol-Islam Muhammad Muhammadi Eshtehardi. 1374.

*Zendegāni-ye por eftekhār-e 'Amār Yāser*. Hojjat ol-Islam Muhammad Muhammadi Eshtehardi. 1373.

*Sirat-e Rasul Allāh*. Trans. Rafi' od-Din Eshaq Muhammad Hamadani. Ed. Dr. Asghar Mahdavi. 1361.

*Sireh-ye Rasul Allāh (PBOH)*. Dr. Zaryab Kho'i. 1376.

*Sireh-ye sahih-eRasul Allāh (PBOH)*. Ja'far Mortazavi 'Amoli. trans. Hosayn Tajabadi. 1373.

*Sha'n –e nozul-e āyat*. Abu al-Hasan 'Ali Vahedi Nishaburi and Jalal od-Din 'Abd al-Rahman Soyuti. trans. Dr. Muhammad Ja'far Eslami. 1362.

*Sharaf on-nabi (PBOH)*. Abu Sa'id Va'ez Khargushi. trans. Najm od-Din Mahmud Ravandi. ed. Muhammad Rowshan. 1361.

*Shahreyār-e Mohabbat*. Mithaq Amir Fajr. 1378.

*Farzandān-e Abu Tāleb*. Abu al-Faraj Ali bin al-Hosayn Esfahani. trans. Javad Fazel. 1362.

*Forugh-e abadiyat*. Ayatollah Ja'far Sobhani. n.d.

*Farhang-e Fārsi*. Dr. Mohammad Mo'in. 1362.

*Qur'ān-e Karim*. trans. Abd al-Hamid Ayati. 1367 (and other translations).

*Muhammad payamāvar-e āzādi*. Abd al-rahmanSharqavi. trans. Hasan Akbari Marznak. 1356.

*Muhammad, payghambari keh az now bāyad shenākht*. Constantine Virgil Giorgio. trans. Zabih Allah Mansuri. 1376.

*Muhammad (PBOH) Khātam-e payāmbarān*. Group work (article "Az ba'sat ta hejrat" by Dr. Sayyid Ja'far Shahidi.) 1363.

*Moruj oz-zahab*. Abu al-hasan Ali bin Hosayn Mas'udi. trans. Abu al-Qasem Payandeh. 1370. Mos'ab bin 'Omayr. 'Adnan al-Tawil. trans. Entesharat-e Towhid. 1369.

*Nehāyat al-Mas'ul fi revāyat al-rasul*. Sa'id al-Din Muhammad bin Mas'ud Kazaruni. Trans. Abd as-Salam bin Ali bin al-Hosayn Alabarquhi. trans. and ed. Muhammad Ja'far Yahaqqi. 1366.